"WAR IS HELL. But the invasion of Grenada was actually very cool. John Bachman takes us through the thrilling tactics and the monumental strategic impact of this not to be forgotten conflict."
—GREG KELLY, host of NEWSMAX Greg Kelly Reports, author of *Justice for All*, and retired marine

"John Bachman has written a necessary history of how the Cold War was actually won. *Turning Point* is beautifully written and tells the story of the war that changed the world. A great read!"
—KAROL MARKWITZ, host of The Karol Markowitz Show podcast, *New York Post* columnist, and author of *Stolen Youth*

"A story that needed to be told, and now John Bachman has told it, and tells it well."
—CRAIG SHIRLEY, presidential historian, and *New York Times* bestselling author of *December 1941*

"Four days of intense fighting in a remote corner of the planet turned the tide in a global struggle that lasted almost a half century. John Bachman brilliantly explains how this happened."
—GORDON CHANG, bestselling author of *PLAN RED: China's Project to Destroy America*

"I'm thrilled to see this book. For over 40 years, I have insisted to the world that the Reagan administration's tremendously successful and pivotal liberation of Grenada was a turning point in the Cold War. It was a singularly transformative event. One almost had to live through it to understand that. For decades, I've urged fellow Reagan writers to take up a history of Grenada and teach the world why that event was so crucial. Huge kudos to Bachman for telling this story and for reminding the world what it forgot."
—PAUL KENGOR, Ph.D., *New York Times* bestselling author of *God and Ronald Reagan*, *The Crusader: Ronald Reagan and the Fall of Communism*, and *Pope Leo XIV: The First American Pontiff*

# TURNING POINT

## HOW REAGAN LIBERATED GRENADA AND WON THE COLD WAR

### JOHN BACHMAN

#### EDITED BY CRAIG SHIRLEY

**Humanix Books**
www.humanixbooks.com

Humanix Books
Turning Point
Copyright © 2026 by Humanix Books
All rights reserved.

Humanix Books, P.O. Box 20989, West Palm Beach, FL 33416, USA
www.humanixbooks.com | info@humanixbooks.com

No part of this book may be reproduced or transmitted in any form or by any means, electronic or mechanical, including photocopying, recording, or by any other information storage and retrieval system, without written permission from the publisher.

Humanix Books is a division of Humanix Publishing, LLC. Its trademark, consisting of the words "Humanix Books," is registered in the United States Patent and Trademark Office and in other countries.

Humanix Books titles may be purchased for educational, business, or sales promotional use. For information about special discounts for bulk purchases, please contact the Special Markets Department at info@humanixbooks.com.

Cover photos © Getty Images/Historical/Contributor, Getty Images/Handout Grenada, and Associated Press/stf.

Cover and Interior Design: Ben Davis

ISBN: 978-1-63006-288-0 (Hardcover)
ISBN: 978-1-63006-289-7 (E-book)

*Printed in the United States of America*
10 9 8 7 6 5 4 3 2 1

*To my father Stephen.*
*This book would not have been possible*
*without your love and support.*

# Evil Empire

"Any objective observer must hold a positive view of American history, a history that has been the story of hopes fulfilled and dreams made into reality. Especially in this century, America has kept alight the torch of freedom, but not just for ourselves, but for millions of others around the world.... We will never compromise our principles and standards. We will never give away our freedom. We will never abandon our belief in God. And we will never stop searching for a genuine peace.... We must find peace through strength.... Let us pray for the salvation of all of those who live in that totalitarian darkness—pray they will discover the joy of knowing God. But until they do, let us be aware that while they preach the supremacy of the State, declare its omnipotence over individual man, and predict its eventual domination of all peoples on the earth, they are the focus of evil in the modern world.... If history teaches anything, it teaches that simpleminded appeasement or wishful thinking about our adversaries is folly. It means the betrayal of our past, the squandering of our freedom.... I urge you to beware the temptation of pride—the temptation of blithely declaring yourselves above it all and label both sides equally at fault, to ignore the facts of history and the aggressive impulses of an evil empire, to simply call the arms race a giant misunderstanding and thereby remove yourself from the struggle between right and wrong and good and evil.... While America's military strength is important, let me add here that I've always maintained that the struggle now going on for the world will never be decided by bombs or rockets, by armies or military might. The real crisis we face today is a spiritual one; at root, it is a test of moral will and faith.... I believe we shall rise to the challenge. I believe that communism is another sad, bizarre chapter in human history whose last pages even now are being written. I believe this because the source of our strength in the quest for human freedom is not material, but spiritual. And because it knows no limitation, it must terrify and ultimately triumph over those who would enslave their fellow man. For in the words of Isaiah: 'He giveth power to the faint; and to them that have no might, He increased strength. But they that wait upon the Lord shall renew their strength; they shall mount up with wings as eagles; they shall run, and not be weary.' Yes, change your world. One of our founding fathers, Thomas Paine, said, 'We have it within our power to begin the world over again.' We can do it."

*Ronald Reagan*
"Evil Empire" speech
March 8, 1983

---

*Sources:* https://en.wikisource.org/wiki/Evil_Empire_speech and https://www.reaganlibrary.gov/archives/topic-guide/evil-empire-speech-03081983

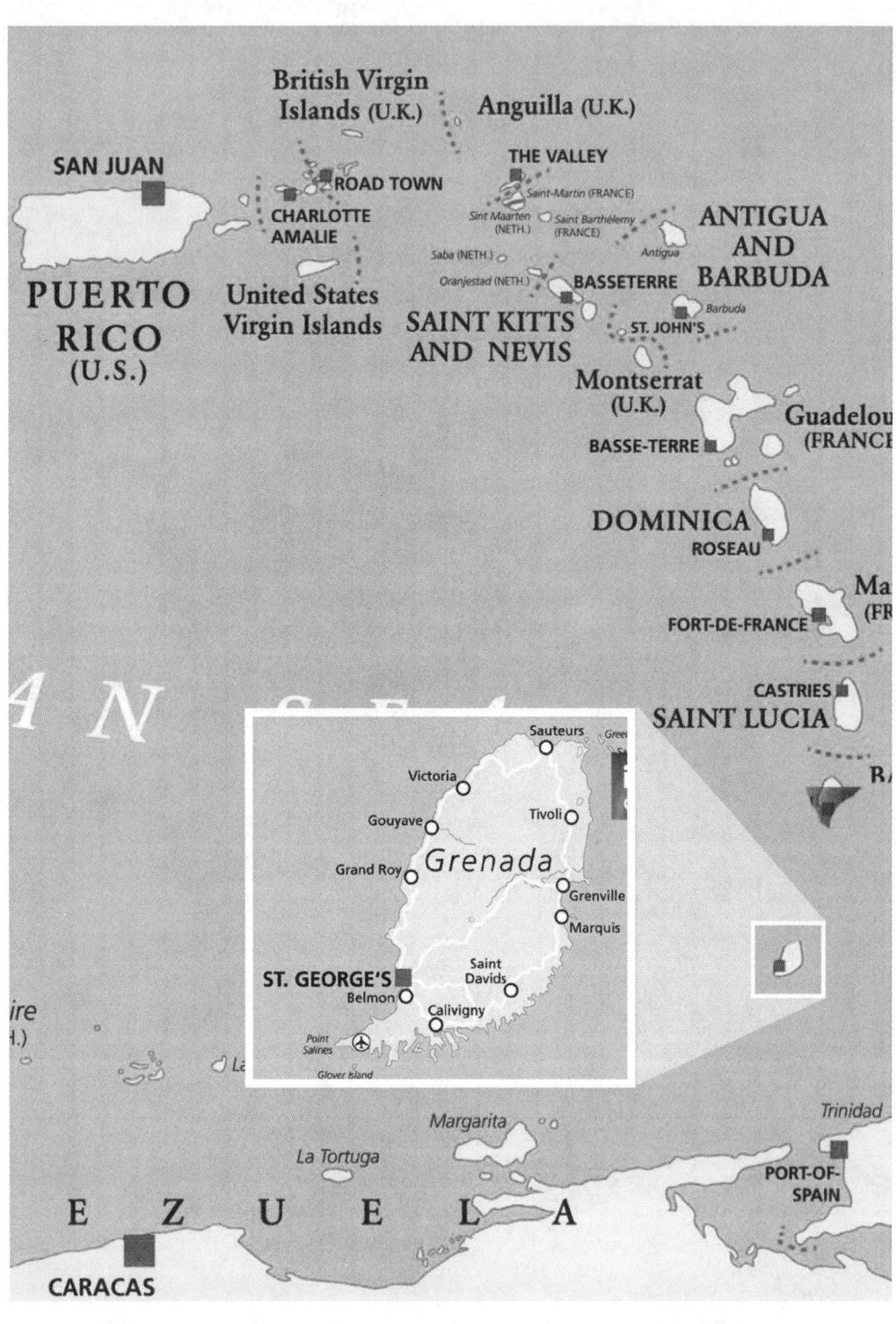

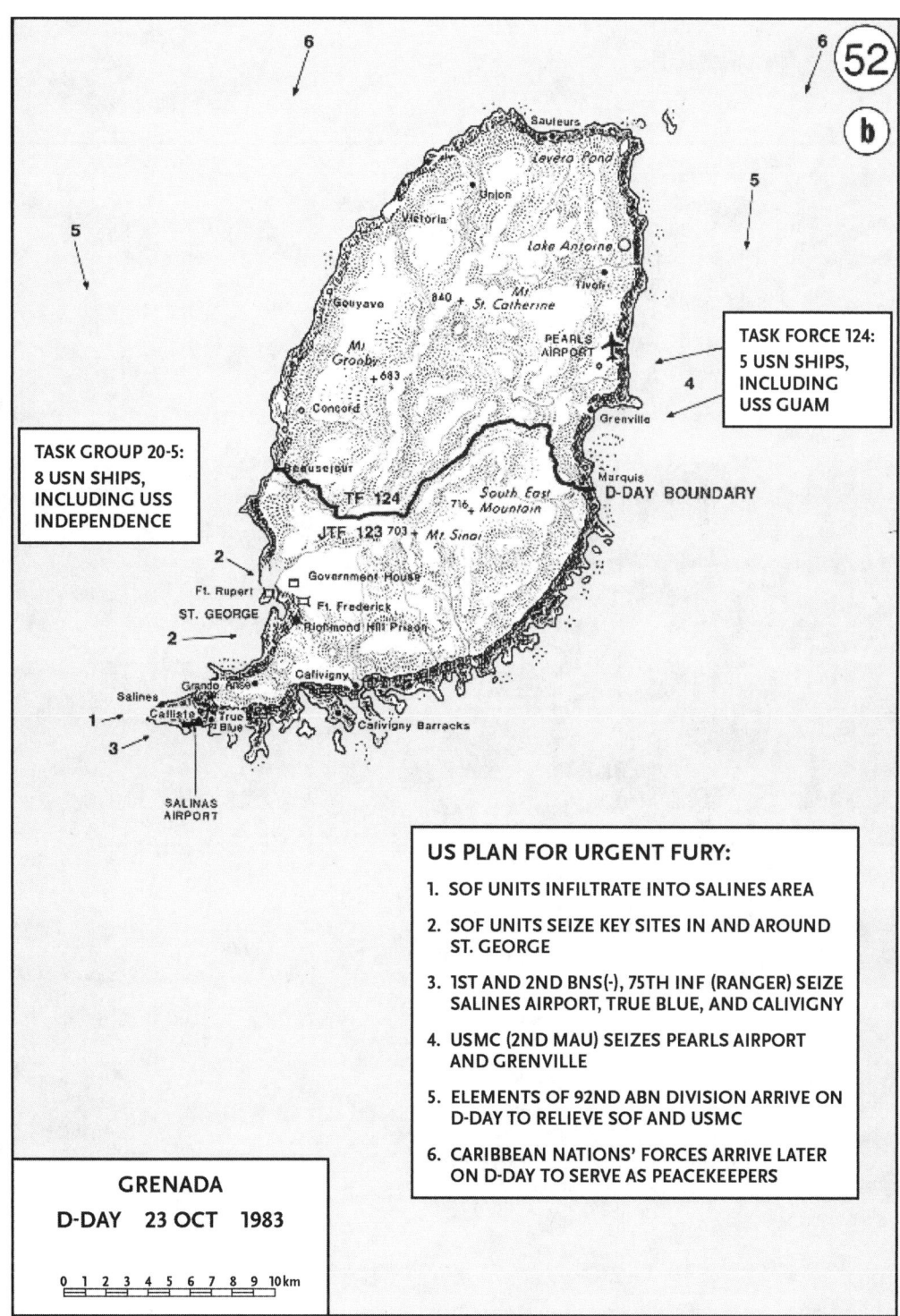

# Contents

Foreword by Craig Shirley . . . . . . . . . . . . . . . . . . . . . . . . . . . . . . . . . xiii
Author's Note . . . . . . . . . . . . . . . . . . . . . . . . . . . . . . . . . . . . . . . . . . . xvii
Preface . . . . . . . . . . . . . . . . . . . . . . . . . . . . . . . . . . . . . . . . . . . . . . . . . xxi

## PART ONE

**CHAPTER 1**
The Metastasis of Marxism in the Western Hemisphere . . . . . . . . . . . 3

**CHAPTER 2**
Reagan's Rise . . . . . . . . . . . . . . . . . . . . . . . . . . . . . . . . . . . . . . . . . . . 23

**CHAPTER 3**
The Resignation of Al Haig . . . . . . . . . . . . . . . . . . . . . . . . . . . . . . . 49

**CHAPTER 4**
The Soviet Gerontocracy . . . . . . . . . . . . . . . . . . . . . . . . . . . . . . . . . 83

## PART TWO

**CHAPTER 5**
Ripe for Revolution . . . . . . . . . . . . . . . . . . . . . . . . . . . . . . . . . . . . 115

**CHAPTER 6**
Contingency Plans . . . . . . . . . . . . . . . . . . . . . . . . . . . . . . . . . . . . . 169

**CHAPTER 7**
The Special Relationship . . . . . . . . . . . . . . . . . . . . . . . . . . . . . . . . 223

# PART THREE

**CHAPTER 8**
Operation Urgent Fury........................................261

**CHAPTER 9**
A Nation with Global Responsibilities........................329

Epilogue ....................................................365

**APPENDIX A**
President Ronald Reagan's "Evil Empire" Speech to
the National Association of Evangelicals......................369

**APPENDIX B**
President Ronald Reagan's Address to the Nation on Events
in Lebanon and Grenada .....................................383

**APPENDIX C**
President Ronald Reagan's Remarks at a White House Ceremony
Marking the First Anniversary of the Grenada Rescue Mission ..397

Acknowledgments............................................403

Notes......................................................405

Photography Credits........................................413

Index......................................................415

About the Author ..........................................433

# Foreword

This is John Bachman's first book with many more to hopefully come. He is a wonderful writer and researcher. By day, he works for Newsmax but by night, he writes and conducts exceptional research.

And that is the key to good nonfiction writing. *Research.* In a nonfiction book, the writing is only as good as the research and John dug deep to tell this important story accurately.

And what a story.

By now, the reader, you, must know this fact and good for Humanix Books to have the wisdom to publish this important work of history. It is a story that has not been told before.

The biggest story of the twentieth century—the fall of the Soviet Union—starts with the battle for Grenada. It is the first time the West and the United States successfully pushed back against the Soviets and communism. Since the end of World War II and the rise of Soviet communism, the story had often been about America losing and the Soviets winning. Too many times.

In Korea, we ended up with a stalemate against Communist China, backed by the Soviets.

The Cuban Missile Crisis was scored as a public relations win for America and President Kennedy, but the Russians got what they wanted—the removal of our nuclear missiles from Turkey and a pledge by the Kennedy Administration not to invade Cuba. And the Soviets still maintained their forward operating post.

We all know what happened in Vietnam, but also Laos and Cambodia. They all fell to communism. The Soviets were also in Africa and Central American, in direct violation of the Monroe Doctrine and the Treaty of Rios—United States initiatives that told outsiders to stay out of the affairs of our hemisphere.

In President Kennedy's magnificent phraseology, he called the Cold War a "long, twilight struggle" but it was sometimes a hot struggle too, and the battle from Grenada was indeed hot. We won and evicted the communists and John tells it in gripping detail.

*Turning Point* tells the story of the liberation of Grenada, a critical time in the Cold War: a turning point from Soviet advances towards the United States' eventual victory over the Soviet state—the fall of the Berlin Wall, the fall of the Warsaw Pact countries, and eventually the Soviet republics, and eventually, Russia itself.

Grenada was more than just a story about a small battle in a Caribbean nation, It was the beginning of the end of the Soviet Union. A new president was in town, and he rejected the co-existence and détente policies of previous presidents.

No, this president, Ronald Reagan was going to hit this "Evil Empire" with everything.

First, he rejected the Strategic Arms Limitation Talks II (SALT II), the Jimmy Carter-inspired treaty with the Soviets, deeming it as "knuckling under" to Soviet intentions. He'd already rejected the previously negotiated Helsinki Treaty, which codified Soviet domination of the Eastern Block.

He rebuilt American defenses. He put the world on notice that America was no longer the "pitiful giant" on the world stage.

He increased the funding for Radio Free Europe and Radio Marti. He stepped up our covert operations and aided the freedom movements throughout the world including the Velvet Revolution in Czechoslovakia.

Reagan often spoke out against the Soviets, saying America would transcend the Soviet state and cosine it to "the ash heap of history."

An important point had been reached on world affairs. The Soviets were on the run.

In a *coup de grâce*, Reagan unveiled his plan for the Strategic Defense Initiative. It was a planned land- and space-based system that would shoot down Soviet ICBMs.

The Soviets were scared shitless. So much so that at the Reykjavik Summit, Soviet Premier Gorbachev offered to eliminate an entire class of Russian missiles if Reagan would give up his beloved SDI.

Reagan said "no."

It was the "no" heard round the world.

After that, the handwriting was on the wall. The Soviets gave up their invasion of Afghanistan. And, after a fashion, the breakaway republics in Eastern Europe, well, broke away.

Then, the Berlin Wall fell. Reagan had left office several months before, but all credit was due him.

Ronald Reagan won the Cold War by standing firm against Soviet hegemony.

The Chinese say a journey of a thousand miles starts with a first step. And the first step in the defeat of Soviet communism began prophetically in a small Island named Grenada.

It's a story that needs to be told and now John Bachman has told it and tells it well.

*Craig Shirley*

# Author's Note

Some backstories: It was my first big, truly international news story with the global media assembled. Well, perhaps aside from the Daytona 500 which I had covered a few months before. But sports were not my primary area of interest. I was 24-years-old in June 2004, and I wanted to focus my reporting on politics, war, and national security. I was a young man in a hurry, rushing through my time in local news, jumping from story to story, eying a future as a war reporter, White House correspondent, and then the anchor chair.

At the time I was deeply invested in covering the presidency of George W. Bush. I had helped register voters on behalf of the Bush Campaign in 2000 while I was a student at the University of Georgia. I watched the dramatic disputes over ballots and hanging chads from my college apartment in Athens, Georgia with great intensity. We high fived and bro hugged when Bush was finally declared the winner. The next year, I woke up one morning in a stupor to see the World Trade Center and the Pentagon had been attacked. The live coverage on TV was ubiquitous. Even MTV was broadcasting CBS News. Not long after that, my naive optimism for the presidency of George W. Bush was getting bogged down in the Middle East.

We were at war. The United States had invaded Afghanistan and Iraq after that. I had covered the buildup and deployments at Fort Gordon, near Augusta, Georgia. And prior to that as a college student at the University of Georgia, which allowed me to get credentialed for a couple of President Bush's speeches as he sold the public on the idea of a "global war on terror."

By October and November 2003, you could sense the nervous excitement among the soldiers who were being deployed to "Southwest Asia" and the front lines of a new war for the first time in a decade. I also watched them come home after they saw what they were up against firsthand. Most of America believed we would be in and out of Iraq quickly. The looks on the soldiers' faces when they saw their wives and loved ones told me otherwise.

On June 5, 2004, I found myself headed to the G-8 Summit, as it was called before Russia was expelled and the conference was reduced to the G-7. The meetings were set amid the backdrop of the super exclusive community of Sea Island, Georgia. I was working for Augusta's CBS affiliate WRDW-TV. I arrived in Savannah, which was where most of the media were based, and the main filing center for the press. The moment I picked up my credentials was a surreal experience. I was so close, yet so far away from reaching my childhood career goal of being where history was happening, when it was happening.

I remember the day vividly—the thick and humid air of coastal Georgia was mixed with uncertain anticipation of international leaders and their entourages—all planning for a post 9/11 world.

There was a different type of gravity in the air. It felt far removed from my usual local stories. As helicopters circled above and satellite trucks lined the streets, I was overwhelmed and thrilled. I was finally working among seasoned journalists, some of my favorites, from around the world. That day wasn't just an assignment; it was the moment I knew journalism would always be about more than just people and their stories—it was also about being in the right place at the right time. I and everyone else seemed to be in my home state of Georgia three days before the summit.

That was the same day Ronald Reagan died, everyone's attention shifted from Sea Island to Bel Air, California, with a sense of urgency and sadness. Newsrooms nationwide were abuzz as headlines blared across every screen. "Ronald Reagan, 40th President, Dies at 93" was the *New York Times*' somber banner. The *Washington Post* followed with, "Reagan Remembered: Legacy of a Conservative Icon." For CNN, it was simply, "Farewell to a Legend," as images of Reagan's iconic salute on Air Force One and his hopeful, steady smile played in loops.

Everyone's Sea Island coverage plans for the day were scrapped instantly, replaced by in-depth retrospectives, reactions from global leaders, and segments recalling his speeches that had moved a generation. Locally, we quickly gathered reaction statements from the community and looked to tell Reagan's story through the eyes of Georgians, who shared both admiration and nostalgia for the "Great Communicator."

That day I also remember hearing a quote from Reagan's 1967 gubernatorial inauguration:

> Freedom is a fragile thing and it's never more than one generation away from extinction. It is not ours by way of inheritance; it must be fought for and defended constantly by each generation, for it comes only once to a people. And those in world history who have known freedom and then lost it have never known it again.

Here we are, a generation after Reagan's death and the viability of freedom is once again an open question in our own backyard.

There is no question Donald Trump's second election in 2024 is a response to the emerging threats we face, but those threats are many, and sadly familiar. The reawakening of socialist- and communist-leaning regimes in Central and South America continues. Chile elected Gabriel Boric, in 2021, while Bolivia's Luis Arce of the Movement for Socialism triumphed in 2020. Meanwhile, Nicaragua's Daniel Ortega of the socialist Sandinista party maintained power in a controversial 2021 re-election, and Venezuela's Nicolas Maduro of the United Socialist Party secured another term in 2024 amidst widespread international skepticism. Colombia's Gustavo Petro was elected president in 2022. Petro, previously a guerrilla, and mayor of Bogotá, ran under the Historic Pact for Colombia coalition, which includes socialist, environmental, and feminist movements among others.

At the same time, we have watched China's strategic investments in Central and South America, ranging from infrastructure to natural resources, not only expand its economic influence but we've also seen how they've fueled the rise of anti-American political factions in the West. By offering attractive financial deals and development projects without the political strings often attached by Western lenders, China has become an appealing partner for countries looking to move away from U.S. influence. Not enough people are talking about the geopolitical parallels between the expansion of Marxist-Leninist regimes in late 1970s and early 1980s and what's happening right now. The expansion of China's influence, and therefore socialism, will not stop until someone stops them.

*John Bachman*

# Preface

## Toronto, Canada—November 8, 1993

Margaret Thatcher stepped onto the stage at the Fraser Institute in Vancouver, Canada. She was no longer the United Kingdom's Prime Minister, but she still rightfully carried herself like someone who had helped change the course of history after a long victorious war. The Cold War was over. The Soviet hammer-and-sickle had been hauled down from the Kremlin's ramparts. In its place, the tricolor of the Russian Federation now flew over their government buildings. The West was busy writing its victory script, and Thatcher was in Canada to make sure the plot was told her way. Standing straight, voice crisp, she delivered the line, "Apart from Vietnam and Korea, the Cold War was won without a shot being fired."[1] It was the kind of statement that fit neatly into a headline, but it wasn't the whole truth. The Cold War had flared into white hot combat several times—in Angola's bush, in the jungles of Central America, and on a small Caribbean island that had briefly become one of the most dangerous theaters of the conflict.

That island was Grenada. In October 1983, American Army Rangers, Marines, and Special Forces including Navy SEALs, and Delta Force operators landed there to liberate a nation and rescue Americans. Their target: a brutal Marxist regime backed by Cubans and Soviets who were armed to the teeth. The local Grenadian soldiers were ready to fight for every block. Operation Urgent Fury was short, but it was no cake walk. Firefights erupted in the streets of St. George. Helicopter gunships strafed enemy positions cut into the hillsides. U.S. forces fought through ambushes, extracted trapped students under fire, and cleared the runway at Point Salines while anti-aircraft tracers clawed across the sky.

For Thatcher, it was more than a battle—it was a political minefield. Grenada was part of the British Commonwealth, and the U.S. led liberation, Operation Urgent Furry, had gone ahead without her consent, straining her otherwise close alliance with Ronald Reagan. She left it out of her victory speech in Toronto, choosing instead to cast the Cold War as a bloodless chess match won by resolve and deterrence.

## The Atlantic Ocean—October 22, 1983

Lance Corporal Bradley Garfield, a machine gunner attached to Echo Company (part of the 2nd Battalion, 8th Marines) was on board the USS *Guam*, an amphibious assault ship, as it steamed due east from Morehead City, North Carolina. The vessel was part of a 10-ship task force that included 1,900 Marines. They were headed to Lebanon to relieve the 1st Battalion 8th Marine Regiment—part of the Multinational Peacekeeping Forces in Beirut. Bradley and many of the other Marines on the *Guam* were headed to the Mideast for a security detail rotation, for some of the men it was their second deployment to Beirut. The bombing at the U.S. Embassy had just happened in April. The men on board were hardened and preparing for the worst.

"In those days, you could still smoke cigarettes in the ship's berthing areas," Garfield said. "It smelled like shit on board. It was a combination of smoke, body odor, and jet fuel. It felt like it was 100 degrees in our quarters."

Bradley and the men in his platoon were shacked up under *Guam*'s flight deck in an area that was about the size of an RV. When they weren't sleeping, the Marines were working out, playing spades on picnic tables, and listening to music.

"It was the era of the big boombox," Bradley told me during an interview. "From one corner a boombox would blare loud rap music, from the opposite corner of the room another boombox would blast country music."

"A few days into our voyage, we all noticed that we were now heading in a southern direction," Bradley said, adding they had no idea why until the Captain of the ship made an announcement on the intercom. President Reagan had diverted their task force to assist some Caribbean forces with taking back control of the island of Grenada.

The Pentagon spokesman told the press, it was just a precautionary measure.[2] There were approximately 1,200 Americans on Grenada who were now endangered by political unrest on the island. Government officials said they were in no immediate danger. The truth was everyone was in a lot of danger.

During the early morning hours of October 24, the Marines were awakened and summoned to the *Guam*'s hangar bay for a briefing with their battalion landing team commander, Lt. Col. Ray "E-tool" Smith. Smith had earned a Navy Cross and two Silver Stars in Vietnam. Bradley said Smith gave the men an effective "pep talk." Bradley also said the Marines were told that they had been ordered by President Reagan to conduct a Non-combatant Evacuation Operation on a small Caribbean island, and that they should expect resistance from an estimated 1,000 well-armed Cuban construction workers. He added that "many of my fellow salty Marines, who had already completed one tour of duty in Beirut, speculated that it was a drill and that we would not end up executing the mission."

The ship's commanders also scrapped the original movie they had planned for the men that night in the hangar bay and replaced it with the *Sands of Iwo Jima* starring John Wayne. The idea, according to the Marines, was to "put the men in the proper frame of mind for the landing."[3]

## Peals Airport, Grenada—October 25, 1983

Lance Corporal Garfied and the rest of the men in his regiment were awakened at 1:00 a.m. They were ordered back to the *Guam*'s hangar bay. Garfield said the "reality of the proposed invasion became evident" at that moment. The ammo technicians began issuing out small arms ammunition, hand grenades, anti-tank rockets, and other explosive devices. "Now, we all came to the realization that the mission was a go," Garfield said. A few hours later Garfield was on board a CH-46 Sea Knight helicopter as it took off from the *Guam*.

Bradley's would be the first helicopter to land at 5:00 a.m. on Grenadian soil. As they approached the island Garfield said they were getting peppered by anti-aircraft fire coming from two positions on the ground. "As we were landing in LZ Buzzard, I started seeing green tracer rounds. Bradley thought to himself, "holy shit this is real. . . those are actual bullets."

He recalled the pilot never actually touched the ground— Bradley says he just opened up the tailgate and "dumped us all out the back." His mission was to lay down a base of covering fire. And he remembers hearing his team leader yell, "GET

THE MACHINE GUN UP!" And Bradley says he "engaged the enemy—didn't hesitate."

He then watched two AH-1 Cobra gunships engage the anti-aircraft weapons with their 20mm canons and 2.75 inch rockets. "My adrenaline was through the roof! This was my first firefight! After the AA gun was silenced, we began our patrol toward Pearls airport. Along the way we encountered sporadic small arms harassing fire from the enemy. We pursued them and captured a few, what appeared to be, Cuban soldiers. The conditions were challenging the Marines like Lance Corporal Bradley were "humping a 70-pound pack, a 30-pound machine gun, and 700 rounds of ammunition through the jungles, chasing after evading combatants wearing T-shirts and shorts."

As the Marines moved south from the airport at Pearls and the town of Grenville, they were welcomed like conquering heroes. Bradley described the "exuberance of the Grenadian people who welcomed us with open arms and even assisted us with locating enemy combatants. They brought us food and drinks, hugged us, and graciously thanked us for freeing them from the oppression of the Soviet-backed Cubans who had killed their leader and taken over their island by a military coup, just days prior."

The Army Rangers and Special Operators tasked with taking the southern part of the island had a much different experience.

## Calliste Ridge, Grenada—October 26, 1983

The order came down just before first light. Bravo Company, part of the 2nd Battalion, 325th Infantry Regiment of the Army's 82nd Airborne Division, was to push beyond the secured perimeter of Point Salines and sweep the ridge overlooking the airfield. Their primary objective was to clear a suspected Cuban observation post near the village of Calliste. Intelligence reports described it as light resistance—maybe stragglers, certainly nothing organized.[4]

Captain Michael F. Ritz knew better. The terrain alone told him to be leery. The ridgeline was high, with a view to the northeast and access to the roads leading into the capital. The area was strategically vital. If the roles were reversed, and Ritz was tasked with defending the area, he'd put his men up there too—and have them dig in deep.

Ritz had always been destined for command. The son of Colonel Michael F. Ritz Sr., a decorated veteran of Korea and Vietnam, he grew up in military housing and on parade fields. His father was in the old-school Army. Polished boots. No nonsense. Mission first.

"Michael loved life," his father told the *Washington Post*, "since he was a boy and had a GI Joe. He was in the sea scouts and sea cadets, did the Outward Bound program in Germany. He was doing what he believed in, what he was trained to do."[5]

Michael's oldest brother, William, who also served in the Army wrote an article for *The Denver Post*, "When he was growing up, we called him Mikey. He was much like any other little boy—playing cowboys, climbing trees, riding sleds, throwing footballs and gradually warming to the idea that girls weren't so bad after all. He was a superbly gifted athlete and earned all-conference honors in football and soccer...."

Ritz graduated from West Point in 1979, then completed Infantry Officer Basic and Airborne School. He earned his Ranger tab the following year. One of the youngest company commanders in the 82nd, he was known for leading patrols himself—refusing to send his men into danger without seeing it first hand himself.

The jungle was eerily silent as Bravo company ascended towards the ridge line over Port Salines. The air was thick with dew and heavy tension. Captain Ritz moved to the front of the patrol, flanked by Staff Sergeant Gary Epps.[6] They found signs of the enemy including cigarette butts, rations, fresh foot prints. A recoilless rifle sat in a dugout area, covered in burlap and makeshift camouflage.

Ritz moved forward to check out the weapon. The other members of Bravo Company fanned out behind him. His hand rose with his palm open, the sign language of Airborne leaders: follow me. Then, suddenly, a flare exploded above him. Every man froze. The still of the moment was shattered by enemy gunfire.

The ridge line erupted in a thunderstorm of bullets. Cuban and Grenadian forces, dug into hardened fighting positions in an L-shaped ambush, opened up on Bravo's Company lead element. Ritz was the first man hit. One round struck him in the head, another pierced him through the chest. He dropped instantly, face down in the mud. No time to fire back. No final order. The Cubans kept firing. They had been waiting for this moment with belt-fed machine guns, rifles, and grenades. They had the high ground—and the element of surprise.

Epps died where he stood. Rifle still in hand. Epps had a choice: hold back or move forward. He moved. Always forward. He didn't want to leave Ritz's body. He wouldn't retreat until it was clear his men had a shot at surviving. He never made it off the ridge.

The firefight at Calliste lasted only 12 minutes. But it felt longer. The Cubans eventually broke contact. Bravo Company held the ground—bloodied but intact.

The loss hit hard. Two of the unit's finest, gone in the same burst of fire.

Ritz's body was flown home under escort and buried at Arlington National Cemetery, Section 60. His father, a two-war combat veteran, stood ramrod straight at the funeral.

Ritz's and Epps's deaths were just two of the 19 Americans killed during Operation Urgent Fury.

Bradley Garfield would go on to serve more than 30 years in the Marine Corps, retiring as highly decorated Chief Warrant Officer 5. Like many OUF veterans, he feels like this story has never received the attention it deserves.

"I'm sure there are a lot of special operations guys who would dispute Thatcher's quote," about winning the Cold War without firing a shot. I was there for the first time we actually engaged the Soviets—were fighting communism."

"If you poll 100 high school students, I don't think 1 of them could tell you what happened in Grenada. Or where it is. They don't know that we liberated an island and restored democracy."

This is the story of how it happened.

# PART ONE

CHAPTER 1

# The Metastasis of Marxism in the Western Hemisphere

*"I feel, and I want you to tell the world that the Nicaraguan people have not thrown me out. It is an insurrection orchestrated and backed by Governments who are afraid of the Communists and who backed them."*
—Anastasio Somoza Debayle to the *New York Times*, July 17, 1979

## THE FALL OF NICARAGUA

By early 1979, President Jimmy Carter had grown disillusioned with Nicaragua's Somoza regime. Just a year earlier, he had praised President Anastasio "Tachito" Somoza Debayle for allowing a human rights commission into the country. But behind the scenes, Carter had already started cutting aid—money Somoza badly needed as Nicaragua slipped into civil war. That decision helped ignite a revolution. Fueled by Soviet and Cuban support, it was led by Marxist rebels known as the Sandinistas. They promised democratic reforms and an end to dictatorship. Tachito Somoza, the last of his family to rule Nicaragua, would soon be forced to flee.

The Somoza dynasty had begun decades earlier. Like many former Spanish colonies, Nicaragua gained independence in the 1820s. As civil unrest spread, the United States, invoking the Monroe Doctrine, moved to block European influence in Latin America. In 1853, U.S. troops, including Marines, landed in Nicaragua to restore order and oversee elections. By the late 1800s, America's growing military power gave it more weight in the region. In 1904, the Roosevelt Corollary established that the United States could intervene in the hemisphere to stabilize nations and protect creditors—often its own.

Following the Spanish-American War, the United States secured similar control in Cuba through the Platt Amendment. That pattern of influence extended across the region. By World War II, U.S. intervention stretched as far north as Canada and Greenland. After the war, new agreements like the Rio Treaty and the Organization of American States helped solidify U.S. hemispheric dominance. And in 1962, American strength helped resolve the Cuban Missile Crisis.

Anastasio "Tacho" Somoza García became president in 1936 after a coup. Born into a wealthy coffee family, he studied in Philadelphia, married into Nicaragua's elite, and spoke fluent English. His ties to U.S. Marines and control of the National Guard made him a powerful figure. He staged a coup, suppressed rivals, and united Nicaragua's political factions under his control. Even after stepping down, he rewrote the constitution to return to office—against Truman's objections—and won re-election in 1950. He ruled until his assassination in 1956 by a socialist poet.

His eldest son, Luis, took power and supported the failed 1961 Bay of Pigs invasion, allowing CIA-backed Cubans to launch from Nicaraguan soil. That same year, the Sandinistas began their armed rebellion. Luis eventually stepped aside but kept influence until his death in 1967. His younger brother, Tachito, had trained at the U.S. Naval Academy and followed the family path through the National Guard's ranks.

By the late 1970s, Nicaragua was boiling. Years of repression, corruption, and a failed earthquake recovery had turned the public against the Somozas. In 1978, the murder of newspaper editor Pedro Chamorro—an outspoken Somoza critic—sparked nationwide outrage. Though Somoza's involvement was never proven, most Nicaraguans blamed him. *La Prensa*, Chamorro's paper, became a rallying point for the opposition.

Seeing the unrest, Fidel Castro invited Sandinista leaders to Havana in early 1979. There, they trained in tactics drawn from Khrushchev's playbook—take power under the banner of democracy, then consolidate it under Marxism. Castro had seen Carter's soft responses in places like Iran, Angola, and Afghanistan. Between 1970 and 1979, more than a dozen pro-Western governments had already fallen to communist revolutions. Nicaragua was just one of them.

Despite intelligence warnings, the Carter administration started backing the Sandinistas. They coordinated with countries like Mexico, Venezuela, and Colombia to strip diplomatic recognition from Somoza's government. Promises of a "minimal military" and "genuine democracy" followed. None would be kept.

In 1977, the State Department had labeled the Sandinistas a small, Marxist, pro-Castro terror group. By 1979, they had swelled to a 6,000-strong fighting force. With U.S. support withdrawn, Somoza lost his grip on the National Guard and the presidency.

On July 17, 1979, he stepped down and fled to Miami. When the United States pressed him to leave, he moved to the Bahamas, then Paraguay. Over four decades, the Somoza family had built a $900 million fortune. But for their Marxist enemies, exile wasn't punishment enough. They wanted the dynasty dead and buried—for good.

## THE ASSASSINATION IN ASUNCIÓN

The sunrise over Asunción, Paraguay, came with a noticeable chill on the morning of September 17, 1980. At first, the skies were clear, but as the city began to come alive, thick clouds started rolling in. The clouds were hanging low in the sky, almost blanketing Asunción. They also cast an ominous shadow over a man who had been warned, by friends and foes alike, that his life was in danger. Tachito Somoza would be dead before lunchtime, consumed in a storm of M16 and RPG fire. His assassination would also send a message to Soviet and Cuban–backed Marxists factions all over the world. It was open season on America's allies, past and present. Not only was treacherous behavior being tolerated, it was also being rewarded.

Tachito Somoza's white Mercedes-Benz limousine was conspicuous but fitting for a man who always seemed to relish his reputation as an international playboy, even after his removal from the Nicaraguan presidency. On the day of his assassination, he was accompanied by his driver and his financial advisor. They were headed to the bank for some routine business transactions. Their errands came one day before a trip Tachito had scheduled to visit his hacienda, which was in a remote village in northwestern Paraguay. They departed Somoza's gated mansion around 10:00 a.m., around the same time the clouds started to gather in the skies above Asunción.

Tachito's white Mercedes was followed by a red compact car carrying four bodyguards—all of whom were members of the Paraguayan national police force. As the two cars approached Asunción's Avenida España, en route to the city's financial district, a stolen blue pickup truck, carrying three men inside, lurched into the road. Somoza's white limo stopped suddenly.

Nearby, an assassin, known to the CIA as "Captain Santiago," stood on the balcony of a house overlooking the busy street. He was holding an RPG launcher, which he had trained on Somoza's white Mercedes as it approached. The blue Chevy pickup had pulled out into the street perpendicularly, blocking Somoza's two-car motorcade. Captain Santiago squeezed the trigger on his RPG launcher, but it misfired. Tachito's entire entourage were now fully aware that they were the target of what would prove to be a well-coordinated and explosive assassination attempt.

The bodyguards jumped out of the red compact car in a panic. Another assassin, Gorriarán Merlo, was stationed in the front yard of the same house with the balcony where Captain Santiago was stationed. Merlo charged toward Tachito's Mercedes with his M16 firing at a rate of 800 rounds per minute, the bullets penetrating the car with ease.

Merlo emptied one magazine, reloaded, and then turned around to face the bodyguards who were exchanging fire with the other assassins, who had jumped out of their blue truck and were firing at Somoza from behind it in the road. On the balcony above the street, Captain Santiago reloaded and fired a second RPG from his perch—this time successfully striking his target.

Suddenly, a blinding white flash enveloped the intersection, followed immediately by a deafening explosion that shattered the air and rattled the ground and the surrounding buildings with a concussive blast. The second RPG had peeled off the hood and roof of Somoza's white Mercedes. The remains of the car, riddled with bullet holds, looked like a giant sardine tin that had been torn open, stomped on, and set on fire. Thick black smoke was pouring out of the engine compartment. There was no doubt about the outcome. If the barrage of M16 rounds hadn't killed Tachito first, the RPG blast had certainly finished the job.

By 10:15 a.m., it was all over. Anastasio "Tachito" Somoza Debayle lay dead inside his car, and there were no survivors among his entourage. Captain Santiago started racing down the stairs from the balcony of the house his crew had recently rented for the sole purpose of killing the former Nicaraguan president. He joined Gorriarán Merlo, who was already down on the street. Both men jumped into the bed of the blue Chevy pickup truck, which was waiting to hurry them away from the scene. The truck's driver, nicknamed "El Gordo" because of his stocky build, stomped on the accelerator and sped away. Police wouldn't arrive on the scene for another 25 minutes.

The pickup truck was later found abandoned several blocks away. The *Washington Post* reported that authorities had found two-way radios, copies of popular Spanish-language comic books, sausages, and bread inside the truck. The men had been stalking Tachito Somoza for who knows how long. When Paraguayan investigators searched the rented home from which the attack had been staged, all they found were one of the two-way radios and the RPG launcher used in the assassination.

Two days later, the Paraguayan police cornered and killed Captain Santiago, whose real name was Hugo Alfredo Yrurzum. In the first chaotic days after the assassination, they incorrectly believed that Yrurzum had been the mastermind behind the attack. Some of the other assassins had escaped, including Gorriarán Merlo. The Paraguayan government never even officially acknowledged Merlo's presence in their country, according to the CIA's archives, which identifies Merlo as the main player in the attack.

And despite their well-publicized claims that they never authorized the hit on Tachito Somoza, the Sandinistas paid Gorriarán Merlo $33,000 for the attack, according to one of his associates who was interviewed by the *Miami Herald* years later.[4] Merlo himself would later comment publicly that he and his fellow assassins had carried out "revolutionary justice" by killing Somoza and relieving Nicaragua of what the Sandinistas and Marxists everywhere considered to be the country's "national shame."

The assassination was not conducted by amateurs. Nor by an impassioned poet, as was the case with Tachito's father. Merlo's crew was full of battle-hardened Marxists. The plot was planned and carried out by former members of the Argentine People's Revolutionary Army (Ejército Revolucionario del Pueblo, or ERP) on behalf of the new Sandinista government in Nicaragua.

Before the ERP's defeat and collapse inside Argentina, they had fought alongside Fidel Castro's revolutionaries in Cuba, proving once again how resilient the Marxist threat was and how far it had spread.

Gorriarán Merlo, the real ringleader of the Somoza assassination squad, had recruited militants like Osvaldo "El Gordo" Farfan, the driver of the getaway vehicle. "Captain Santiago" Hugo Alfredo Yrurzum, the CIA later discovered, infiltrated Paraguay using a phony passport along with the rest of the team, including a woman who went by the name Silva Mercedes Rodgers. Her name was used to sign the lease on the house they rented in Asunción That house was just two blocks away from the U.S. embassy.

For committed Marxists, including Fidel Castro, Nicaragua was now a fully functioning launch pad for the next wave of communism in the Western Hemisphere. Aspiring dictators saw the assassination of a resilient, U.S.-educated anti-communist like Tachito Somoza and acted accordingly.

During their training, the members of Merlo's squad had joined up with a Sandinista-affiliated militant leader named Eden Pastora, also known as "Commander Zero" ("Comandante Cero"). Pastora operated a training compound just over the Nicaraguan border in Costa Rica and had trained Marxist guerrillas before and after the fall of Somoza's government.

Pastora gained global notoriety in 1978, when he orchestrated a bold insurgency, leading a band of guerrilla fighters on a raid in which they seized Nicaragua's national congress and held the government hostage. The mission forced Somoza's government to free sixty imprisoned Sandinista comrades, and it delivered a seismic blow to the Somoza government in Nicaragua. However, as time passed, ideological divisions within the Sandinista movement caused a rift. Pastora found himself at odds with his more ideologically radical comrades, and disillusionment set in. Gradually, he distanced himself from the Sandinistas and their charismatic leader, Daniel Ortega. The story of Pastora is an important and common tale inside many Marxist revolutions: The people who truly believe in the cause, yet refuse the lavish trappings available to leaders, wind up jaded, marginalized, or worse—dead.

Merlo's assassination squad was also heavily influenced by one of the original founders of the Sandinista movement, Tomás Borge, who would eventually become Nicaragua's interior minister under President Ortega and his new Sandinista government.

Borge was extremely close to Ortega. Ortega, who was often referred to as "El Comandante," exhibited an unyielding and authoritarian leadership style in the early days of the Sandinista government. But as the revolution unfolded, Ortega's commitment to socialist principles gave way to his ruthless determination to consolidate power. Ortega's proclivity for silencing dissent became increasingly pronounced. The early promise of a more equitable Nicaragua, championed by the Sandinista movement, was gone. Ortega was orchestrating his own version of human rights, which were as bad as, if not worse than, anything the country had experienced under the Somozas. This descent into a violent dictatorship occurred despite the warm welcome the Carter administration had given to Ortega and the upstart Sandinista movement. President Carter even invited Ortega to the White House in September 1979. Under the Carter administration, the U.S. government would provide $118 million of direct aid to the Sandinistas. They would get another $260 million in aid from U.S.-funded international development banks. Half a billion dollars in private bank loans would be refinanced on very generous terms. All of that during the first two years of the new Nicaraguan government.

There had been numerous offers to kill Somoza, including at least six from Merlo's group of Argentine ERP veterans, prior to their offer finally being accepted. The Sandinistas, under the leadership of Ortega, and Borge had rejected offers to kill Somoza. And publicly Borge said Tachito was "more useful alive than dead," because "he is the monkey that scares the people." We now know that was just lip service, because Merlo's ERP hit squad would ultimately become Somoza's judge, jury, and executioner not long after Borge spoke those exact words.

Several years after Tachito's assassination, the *Miami Herald* interviewed the surviving members of Gorriarán Merlo's hit squad. They claimed their group had developed a total of 14 separate assassination plans, including a raid on Somoza's gated mansion. Ultimately, they felt their best chance of success was a bold daylight ambush on the streets of Asunción. Perhaps they wanted the public to see Somoza's assassination up close and personal to send a message. One of the assassins also recalled that he was surprised by how easily the bullets shredded Somoza's car door. He said he thought Somoza, who had many enemies, would be riding in an armored car. The CIA's records show Tachito Somoza had been warned by Paraguayan authorities for over a year that he would be the target of an assassination attempt. But Somoza refused to alter his lifestyle.

One *Washington Post* report noted that "the method of the assassination, with its bazooka shot and multiple machine guns and getaway cars," was initially "a mystery to some in the diplomatic community."[5] One observer interviewed by the paper noted that Tachito Somoza used to go down to the Armed Forces track every day. And an assassin "could have gotten him with a bullet." So, why so much firepower?

Chaos and confusion naturally followed the explosive assassination, and wild rumors quickly began to swirl about the possible motives behind the former Nicaraguan president's murder. Somoza reportedly had had a falling out with the son-in-law of

Paraguay's anti-communist president General Alfredo Stroessner over an affair Somoza had been having with the son-in-law's mistress. Because of this, some of President Stroessner's friends in the diplomatic community initially said the assassination was more likely a domestic dispute than a political one. News cameras captured Somoza's distraught paramour weeping at the scene of his demise.

A disgraced British spy named John Banks later claimed that it was none other than U.S. President Jimmy Carter's Central Intelligence Agency that ordered the assassination of Somoza.[6] Banks, who was later convicted in 1980 of extorting $250,000 from the Nicaragua embassy in London, in exchange for information about a previous attempt on Somoza's life, alleged in court testimony that he had been one of six British and American mercenaries hired by the CIA to carry out the hit in Asunción. However, Banks claimed that he and his fellow mercenaries had been reluctant to follow through with the assassination plan themselves and instead had chosen to hire the Argentine hit squad on behalf of the CIA. Despite vehemently denying the extortion charges, Banks was convicted and sentenced to prison. He later escaped, only to be recaptured and imprisoned again in late 1981. An associate of Banks claims that by 1982, the former British spy had been released and had taken up a new role as a security advisor for Libyan leader Muammar Gaddafi.

After the initial chaos and sensational headlines, the assassination story quickly faded from front pages of American newspapers, as well as TV and radio newscasts. At the time, Nicaragua seemed much less significant than the inflamed Islamic Revolution in Iran, inflation, and the high price and limited availability of gasoline in the United States. And, of course, the looming presidential election. So did an even smaller country, the tiny island nation of Grenada.

## GRENADA'S BLOODLESS REVOLUTION

The Marxist revolution in Grenada, part of the British Commonwealth, had slid under the radar of the international press and the public eye. In the early hours of March 13, 1979, the New Jewel Movement, spearheaded by Maurice Bishop, orchestrated a remarkably bloodless coup, unseating Prime Minister Sir Eric Gairy. The atmosphere on the island was charged with a sense of anticipation. Bishop was promising a new era of progressive socialism.

Under Bishop's government, Grenada embarked on an ambitious agenda aimed at restructuring the nation. Land redistribution initiatives sought to address long-standing issues of inequality, and the nationalization of key industries signaled a departure from the country's reliance on traditional Western powers. Grenada, once a tranquil Caribbean haven, now found itself navigating the currents of international socialism while flirting with countries like Cuba and the Soviet Union. The beginning of Grenada's Marxist revolution was quieter than Nicaragua's, but its end would mark a turning point in the battle against the spread of communism. Much of the West, including the U.S. government, seemed to have more pressing matters than a small island nation in the Caribbean. But for both Castro and the Soviets, Grenada's strategic location made it a prize worth pursuing.

The allure of socialist ideals drew Bishop toward the Soviet Union. In July 1982, Bishop signed significant economic and political agreements with the Soviet government during his first visit to Moscow since seizing power.[7] The *New York Times* reported that he had secured $1.4 million for the acquisition of 500 tons of steel, 400 tons of flour, and other essential goods.[8] Additionally, the Soviet Union provided Grenada with a 10-year credit of $7.7 million for the purchase of equipment. The Soviets, in turn, saw in

Grenada an opportunity to extend their influence in the Western Hemisphere. As the ink dried on these accords, the Caribbean breeze carried the weight of shifting alliances, and Grenada found itself entangled in the intricate dance of superpower politics.

Parallel to his dalliance with the Soviets, Bishop turned his attention to the charismatic allure of Cuba. In Havana, where the pulse of Marxist revolution beat most loudly, Bishop found a kindred spirit in Fidel Castro. Their friendship, solidified over shared aspirations and a shared disdain for Western hegemony, laid the groundwork for unprecedented cooperation. Cuba, with its revolutionary fervor and military might, became a key ally in Bishop's grand design for Grenada's future.

Central to Bishop's vision was the development of an airport that could serve both military and touristic purposes—an ambitious endeavor with implications that rippled far beyond the shores of Grenada. The construction of Point Salines International Airport became a symbol of the island's pivot toward a dual-purpose identity. Strategically positioned, the airport not only opened the doors to increased tourism but also raised eyebrows in Washington, D.C., where concerns about its potential military applications began to foment.

In Bishop's eyes, the airport represented not just concrete and tarmac but also a bold assertion of Grenada's newfound sovereignty. It was a declaration that this Caribbean nation, once a pawn on the geopolitical chessboard, was now making its own moves. The airport project, entwined with his alliances with the Soviets and Cubans, became the nexus of a complex geopolitical game—one that would ultimately contribute to the escalating tensions leading to the dramatic events of 1983. As the runway stretched out toward the horizon, so did the geopolitical ramifications of Bishop's intricate dance with global powers.

## MEXICO'S TILT TOWARD MARXISM

There were legitimate concerns that extended into and beyond smaller countries like El Salvador, which looked like it would be the next domino to fall to Marxism in Central America. Communism was pulsing through Central America. What was next? Maybe Mexico.

In early 1979, conservative scholar Constantine Menges wrote an article titled "Mexico: The Iran Next Door?"[9] Menges drew a parallel to the recent downfall of the shah of Iran and the contemporary state of Mexican politics. Menges argued that Mexico, a significant yet troubled ally of the United States, might follow a trajectory like Iran's. He also envisioned a scenario for Mexico that mirrored the Sandinistas' triumph earlier that year against Anastasio "Tachito" Somoza in Nicaragua—only he predicted Mexico's revolution would unfold on a grander scale.

During the 1970s oil boom, Mexico obtained the ability to borrow and spend without any serious restraint. The revelry, however, met an abrupt end when the Federal Reserve Board started to jack up U.S. interest rates to quell inflation, triggering a harsh economic reckoning south of the border. Mexico's Institutional Revolutionary Party ("Partido Revolucionario Institucional," or PRI), later dubbed "the perfect dictatorship" by Nobel laureate and Peruvian writer Mario Vargas Llosa, found its grip on power weakening against the rising tide of political dissent. Corruption, an ever-present factor in Mexican politics, took a darker turn as officials sought funds from narcotics cartels and other foreign influences to fill the void left by dwindling oil revenues.

In his book *Inside the National Security Council*, Constantine Menges wrote that Mexico was hedging its bets by pursuing a two-track foreign policy strategy that sought to maintain relations with existing governments like the U.S. government, while also providing active support to insurgent movements like the Sandinistas. In May 1979, Mexico's president José López Portillo welcomed Castro as a "vindicated hero," according to the *Washington Post*.[10] Mexico had even allowed the Sandinistas and other guerrilla movements to set up political and propaganda shops inside Mexico. Following Castro's visit, President Portillo joined the calls for removal of the Somoza government. Portillo was also working with Costa Rica, Venezuela, Panama, Colombia, and Cuba to provide aid for the Sandinista rebels, while at the same time Mexico was also working with the Carter administration and the OAS to withdraw official diplomatic recognition of Somoza's government.

## A WARNING FROM CONGRESS

About two weeks after Somoza's assassination, on October 2, 1980, the topic of Nicaragua was raised by Congressman Bill Young. Representative Young, a Republican from Florida, spoke up during a House Foreign Affairs Subcommittee hearing on Capitol Hill.[11] Young, unlike the current commander in chief, seemed to understand that Somoza's downfall would have a profound effect on American foreign policy. Young stated that key members of Congress, and their staffers, who held top-level security clearances were being blocked by the intelligence community and the State Department as they attempted to investigate the Sandinistas' ties to Somoza's assassination. Representative Young implored his colleagues to act.

"There are documents which the Intelligence Committee staff have requested which they have not received," Young declared.

> Mr. Chairman, on September 12, the president of the
> United States signed a certification in which he swore

that the government of Nicaragua "has not cooperated with or harbored any international terrorist organization or is aiding, abetting, or supporting acts of violence or terrorism in other countries," the intelligence information available to the president proves the opposite.

I have had the opportunity to examine information made available to the president by our intelligence agencies, and no reasonable man, after examining that evidence, could reach the same conclusion contained in the president's certification.

Young was exposing the deceitful nature of the new Nicaraguan regime. He passionately argued that the Sandinistas had made it clear that they had no intention of upholding the promises they had made to obtain a $75 million loan and other aid from the U.S. government.

During his speech, Young quoted the Sandinistas' Interior Minister Tomás Borge, one of the founders of the movement, who said, "If the Americans could buy us with $75 million or with one billion dollars, we would stop being revolutionaries. We revolutionaries would rather starve, if necessary, before falling on our knees in the face of Yankee imperialism."

Young also stressed that the Sandinistas were actively supporting other Marxist terror groups in Latin American countries, like El Salvador. Not only that, but they were also working directly with another Soviet-backed terror organization in the Middle East, the Palestinian Liberation Organization. The Sandinistas' and PLO's unholy partnership was born out of a shared appetite for destruction and chaos and a mutual admiration of Marxism.

Young also cited news reports including an interview with Jorge Mandi, who was a Sandinista attaché in Europe, granted to the Kuwaiti newspaper *Al-Watan*.[12] Mandi said there was "a long-standing blood unity between the Sandinistas and the historical efforts of Arab countries supporting the Palestinians." He continued, "We have long had close relations with the Palestinians."

"Many of the units belonging to the Sandinista movement were at Palestinian revolution bases in Jordan," Mandi boasted during the interview.

The implications of this statement were staggering—it meant that the PLO had been actively supporting the Sandinistas, providing them with a safe haven to train and organize their fighters. That was in addition to the support the Sandinistas were already getting from the Soviets, Cuba, Mexico, and the United States.

Congressman Young hinted that the news reports supported the intelligence he had been allowed to see. Young again urged his colleagues to act immediately and end the federal government's financial support for the new Sandinista regime in Nicaragua.

Congressman Young also recalled the story of a leftist terrorist captured by the El Salvadoran government who, during an interview on a local radio station, said his group had gone to the border of Honduras to receive weapons from the Sandinistas, and those weapons came "directly from the Soviet Union and the Socialist Republic of Cuba."

"Yet, somehow," a visibly frustrated Young said, "the Sandinistas had already received $15 million of the [U.S. government] loan."

Rep. Young also emphasized that several terror groups in El Salvador were now unifying into "a single army," just like they had in Nicaragua prior to the Marxist revolution there, as well as every other country that had fallen under the spell of a communist dictator during the Carter administration.

Furthermore, Representative Young mentioned a story published in May 1980 by the *Jewish Press* newspaper.[13] The paper reported that during the revolution, Nicaragua's entire Jewish community had disappeared, some 70 families, a total of 350 people. The *Jewish Press* had interviewed anti-communist Nicaraguan Jewish exiles, who claimed the Sandinistas had employed a combination of anti-Semitic threats and private property confiscation to force out the country's Jewish community. Later in 1983, the *Washington Post* reported that Anthony Quainton, the U.S. ambassador to Nicaragua under Ronald Reagan, said he found no credible evidence to corroborate the allegations of systemic anti-Semitism by the Marxist Sandinista regime.[14] However, the Anti-Defamation League, which conducted its own investigation, found that Nicaragua's small Jewish minority had been indeed subjected to the most insidious forms of persecution by the Sandinistas. The anti-Semitic tactics stemmed from a festering animosity over Israel supplying weapons to the army of former president Anastasio Somoza, Tachito's father. There was no indication the Sandinistas were going to forget that. And despite the friendly treatment from the Carter administration, Nicaragua's Marxist regime worked to undermine the Camp David Peace Accords and Carter's broader Mideast peace efforts through their unwavering support for, and collaboration with, the Palestine Liberation Organization.

Young closed his remarks with this: "What we have is a case of the intelligence community being manipulated by the executive branch to protect a political sensitivity."

CHAPTER 2

# Reagan's Rise

*"We must go forth from here united, determined
and what a great general said a few years ago is true:
There is no substitute for victory."*

—Ronald Reagan, in his speech at
the Republican National Convention, 1976

## The News World

### NEWS WORLD PREDICTION

# Reagan landslide

Will win by more than 350 electoral votes and carry New York as well

News World Election Prediction

## ONE DEBATE FOR ALL THE MARBLES

*October 28, 1980*
More than 80 million Americans tuned in to witness what would become the defining moment in the 1980 presidential campaign. Ronald Reagan and Jimmy Carter squared off in the one and only nationally broadcast debate featuring the two major party presidential candidates. The backdrop was Cleveland, Ohio, and a nation at a crossroads. The Carter administration was grappling with multiple international crises, a faltering economy, and a pervasive sense of uncertainty among American voters. The prime-time showdown came just one week before the election and at a time when most of the polls showed a very tight contest.

Carter, facing the dire circumstances of the Islamic Revolution, including a hostage crisis, and a troubled economy, would later be accused of trying to explain away the nation's "malaise" by diving too deeply into policy details. Carter sounded like a preachy policy wonk. In contrast, Reagan, already known for his mastery of stagecraft, exuded confidence and charm.

During the heart of the debate, Reagan delivered an attack line that landed like the first punch of a boxer's one-two combo.

The former governor of California had to respond to President Carter's criticism of Reagan's views on Medicare. President Carter had called for a nationalized health insurance program, and when he did this, the camera cut to Reagan, who chuckled and shrugged as if a window of opportunity had just opened right in front of him. His rebuttal came with a cool smile, and the iconic line, "There you go again." What Reagan said was less important than how he said it. The confident Reagan stood in stark contrast to Carter, who seemed uneasy throughout the entire debate.

The second punch from Reagan's rhetorical one-two combo would come during the closing arguments. Reagan asked the audience a simple question: "Are you better off than you were four years ago?" This carefully rehearsed and powerfully delivered line struck at the core of Carter's aspirations for a second term.

As Rick Shenkman, a presidential historian at George Mason University, told *U.S. News & World Report*, "Certainly no one remembers what the hell Carter said that night. It was Reagan's debate."[1]

The election's results validated Shenkman's sentiment, as Reagan secured a landslide victory, winning the popular vote, 44 states, and 489 electoral votes to Carter's 49 electoral college votes.

Reflecting on the historic night, reporter Howard Wilkinson, who witnessed the debate firsthand, likened it to "watching an American presidency go down the chutes." But the prevailing media coverage, including the front page of the Cleveland *Plain Dealer*, attempted to downplay Reagan's televised victory.[2] The paper's headline yelled, "Carter and Reagan trade punches but both on their feet at the bell—Each candidate leaves the ring without errors." However, there were plenty of people who disagreed.

In a surprising turn during the debate, Carter invoked the name of his 13-year-old daughter, Amy, to emphasize the significance of negotiating a weapons treaty with the Soviet Union. The move was intended to highlight Amy's concern about the future and nuclear warfare including the Strategic Arms Limitation Treaty (SALT).

"To close out this discussion, I think it would be better to put into perspective what we are talking about. I had a discussion with our daughter, Amy, the other day before I came here to ask her what the most important issue was. She said she thought it was nuclear weaponry, and the control of nuclear arms," Carter stated.

UPI later reported that groans were heard from some of the reporters covering the event.[3] On the nationally broadcast radio program *The Larry King Show*, which aired shortly after the debate that night, several callers pointed out that Carter's use of his daughter was a memorable gaffe. "The general consensus was that it was absolutely outrageous," commented Jack Kirby, producer of *The Larry King Show*.

Still, the *Plain Dealer*'s tilt toward the incumbent echoed what was said about Reagan by a lot of the most prominent media after the debate. Most of the press had obviously failed to capture the reality of the situation and the groundswell of support that Reagan had already earned. The debate was Reagan's, and thus so was the presidency.

Cuyahoga, Ohio, GOP Chairman Bob Hughes said in the immediate aftermath of the debate, "I think he just won the election."[4] Hughes was obviously biased, but his optimism better reflected the reality of the moment than a lot of the media coverage the following day. Two thousand jubilant Reagan supporters attended the post-debate watch party. Hughes said they had to turn away an additional 3,000 people, many of whom had shown up spontaneously to bask in Reagan's debate victory.

Reagan's background in acting and previous warm-up debates during the primary left him well prepared for that pivotal moment. President Carter had chosen to skip the previous debate due to the inclusion of independent candidate John Anderson. Carter felt that debating Anderson was beneath him.

Anderson was still in the race at the end and attacked Carter in the days after the Cleveland debate. While campaigning in Philadelphia, Anderson, who was excluded from the October 28 debate, remarked: "If I could have gotten Amy's ear, I would have said, 'Honey, you just tell your daddy it's important for the American people to hear John Anderson's ideas on nuclear proliferation too." Anderson also hinted at the possibility of having to disappoint Amy, stating that he would also have pointed out Carter's contradiction regarding nonproliferation.

He added a pointed comment, alleging, "[Y]our daddy who professes this great passion for nonproliferation did sell 38 tons of enriched uranium to India a few weeks ago." Anderson didn't stand a chance of winning, but he echoed Reagan's criticisms of Carter's foreign policy miscalculations, and he was still getting press coverage until the end.

William Albers, who was the Virginia coordinator for the 1980 Carter-Mondale campaign, defended the mention of Amy, suggesting that many fathers and daughters could relate to the sentiment expressed by Carter.

In 1989, PBS anchor Jim Lehrer would interview both Reagan and Carter about the debate and Carter's reference to his young daughter. Reagan, emphasizing the advantage he gained from the moment, highlighted the public's skepticism about a major policy being influenced by a child's opinion. Carter, finally admitting it was a mistake, acknowledged how the episode had cost him credibility at a critical moment during the climax of a presidential campaign.

## WHY REAGAN RAN AGAIN

Ronald Reagan's pursuit of the presidential nomination was anchored in a strategic vision that transcended party lines. The genesis of this vision can be traced back to a pivotal moment in late June 1975 when President Gerald Ford, guided by advice from his National Security Council and explicitly by his Secretary of State Henry Kissinger, refused to meet with Aleksandr Solzhenitsyn, the Nobel Prize–winning Russian dissident and author of *The Gulag Archipelago*, a book that laid bare the harsh realities of life under Stalinist regimes in the Soviet Union.

Solzhenitsyn, who had endured imprisonment in Siberia and persecution for criticizing Joseph Stalin, received an ice-cold reception from American officials. Only two U.S. senators, Joe Biden and Jesse Helms, publicly greeted the Soviet dissident in Washington, D.C. Reagan, the now-former governor of California, made meeting with Solzhenitsyn a top priority. He, unlike virtually every member of Congress and the Ford administration, clearly recognized the moral importance of engaging with a man who was not only a hero to Reagan personally, but also the embodiment of the resistance against Soviet tyranny.

Fast-forward to a few months later in September 1975 in Orlando, Florida, where Reagan, during a news conference, questioned the policy of détente pursued by the Ford administration and Kissinger. He challenged the notion of making preemptive concessions to the Soviet Union while it engaged in military and diplomatic adventures around the world including in the United States' own backyard. Reagan's rhetoric reverberated with a firm belief that the United States had given away too much without receiving commensurate benefits from the Soviet Union. Reagan highlighted Ford's snub of Solzhenitsyn as a symbol of his misguided foreign policy.

Reagan's persistent critique of Ford and Kissinger's policies continued through the 1976 GOP Republican primaries, even as he did his best to adhere to his unwritten "Eleventh Commandment," which was not to speak ill of fellow Republicans. While his focus on the threat of Soviet-style Marxism and the proximity of Communist Cuba proved effective at wounding Ford in the polls, Reagan still faced a string of GOP primary losses up until March 23, 1976, when, with the support of Senator Jesse Helms, Reagan secured an upset victory in North Carolina.

The slugfest between Ford and Reagan during the summer of 1976 resembled two stacked Major League Baseball teams vying for a pennant. Reagan racked up impressive victories, including Texas, Georgia, Indiana, and Nebraska. But they were countered by Ford's successful campaigns in West Virginia, Maryland, and Michigan. The race remained too close to call until the GOP convention in Kansas City, Missouri, in August 1976.

The convention was a tumultuous spectacle, which was broadcast live each night on all the national television networks. Reagan biographer Craig Shirley called the convention "riotous." Reagan's operatives were openly fighting with Ford's operatives inside the convention hall. There was an atmosphere of unprecedented disorder.

One of Ford's delegates, who broke her leg during the turmoil, faced an unusual predicament. Fearful that her replacement might cast a vote for Reagan, she endured the pain of her fractured limb and fastened a makeshift brace out of convention programs so she could participate until the voting concluded.

Behind the scenes, Kissinger worked to make sure Ford maintained the incumbent's advantage. Witnesses recall the secretary of state "raising hell," going as far as threatening to resign and insisting on a roll call of delegates, some highly intoxicated, as they engaged in crucial deliberations.⁵ Ultimately, Ford would secure the votes, and the nomination.

There was some speculation that Reagan would be Ford's vice-presidential nominee, replacing Nelson Rockefeller. Michael Reagan, the president's son, told *Politico Magazine* years later, "I remember after Ford was nominated we were up in our suite with my dad waiting for Ford to come up. My sister and I were thinking, 'If he offers [the VP slot] take it. You're too old to get another shot at this. You're too old. If he offers it take it, and go from there.' When Ford came up, they went into a private room. He came out, and we all went, 'What happened? What'd he say?' He said, 'He never asked me, he just chose Bob Dole.'... That's how we found out Bob Dole was chosen."⁶

Michael Reagan also recounted the backstory of his father's iconic speech at the convention. Reagan says an inebriated convention "bigwig" from California had come to the convention booth where the Reagan family and Reagan's closest associates were hanging out. The convention official was looking for Michael Deaver, a longtime aide and personal friend of Reagan's.

Michael Reagan recalled the convention official saying, "Here's what going to happen... the president of the United States is going to speak, and when he gets done speaking, he's going to look up at the booth, and say 'Ronnie, why don't you come down and say a few words, and bring your lovely wife, Nancy.' And then he left." According to Michael Reagan, the convention official said, "Please tell Michael Deaver this, so he can relay it to the governor." No one told Deaver, because the convention official was so drunk, according to Michael Reagan, that no one actually believed the president would invite Reagan down to speak.

As President Ford began his speech, occupants of the Reagan family's booth, including Maureen (Reagan's firstborn daughter), her husband, and Colleen (Michael's wife), discreetly exited, choosing to avoid the crowd at the convention hall. Across the street at the hotel bar, the Reagans tuned in to watch President Ford conclude his speech on television. To their astonishment, when he finished his speech, Ford looked up and invited Ronald and Nancy Reagan to join him on the convention stage.

Reagan faced a dilemma. Declining the invitation would make him "look like a sore loser." Aware of the optics, Reagan embraced the opportunity, stepping onto the convention stage with no prepared remarks. What followed was an impromptu speech that would become "the defining moment" of the entire convention and a preview of what his presidency could be.

Reagan had been the first presidential primary challenger to defeat a presidential incumbent in a state contest since Estes Kefauver defeated Harry Truman in the 1952 New Hampshire contest. While Ford ultimately secured the nomination, Reagan had an impact on the general election, as highlighted by former Texas Governor John Connally, suggesting that Reagan's attacks had weakened Ford against his eventual successor, Jimmy Carter.

Reagan sounded the alarm about the danger of nuclear weapons and wondered aloud if the American people would still be free in 100 years. And he closed his speech with this: "We've got to quit talking to each other and about each other and go out and communicate to the world that we may be fewer in numbers than we've ever been, but we carry the message they're waiting for. We must go forth from here united, determined and what a great general said a few years ago is true: There is no substitute for victory."

## THE 1980 GOP PRIMARY

Reagan's decision to run again in 1980 was directly tied to his experience in 1976 and the foreign policy decisions that were pursued by Presidents Ford and Carter. Reagan, a Washington outsider, labeled by the press as a "far-right darling," would face tough challenges in Iowa, New Hampshire, Maine, and Michigan, where George H. W. Bush, a much more comfortable fit for the traditional Republican Party member, claimed early victories.

But Reagan possessed an uncanny ability to break through the media's coverage of the 1980 campaign with a straightforward, folksy style, especially during the GOP primary debates.

What would become the first Reagan-Bush debate was set to take place just three days before the New Hampshire primary in late February. The debate was sponsored by the *Nashua Telegraph*, but it faced regulatory issues and scrutiny from the Federal Election Commission, which said the newspaper-sponsored debate would violate election rules if it did not invite all seven Republican candidates.[7] In response, then-candidate Ronald Reagan financed the debate using his campaign funds.

Despite Reagan's funding, the *Nashua Telegraph*'s editorial staff remained in charge of moderating the debate, inviting only frontrunners Reagan and George H. W. Bush for a one-on-one matchup.

Reagan, desiring the participation of all the GOP candidates on stage, argued for a say in the ground rules since he was financing the debate. Consequently, the debate's unusual start featured Reagan and Bush on the main stage with the moderator, while four trailing candidates stood off to the side. The *Telegraph*'s publisher clarified that these candidates could make closing arguments but not participate in the actual debate.

During the debate, Reagan protested when the moderator attempted to lay out ground rules and prepare the first question. Though Reagan wanted to make an introductory statement and was displeased that other candidates couldn't be included, his microphone was temporarily turned off by the moderator, prompting boos from the crowd.

Reagan, angered, tapped the microphone, saying, "Is this on? Mr. Green ... you asked me if you would ... I am paying for this microphone, Mr. Green!" The crowd cheered.

Despite the initial tension, Reagan eventually stayed on stage with Bush, and the two had a respectful debate. Although they didn't agree on everything, they found common ground on one issue: whether Reagan's age disqualified him from the presidency.

When the moderator asked Bush if he thought Reagan was too old to be president, CBS News reports that Bush responded, "No, I don't." Reagan concurred, saying, "I agree with George Bush."

Then on April 23, 1980, in Houston, American voters would get to see an even more contentious debate between the two front-runners. It would also serve as a preview of Reagan's deft debate skills that he would later use to finish off Jimmy Carter's reelection campaign. The venue was the Albert Thomas Convention Center. The day was hot, and the air was heavy with humidity and intraparty tension.

As the doors swung open, revealing the vast expanse of the convention center, the audience streamed in. The venue's colossal ceilings echoed with the hum of anticipation as candidates and spectators alike settled into their places. The stage, bathed in a spotlight's glow, awaited the rhetorical battle that would soon commence. Howard K. Smith, the seasoned moderator, took his position, his voice resonating through the cavernous space.

The spotlight turned to Bush. Smith raised the topic of Cuba, a Soviet outpost on America's doorstep. The communist island country would provide viewers with a stark ideological divergence between the two candidates.

Bush, his words measured, dissected Castro's calculated decisions to export revolution. The audience hung on every syllable as he detailed the intricacies of Soviet and Cuban influence, from Grenada to Central America. However, the Texas heat seemed to intensify inside the venue as Bush started to struggle and Reagan gained the upper hand in the debate.

Regarding Cuba, Reagan said, "Here we have a Soviet satellite ninety miles off our shore. And instead of threatening sanctions or threatening the Olympics or anything else, why couldn't we blockade Cuba and then say to the Soviets, 'When your troops get out of Afghanistan, we will drop the blockade around Cuba.' And I think this could exert great pressure."

Bush countered by pointing out that he had a "fundamental difference" with Reagan's proposed strategy, "Because it wasn't Cubans that invaded Afghanistan; it was Russians. And we have a hemispheric problem today, it seems to me, and I believe that if you will go back and, look, blockage connotes in naval parlance, war, interdiction of shipping, interdiction of aircraft."

It would not be the last time someone would worry out loud that Reagan's willingness to be more assertive with both the Cubans and the Soviets than any other Republican president would turn the Cold War into a hot one.

Reagan continued, "Russia provides, and I guess, about a tanker a week with oil for Cuba. I don't think they could stand a blockade very long, and I think a little call on the hot line with this kind of a threat might get the withdrawal of the troops from Afghanistan, because it would be a pressure on them."

As the audience dispersed, the echoes of that exchange lingered, shaping the narrative of the candidates' stances on the global stage.

Reagan's stance on foreign policy, articulated in the debate with Bush, foreshadowed his presidency's approach. Reagan highlighted the need for a nuanced and strategic response. As the primary season concluded in the early summer of 1980, Reagan emerged as the Republican nominee, ready to face the challenges of the general election with a clear and visionary approach.

## PRESIDENT CARTER'S PRIMARY CHALLENGES

On December 4, 1979, against a backdrop of familial support, loyal staff, and ardent campaign enthusiasts, Jimmy Carter rolled out his formal announcement to seek reelection as president of the United States. In a five-minute videotaped address aired on CBS, Carter, exuding confidence, spoke from the East Room of the White House. The president unequivocally declared, "I intend to be renominated by the Democratic Party, and I intend to ask the Democratic Convention to renominate the most effective Vice President in the history of the United States—Walter Mondale. We intend to lead the Democratic Party to victory next year, and we also intend to lead the Nation in continuing the good work which all of us have begun together."[8]

For those immersed in the intricate dance of Washington politics, Carter's assurance might have appeared enigmatic. President Carter's acknowledgment of his vice president stirred discontent within his national security team and mirrored a broader rivalry among Carter's advisors. A faction known as the "Mondale Mafia" existed within the White House, with members including President Carter's Deputy Assistant for National Security David L. Aaron. While reporting directly to National Security Advisor Zbigniew Brzezinski, Aaron also maintained a close relationship with Vice President Mondale.

Aaron's government service began in the early 1960s as a Foreign Service officer, followed by roles in various national security positions over the next decade. These included assignments at the headquarters of the North Atlantic Treaty Organization in Brussels and at the Arms Control and Disarmament Agency, and as a member of Henry A. Kissinger's staff during the first Nixon administration.

According to a 1979 report by the *New York Times*, White House aides hinted at disagreements between Aaron and Brzezinski.[9] Like Kissinger and Vice President Mondale, Aaron supported direct negotiations with Moscow, diverging from his hawkish image in dealing with Russian issues in third-world regions.

Consequently, some characterize Mr. Aaron and certain national security aides as part of the "Mondale Mafia" in foreign policy. This group was perceived to hold views distinct from both Brzezinski and Secretary of State Cyrus Vance.

Brzezinski, who would explicitly cite the Monroe Doctrine to Carter, had consistently urged the president to be more proactive about the Marxist threat in the Western Hemisphere. At one point he sent a memo to CIA director Stansfield Turner warning about "the growing Cuban presence on Grenada." Brzezinski had convinced Carter about the urgency of the matter and the need "to focus international press attention on this development."

But Brzezinski and Turner were up against the so-called Mondale Mafia, which had cleaved through the Carter foreign policy team and the National Security Council, a shadowy influence that left political observers questioning the dynamics at play and the lack of success when it came to Carter's foreign policy and national security objectives.

Carter, in his prerecorded announcement, candidly acknowledged the challenges already facing his presidency. He admitted, "As President, I have had to make some very difficult decisions, and I expect to make some more. I've made some mistakes, and I have learned from them. I've fought some bitter fights against selfish special interests, and I expect to go on leading the fight for the common good of the American people. I carry some scars, and I carry them with pride."

One of those scars was a bruising funding battle with Senate Democrats on the Armed Services Committee. Carter engaged in a high-stakes veto of a $37 billion defense authorization bill that irked Senator John C. Stennis, the committee's Democratic chairman.

Carter's veto, part of his strategy to curtail military spending and emphasize diplomacy and human rights, included a symbolic rejection of a $2 billion nuclear-powered Nimitz-class aircraft carrier. In a move to project a more responsible and peaceful foreign policy, Carter deemed the carrier a symbol of Cold War excess that did not align with modern American values.

As the *Washington Post* reported, some members of Congress opted to support Carter on the veto, viewing it as a temporary truce in preparation for more contentious battles that lay ahead.[10] Despite differing views, the sentiment among some representatives reflected a reluctance to intensify attacks on the president.

Representative George Mahon, a Democrat from Texas, urged his colleagues to rally behind Carter, emphasizing the need for unity in the quest for peace in the Middle East. However, the controversial veto would later be overshadowed by the eruption of the Iran hostage crisis. It was clear that the leaders of the Islamic Revolution, including Ayatollah Khomeini, did not respect the Carter administration's efforts to project "a more responsible and peaceful foreign policy."

The Carter administration was trying to leverage the political capital it had gained from the Camp David Accords.

Ironically, a year later, Congress, now grappling with the severity of the situation in Iran, approved the very carrier Carter had once vetoed. CVN-71, now known as the USS *Theodore Roosevelt*, sailed into the pages of history, emblematic of the unpredictable tides that defined Carter's presidency.

## THE TRANSITION AND THE END OF THE IRAN HOSTAGE CRISIS

In the waning days of 1980, with Ronald Reagan poised to assume the presidency, the Iran hostage crisis loomed large. The transition from the Carter administration to Reagan's team fueled speculation about the approach Reagan would adopt to resolve the prolonged captivity of American diplomats in Tehran.

Reagan's sudden and unequivocal denunciation of the Iranian regime as "criminals" engaged in kidnapping and barbarism prompted questions about the future of United States-Iran relations under his leadership. The people who seemed to be most concerned about the president-elect's strong words were the same people who had missed the explicit warning about the Islamic Revolution.

In his book *Inside the National Security Council*, Constantine Menges wrote about a meeting he had with William Casey, who succeeded Stansfield Turner as the director of the CIA. Menges told Casey of his firsthand experiences of trying to warn Carter administration officials about diverse groups that were rallying together to overthrow the shah. Menges wrote that one Carter administration official cited Carter's 1978 state visit to Tehran, where the U.S. president had been hypnotized by the pomp and circumstance of the visit. Carter told the shah, "I can see how you are loved by your people."

Menges told Casey at the time that he had "serious questions about the competence of the career foreign policy and intelligence agencies, including the CIA. I know there are many dedicated and skilled people, . . ." Menges added. "But during the Carter years these organizations just didn't foresee—much less prevent—some real disasters."

Reagan, during the campaign, had vowed to course-correct U.S. foreign policy. And he didn't seem concerned about his strong rhetoric making the situation worse than it already was. But plenty of people were. On New Year's Eve 1981, a *Washington Post* story asked, "Why did President-elect Ronald Reagan suddenly break his silence on the hostage issue?"[11] And "Does this portend a much tougher American line three weeks from now, when in all probability the hostage problem will be President Reagan's to solve?"

Reagan had challenged the notion of paying "ransom for people who have been kidnapped by barbarians." His tough talk signaled a departure from the more diplomatic language used by the outgoing Carter administration.

The *Washington Post* even went so far as to speculate that "any breakthrough on the hostages will not be as a result of a new Reagan 'hard line.' Conceivably, it could come out of an uncharacteristic consensus among Iranian authorities to do business with President Carter, rather than wait for the unknown of Ronald Reagan."

As pundits speculated on whether Reagan's statements heralded a return to the initial hardline position taken when the hostages were first seized, the historical context suggested a more complex reality. The lessons of 1980 underscored that dealing with Tehran's anarchic revolutionary government required an understanding that traditional diplomacy and military force might not be effective. The internal upheavals in Iran, marked by power struggles and a lack of coherent governance, posed a significant challenge to any administration seeking to navigate the complexities of Iranian politics.

Reagan's supporters argued that his firm leadership could give pause to Iranian authorities, but the prevailing view was that the revolutionary government, under Ayatollah Khomeini, resisted conventional diplomatic approaches. The backdrop of an Iran grappling with war with Iraq, economic sanctions, and internal strife painted a picture of a government on the verge of collapse.

Reports from observers on the ground hinted at a disintegrating and fragile regime, with elements within Iran anticipating a counterrevolution led by a combination of the military and moderates. The harsh realities of rationing, hunger, and cold in parts of the country fueled speculation that the Khomeini government's grip was slipping.

Reagan's harsh rhetoric against the Iranians served a dual purpose. While he claimed to be expressing his genuine feelings, the underlying message was strategic. By signaling a potentially tougher stance than the Carter administration's, Reagan aimed to influence the Iranians not to wait for his inauguration before seeking a resolution to the hostage crisis.

The question lingered: Did Reagan's sharp words foreshadow his actual approach to the hostage problem once in office? Given the unpredictable and volatile nature of Iranian internal affairs, such assumptions remained precarious. The complexities of the hostage dilemma, intertwined with the tumultuous landscape in Iran, set the stage for a pivotal moment in Reagan's early presidency—one where tough talk would need to be met with astute and nuanced diplomatic maneuvering. Reagan proved he was up to the task.

Surprisingly, the Carter administration accepted Reagan's explanation and, according to insiders, even welcomed the president-elect's strong words. The hope among Carter's negotiators was that Reagan's apparent toughness might spur the Iranians to reach an agreement before Inauguration Day. Despite the Carter administration's foreign policy missteps, Carter himself was genuinely concerned about the hostages and making sure they returned home.

But there were other actors who had their own motivations. The *New York Times* unfurled a tale that pierced the veneer of historical assumptions. The protagonist of this drama was Ben Barnes, the former Texas lieutenant governor, who at the age of 85 decided to come clean about his clandestine role in John Connally's attempt to free the American hostages in Iran. The scheme was designed to ensure that Carter's reelection campaign would not reap the benefits of an early release of the U.S. hostages in Tehran.

Connally, once wounded while riding in the same car as John F. Kennedy when he was assassinated, had transcended his notoriety to become a political fixer of formidable influence. He was a protégé of Lyndon B. Johnson. Connally had also played a pivotal role in convincing Richard Nixon to impose wage and price controls to combat inflation.

Amid these challenges, a deeply divided Democratic Party and a robust primary challenge from Ted Kennedy further strained Carter's reelection prospects. The unique coalition that propelled him to victory in 1976 proved difficult to sustain against the ideological juggernaut of Reagan.

## CARTER AND EL SALVADOR

As 1980 turned into 1981, the situation in El Salvador came to the forefront of a crisis that needed urgent attention. The political situation in El Salvador was perilous—that nation, like Iran, was ensnared in political turmoil and social unrest. Carter's strategic decisions, which would be a stark departure from his previous moves, showed that he realized he needed to change his approach as the transition to the Reagan administration loomed.

The White House, adorned with festive decorations for the holiday season, bore witness to a flurry of meetings and deliberations on the subject of El Salvador. Carter, surrounded by his advisors, grappled with the complexities of the country's internal strife. José Napoleón Duarte, who had just been appointed as the head of a new civil-military junta, had implored the United States for assistance.

The Salvadoran government faced a formidable insurgency, with leftist rebels seeking to overthrow the established order as the Sandinistas had done in Nicaragua. The ideological struggle mirrored the broader Cold War dynamics, with the United States apprehensive about the spread of Soviet influence in its backyard.

In the Oval Office, Carter, shouldering the gravity of presidential responsibility, convened with his national security team. The atmosphere was charged, and the decisions made within those walls would echo beyond the confines of the room. Carter seemed to be cognizant of the potential consequences of inaction, and he grappled with the moral and geopolitical dimensions of the crisis.

On Capitol Hill, congressional debates raged on. The proposed aid package for El Salvador became a battleground of conflicting ideologies. Carter faced opposition from some quarters, with critics decrying the potential entanglement in a foreign conflict. Meanwhile, proponents argued that supporting El Salvador was a strategic imperative to thwart the spread of communism in the Western Hemisphere.

Against this backdrop, Carter made the fateful decision to provide military and economic aid to El Salvador. The aid package, a calculated maneuver in the twilight of his presidency, aimed to bolster the Salvadoran government's efforts against the insurgency. Carter, aware of the imminent transition to the Reagan era, sought to lay the groundwork for a policy that would extend beyond his tenure.

Carter's decision became a focal point of scrutiny. Some saw it as a principled stance against the encroachment of communism, while others criticized it as entangling the United States in a quagmire with unclear outcomes. Carter had just decided to pull aid from El Salvador a few weeks earlier after a messy incident in which four American missionaries were killed by Salvadoran security forces.

The Reagan administration was about to inherit the remains of Carter's foreign policy, a policy fraught with challenges and implications. The aid to El Salvador was born out of the acknowledgment of previous failures. In 1979 alone, Marxist rebels, backed by Soviet support, had achieved significant gains in Ethiopia, Angola, and Mozambique. Vietnam had assumed control of Cambodia from the brutal Khmer Rouge regime after a border battle with China. Additionally, toward the end of the same year, the Soviet Union had invaded Afghanistan to bolster a Marxist regime there.

By the end of his presidency, Carter had made a notable shift in his perspective on both the Soviet Union and the guidance of his advisors. Initially leaning toward Secretary Cyrus Vance's negotiation-oriented policy, Carter had become more amenable to National Security Advisor Zbigniew Brzezinski's more confrontational approach. This shift reignited open conflict between the National Security Council and the Department of State—a problem that would carry over to the next administration.

But even before Reagan assumed office, his transition team, which consisted of some of his closest friends and advisors, faced a power struggle. Constantine Menges wrote that President-elect Reagan's pick for secretary of state, Alexander Haig, a career military officer, met only once with Reagan's foreign policy experts. Haig thanked them for their service and their transition report and then dismissed them. Menges also wrote that he realized that neither Reagan nor the key members of his team in California grasped the challenge they were already facing inside Washington, D.C.'s foreign policy agencies. Menges believed that "unless a new president, Republican or Democrat, appointed his own competent people to the top policy jobs, the powerful Washington bureaucracies would naturally push their own agendas rather than the president's."

## THE INAUGURATION

The night before Ronald Reagan's inauguration, the nation witnessed a spectacle that would signal the dawn of a new era. As a 69-year-old Republican, poised to ascend the highest political summit, the president-elect participated in an "All-Star Inaugural Gala" that aired on ABC on January 19, 1981. Emcee Johnny Carson, his quips cutting through the opulence, dubbed it the "first administration to have a premiere." The event, produced by Frank Sinatra, harkened back to a bygone era.

Reagan gazed upon a stage populated by performers who mirrored his vintage. Ethel Merman, at 73, belted out show tunes; Jimmy Stewart, age 72, extolled his friend "Ron"; and Bob Hope, a sprightly 77, delivered soft-hitting jokes, humorously noting Reagan's lack of expertise in lying, exaggerating, or cheating—a job always left to his agent.

The following day, a record-breaking 41.8 million TV viewers tuned in to witness Reagan's inauguration. His predecessor, Jimmy Carter, had been president during challenging times: the worst recession since the Great Depression, soaring rates of inflation and unemployment, the Soviet invasion of Afghanistan, the Iran hostage crisis, and a pervasive sense of defeatism lingering in the wake of Vietnam and Watergate.

Yet Reagan, in his inaugural address, painted a vivid tableau of American renewal. In plainspoken yet stirring language, he invoked the "moral courage of free men and women," urging Americans to rededicate themselves to noble causes. Rejecting the self-loathing politics of the Left, he resurrected the concept of American exceptionalism, rallying a dispirited citizenry.

Despite Carter's campaign descending into personal attacks, Reagan remained dignified. He thanked Carter for his "gracious cooperation in the transition process," delivering a stunning message of unity: "Mr. President, I want our fellow citizens to know . . . you have shown a watching world that we are a united people pledged to maintaining a political system which guarantees liberty to a greater degree than any other." Reagan seized every opportunity to educate the world about America's democratic achievements.

Anticipating the rise of identity politics, Reagan championed the common good, lauding the American democratic ethos that transcends ethnic and racial divisions in times of crisis. His vision encompassed a vibrant, dynamic free-market economy—the antidote to the stifling grasp of massive government spending and tax increases. Reagan spoke to the populist and egalitarian impulses that shaped American political life, addressing the struggles of the unemployed and the burden faced by those who worked under a punitive tax system.

Born into poverty in a small Midwestern town, Reagan drew on his experiences during the Great Depression and the resilience of the nation during World War II. His inauguration speech underscored the quiet courage of ordinary citizens, from professionals to industrialists, shopkeepers to truck drivers, who served others.

Reagan proclaimed, "Government is not the solution to our problem; government is the problem." Yet he pledged that the dreams, hopes, and goals of the citizens would be central to his administration. Long before the term "compassionate conservatism" became popular, Reagan envisioned a government partnering with its citizens, reflecting the compassion inherent in the American spirit.

It would be the first time a U.S. presidential inauguration would be held on the west-facing side of the Capitol. From that perspective, Reagan looked out and gazed upon half a million people. The Washington Monument and the Jefferson and Lincoln Memorials framed the scene. Beyond the Reflecting Pool lay the graves at Arlington National Cemetery, a testament to the price paid for freedom.

Reagan, with a simple tribute, emphasized that whoever sought the meaning of America could find it in the life of Abraham Lincoln. As he looked beyond the monuments, Reagan paid homage to the heroes who fought and died in Vietnam, determined to honor them in the face of the Left's contempt.

Just moments after Ronald Reagan was sworn in as the fortieth president of the United States, the 52 American captives held at the U.S. Embassy in Tehran, Iran, were released, bringing an end to the 444-day Iran hostage crisis.

## REAGAN'S FIRST TELEVISED PRESS CONFERENCE

On the brisk afternoon of January 29, 1981, President Ronald Reagan unveiled a strategic shift in American foreign policy during his first live televised press conference in the Old Executive Office Building adjacent to the White House. The masterful display of Reagan's communication skills, honed during his 1980 campaign, signaled a sharp departure from the détente policies of his predecessors, including President Jimmy Carter.

ABC News correspondent Sam Donaldson set the stage by questioning Reagan about his plans for dealing with the Kremlin and the long-term goals of the Soviet Union. The key moment came when Donaldson inquired whether Reagan believed "the Kremlin is bent on world domination" and if this trajectory might perpetuate the Cold War. Moreover, Donaldson probed Reagan on the viability of détente.

Reagan's response was both firm and strategic. He characterized détente as a one-way street exploited by the Soviet Union for its own gains. With his signature subtle smile, Reagan articulated his awareness of the Soviet leadership's repeated declarations of pursuing global revolution and a one-world socialist or communist state. Crucially, Reagan emphasized the fundamental disparity in moral standards between the United States and the Soviet Union.

"Well, so far detente's been a one-way street that the Soviet Union has used to pursue its own aims," Reagan declared. "I think when you do business with them, even at a detente, you keep that in mind," said the president.

The smile on Reagan's face always seemed to hint at a deeper meaning. It wasn't merely a divergence in economic philosophies but a profound departure from the Carter administration's approach. Reagan conveyed that under his leadership, the United States would operate under a different set of standards. This subtle yet impactful message reverberated not only through the press conference room but across the global stage.

Reagan's mastery of the press conference was apparent. He skillfully put the Soviets on notice and signaled a paradigm shift in U.S. foreign policy. The confident smile was emblematic of Reagan's ability to articulate complex ideas with ease and charm. It also reflected his opportunity to directly communicate his vision for confronting the Soviets to the American people, unfiltered by the foreign policy establishment. Reagan's chess moves at the press conference marked a profound moment, setting the stage for a new era in U.S.-Soviet relations under his administration. But very quickly, Reagan's efforts to pursue this new foreign policy vision would be hindered.

CHAPTER 3

# The Resignation of Al Haig

*"Every president has to make sure that his secretary of state understands who is the president and who is the secretary of state."*

—Dean Rusk, Secretary of State,
to John F. Kennedy and Lyndon Johnson

## "THE MEANEST SON OF A BITCH"

In the initial days of Ronald Reagan's presidency, the relationship between Reagan, the commander in chief, and his first secretary of state, Al Haig, resembled a discordant symphony. Haig, self-anointed as the "vicar" of Reagan's foreign policy, envisioned himself as the architect of its formulation and its chief executioner. However, the reality was far from what Haig had envisioned.

Contrary to Haig's aspirations, the Reagan administration was not built on a policy of careful coordination between the State Department and the National Security Council at the White House. Early on, the administration was accused of speaking with multiple voices on foreign policy matters, which critics say created confusion and disarray. Despite an agreement between Reagan and Haig to present a unified front, the pact proved challenging, especially since Reagan was unwilling to fully outsource his foreign policy to the State Department.

Described by Richard Nixon as "the meanest, toughest, most ambitious son of a bitch I ever knew,"[1] Haig openly pursued power. On paper, Haig had seemed like a strong choice for a secretary of state for a Republican president who had promised the American people a more assertive foreign policy than that of his recent predecessors. Haig was the youngest four-star general in Army history. His military career spanned three decades and included service on General Douglas MacArthur's staff in Japan, an appointment as vice chief of staff of the Army, and a stint as the supreme allied commander of NATO.

Haig also had notable policy expertise, as highlighted by Duke University Professor Simon Miles in an essay about his rocky tenure in the Reagan administration.[2] The contrast of Haig's style with Reagan's was stark. "Haig's was not a personality suited to quiet diplomacy," Miles wrote. "But that was the order of the day so long as Reagan felt U.S. power was inadequate to the task of making the type of diplomatic deals that would benefit the United States over the Soviet Union." Haig "wanted the splashy summits that Reagan doubted were in the U.S. interest in the climate of that time."

Haig believed that his struggle to develop a close personal relationship with Reagan, coupled with his limited access to the Oval Office, hindered his objectives.[3] The president's aides within the White House, some pursuing their own power plays, tightly controlled Haig's interactions with Reagan.

In February and March 1981, Reagan's National Security Council was engaging in discussions on how to address the intensifying civil war in El Salvador and the need for a comprehensive strategy for the Caribbean, as well as Central and South America. El Salvador was one of the many foreign policy problems that had carried over from the Carter administration, and perhaps was the most pressing at the time. During his second National Security Council meeting, Reagan declared that "if the Junta falls in El Salvador, it will be seen as an American defeat."[4] He added, "We must not let El Salvador become another Cuba on the mainland. It cannot happen."

Haig had proposed a strategy of "going to the source," to deal with the root problems plaguing Central and South America and the Caribbean. Haig suggested an invasion of Cuba to bring an end to the Castro regime and its influence in the Western Hemisphere. Despite the president's initial interest, Haig was disappointed to find that none of his colleagues shared his enthusiasm for kicking off the new administration with a foreign war.

Haig sought the quick decisive action that he believed could have prevented the stalemates he'd personally experienced in Vietnam and Korea. During one National Security Council meeting, Haig infamously declared, "You just give me the word, and I'll turn that fucking island [Cuba] into a parking lot."[5]

The consensus opinion inside the Reagan administration was that Cuba was, in fact, a source of the major problems in the region. Containing Fidel Castro was crucial for U.S. national security. Haig also stated that he believed Castro was afraid of Reagan; however, he stood out among the new president's cabinet members as the only one firmly advocating for a full-blown invasion of the communist island nation. Despite Reagan's refusal to revoke the non-invasion commitment, in place since the end of the Cuban Missile Crisis, and his colleagues' reminders about the lack of public support for such an action, Haig remained persistent and indignant.

While Reagan clearly wanted to reinforce the Monroe Doctrine, he was measured in his approach, opposing Haig's call for an override of the 1962 Kennedy-Khrushchev understanding. That agreement came after the Soviets committed to dismantling their nuclear weapons in Cuba and transporting them back to the Soviet Union, with UN verification. In exchange, the United States publicly agreed not to invade Cuba ever again. Haig's colleagues, though sharing a disdain for Castro and acknowledging the need for firm measures against the regime, never fully grasped why the secretary of state was so determined to invade Cuba, potentially sparking a full-blown nuclear conflict with the Soviet Union that could drag the United States into a third world war. Haig also supported the idea of returning and abandoning thousands of rejected Mariel Cubans near the island, a stance almost everyone else in the State Department, National Security Council, Defense Department, and the CIA disagreed with.

In his memoir *Inner Circles: How America Changed the World*, Haig wrote about his conviction that the United States should, or at least could, have emerged victorious in its Cold War conflicts in Korea and Vietnam. Haig believed that warfare had become too political. And he viewed Cuba as an opportunity to assert America's military strength and send a clear message to the Soviets. Just about everyone else thought he was mad for suggesting a war with Cuba.

According to Edwin Meese, one of Reagan's closest counselors and future attorney general, the trouble with Haig was more style than substance. Meese said, "Well, actually, there were basic differences, generally, between Cap [Caspar] Weinberger in the Department of Defense and Haig in the State Department, and of course those two departments were always battling traditionally, but Haig was a more aggressive warrior than they generally had."

The rift between Haig and Reagan's other advisors grew even wider after a Senate Foreign Relations Committee meeting on March 19, 1981, that resulted in public embarrassment for both Haig and the Reagan administration. Haig was called to testify. Committee members were discussing a brutal incident that had occurred in December of the previous year. Four Catholic missionaries, including three nuns and one layperson from the United States, were raped and murdered by five members of the El Salvadoran National Guard.

During his testimony Haig suggested that he'd "like to propose that some investigations hint at the possibility that the vehicle carrying the nuns might have attempted to pass through a roadblock, or perhaps was mistakenly perceived to have done so. There might have been an exchange of fire, and then those responsible for the casualties might have sought to conceal it."

Haig's remarks didn't seem to jibe with the FBI's conclusions, which had dismissed allegations that the U.S.-supported Salvadoran government was uncooperative in the inquiry into the deaths of the four Americans.

"I want to assure you that discussions between the Salvadoran government and the FBI regarding this atrocious crime—and I use that term without reservation—are ongoing," Haig informed the congressional committee. "It is a complex matter," he added. "The details are not sufficiently clear for anyone to formulate a conclusive judgment."

Haig's theory was met with immediate criticism from the victim's families, members of Congress, and others. The *Washington Post* reported, "One diplomatic source said he feared that Haig's comments were particularly ill-timed and might be read as a sign that the United States was easing pressure on Salvadoran authorities to pursue the investigation."[6]

Congressman Richard Ottinger, a Democrat from New York who represented the district that was home to the deceased nuns' Maryknoll order, released a statement criticizing Haig's comments.

"If Secretary Haig possesses concrete information, he should disclose it immediately. Otherwise, he is engaging in shocking and thoughtless speculation that could only encourage terrorism and jeopardize American lives in El Salvador and around the world," wrote Ottinger.

In Ossining, New York, Sister Martha Bourne, a spokesperson for the Maryknoll sisters, mentioned that the community has not received any information from their sources in El Salvador indicating that the nuns attempted to run a roadblock. "I can't fathom anyone in their right mind attempting such a thing," she expressed.

UPI reported that the FBI had informed the Senate Foreign Relations Committee that the bureau was "completely satisfied" with the Salvadoran government's cooperation.[7] And the FBI was currently reviewing evidence and fingerprints received from El Salvador. Investigators acknowledged that "some witnesses had been hesitant to cooperate," but as of the time of Haig's testimony, the identity of the murderers remained unknown.

Haig was ultimately forced to backtrack on his theory that the nuns attempted to avoid the roadblock. The secretary of state had made it look like the Reagan administration was blaming the three nuns and one missionary for their own brutal murders. It was a massive distraction the nascent administration could not afford.

## "I'M IN CONTROL HERE"

Just two weeks before the assassination attempt on President Reagan, Secretary Haig graced the cover of *Time* magazine along with a headline that read "The Vicar Takes Charge."[8] The article opened with a story about how, right after Reagan took his inaugural oath, Haig wasted no time in proposing a comprehensive reorganization of foreign policy decision-making to Edwin Meese, as mentioned above, one the president's closest advisors, official counselor, and future attorney general. Haig's memo envisioned a restructuring that would elevate the secretary of state to a supreme position within the administration. Within two weeks, Reagan approved a directive that granted Haig most, if not all, of the authority he sought. Haig then assembled a team of handpicked subordinates, surpassing the pace of other Cabinet members. Reagan formally nominated several individuals from Haig's team within a week. The move faced objections from Reagan allies and conservative members of Congress. Critics contended that Haig's chosen lieutenants, much like Haig himself, were too deeply rooted in the era of détente associated with Henry Kissinger.

Haig's confrontational demeanor, fondness for the dramatic, and inclination for behind-the-scenes maneuvering and manipulation ultimately led him astray from the rest of the administration. While he sought control, he evidently lacked the acumen to secure it.

On March 30, 1981, the fabric of American democracy was nearly ripped apart. President Ronald Reagan, the leader of the free world, became the target of an assassination attempt by John Hinckley Jr. The incident unfolded after a speaking engagement where President Reagan addressed roughly 5,000 members of the AFL-CIO, one of the country's most powerful labor unions, at the Washington Hilton in D.C.

The day was already dreary and rainy. As President Reagan was making his way back to his limousine from the hotel, the scene was shattered by an abrupt eruption of gunshots, leaving the nation in shock and disbelief. One of the six .22 caliber bullets fired by Hinckley found its mark, piercing the president's body. A bullet struck White House Press Secretary James Brady in the head. Another hit District of Columbia police officer Thomas Delahanty in the back of his neck as he shielded Reagan. Another overshot the president, hitting a building's window. As Special Agent in Charge Jerry Parr shoved Reagan into the limousine, another bullet hit Secret Service agent Timothy McCarthy in the abdomen.

President Reagan had been in office only 70 days when he was shot. At the time Vice President George H. W. Bush was on a plane over Texas, without secure voice communication.

At the White House and the Department of State, a trio of witnesses including G. Philip Hughes, the vice president's deputy foreign policy advisor; Samuel Gammon, the executive assistant in management at State; and John Kelly, in the Secretariat at the Department of State, found themselves intertwined in the unfolding drama of what would later be known as the Haig Incident, which would further reveal Haig's lone-wolf approach to governance and his isolation from Reagan's other advisors.

Hughes had watched firsthand as Haig's failure to forge alliances within the cabinet set the stage for his dismissal. The man who had steered the government during the Nixon era seemed out of step, operating as if he alone comprehended the necessary course of action after the president was shot.

Hughes recalled Haig hastily convening a meeting of the National Security Council at the White House. The public, gripped by anxiety, awaited a statement that would provide reassurance and clarity. There was a sense of responsibility to address the press by someone in the cabinet, with more authority than Larry Speakes, the deputy press secretary. Haig volunteered for the task, and it proved to be an ill-fated choice.

Hughes, watching from his office, recalled witnessing Haig's breathless entrance into the press room. The secretary of state's "flushed and frazzled" appearance amplified the heightened tension of the moment.[9] Haig clearly did not exude the type of quiet confidence needed to calm the situation and assuage the fears of hundreds of millions of people wondering who was in control of the most powerful nation on earth.

"Constitutionally, gentlemen, you have the president, the vice president, and the secretary of state, in that order, and should the president decide he wants to transfer the helm to the vice president, he will do so," Haig stated.[10] He was nervous and sweaty.

But Haig either forgot or intentionally failed to mention that the Speaker of the House and then the Senate's president pro tempore come before the secretary of state in the line of presidential succession. And then, to the amazement of many, the secretary of state declared, "As of now, I am in control here, in the White House, pending the return of the vice president and in close touch with him. If something came up, I would check with him, of course."[11]

What followed was an unintended chain reaction of perceptions. Instead of projecting steadiness in a moment of crisis, Haig's choice of words fueled existing suspicions that the secretary of state harbored vast ambitions of power within the administration. The fallout from this pivotal moment led to deep internal battles, a gradual sidelining of Haig, and ultimately his resignation.

Samuel Gammon, an executive assistant at the State Department, recalled Haig's televised address and what followed behind the scenes. Gammon was in the State Department's Operations Center, where officials had gathered from the afternoon until late into the night. The initial reports had suggested that President Reagan was unharmed, leading to a belief that the situation was less severe than it truly was. However, the gravity of the shooting became clear later, challenging the team to reassess their emergency procedures. It was total chaos.

There was an emergency manual, known as the Carter-Mondale Book, but it proved insufficient. It primarily addressed the aftermath of a fatal event, drawing from the Kennedy assassination. However, the nature of President Reagan's injuries, initially downplayed as minor, prompted a reevaluation of the existing contingency plans with an incapacitated but living president.

Recognizing the gaps in preparedness, John Kelly, in the Secretariat at the Department of State, acted. The following day, he directed the Ops Center to revise the emergency manual, incorporating considerations of the Twenty-Fifth Amendment and accounting for scenarios beyond the fatal or abrupt termination of the presidency. While the final product remained unseen, this initiative reflected a commitment to comprehensive and adaptable planning in the face of unforeseen challenges.

Within the State Department, recognizing the imperative of projecting stability to allies and adversaries worldwide, Hughes and a colleague drafted a "flash" message. This missive, disseminated to U.S. Embassies globally, conveyed the known details of the situation, including President Reagan's medical condition. The embassies were instructed to relay reassurance to their host governments, emphasizing that despite the temporary incapacitation of the president, the U.S. government was firmly in control.

Simultaneously, assistant secretaries engaged in direct conversations with foreign leaders, addressing concerns that might have lingered after interactions with other officials. The collective response orchestrated by State Department staff underscored the necessity of prompt and coherent communication during moments of crisis, demonstrating a commitment to restoring order and confidence in the face of unprecedented challenges.[12]

Reagan National Security Advisor Richard Allen later wrote that "Haig had been objecting so vociferously to any National Security Council structure or crisis plan for so long that we barely had one in place when the president was shot."[13]

While inside the White House Situation Room, Allen recalled that when "the president was readied for surgery, he [Haig] rounded up the key players in the administration." Allen also grabbed his tape recorder, placed it on the table, and opened a discussion on what would come next, despite Haig's assertion that he was in control. What followed, according to Allen, was nearly six hours of deliberations between senior administration officials. The people in that room knew Haig's statement had violated both the tradition and rules of the executive branch. Allen said his recorder was not hidden and it captured the honest reaction of the officials present.

"What's this all about? Is he mad?" asked Treasury Secretary Don Regan.

"He's wrong! He doesn't have such authority," said Defense Secretary Caspar Weinberger.

Allen writes that when Haig returned to the Situation Room a few minutes after his now infamous press conference, "he continued picking fights, even as other top aides tried to figure out whether Hinckley was a lone wolf or part of a coordinated attack requiring them to raise the nation's threat level."

The nation would later learn that Hinckley was motivated by a desire to impress actress Jody Foster and inspired by the movie *Taxi Driver*, which included a scene eerily like the assassination attempt on Reagan.

The White House Press Room, usually a hub of information dissemination, was now filled with confusion and disorder. Within and around White House Chief of Staff James Baker's office, there was shouting and uproar. The gravity of the situation was further complicated by the fact that Press Secretary Jim Brady had also sustained severe injuries in the incident.

In those critical hours preceding the vice president's return from Texas to Washington, Al Haig had thrust himself into the center of a power struggle. Throughout the afternoon, not only did he contest control of the White House, but he went further, asserting authority over the national command structure and even questioning Caspar Weinberger's role as defense secretary.

The attempt on Reagan's life came simultaneously as Soviet submarines, with their nuclear warheads, had moved close enough to the U.S. mainland to reach Washington, D.C., in just 11 minutes. As the discussion shifted from the health of the president to the succession of power, the nuclear threat also came into focus. Haig discussed the possibility of deploying the airborne command center and debated Weinberger's decision to have nuclear bomber crews move closer to their planes. Allen wrote that Haig suggested the defense secretary's order involved a change in the DEFCON, or Defense Condition, when it did not.

The tension then reached a boiling point. "I'm discussing it from the point of view that at the moment, until the vice president actually arrives here," Weinberger said, "the command authority is what I have … and I have to make sure that is essential that we do everything that seems proper."

Haig exploded. "You'd better read the Constitution!"

Weinberger was incredulous. "What?"

Haig laughed. "You'd better read the Constitution!"

However, the heart of the matter was lost on Haig—the crisis was about more than a constitutional power struggle. Rather, for everyone else in Reagan's cabinet the real issue was the will and the condition of the wounded president lying near death in a hospital. The procedures Reagan had previously approved were set in motion, and despite the disputes, the Situation Room remained focused on the tasks at hand.

As Vice President George H. W. Bush quietly assumed command upon his return, the confusion and power struggle subsided. And that's only because, under the advice of his closest advisors, Reagan had rejected Haig's early proposals for an executive branch crisis management structure that would've put Haig, the secretary of state, in charge of almost everything.

Traditionally, the role of coordinating information during a national security crisis had been assigned to the national security advisor. This position, with proximity to the president, is strategically positioned to oversee the influx of information from various sources such as the Defense and State Departments, the CIA, the FBI, the National Security Agency, and the Defense Intelligence Agency. This coordination ensures a comprehensive and unified approach to addressing national security challenges.

The State Department, despite being stuffed with seasoned professionals, faced functional and institutional limitations that hindered its ability to manage such a complex and coordinated effort. Bureaucratic habits alone posed significant impediments to effective coordination within the department, Richard Allen noted.

Allen had proposed a strategic solution to the president to control Haig's ambitions, suggesting the appointment of Bush to lead Reagan's national security crisis management team, while the national security advisor and his staff would handle the actual management. This proposal presented an ideal resolution: Bush brought a wealth of experience in foreign affairs and intelligence matters, having been the director of the CIA and serving in Congress. In 1971, President Nixon appointed George H. W. Bush as the U.S. ambassador to the United Nations. Later, in 1974, President Ford appointed Bush as the chief of the Liaison Office to the People's Republic of China. Unlike Haig, Bush was known for his cooperative nature. And more crucially, Bush held a higher rank than Haig in the line of succession.

The president had finally embraced Allen's proposal, signing a "Decision Memorandum" on March 24, 1981. With this decision, the groundwork was laid for a more efficient and cohesive crisis management structure, allowing the team to move forward with a clear and established hierarchy.

The president's decision on crisis management proved to be timely, the assassination attempt occurring just six days after Reagan signed the directive. The establishment of the crisis management structure played a pivotal role in ensuring a coordinated and effective response during this critical period and beyond. Moreover, it prevented Haig from controlling the administration in a way that would have further alienated the same advisors that would play key roles in Reagan's most significant national security and foreign policy achievements.

## THE BEGINNING OF THE END

In a revealing exposé in May 1981, the *New York Times* delved into the intricate internal dynamics of the Reagan administration, attempting to unveil the complex interplay of ideologies that spanned from what they considered "far-right" to the Kissingerian left. There had been an intricate dance of shifting alliances within the administration, and the press was starting to notice now that Reagan was on the mend.[14]

At this point in the Reagan presidency, there were two key figures playing an increasingly larger role coordinating this intricate and tense dance among White House advisors and cabinet members: Presidential Counselor Edwin Meese and White House Chief of Staff James Baker. Both men acted like a fulcrum between Secretary of State Al Haig and men like Richard Allen, William Clark, William Casey, and NSC staffer Constantine Menges, all of whom seemed way more committed to the president's objectives than their own, unlike Haig.

## "REMEMBER, EVERYONE STOCK UP ON VODKA."

One incident that helped expose the growing rift inside the administration occurred during a meeting of the National Security Council just before Christmas on December 21, 1981. The subject of the meeting was Poland, and President Reagan wanted to use the burgeoning Solidarity movement as leverage against the Soviets. Lech Walesa, the leader of the movement, was believed to be in prison, and the Polish government, a proxy of Moscow's, had declared martial law and was cracking down hard on the Catholic Church and other "troublemakers" in the country.

The members of the National Security Council who attended that meeting included Vice President Bush, Deputy Secretary of State William Clark, Defense Secretary Caspar Weinberger, his deputy Frank Carlucci, William Casey, UN Ambassador Jeane Kirkpatrick, Edwin Meese, and a select few other key players.[15] Secretary of State Al Haig was also there, and when asked to give his assessment of what to do in response to the Polish government's crackdown on its citizens, Haig asked, "Is some degree of repression tolerable from our standpoint or do we stand only for total victory and are we prepared to pay the price for total victory?"

After laying out some of the different options, Haig cautioned the president about doing anything that would provoke the Soviets. "I think we should delay action until we further assess the situation," cautioned Haig.

Reagan responded by saying, "This is the first time in 60 years that we have had this kind of opportunity. There may not be another in our lifetime."

The president was able to see that the world was watching Poland and the Solidarity movement—and the cracks it was creating in the Iron Curtain. The president and the White House had also been working with the Vatican and Pope John Paul on this issue. The two men had bonded over the assassination attempts on their lives and shared a great concern for the prospect of nuclear war. More importantly, both the Pope and President Reagan understood that they had the moral authority to use the situation in Poland to apply extreme pressure on the Soviets—both politically and in the global court of public opinion.

"Can we afford not to go all out? I'm talking about a total quarantine of the Soviet Union. No detente!" Reagan exclaimed. "We know—and the world knows—that they are behind this [martial law]. We have backed away so many times!"

What Reagan suggested next would soon be rejected by Haig as a dangerous misstep. It would also mean that companies like Caterpillar Tractor and International Harvester would have to pay significant financial costs because of the new trade sanctions. All three U.S. companies had recently signed deals with the Soviets to sell them equipment. But that was not Reagan's primary concern.

The president pointed out that the Soviets had "violated the Helsinki Accords since the day it was signed. They have made a mockery of it. And we are not going to pretend it is not so."

Everyone in the meeting took a moment to absorb Reagan's statement. Vice President Bush was the first to speak up and back the president and said, "We have a real turning point."

Then Defense Secretary Caspar Weinberger agreed with the president and vice president and added that the United States could not maintain the moral high ground while also selling hundreds of millions of dollars of heavy equipment to the Soviets after they used the Polish government to implement martial law. William Casey added his belief that the United States would lose all credibility if they refused to follow through with a stern response to the Polish situation.

Reagan listened to a few comments from some of his other advisors and then drew back on his days in Hollywood and told the meeting's attendees about a movie produced by Warner Brothers called *Confessions of a Nazi Spy* in 1939. "Interests that wanted to continue selling movies in Germany even though the Holocaust had already started offered to buy the film, including a profit for the makers, to prevent it from being shown," Reagan said.

The object was to make sure other American films could still be sold to the German market. But Reagan told his advisors that Warner Brothers balked at the idea. Adding that "the film was run and had as much impact as anything" when it came to awakening the public to the horrors of Nazi Germany.

Once that happened, other Hollywood studios followed Warner Brothers' lead. MGM released *The Mortal Storm* and *Escape* in 1940, while 20th Century Fox released *The Man I Married* and *Man Hunt* in 1941. Additionally, Charlie Chaplin's *The Great Dictator* both was directed by and starred Chaplin himself. These films were part of the broader collection of anti-Nazi movies released before the United States entered World War II.

Reagan then told his advisors, "If we show this kind of strength—and we have labor and people with us; if we demand that Solidarity gets its rights; if that happens—nothing will be done. But if not, then we invoke sanctions and those who do not go along with us will be boycotted, too, and will be considered against us."

Haig objected and urged the president not to move forward with his ultimatum to the Soviets and instead warn them first in an "unequivocal way" with a speech and a letter.

Reagan again rebuffed Haig and said, "If we don't take action now, three or four years from now we'll have another situation and we wonder, why didn't we go for it when we had the whole country with us? I am tired of looking backward."

Haig tried one more time to persuade the president to hold off on his plans. "This is a matter of life and death for the Soviet Union. They would go to war over this."

A few of the other advisors responded, but then Meese alerted everyone that the meeting had already run over its scheduled end time by 15 minutes. The president, having just been warned by his secretary of state about the prospect of war with the Soviet Union, prepared to leave the room, and as he was walking out joked, "Remember, everyone stock up on vodka."

## A "NIGHTMARE" TRIP TO EUROPE AND THE 1982 WAR IN LEBANON

The president's European tour of 1982 was, according to those who went on the trip, the real beginning of the end of Al Haig's tenure as secretary of state. Clayton E. McManaway, who served in the Staff Secretariat in the Department of State during this tumultuous period, provided insights into the inner workings and challenges that beset Haig during an oral history interview with journalist Charles Stuart Kennedy for the Association of Diplomatic Studies and Training.[16]

The overscheduled itinerary, culminating in a moment when President Reagan fell asleep during a meeting with the Pope on worldwide television, underscored the overwhelming nature of the journey. The signs of a brewing attitude toward Haig became evident during the planning stages, hinting at a disconnect that would later boil over.

The European excursion, intended to strengthen diplomatic ties, turned into a logistical nightmare. McManaway, involved in the advance planning, warned Haig's staff against an overly ambitious schedule that left the president fatigued. The heavy agenda, featuring back-to-back summits and a visit with the Pope, resulted in a grueling ten-day itinerary, with McManaway averaging a mere three hours of sleep per night.

The secretary of state's positioning in the presidential motorcade became a matter of careful consideration, indicative of the growing disconnects and misplaced priorities. McManaway found himself trying to navigate the complexities of securing adequate hotel space for the staff while also ensuring support for Haig himself.

A revealing incident unfolded when McManaway discovered Reagan's plan for an additional day in Paris, unbeknownst to Haig and the State Department team. Faced with resistance from the White House in providing sufficient space and communication with the secretary, McManaway said he took matters into his own hands. By reserving hotel space at the Crillon, he orchestrated a strategic move that later allowed him to negotiate for the required resources. But things continued to deteriorate.

During the trip, the situation shifted from protocol and logistical concerns to substantive foreign policy issues. Al Haig found himself repeatedly bypassed, with Deputy Secretary of State William Clark directly engaging the president on matters like UN votes.

While Reagan was in Europe, Israel invaded Lebanon in response to the attempted assassination of the Israeli ambassador to the United Kingdom by Lebanese terrorists. The conflict prompted the dispatch of career diplomat and Mideast policy expert Phil Habib for a presidential briefing at Versailles. Habib accurately predicted Israel's actions, leading to a critical moment when Clayton E. McManaway discovered a letter from Reagan to Israeli President Menachem Begin urging a ceasefire.

Facing a dilemma, McManaway contacted Executive Secretary Jerry Bremer for clarification. Despite initial denials, McManaway insisted he had the signed letter in his possession.

"Jerry, this letter, it is signed. Do you know anything about it? What am I going to tell the Secretary of State?"

Bremer first said, "There is no such letter like that."

But McManaway rebuffed him, "Jerry, I am looking at the letter."

Bremer then promised, "I will be right back to you."

Bremer then called Robert "Bud" McFarlane, who was then the deputy national security advisor to William Clark. And McFarlane denied it at first.

Bremer then called McManaway back and again said that there was no such letter.

McManaway responded, "Jerry, God damn it, I am looking at it. I can't send it to you, but I will read it to you. And it is signed."

Bremer was ultimately forced to admit the letter had been sent without Haig's knowledge.

According to McManaway, such incidents appeared orchestrated to undermine Haig. The secretary of state, at times threatening resignation, was continually placed in compromising situations. But this was a result of Haig's own diplomatic missteps within the administration.

The aftermath of the European journey reflected the strains within the administration and hinted at the challenges that lay ahead for Haig. The trip, meant to solidify international relations, instead laid bare the internal discord and signaled a turning point in the trajectory of Haig's role as secretary of state.

## CHINA AND TAIWAN

The issue of arms sales to Taiwan became another example of Haig's failure to fully grasp President Reagan's disdain for communism and the new direction in which American foreign policy was heading under Reagan's leadership.

In the initial months of 1982, the Reagan administration began engaging in negotiations with Beijing. The discussions focused on America's ongoing arms sales to Taiwan, a matter that gained significance following the diplomatic shift of U.S. relations to China in 1979. Even the Carter administration maintained that, considering congressional approval of the Taiwan Relations Act of 1979, sustaining limited arms sales to Taiwan was a political imperative.

However, this stance posed a significant challenge to the continued amicable relations with Beijing first established under President Nixon less than a decade prior. Advocates of the burgeoning United States-China relationship, including Haig, had perceived these arms sales as a stumbling block and expressed their concerns on this matter to anyone who would listen.

During the spring of 1981, Beijing issued strong warnings, indicating its intention to significantly diminish its relationship with the United States unless decisive action was taken to limit arms sales to Taiwan.

On the eve of Haig's arrival in China for three days of meetings, the *New York Times* published an article that outlined the evolving nature of Sino-American relations since Haig last visited China in early 1972 to prepare for President Richard M. Nixon's pivotal visit.[17] Since then, China had started bottling Coca-Cola, Fujian Province was now making Camel cigarettes, and Chinese movie studios had started using Kodak film. Direct trade between China and the United States was on the cusp of exceeding $6 billion by 1982. Joint business ventures were openly encouraged, and thousands of students and scholars had been exchanged. United States oil firms were preparing to bid on exploration tracts in the South China Sea.

While on the campaign trail in 1980, Ronald Reagan, as described by China's state news agency, Xinhua, had "insulted one billion Chinese" by advocating for renewed "official" ties with Taiwan.

Leonard Woodcock, the American ambassador to China under Jimmy Carter, noted that these campaign remarks had the potential to disrupt the still delicate Chinese-American relationship. Since Reagan's election, this issue had loomed like a dark cloud over the Chinese leadership.

Secretary of State Alexander Haig held a firm belief that "in the last quarter of the twentieth century, China may well be the most important country in the world" concerning American interests. Haig exerted substantial pressure and effectively advocated for a form of compromise with Beijing. However, his ultimate proposal, suggesting a halt to arms sales to Taiwan, did not gain approval.

Again and again, it appeared as if Haig, the secretary of state, had not been paying attention to Reagan's public statements about what was truly motivating his presidency. During his 1981 commencement address delivered to Notre Dame's graduating class, President Reagan recalled one of his early acting roles, playing George Gipp in a movie about legendary Notre Dame Coach Knute Rockne. Gipp, a legend himself, had died from illness at just 25 years old, but before doing so, he urged his coach to "Win just one for the Gipper." Reagan focused on the significance of the story:

> Rockne could have used Gipp's dying words to win a game any time. But eight years went by following the death of George Gipp before Rock revealed those dying words, his deathbed wish.
>
> And then he told the story at halftime to a team that was losing, and one of the only teams he had ever coached that was torn by dissension and jealousy and factionalism. The seniors on that team were about to close out their football careers without learning or experiencing any of the real values that a game has to impart. None of them had known George Gipp. They were children when he played for Notre Dame. It was to this team that Rockne told the story and so inspired

them that they rose above their personal animosities. For someone they had never known, they joined together in a common cause and attained the unattainable.[18]

George Gipp's real life story and that Notre Dame team had become somewhat of a metaphor for Reagan's own administration. Unlike Gipp, Reagan has survived, of course. But not only was the president trying to inspire the Notre Dame graduates; it was as if he were trying to inspire his own administration to put aside their own personal ambitions to attain the unattainable. Reagan then said:

> The West will not contain communism; it will transcend communism. We won't bother to denounce it; we will dismiss it as a sad, bizarre chapter in human history whose last pages are even now being written.

The president also mentioned both William Faulkner and Pope John Paul II as he outlined the overarching intentions of his presidency:

> William Faulkner, at a Nobel Prize ceremony some time back, said man "would not only [merely] endure: he will prevail" against the modern world because he will return to "the old verities and truths of the heart." And then Faulkner said of man, "He is immortal because he alone among creatures . . . has a soul, a spirit capable of compassion and sacrifice and endurance."
> 
> One can't say those words—compassion, sacrifice, and endurance—without thinking of the irony that one who so exemplifies them, Pope John Paul II, a man of peace and goodness, an inspiration to the world, would be struck by a bullet from a man towards whom he

could only feel compassion and love. It was Pope John Paul II who warned in last year's encyclical on mercy and justice against certain economic theories that use the rhetoric of class struggle to justify injustice. He said, "In the name of an alleged justice the neighbor is sometimes destroyed, killed, deprived of liberty or stripped of fundamental human rights."

For the West, for America, the time has come to dare to show to the world that our civilized ideas, our traditions, our values, are not—like the ideology and war machine of totalitarian societies—just a facade of strength. It is time for the world to know our intellectual and spiritual values are rooted in the source of all strength, a belief in a Supreme Being, and a law higher than our own.

Ten months after his commencement address at Notre Dame, President Reagan sat for an interview with the *New York Post*'s editorial board. He was asked a question about the Soviet Union and the Eastern bloc's deteriorating economic conditions. During the interview one can get a sense of the clarity of Reagan's personal objectives and which country he believed would be the most important as it related to the future of the United States' standing in the world. Reagan told *New York Post*'s editors that the Soviet Union had "run out of hard cash and they economically are very vulnerable right at the moment." He explained:

> They've deprived their people; they've lowered their standard of living just to continue with this massive buildup. And I must say they've been tremendously successful with it. They're—not only quantitatively but qualitatively—militarily they have been an industrial

giant. And this is one of the reasons why we can't retreat on what we're doing, because I believe we've come to the point that we must go at the matter of realistically reducing, if not totally eliminating, the nuclear weapon, the threat to the world.

And I think to do that we have to sit across the table from them with the strength that we haven't had for the last decade in which they've got a stake in maybe doing something of this kind, and particularly now in their economic situation. But before this we were unilaterally disarming. They didn't have to give in and make any deal about disarming. And I think what we're doing in Geneva reveals something about their lack of sincerity now in this whole matter, because we don't have anything there and they have 300, and we're saying we won't put anything there if you'll take your 300 away. And they so far haven't been willing to meet.

But I think that's a pretty good indication of how important it is that you sit on the other side of the table with some chips of your own that you can throw in the pot.[19]

## THE FALKLANDS

In 1982, during the Falklands War, the United States nearly sided against its key ally, the United Kingdom, largely due to Secretary of State Alexander Haig's diplomatic efforts. Initially, Washington remained neutral, and Haig engaged in shuttle diplomacy between Buenos Aires and London, seeking a settlement. However, after Argentina's military junta rejected his proposal, the United States reconsidered its stance.

Declassified documents from an April 30, 1982, National Security Council meeting, released by the Reagan Library in 2012, show internal White House deliberations.[20] One key revelation was how Haig's compromise plan leaned toward Argentina, potentially granting it sovereignty over the Falklands, which the islanders might have accepted over time.

However, doubts lingered as to whether the islanders would indeed accept Argentine sovereignty, and whether Haig genuinely considered their interests. His previous remarks to U.S. congressmen, suggesting that the principle of "self-determination" did not fully apply to them, raised concerns. Additionally, an inappropriate joke he made about their sexual practices underscored his lack of empathy.

Despite Haig's efforts, he expressed bewilderment and frustration at the junta's response, noting that their proposals amounted to a veiled transfer of sovereignty, which the Argentine foreign minister acknowledged. Yet the junta remained unwilling to accept them. This apparent stance fueled suspicions among some British officials that the United States was favoring Buenos Aires throughout the conflict. However, the meeting minutes contradict this notion in two key ways.

First, the NSC meeting was convened to discuss and ultimately decide on leaning toward Britain. While this tilt was more symbolic than practical at this stage, a White House statement attributed the breakdown of negotiations to Buenos Aires, with plans to resume talks soon. Second, Haig found an unexpected ally in UN Ambassador Jeane Kirkpatrick, usually his adversary. Meanwhile, influential figures like Defense Secretary Caspar Weinberger and CIA Deputy Director Bobby Inman favored a stronger alignment with Britain.

During an interview for this book, K. T. McFarland, who was working in the Pentagon as an aid to Defense Secretary Caspar

Weinberger, said it was known throughout the administration that "Al (Haig) had a healthy ego. . . . So, he really felt that he could take the lead on a lot of these things. The time that it really was the most obvious was in the Falklands. The United States was, of course, going to support our ally, Great Britain. That's what the president wanted to do. That's what the secretary of defense wanted to do. Al Haig said, 'No, no, no. I think we should have an opportunity to negotiate here.'"

McFarland explained that Haig "tried to negotiate between the generals, the junta in Argentina, and the Brits. And everyone thought, 'Oh, really? I mean, we're going to support the Brits, right?'" McFarland also says President Reagan gave Al Haig "about a week to see if he could do any negotiating Henry Kissinger style, and he was not able to."

She called the Falklands War "a great military exercise" for the British. But more importantly, "it was real proof that Britain was going to protect its country and its land. And it really put Margaret Thatcher on the map."

President Reagan maintained a calm and detached demeanor throughout the discussion. He had articulated a clear U.S. stance from the outset: neutrality regarding sovereignty over the Falklands but firm opposition to resolving the issue through military aggression. This position remained unchanged.

While the British had hoped for U.S. support on both fronts, they received substantial backing, particularly in endorsing a principle that allowed Washington to provide robust material support for their military campaign. Reagan granted his cabinet secretaries considerable autonomy in interpreting this principle. Weinberger and Haig left the NSC meeting with approval for further military aid and shuttle diplomacy.

Three weeks later, British troops landed at San Carlos Bay, marking a turning point. The modest U.S. tilt toward Britain at the meeting became more pronounced as diplomacy waned and military action determined the outcome. Military aid emerged as Washington's most significant contribution to the conflict.

Thatcher's resolve and strategic acumen were tested, and she twice accepted compromise proposals that could have ended her career had the junta agreed to them. However, she correctly surmised that the junta would not agree to withdraw its troops from the islands, ultimately leading to a British victory.

Despite differing opinions within the NSC that day, almost everyone benefited from Britain's triumph. The junta fell, free elections were held in 1983, and Argentina enjoyed a period of political and economic stability. Reagan and Thatcher emerged as winners, with Thatcher solidifying her dominance in British politics and Reagan securing a steadfast ally in the Cold War struggle. In hindsight, the wisdom of the tilt toward Britain is evident, underscoring the prescience of figures like Weinberger and Inman.

## THE FINAL STRAW

On June 26, 1982, Haig's troubled tenure with the Reagan administration finally ended. He would later tell journalist James Rosen "the appalling part of it was that you assemble people around you to be on a team, and yet you tolerate it when they don't play on that team. And I quit Ronald Reagan for exactly that reason." Haig recalled:

> When we got into the Middle East war, in Lebanon, we could have settled that war, on terms in which we wouldn't be confronted with what we were confronted with today. We would have returned Lebanon to the sovereign control of their people. . . . I went to the president, and I said: "Hey, you're going to have big, big

problems. And I don't want to be a part of it. Now you either are going to let me do what you hired me to do or get another guy." "Well," he said, "well, Al, please stay here and settle this Middle East thing."

I settled it twice. The first time I got it settled was before the funeral of [Saudi Arabia's] King Khalid. We had a withdrawal schedule for [Israeli troops in Lebanon]. That's why I created a multinational force to go into Beirut. Not to keep the Israelis from brutalizing the PLO, but to supervise the withdrawal of Syria, the PLO and Israel. Now, what happened? [Vice President] Bush, [Defense Secretary] Cap Weinberger, designated by Jim Baker to go to Khalid's funeral. And do you know what they had—went in, in a meeting, a secret meeting, and said, "Boys, Haig doesn't speak for the U.S.—United States government." And therefore, they immediately jumped off that agreement, which I had to twist their arms to accept."

Rosen asked, "How did you learn about that?" Haig told Rosen that he confronted the president privately and said: "You can't run a government this way. People are getting killed." Haig claimed that Reagan again begged him to "Please stay on." This claim was disputed by others. Haig said:

I stayed on. I rebuilt the whole thing by brutalizing the Saudis. And the next thing I know, I tell the president, I said: "Mr. President, I think we've got it now. But it's very delicate. And it's got to be handled very carefully." I went down to Greenbrier for the weekend. I got a call from [Reagan aide] George Shultz. He said, "Al, the president has said now's the time." And I said: "George, you're not going to tell me that. You tell the president to tell me that." So, the president called me 30 minutes later. He said, "What George told you is so."

Prior to Haig's resignation, and to address the mounting tension in the Cabinet, Ed Meese told me Reagan . . . [had been] developing this idea where just [Defense Secretary Caspar] Weinberger, Haig, [The Director of National Intelligence William] Casey, and [National Security Advisor] Bill Clark would get together privately to try to work things out among them.

And so, we did that for several months. And Casey and Clark were obviously more supportive of Reagan taking the lead in the decision making than Al Haig. And so was Weinberger. Al Haig was basically one against three. And at that point, it probably became clear that the writing was on the wall, that it wasn't gonna work out.

Meese added that Haig "was using the resignation as leverage, knowing that Ronald Reagan didn't like controversy. I mean, he liked disagreement, civil disagreement, but not controversy. Yeah, not the coercive type of disagreement."

Shultz would be quickly confirmed as Haig's successor, but in the interim Haig would stay on. Meanwhile, a classified memo circulated among the National Security Council members including Bud McFarlane, Judge Clark, and John Poindexter.[21] The memo sought to redefine the relationship between the new secretary of state, the State Department, and the Reagan White House. The memo said that to prevent past conflicts, like the ones experienced with Haig and his staffers at the State Department, it was crucial to establish ground rules with the new secretary early on.

Under the Reagan administration, the memo stated, the White House Personnel Office would operate with a commitment to fairness. While they respected the autonomy of each department, the White House Personnel Office also had a responsibility to ensure that appointees possess integrity, competence, and most importantly an alignment with the administration's goals. The memo proposed a collaborative system to recommend candidates for vacancies, fostering mutual confidence between the White House and the State Department. And the following recommendations were made.

Recommendations for presidential appointments should be a joint effort between the Department of State and presidential personnel. Changes desired by the new secretary should be made in consultation with presidential personnel, benefiting from insights into past issues and concerns. The undersecretary for management's responsibilities should be reduced to allow greater focus on personnel matters, separate from other roles. A thorough review of regional bureaus and senior noncareer positions was necessary to ensure competence and alignment with the secretary's philosophy. They also suggested that the new secretary should establish a management structure that correlated day-to-day policy decisions with his foreign policy objectives.

And for a brief period at least, these recommendations seemed to work.

# CHAPTER 4

# The Soviet Gerontocracy

*"The clique of elderly gentlemen that has ruled the Soviet Union so far during the 1970s remains in control."*
—*New York Times*, March 7, 1976

## THE GHOSTS OF STALIN'S PURGE

By the late 1970s, the Soviet Union's Politburo was deeply scarred by Joseph Stalin's ruthless purge of his rivals from the Communist Party. Stalin had orchestrated a brutal campaign that eliminated any real or perceived threats to his supremacy. His tactics led to a pervasive fear that lurked in every echelon of the Kremlin. A peculiar gerontocracy remained in Moscow. The aging vanguards of the USSR's Communist Party, survivors of Stalin's purge, now held the reins of power. This gerontocracy was grappling with the ghosts of the past while also trying to navigate the uncertainties of the present.

After Stalin's death in early March 1953, a fierce power struggle unfolded within the Communist Party's Central Committee, ultimately leading to the ascension of Nikita Khrushchev as the first secretary. Khrushchev boldly denounced Stalin's purges and pursued policies aimed at mitigating repression. One significant policy shift involved substantial reduction in the USSR's conventional military forces, combined with a strategic pivot toward relying on Soviet missiles for national defense. This move faced a critical test during the Cuban Missile Crisis, which exposed a perception of weaknesses in Khrushchev's leadership. It also emboldened his political adversaries within the Politburo. Khrushchev's popularity waned, eventually leading to his ouster in October 1964. Unlike some of his predecessors who died or were killed while still holding office, Khrushchev was peacefully pensioned off into retirement. He lived out his final years splitting his time between a Moscow apartment and a dacha in the Russian countryside until his death from a heart attack in 1971. And even though Khrushchev was allowed a quiet retirement, paranoia remained among Soviet leaders.

In early March 1976, the *New York Times* reported that the Soviet gerontocracy was "alive and well in the Kremlin." Their report came shortly after the Communist Party's 25th Congress in Moscow. "The clique of elderly gentlemen that has ruled the Soviet Union so far during the 1970s remains in control," the *Times* reported.[1]

That clique included Khrushchev's successor as first secretary, Leonid Brezhnev; Alexei Kosygin, who would serve as the premier of the Soviet Union from 1964 to 1980 and was one of the Kremlin's most influential policymakers; Mikhail Suslov, the Communist Party's second secretary and its unofficial chief ideologue; Nikolai Podgorny, who served as the chairman of the Presidium, which was the head of state of the Soviet Union; and Yuri Andropov, who was the chairman of the Committee for State Security, also known as the KGB. The average age of the USSR's leadership "clique" when the *New York Times* article was published was well above 70.

By 1981, the average age of the USSR's 14-man Politburo had fallen to 69, but only after Kosygin died in 1980. And even though Reagan was 69 years old at his inauguration, the Politburo's average age was still 13 years older than the average age of Reagan's cabinet at the same time, the *Washington Post* observed in one of its reports.[2]

There was a belief, at least in the media, that the ruling Soviet 70-year-olds were "hardly likely to push an adventurous course that would pose serious risks of thermonuclear war. Their instinct for aggression seems more likely to be expressed in trying to capture isolated targets of opportunity—future Angolas where the dead can be Cubans or Africans rather than Russians." Grenada would fit into this category, as would many of the Central and South American nations teetering on the brink of falling into Marxist hands at the time.

In 1979, with the success of the Nicaraguan Revolution and the rise of the New Jewel Movement in Grenada, the Soviet Union conducted a fresh evaluation of its geopolitical posture.

Grenada's New Jewel Movement attempted to build a Marxist-Leninist outpost in the Caribbean. It rapidly turned into a radical dictatorship allied politically and militarily with the Eastern bloc. By 1983 the Marxist movement in Grenada started to stall out. Maurice Bishop started to grow frustrated with the lack of resources he was getting from his Cuban and Soviet allies. He started looking elsewhere for help, including the United States. That proved to be a fatal decision. Shortly after his appeal to the Reagan administration, Bishop was deposed in a coup and murdered by an even more radical faction of his own party loyal to his childhood friend Bernard Coard. Coard was provoked to action by Bishop's attempt to work with Washington. The Soviets also saw the move as a sign of ideological backsliding. The violent downfall of Maurice Bishop was viewed as beneficial to the Soviets and Cubans since it temporarily brought to power a regime even more pro-Soviet than Bishop's had been. Grenada looked like it could be a geographically strategic addition to the Soviet bloc's intelligence apparatus that was expanding, despite its financial limitations.

This reevaluation, in turn, also led to an intensified focus on Latin America as a breeding ground for revolutionary activities.

The increased Soviet support for Salvadoran guerrillas and similar groups reflected these shifts in opportunities and strategies.

Brezhnev, like Khrushchev and Stalin, hoarded power and was reluctant to share it with a newer generation of Soviet leaders. And the *New York Times* predicted that "when the time comes for new leaders, the battles in the Kremlin will be more difficult than they would have been had today's gerontocrats been willing to retire gracefully before death or illness forced them to."[3]

President Reagan even once joked that Soviet leaders "kept dying" on him during his first few years in office.[4] And this was true. Brezhnev, who led the USSR for 18 years, died at 75 in 1982. He was followed by Yuri Andropov, who died in 1984 at 69. Andropov's successor, Konstantin Chernenko, died in 1985 at 73 and was succeeded by Mikhail Gorbachev.

Stalin was long gone, but the mental scars left behind by the intelligence failures preceding the German invasion of Russia in June 1941 remained. And those scars would play a significant role in how the Soviet leadership and intelligence community responded to Reagan's rhetoric and his emerging strategy to confront the USSR. Both Brezhnev and Andropov had lived through Operation Barbarossa, and it became the "formative experience of their political lives," according to the CIA's analysis.[5] Stalin's clandestine sources provided him with timely and detailed warnings about the Nazis' impending attack. But Stalin gambled on his belief that Hitler wouldn't invade without issuing an ultimatum first. Stalin also could not comprehend a strategy that would put the Nazis in a two-front war. Stalin didn't trust his intelligence and was known to discount reports from his agents because he believed they could be controlled and corrupted by the enemy. So Stalin also insisted that Soviet intelligence agents bolster their assessments with other examples of war-planning. One example is when Stalin had his intelligence assets in Nazi-occupied Europe monitor the price of mutton. The rationale for this strategy was based on the idea that German soldiers would need sheepskin coats to survive a winter campaign in Russia. If the Nazi purchased all the sheep for their skins, the market would be flooded with cheap mutton. The problem with this strategy was Stalin's failure to account for Hitler's wrongheaded belief that the Nazis could defeat the Red Army in just five months, before the winter cold set in, and so he never prepared his troops for the harsh winter ahead. The blame for the intelligence failures before the Nazi invasion of Russia belongs to Stalin, but he chose to blame his intelligence officers, many of whom became victims of his great purge after World War II. This, experts believe, became a guiding factor in KGB Chief Yuri Andropov's reactive decision-making in the early 1980s.

## REDEFINING "DÉTENTE"

Over the course of his presidency, Reagan's approach toward the Soviets would evolve from a "militant distrust for the Soviets to one of almost respectful appreciation for [Chernenko's successor] Gorbachev."[6] But that was still years away.

During the 1980 election, Reagan told the *Washington Post* that the arms buildup he favored would restore a U.S. military capability that had been declining since the Vietnam War.[7] Reagan knew that his rapid acceleration of the United States' ongoing military buildup, which only began under his predecessors, would lead to serious arms talks and his goal of eliminating all nuclear weapons. And in the short term, it would prevent more Soviet aggression. Reagan's perspective was based on his belief that the Soviet economy was way too far behind the United States' economy to compete effectively with the United States in a high-technology arms race. Reagan's strategy for pressuring the

USSR would also rely on the lack of morality that he knew existed among most Soviet leaders.

*Washington Post* White House correspondent Lou Cannon wrote, when he became the commander in chief, "Reagan held a primitive view of the Soviets that had changed little since the late 1940s, when Joseph Stalin was in power and Reagan was a movie actor and president of the Screen Actors Guild at a time of emotional congressional investigations of Communist influence in Hollywood."[8] In his 1965 autobiography *Where's the Rest of Me?* Reagan referred to his encounters with communists and their sympathizers in Hollywood as the seminal experience in forming his harsh but accurate view of communism.

Reagan's opinion on Soviet immorality was reinforced during his work with Barry Goldwater's unsuccessful 1964 presidential campaign. And then again during Reagan's own campaign against Gerald Ford for the Republican presidential nomination in 1976.

According to former Russian double agent Oleg Gordievsky and the British intelligence officials who worked with him, Moscow had expected Ronald Reagan's anti-Soviet rhetoric to mellow after his election to the presidency. The opposite would occur.

President Reagan, unlike Governor Reagan, now had access to classified intelligence reports that confirmed his opinions about the Soviets and their activities. The Soviets were not prepared financially nor psychologically for what the new American president had in store.

While the 1976 campaign didn't work out the way Reagan had hoped, the future president successfully managed to redefine "détente" in that race. Reagan knew his predecessors' previous application of détente was a flawed strategy that allowed the Soviet military to continuously build up its weapons with the goal of achieving world domination. Reagan's critiques were so effective that President Ford abruptly announced he was renaming his policy "peace through strength."⁹

Reagan had originally discussed this idea during his 1964 "A Time for Choosing" speech, which Reagan simply called "the speech."¹⁰ He said:

> You and I have the courage to say to our enemies, "There is a price we will not pay." "There is a point beyond which they must not advance." And this—this is the meaning in the phrase of Barry Goldwater's "peace through strength." Winston Churchill said, "The destiny of man is not measured by material computations. When great forces are on the move in the world, we learn we're spirits—not animals." And he said, "There's something going on in time and space, and beyond time and space, which, whether we like it or not, spells duty." You and I have a rendezvous with destiny.

Ford also proposed an *increase of $7.4 billion* for the 1977 defense budget. The military buildup would continue under Carter, thanks to pressure from Congress, but the military buildup under President Reagan increased exponentially.

Reagan also knew the military strength he sought would not be possible unless he first worked to strengthen the U.S. economy. During his first year in office, Reagan slashed taxes and domestic spending. These moves proved successful later, but they would also cost Reagan and the Republican Party during the 1982 midterms. The GOP saw a loss of 26 seats in the House of Representatives, and Democrats gained 7 new governorships.

Reagan continued with his plans undeterred by the midterms' political consequences. He understood that the Soviet economy was faltering and was in a much worse position than the U.S.

economy, even though some were trying to blame Reagan for the unemployment rate, which was stubborn and still at a post-depression high during much of his first term. Reagan's optimism and his underlying belief in American exceptionalism were dismissed by many.

After a trip to Moscow, historian Arthur Schlesinger claimed that he "found more goods in the shops, more food in the markets, more cars on the street—more of almost everything except, for some reason, caviar." Schlesinger also discounted the opinions of people like President Reagan "who think the Soviet Union is on the verge of economic and social collapse . . . with one small push to go over." Schlesinger added that both the United States and the Soviet Union had "economic troubles; but neither is on the ropes."

Harvard economist John Kenneth Galbraith said, "[T]he Russian system succeeds because, not in contrast to the Western industrial economies, it makes full use of its manpower."

The Soviet decline was temporarily obscured by elevated prices for Soviet oil exports. However, this temporary support eroded in the early 1980s. By November 1985, the price for crude oil stood at $30 per barrel, but by March 1986, it plummeted to just $12.[11]

Reagan's close friendships with fellow conservative political leaders like Margaret Thatcher in Britain, and then later with Prime Minister Brian Mulroney in Canada, would prove critically important to his goals. Reagan successfully managed to leverage those friendships to strengthen American alliances with other countries as he shifted his focus from the U.S. economy to his foreign policy and the need to directly confront the Soviets. Mulroney's predecessor, Pierre Trudeau, who was Canada's prime minister until 1984, had a much different foreign policy vision than Reagan's. And neither Reagan nor Trudeau seemed to care about keeping their differences a secret.[12] Trudeau's outward animosity to Reagan between 1981 and 1983 was the result of Trudeau's close relationship with Marxists like Cuba's Fidel Castro.

As he recovered from the gunshot wounds suffered during the March 1981 assassination attempt, Reagan's goal of ending communism became a prominent feature of his public speeches. That included the commencement address President Reagan delivered on May 17, 1981, at Notre Dame University.[13] In addition to telling the story of his role in *Knute Rockne, All American*, Reagan also wove in his prediction of what was about to happen to communism across the globe. "The years ahead will be great ones for our country, for the cause of freedom and the spread of civilization," the president told graduating students unapologetically. "The West will not contain communism; it will transcend communism. We will not bother to denounce it; we'll dismiss it as a sad, bizarre chapter in human history whose last pages are even now being written."

In public, the Reagan administration still looked like it was conducting a quasi-normal diplomatic relationship and arms control posture with the Soviets, albeit with sharper rhetoric. But behind the scenes, and under Reagan's direction, the U.S. military and intelligence community conducted covert political and psychological operations designed to exploit Soviet vulnerabilities. Fred Ikle, who served as Reagan's under secretary of defense, said, "[N]othing was written down . . . so, there would be no paper trail." Reagan's closest advisors in the White House wanted to play on the Soviet perception that America's fortieth president was a "cowboy and a reckless practitioner of nuclear politics," according to now declassified internal CIA documents.[14]

Those same documents included interviews with General Jack Chain, who ran the Strategic Air Command at that time.

General Chain explained that they would send bombers over the North Pole just to ping the Soviet's radar. They would also send other aircraft to probe the periphery of the USSR's Asian and European borders. "As quickly as the flights began, they would stop, only to begin a few weeks later, they would stop, only to begin a few weeks later," the general recalled.

Dr. William Schneider, who served at the State Department, said, "It really got to them." Dr. Schneider had access to the classified after-action reports of these missions. He recalled that the Soviets "didn't know what it all meant. A squadron would fly straight at Soviet airspace, and other radars would light up units and would go on alert. Then at the last minute the squadron would peel off and return home."

The Navy was also involved and would play an even larger role in Reagan's PSYOPs with the Soviets. In early March 1981 President Reagan, before he was shot, greenlit operational plans for the Navy to sail into waters the U.S. fleet had rarely—if ever—sailed into before. Major naval exercises conducted in these areas would demonstrate the U.S. Navy's global reach. Some of these classified naval operations were quite daring, like the ones involving carrier-launched aircraft used to penetrate Soviet air defense systems. The U.S. chief of naval operations summed up one of these exercises by stating that the Soviets were "as naked as a jaybird" on the Kamchatka Peninsula, "and they know it."

On April 4 at least six U.S. Navy planes from the USS *Enterprise* and the USS *Midway* simulated bombing runs over Soviet Zeleny Island, located between the Kamchatka Peninsula and the Japanese archipelago. The two carriers were part of a 40-ship armada patrolling the northern Pacific. According to journalist Seymour Hersh and a Soviet order he referenced in an article he wrote for the *Atlantic*, the Navy aircraft flew 20 miles inside Soviet airspace and remained there for as much as 20 minutes.[15] The Soviet air defense organization was put on alert for the indefinite future. Some officers were dismissed; others were reprimanded and transferred. Yuri Andropov issued an order that readiness be increased and that any aircraft discovered in Soviet airspace be shot down.

Over the spring of 1982, the Reagan administration started to formalize their new strategy against the Soviet Union and officially outlined it in National Security Decision Directive 32 (NSDD 32).[16] The document outlined a total of 11 global objectives that would come to define the Reagan Doctrine and help shape his administration's national security policy moving forward.

The primary goals included deterring military attacks by the USSR and its allies, strengthening U.S. influence globally through alliances and diplomatic efforts, and containing and reversing Soviet expansion and military presence worldwide. The directive aimed to increase the costs of Soviet support and the use of proxy, terrorist, and subversive forces.

Over the next several months, Reagan would continue to refine and sharpen his rhetoric. On March 8, 1983, after a visit to Epcot Center at Walt Disney World in Florida, Reagan headed to address the National Association of Evangelicals at an Orlando hotel. The speech included a discussion on religion and a condemnation of anti-Semitism and other forms of racial hatred.

But then the president turned his attention to United States-Soviet relations and said, "Whatever sad episodes exist in our past, any objective observer must hold a positive view of American history—a history that has been the story of hopes fulfilled and dreams made into reality. Especially in this century, America has kept alight the torch of freedom, not just for ourselves but for millions of others around the world."

President Reagan then harkened back to his first press conference as president and underscored that "being committed

Marxist-Leninists, the Soviet leaders have openly and publicly stated that they only acknowledge the morality that advances their cause—namely, world revolution." Then Reagan pressed his audience to make sure they didn't "ignore the facts of history and the aggressive impulses of an evil empire, to simply call the arms race a giant misunderstanding and thereby remove yourself from the struggle between right and wrong and good and evil." And the president predicted that communism would eventually collapse, again saying, "I believe that communism is another sad, bizarre chapter in human history whose last pages are even now being written."

Then on June 8, 1982, while on that tour of Europe that would factor into Secretary Haig's resignation, the president delivered a powerful speech in front of the British Parliament. The speech would also prove to be one of his most important. Reagan articulated his emerging foreign policy strategy to a global audience. He stressed again that the Soviet Union was in a deep economic crisis. Not only that, he said, but the long-term existence of the USSR "runs against the tide of history by denying human freedom and human dignity to its citizens." He stated:

> We're approaching the end of a bloody century plagued by a terrible political invention—totalitarianism. Optimism comes less easily today, not because democracy is less vigorous, but because democracy's enemies have refined their instruments of repression. Yet optimism is in order, because day by day democracy is proving itself to be a not-at-all-fragile flower. From Stettin on the Baltic to Varna on the Black Sea, the regimes planted by totalitarianism have had more than 30 years to establish their legitimacy. But none—not one

regime—has yet been able to risk free elections. Regimes planted by bayonets do not take root.

The strength of the Solidarity movement in Poland demonstrates the truth told in an underground joke in the Soviet Union. It is that the Soviet Union would remain a one-party nation even if an opposition party were permitted, because everyone would join the opposition party.[17]

A nervous laughter rippled through the Royal Gallery at Westminster in London, where the MPs had gathered to hear President Reagan's speech. And there were plenty of reasons for jitters. The speech came during a dark period in Europe, which included unsuccessful uprisings against communism in East Germany in 1953 and Czechoslovakia in 1968. The future success of the Solidarity movement in Poland was nowhere near certain yet. Reagan added:

The Soviet Union itself is not immune to this reality. Any system is inherently unstable that has no peaceful means to legitimize its leaders. In such cases, the very repressiveness of the state ultimately drives people to resist it, if necessary, by force.

While we must be cautious about forcing the pace of change, we must not hesitate to declare our ultimate objectives and to take concrete actions to move toward them. We must be staunch in our conviction that freedom is not the sole prerogative of a lucky few, but the inalienable and universal right of all human beings. So states the United Nations Universal Declaration of Human Rights, which, among other things, guarantees free elections.

> The objective I propose is quite simple to state: to foster the infrastructure of democracy, the system of a free press, unions, political parties, universities, which allows a people to choose their own way to develop their own culture, to reconcile their own differences through peaceful means.

It was during this speech when President Reagan asserted that "the march of freedom and democracy" would "leave Marxism-Leninism on the ash-heap of history."

President Reagan used the Parliament speech to advocate for the United States retaking the initiative in the Cold War, emphasizing the need for a global commitment to eradicate communism without resorting to military intervention, recalled Reagan's speechwriter Anthony Dolan, during an interview with the Associated Press.[18] Dolan stressed that Reagan's choice of his draft for the speech marked a significant moment, as there had been no comparable call from Western statesmen, resonating strongly with conservatives. One reason for his abundant confidence in these speeches can be traced back to his well-known love of reading intelligence reports, and what he was learning about the impact his strategy was having on the Soviets.

During an interview conducted for this book, former Reagan counselor and Attorney General Edwin Meese confirmed what Peter Schweizer reported in his book *Reagan's War*. Schweizer included this quote from a CIA liaison to the Reagan White House, "[H]e [the president] enjoyed looking at all of it. He particularly enjoyed information about economic troubles they [the Soviets] were experiencing."

William Clark, one of Reagan's closest friends who would go on to serve as his national security director and secretary of the interior, recalled to Schweizer how persistent Reagan was with questions like "What is Brezhnev thinking about in Europe?" and "How are they dealing with those losses in Afghanistan?"

## OPERATION RYaN

We know that based on accounts from both the CIA and the KGB, Moscow had become convinced that the United States under Reagan was preparing a nuclear attack on the USSR.[19] Around the same time as Reagan's speech at Notre Dame, Brezhnev, the Soviet Union's general secretary, and Yuri Andropov, head of the KGB, briefed the Soviet intelligence community on the Politburo's forecast that the chances of nuclear war were higher in 1981 than at any time during the entire Cold War. The KGB and the GRU, which was the Soviet's military intelligence unit, were both placed on a permanent watch to monitor any indication or warnings of U.S. war-planning.

This new Soviet response to Reagan's fortified national security posture was nicknamed Operation RYaN.[20] RYaN is a Russian acronym for Raketno-Yadernoe Napadenie, or "nuclear missile attack" when translated into English. The years-long operation was the result of both Reagan's accelerated military buildup and his increasingly strident rhetoric aimed at the Soviets, and the biggest factor was deep-rooted Russian paranoia.

The plan was unveiled in Moscow. Yuri Andropov's portion of the presentation before the KGB and GRU proved to be the most dramatic, according to former Soviet spy Oleg Gordievsky. Gordievsky wrote in his book *Top Secret Files on KGB Foreign Operations* that the intelligence community was astonished by Andropov's assessment. Andropov declared that the new American administration was actively preparing for war, and because of this, the Politburo, the KGB, and the GRU would, for the first time ever, cooperate in a worldwide intelligence operation. There was immediate skepticism among the American experts in the Soviet Foreign Intelligence Services; they did not doubt Andropov's concern, but they didn't believe the Americans were capable of a nuclear first strike. Many believed the reaction to Reagan's new policies was designed by the USSR's Defense Minister Dmitri Ustinov, who had served and somehow survived under Stalin as his armaments commissar.[21] According to Gordievsky, Donald Maclean, a British double agent who worked for the Soviets, wrote a secret memo that expressed alarm at the way the Soviet Union appeared "hypnotized by the size and variety of American nuclear forces."[22]

But Operation RYaN moved forward anyway. The GRU was responsible for monitoring the nonexistent preparations for a nuclear strike from the West. The KGB had the primary responsibility of providing advance notice of a decision by the United States and its NATO allies to launch a nuclear attack. And the most prestigious arm of the KGB, the First Chief Directorate (FCD), would plan out the entire operation.

The FCD believed that the USSR's foreign intelligence operations needed to deviate from their peacetime routines to provide a preliminary warning of first-strike preparations. In November 1981 Soviet agents in the West, Asia, and the third world received instructions from Moscow requiring them to submit reports every two weeks concerning the likelihood of a nuclear strike. "Uncovering the process for preparation by the adversary to make the decision for nuclear attack and the subsequent measures to prepare the country for nuclear war would enable us [the Soviets] to increase the period of anticipation needed for a retaliatory strike."

Outside of the USSR, Gordievsky discovered that his colleagues were skeptical of Operation RYaN. The reality of living in the West may have impacted their ability to be as alarmist as the FCD about the prospect of nuclear war. But more importantly, none of them had been willing to risk their careers or their lives to challenge the orders coming from Moscow. This created a "vicious cycle" of foreign agents being required to report alarming information, even if legitimate information of this kind didn't exist. And what was reported alarmed the FCD, and they demanded more of it, regardless of its legitimacy and the skepticism of those who reported it. In February 1983, the FCD sent out even more detailed instructions. This time the top-secret memo was individually addressed to each foreign agent with instructions to keep the document in their personal files. The memo stressed that there was a steadily increasing nuclear threat and "the growing urgency" of discovering the West's plans for a strike on the Soviet Union. However, those plans didn't exist.

Operation RYaN continued after the death of Brezhnev in November 1982. President Reagan, during a nationally broadcast news conference, acknowledged the potential for improved relations between Washington and the Kremlin following the death of the Soviet leader. However, he cautioned that meaningful diplomatic progress requires mutual cooperation, stating, "It takes two to tango." Reagan refrained from speculating on whether Brezhnev's passing, as the key figure in the United States-Soviet détente with Richard Nixon, could lead to heightened East-West tensions.

Reagan emphasized, "We've had periods of tension before," highlighting the unpredictability of future situations. He expressed a commitment to pursuing peace as a fundamental goal but underlined a key principle: "We should not delude ourselves. Peace is a product of strength, not of weakness." This assertion reflected Reagan's belief in maintaining a robust and secure position to contribute to global peace.

## RESPONSE TO THE STRATEGIC DEFENSE INITIATIVE

President Reagan announced the Strategic Defense Initiative (SDI) during a speech on March 23, 1983. President Reagan's intent was to shift the emphasis from mutual assured destruction to strategic missile defense and upset the status quo of the nuclear threat.

Specifically, the president stated during his nationally televised speech to the nation, "What if free people could live secure in the knowledge that their security did not rest upon the threat of instant retaliation to deter a Soviet attack, that we could intercept and destroy strategic ballistic missiles before they reached our soil or that of our allies? I believe there is a way.... It is that we embark on a program to counter the awesome Soviet missile threat with measures that are defensive.... I call upon the scientific community in our country, those who gave us nuclear weapons, to turn their great talents now to the cause of mankind and world peace, to give us the means of rendering these nuclear weapons impotent and obsolete.

The Soviets quickly condemned Reagan's SDI proposal. Four days after President Reagan's speech, Soviet leader Yuri Andropov said that President Reagan's new proposal was "a bid to disarm the Soviet Union" that would launch the two nations into a new strategic nuclear weapons arms race. "This would open the floodgates of a runaway race of all types of strategic arms both offensive and defensive," Andropov said. Andropov directed the Soviet media to launch rhetorical attacks on Reagan unseen since Stalin was in power. They compared Reagan to Hitler. They said the American president was "fanning the flames of war."

Unlike Reagan, Andropov wanted to pivot back to détente and the 1974 agreement between his predecessor Leonid Brezhnev and Soviet Ambassador to the United States Anatoly

Dobrynin that was ironed out with the United States under President Ford and Secretary of State Henry Kissinger in Vladivostok. Andropov said both sides had agreed that no progress in limiting offensive nuclear weapons could be made unless there was "mutual restraint."

The Vladivostok Summit initially looked like a sweeping success. Ford described it as "an appropriate ending to a journey designed to strengthen ties with old friends and expand areas of agreement with potential adversaries" and an experience that "had exceeded my expectations."[23]

At the conclusion of the summit, Kissinger said the American delegation was "exuberant" about the outcome. Kissinger claimed the Soviets had made almost all the concessions.[24] Dobrynin said, "[B]oth sides were satisfied with the results of the meeting," and he even called the Vladivostok Summit the high point of détente between the Soviet Union and the United States, claiming that "for that Ford deserves credit as well as Brezhnev."

But Andropov was learning, the hard way, that Reagan was not Gerald Ford, nor Nixon, and certainly not Carter. Andropov accused Reagan of telling "a deliberate lie" by claiming that the Soviet Union had broken its promise to freeze the deployment of medium-range nuclear missiles in Europe. He also described Washington's attempts to improve the United States' ability to fight and win nuclear wars as "not just irresponsible, it is insane."

The Soviet leader's initial response to the president came from an interview published in *Pravda*, the official newspaper of the Communist Party. An English version of the interview was distributed in advance by the Soviet's official press agency, TASS. The harsh tone of the interview stood in stark contrast to Andropov's more conciliatory tone on United States-Soviet relations shortly after he succeeded Brezhnev. The Soviets seemed to treat the SDI more seriously than White House aides or American scientists did.

In a 1992 article published in the *New York Times*, former Assistant Secretary of Defense Leslie Gelb recalled a revealing off-the-record conversation with Chief of the Soviet General Staff Marshal Nikolai Ogarkov that transpired in 1983.[25] The hard-line Soviet general asserted that, in his view, the Cold War was already over. Ogarkov emphasized the acknowledged technological superiority of U.S. arms, grounded in widespread computer use. He pointed out that even small children in the United States were regularly using computers while the Soviets didn't "even have computers in every office of the Defense Ministry." Ogarkov bluntly stated that catching up with the West in a modern arms race required an economic revolution. "And the question," the general said, "is whether we can have an economic revolution without a political revolution."

But in public, Ogarkov, like Andropov, frequently compared the United States to Nazi Germany. This was common practice among Soviet officials, and according to the CIA, contributed to their growing anxiety and frustration.

## KOREAN AIRLINES FLIGHT 007

On September 1, 1983, just before 3:30 a.m. Moneron Island local time, 2:30 p.m. Washington, D.C., time, a Soviet military jet fired two missiles at Korean Air Lines Flight 007. The missiles hit their target, destroying the 747, killing all 269 people on board. U.S. Congressman Larry McDonald and numerous Americans were on the flight, which was en route from New York to Seoul, South Korea. After stopping in Anchorage, Alaska, for fuel, the plane inadvertently entered Soviet airspace. Soviet air defense units had been tracking the 747 for more than an hour as it flew over the

Kamchatka Peninsula. Orders were given to intercept the civilian plane. The first attempt was made by a MiG-23, which caught up with the 747, but the pilot had to give up the chase because he was running out of fuel.

The reason for the fuel shortage was that after Viktor Belenko's defection to Japan in 1976,[26] the Soviet Air Defense commanders did not trust their pilots. So their planes were given a limited fuel supply to avoid another embarrassing defection. This was more Soviet paranoia at play.

The 747 then flew over the Sea of Okhotsk and then drifted back into Soviet airspace for the second time near Sakhalin Island. Next, two Su-15 interceptors were scrambled from Sokol Air Base, which was in the southern part of Sakhalin Island. The Soviet pilots claimed they tried to contact the crew by radio and fired warning shots from their cannons to force the plane to land. The Korean crew failed to notice the gunfire. Since the warnings were ignored and the plane continued toward the border, orders were given to destroy it.

Two missiles struck the Korean airliner, and moments later it plunged into the Sea of Japan off Moneron Island, south of Sakhalin, disintegrating on impact.

Once word got to Deputy Foreign Minister Georgi Kornienko, he called Yuri Andropov, who was hospitalized with a potentially deadly illness. Kornienko briefed the Soviet premier on the situation. Andropov asked Kornienko to stay on the phone while they reached the Soviet Defense Minister Dmitri Ustinov. In a few moments Andropov came back with the answer.

The Soviet premier told Kornienko, "Ustinov says we shouldn't admit to anything." He added, "Nobody will find out that we shot it down. It is an imperialist provocation." The official line would be that the plane was intercepted over Soviet airspace, that it continued its flight, and that there was no word of its fate. They lied to the world.

Still, Moscow would not publicly respond to the incident until September 9, 1983. Nikolai Ogarkov, the Soviet Army's chief of staff, was joined by other Soviet officials, who tried to blame the United States and prove that the Soviet Union had been within its rights to destroy the flight. They claimed their radar systems had identified the commercial passenger jet as a U.S. military RC-135, and they believed the plane was on an intelligence mission. Once again Andropov bellowed from Moscow, attempting to use the tragedy to stoke the Soviet's anti-American propaganda operation.

Andropov, who was starting to recover from his illness, claimed that an "outrageous military psychosis" had overtaken the United States, adding that "the Reagan administration, in its imperial ambition, goes so far that one begins to doubt whether Washington has any brakes at all preventing it from crossing the point at which any sober-minded person must stop." Andropov made these claims after he received a memo from the KGB that claimed KAL flight 007 had two purposes. "The first purpose was to use the incursion of the intruder aircraft into Soviet airspace to create a favorable situation for the gathering of defense data on our air defense system in the Far East, . . . Second, they envisaged, if this flight were terminated by us, [the U.S. would use] that fact to mount a global anti-Soviet campaign to discredit the Soviet Union."

After the April incursion by U.S. Navy aircraft and Andropov's subsequent "shoot to kill" order, Soviet Air Defense commanders were also warned they would be dismissed if they refused to follow through on Andropov's policy, which had essentially become law. Soviet airspace and its borders were closed to anyone or anything perceived to be an intruder.

Retired CIA veteran Ralph McGehee asserted that Korean Air Lines Flight 007 was intentionally flown over Soviet airspace during a planned Soviet ICBM launch. Drawing on his 25 years of CIA experience, 14 of which were spent overseas, McGehee claimed that the United States orchestrated the event to gather intelligence, believing the Soviets wouldn't shoot down a commercial airliner.

According to McGehee, the Soviets might have mistaken the Boeing 747 for an RC-135 spy plane. He suggested that the United States aimed to obtain information while tarnishing the Soviet image. McGehee, who believed he was under CIA surveillance, criticized the agency for withholding information and stated that the intrusion was a tactic to simulate an invasion, testing Soviet defense radar.

Highlighting a similar incident in 1978, McGehee argued that the United States expected the plane to be intercepted, not shot down, creating a scenario where they gained intelligence while causing embarrassment for the Soviets. He emphasized the challenges of understanding Soviet radar systems due to their intermittent activation, contrasting with continuous U.S. radar operation. McGehee proposed that the RC-135 was equipped to monitor Soviet radar systems during their occasional activation. McGehee also alleged he was being followed by agents of the CIA and said the agency was tapping his telephone.

CIA spokesman Dale Peterson said at the time, "On the record, both of those allegations are absolutely ridiculous. His allegations of intelligence use of the South Korean airliner is utterly irresponsible."[27]

There was a problem with McGehee's claims and the Soviets' public relations effort. Secret American military intelligence stations near the Soviet border had monitored the pursuit of the 747 and its destruction.

U.S. intelligence officers from NSA and the CIA officially concluded the pilot and Soviet air defense commander made an honest, but serious, error, due in part to the fact that the entire Soviet military and all Soviet intelligence officers were in a state of high anxiety.

It was Labor Day weekend, and President Reagan was in California for the holiday. Regardless, the response from the White House to the Soviet's downing of KAL 007 came almost immediately after the tragedy. Secretary of State George Shultz quickly denounced the Soviet act as mass murder during a news conference the day after the plane was shot down, saying, "The United States reacts with revulsion to this attack. Loss of life appears to be heavy. We can see no excuse whatsoever for this appalling act."[28]

Shultz was asked by a reporter if he had "spoken to the President about this matter and what did he say?"

Shultz responded, "I haven't spoken to the President as yet." He added, "[T]he President was fully informed, and I've talked to the West Coast, and the President knows all about this and has been kept fully informed. I haven't personally spoken to him."

Schultz was also asked if the Soviets gave any warning and request to land the plane or attempted to force it down before it was shot down.

Shultz stated, "We have no evidence of that. There was no, apparently no, ability to communicate between the two aircraft. But as the statement says, the Soviet plane that shot the commercial airliner down moved itself into position with a visual contact with the aircraft, so that with the eye you could inspect the aircraft and see what it was you're looking at."

One reporter asked the secretary of state if he or anyone else was aware of any kind of "Soviet military exercises or maneuvers or super-sophisticated radar that might have been in the area, and that they had warned everybody to stay away from?"

Shultz answered bluntly, "No." He added that the White House could "see no explanation whatsoever for shooting down an unarmed commercial airliner, no matter whether it's in your airspace or not."

But in subsequent days following the tragedy, the Reagan White House also wanted to make sure the 269 souls on board didn't die in vain. They worked with producers, including Alvin Snyder, the director of worldwide television for the United States. Information Agency, to produce a video of the incident. Snyder wrote in his book *Warriors of Disinformation: American Propaganda, Soviet Lies, and the Winning of the Cold War* that his team was instructed to make "a slick video" that would be played at a meeting of the UN Security Council on September 6.[29] It would also be broadcast live via satellite to the rest of the world. It was a novel idea, and the video was dramatized for maximum effect.

When the video evidence was presented, it showed the Soviet fighter pilots' comments as they tracked the plane. The video, featuring Russian text and English translations alongside a chronological timeline and route map, strongly supported the claim that the Soviets deliberately shot down a known passenger plane. Notably, no warning shots were fired, and no signals were given to land.

U.S. officials positioned a TV monitor beside the Soviet UN ambassador, Oleg Troyanovsky. This deliberate setup ensured that he and the monitor would be photographed together as the video played. The introduction to the tape was delivered by U.S. Ambassador to the United Nations Jeane Kirkpatrick, who emphasized a particularly alarming revelation from the transcript: "Perhaps the most shocking fact learned from the transcript," she stated, "is that at no point did the pilots raise the question of the identity of the target aircraft."

In the packed chamber, the crowd fell silent, captivated by the unfolding horror on the screen. Amid the intense static, the controlled voices of the Soviet pilots recounted the grim final moments of Flight 007, echoing pilot Osipovich's chilling words, "The target is destroyed." Despite the unsettling narrative, the Soviet ambassador remained defiant, refusing to turn around and confront the monitor directly behind him. In his stoic demeanor, he embodied the epitome of a jowly, arrogant, and unapologetic Soviet bureaucrat.

This visual presentation added to the comprehensive public relations effort orchestrated by Secretary of State George Shultz, as outlined in a memo to President Reagan. The strategy aimed to leverage the incident to raise concerns about Soviet integrity, potentially jeopardizing their peace campaign to dissuade NATO allies in Europe from hosting upgraded American nuclear weapons.

Interestingly, the State Department, unbeknown to the team presenting the video, simultaneously informed President Reagan that Soviet interceptor pilots were allegedly confused about the plane's identity. This revelation, disclosed in a recently declassified memo from Shultz to Reagan, was brought to light through the Freedom of Information Act.

Soviet Communist Party Central Committee member Anatoly Chernyaev wrote about the tragedy in his diary on September 6, 1983. "He initially believes it was an American provocation and that the 'tragedy is that we fell for it.' He blames the United States for the global uproar against the Soviet Union" that followed.

"Reagan started such an anti-Soviet furor around the world," Chernyaev wrote, "that nothing will wash us clean of the stigma as murderers of innocent people in the eyes of regular people around the world." Chernyaev added that Soviet leadership "behaved . . . stupidly, . . . inconsistently, helplessly." And that the incident perfectly "showcased . . . the power and pressure of the 'military complex' over [Soviet] life and politics."[30]

## A NUCLEAR SCARE

It would have been hard to overstate the amount of nuclear-powered tension that existed on the night of September 26, 1983. The Soviet Union found itself on the brink of yet another potential catastrophe. The Oko, the Soviet nuclear early warning system, startled the vigilant eyes of Stanislav Petrov, a lieutenant colonel in the Soviet Air Defense Forces. The system reported the launch of five intercontinental ballistic missiles from the United States, trailed by four more menacing missiles.[31]

Petrov, stationed at the Serpukhov-15 bunker near Moscow, the nerve center of the Soviet early warning satellites, faced a critical decision.[32] His duty entailed observing the satellite early warning network and promptly notifying superiors of any imminent nuclear missile threat. The stakes were high, especially after the downing of the Korean jetliner. The Soviet doctrine of mutual assured destruction mandated an immediate and compulsory nuclear counterattack against the United States upon detection of inbound missiles (launch on warning).

In the eerie silence of the bunker shortly after midnight, Petrov faced a dilemma. The bunker's computers insisted that a single intercontinental ballistic missile was hurtling toward the Soviet Union from the United States. Skepticism crept in as Petrov deemed this detection a computer error. A first-strike nuclear assault by the United States would logically involve a barrage of simultaneous missile launches. Moreover, doubts lingered about the reliability of the new satellite system, intensifying Petrov's suspicion.

With courage and conviction, Petrov dismissed the warning as a false alarm, showcasing his belief that any U.S. first strike would be far more massive. The untested launch detection system fueled his skepticism, coupled with the failure of ground radar to provide corroborative evidence even after several minutes of the false alarm.

The tension escalated when the computers identified four additional missiles targeting the Soviet Union. Petrov, relying on his instincts, suspected another malfunction in the system. The Soviet Union's land radar, incapable of detecting missiles beyond the horizon, left Petrov in a precarious position, relying on intuition to avert disaster.

In the aftermath, it was revealed that the false alarms were triggered by an unusual combination of factors including the alignment of sunlight on high-altitude clouds and the satellites' orbits. Petrov's intuition, coupled with a stroke of luck, prevented a potentially catastrophic chain of events. His decision, rooted in a belief in the illogical nature of the detected missile count and a distrust of the nascent launch detection system, stood as a testament to the critical role individuals play in the face of technological uncertainties that could tip the balance toward devastation.

Petrov reasoned that if the sun glint had triggered the system to report hundreds of missile launches, the Soviet Union might have made a catastrophic mistake by launching its missiles. His decision not to relay the alert to his superiors was grounded in a pragmatic assessment: "When people start a war, they don't start it with only five missiles. You can do little damage with just five missiles." In exercising his judgment, Petrov averted a potentially devastating escalation based on a critical evaluation of the situation at hand.

Many leaders in Europe, including France's François Mitterrand, were accusing Reagan of ushering in a new, more dangerous phase of the Cold War, more dire than the Cuban Missile Crisis in 1962 or the blockade of Berlin in 1948.

# PART TWO

CHAPTER 5

# Ripe for Revolution

*"I have myself seen an unidentified flying object, and I have been overwhelmed by what I have seen."*

—Grenada's Prime Minister Sir Eric M. Gairy, in a speech to the UN General Assembly, October 7, 1977

## ERIC MATTHEW GAIRY'S INDEPENDENCE

Independent Grenada's first prime minister, Sir Eric Matthew Gairy, was born into a peasant family in 1922 in St. Andrew's Parish, which encompasses the middle of the island's east coast. Gairy was educated at the local Catholic school in a community that was brimming with the Catholic faith at the time.[1] When he turned 20, Gairy left Grenada and moved to Trinidad. He eventually found his way to the Dutch colony of Aruba where he started working at the Standard Oil refinery. While in Aruba, Gairy became involved in trade union organizing. He returned to Grenada in 1949 and put his newly acquired organizing skills to work. He was quickly able to recruit a group of 20,000 supporters.

The lush landscapes of rural Grenada, where fields and jungles mix with verdant yet rugged volcanic peaks, stretched across the small island of just 133 square miles. As the twentieth century reached its midpoint, most Grenadians eked out a living as farmers on small plots of land. Some of them supplemented their incomes with seasonal work on the plantations that dotted the landscape or in the hotels that catered to the tourists who were able to reach the southernmost island in the Windward chain.

Per capita income lingered somewhere between $250 and $500 a year.[2]

The Antilles islands, which, besides Grenada, include (among others) Cuba, Jamaica, the Bahamas, and the Leeward Islands, were once extremely prosperous thanks to sugar production and the African slave trade between the sixteenth and nineteenth centuries. The mighty navies of Britain and France battled fiercely for control over islands like Grenada, Saint Lucia, and Dominica.

Grenada was under French rule until 1762 when it surrendered to the British. Through the Treaty of Paris in 1763, it officially became a British territory. Although briefly recaptured by the French in 1779, it was returned to British control in 1783. But the strategic significance of Grenada had faded over time.

By the time Eric Gairy and his larger-than-life ambition returned to the island of his birth, the Grenadian economy was still classified as a small-scale colonial plantation system. An elite group of planters owned the vast majority of land and exported cocoa, nutmeg, and sugar. Most of the island's political power rested with the British governor general, who was assisted by his staff of civil servants.

Gairy was ready to put his legions to work. He openly defied the norms of the colonial system and mocked the political power of the governor general in the capital of Saint George's. Gairy leveraged his brash style to inspire others to stand up to the establishment.

Gairy then formally established the Grenada Manual and Mental Workers Union, followed by the Grenada United Labour Party (GULP). Their aim was to challenge the subservience displayed by former Grenadian leaders, specifically a man named Theophilus Marryshow. Marryshow, in Gairy's opinion, displayed an almost comical deference toward Queen Elizabeth, England, and Grenada's other "colonial masters," as Gairy described them.

Gairy once led a rowdy group of peasant farm workers into a tourist hotel, where they demanded to be served a meal. He further encouraged domestic servants to rise up and strike against the standard 15-hour workday. Gairy quickly earned the love and respect of the masses.

Grenada was experiencing widespread and violent labor strikes, the most severe in the island nation's history.[3] The strikes primarily focused on the sugar industry and were called by Gairy's trade union. The workers demanded increased wages. The British government responded by expelling Gairy and one of his top lieutenants from the island, which only inflamed the situation.

Almost immediately after Gairy was exiled, crowds gathered outside the governor general's residence and called for their leader's release. There were reports of unruly crowds invading estates, attacking plantation owners and their loyal workers, and damaging crops. In at least one instance, women were attacked and beaten up on suspicion that they were "enemies of Gairy," simply because they were white and presumably property owners.

The British governor was forced to negotiate directly with Gairy to quell the demonstrations. As a result, Gairy gained even more legitimacy and power among the masses. The British governor eventually conceded that Gairy was the true leader of Grenada's working class. At this point, the British colonial government also decided to grant all adults the right to vote. Until then, the majority of the Grenadian population had not participated in the political process.

Gairy and his Grenada United Labour Party won the 1951 elections but quickly realized that the British governor still had them on a tight leash. In the 1954 elections Gairy's GULP won six of the eight seats. In 1957 he lost control of the legislature by winning only two seats. But Gairy had established himself as a political force that demanded attention.

## CIA INTERVENTIONISM

Around the same time as Gairy's rise to power, the rest of the Caribbean was awash with socialist revolutions. Fidel Castro's victory in Cuba occurred concurrently with the rise of a Marxist leader named Cheddi Jagan in the South American country of British Guiana (now known as Guyana).[4]

Amid some of the perilous moments of the Cold War in the 1960s, concerns of another communist stronghold emerging in the region forced President John F. Kennedy to greenlight a covert CIA political campaign aimed at influencing national elections in British Guiana.[5] The operation would continue even after Kennedy's assassination.

U.S. intelligence assessments painted Prime Minister Cheddi Jagan as a prominent presidential contender for the upcoming 1964 elections. Jagan's popularity was a problem because he was known to be a communist sympathizer, albeit not directly aligned with Moscow.

In response, Kennedy deemed Jagan's leadership unacceptable and pressed London to collaborate in efforts to oust him. As early as mid-1962, JFK expressed to the British prime minister, Harold Macmillan, his serious reservations about an independent British Guiana led by Jagan. Kennedy believed intervention was necessary to prevent another Castro-like regime in the Western Hemisphere. President Kennedy's decision to initiate covert operations in British Guiana in 1962 came even despite the Bay of Pigs failure. Meddling in foreign elections was not a new phenomenon for the United States. The CIA had been engaging in such activities since the 1948 Italian elections.

Cheddi Jagan was a dentist by profession. He was born to Indian immigrants in British Guiana and educated in Georgetown, its capital city. He went on to study in Washington,

D.C., and Chicago before he returned to South America in 1943. He founded the socialist People's Progressive Party in 1950, which secured a majority in the 1953 elections. However, the suspicions of communist sympathies led the British government to force him out of office. The British abolished his position and imposed a military occupation for seven years. Despite this, Jagan managed to regain political traction, and he and his PPP party won the elections of 1957 and 1961, and Jagan was eventually elected prime minister.

Jagan would make a visit to both the United States and United Kingdom in October 1961. He reportedly wanted to address the festering suspicions surrounding his communist sympathies during a meeting with President Kennedy.[6] Despite the tensions, no significant drama occurred during the meeting, and the United States even pledged to provide some assistance to British Guiana.

Around this same time, a man named Forbes Burnham emerged as a shadowy political rival to Cheddi Jagan and became instrumental in the CIA's efforts against Jagan. In a National Security Council meeting on May 5, 1961, discussions about covert actions against Cuba and the Dominican Republic included plans to prevent a communist takeover in British Guiana as well.[7] Secretary of State Dean Rusk later wrote a letter to British Foreign Secretary Lord Douglas-Home on August 11, 1961, seeking assistance to prevent Jagan's electoral victory. Despite Lord Douglas-Home's response advising against direct intervention, the State Department decided to get involved anyway, and continued to advocate for offers to "help" Guiana by the end of August. This included requests for the British to "nudge" Prime Minister Jagan toward a more pro–American and British stance. The State Department also started initiating a more forceful covert operation to undermine other communist elements. President Kennedy signed off on all of it on September 3, 1961.

The decision reflected the deep concerns about Jagan's political tendencies. A September 4 cable even referred to Jagan as a "possible sleeper agent."[8]

In early 1962, facing significant economic challenges, Jagan's political party, then in the majority, implemented austerity measures combined with tax increases. These decisions were made without consulting the opposition or the people who would be affected the most—the working class. The result was predictable: a violent strike along with widespread rioting in Georgetown. Many parts of Guiana's capital city were destroyed.

From his official residence, known as the Red House, Jagan observed the flames engulfing Guiana's capital city, while he grew convinced the CIA had orchestrated the riots. Neither Jagan nor anyone else was able to prove the CIA was directly involved. Nevertheless, U.S. officials seized upon the chaos that followed as a pretext to discredit Jagan's authority. On February 19, 1962, while the smoke still billowed from the ruins, Secretary of State Dean Rusk again wrote to Lord Douglas-Home, urging "remedial steps" to counter Jagan's "Marxist-Leninist policy."[9] Rusk asserted to London that an independent British Guiana under Jagan's leadership was untenable.

At the White House, presidential advisor Arthur Schlesinger countered that Cheddi Jagan was not a hardline communist but, instead, a naive "London School of Economics Marxist filled with charm."[10] The scheme to raise taxes while cutting spending, he added, had not been Marxist, but instead something suitable for Britain's Labour party.

On March 8, 1962, Kennedy issued a directive specifically addressed to Secretary Rusk and CIA Director John A. McCone.[11] The president sought consultation on his covert action options while expressing his urgent concern about the situation developing in Guiana.

The agency predicted that Cheddi Jagan would win the upcoming election, even if facing a challenge from a coalition of opposition political parties. Additionally, agency analysts concluded that Jagan's government would be unlikely to form a coalition with any other parties, given its overwhelming majority in the Guianese assembly. Moreover, it anticipated that a Jagan administration would pursue a nonaligned foreign policy, potentially leaning toward the Communist bloc.

Kennedy also wanted to know more about the British position—would they be willing to postpone Guiana's independence and hold new elections if Jagan won? Secretary Rusk would meet for discussions in Geneva with Lord Douglas-Home, who revealed the British were still reluctant to do so, prompting Rusk to advocate for covert action, "with or without London's cooperation."[12]

In May 1962, Kennedy and Macmillan held talks, while Forbes Burnham visited Washington. These discussions paved the way for the political portion of the covert action plan. Burnham also preached a form of socialism, but his politics seemed more acceptable than Jagan's, mostly because Burnham was more pliable and open to outside influence from London and Washington. After Kennedy spoke with the prime minister in May, they made the decision to delay independence, which facilitated the CIA intervention.

There were no CIA stations established in British Guiana in 1962; British intelligence also had minimal representation in the country.[13] Their presence consisted of only one regional officer. To augment intelligence-gathering capabilities, the agency recruited an expat psychiatrist whose brother was already serving as an aide to Forbes Burnham, the CIA's preferred candidate. A CIA case officer in Barbados met with the psychiatrist, providing him with a crash course in clandestine communication techniques and other covert practices. The newly trained operative also helped facilitate Burnham's visit to Washington, during which the CIA informed him of the United States' plans for action against Jagan, to which Burnham readily agreed.

The CIA also reached out to a man named Peter d'Aguilar and supported his efforts to establish a proportional representation government in British Guiana. D'Aguilar organized a constitutional convention, which collapsed due to resistance from Jagan's supporters. Tensions escalated, leading to another violent strike in 1963. The CIA again supported the strike, contributing to more unrest and violence in Georgetown.

The violence reached alarming levels during this period, with houses being set on fire at a rate of over five per day, forcing more than 2,600 families from their homes. Nearly 200 murders and 1,000 injuries occurred amid the political turmoil.

President Kennedy closely monitored the situation and discussed British Guiana with Prime Minister Harold Macmillan yet another time.[14] They decided to impose a proportional representation system after the December 1964 election, and if the outcome were favorable to American and British interests, it would pave the way for Guyana's independence.

Jagan reportedly made several attempts to engage with the United States, but they were unsuccessful, and the violence continued to escalate between rival political factions. Even with John Kennedy's assassination and the arrival of President Lyndon B. Johnson, Washington's and the CIA's approach to British Guiana remained unchanged.

Cheddi Jagan, Forbes Burnham, and Peter d'Aguilar were in talks to quell the violence when the headquarters of the People's Progressive Party was bombed. Jagan's reaction captured the shock and devastation of the moment: "My God, it's Freedom House!"

The 1964 U.K. elections brought in a Labour government led by prime minister Harold Wilson, raising the doubts of U.S.

officials about their stance on intervention in British Guiana. The new Labour government in Britain proceeded with the sale of a large shipment of Leyland buses to Cuba despite U.S. objections, in exchange for $10 million.[15] But the shipment would never arrive in Havana. The East German cargo vessel carrying the buses was struck by a Japanese vessel in the Thames River.[16] Considering the sensitive nature of the sale, there were published reports that included rumors and speculation that the collision was orchestrated by the CIA. The East German investigation of the collision seemed to support this theory, but considering the source, it lacked serious credibility. What we do know, according to a biography written about British Minister Rab Butler, is that President Lyndon B. Johnson called Butler to America soon after the collision and dressed him down. President Johnson reportedly waved a stack of dollars in the air, yelling that "if the British needed money, they should ask the United States before doing a trade deal with Castro and the Cubans." Meanwhile, the new Labour government in London continued to distance itself from Cheddi Jagan.

Jagan faced dwindling prospects as the 1964 election approached, with CIA assessments indicating a close race. Despite winning the popular vote, Jagan's PPP gained fewer seats than Burnham's PNC due to the outside electoral manipulation of the CIA. Burnham was given the opportunity to form a coalition government, with Peter d'Aguilar becoming his finance minister.

A CIA memo from February 1965 foresaw Burnham's weaknesses and Jagan's enduring strength as British Guiana approached independence.[17] While Burnham was expected to seek support from the United States, the United Kingdom, and Canada through development projects favoring local populations, he ultimately became corrupted and dictatorial after winning the presidency in 1968. Despite U.S. aid, Burnham adopted radically leftist politics. The CIA's efforts were unsuccessful. In 1992, Cheddi Jagan eventually became Guyana's president, but he suffered a heart attack in 1997 and passed away shortly after receiving treatment, ironically, at Walter Reed military hospital in the United States.

## GRENADA'S PUSH TOWARD INDEPENDENCE

Grenada witnessed a strong shift in its economic landscape, a transformation that caught Eric Gairy politically unprepared. The burgeoning hotel industry offered increased job opportunities in construction, service, and transportation. But those opportunities came at the expense of the agricultural labor pool, which had long been the bedrock of Gairy's political support.

The GULP was returned to power in 1961, but their power was weakened. Allegations of widespread financial mismanagement and corruption started to spread. Undaunted, Gairy called for the suspension of the constitution, pushing off a call for new elections the following year. In this election the GULP lost to the middle-class, business-oriented Grenada National Party (GNP), which went on to run the country until 1967.

Gairy managed to secure another term as prime minister after five years of GNP leadership. The elections of 1967 saw his GULP returned to power, backed by an amended constitution that granted the prime minister greater leeway to manipulate the government to his advantage.

Gairy's new title was premier as Grenada became an Associated State in its relationship with Britain. This new dynamic meant that Grenada, led by Gairy, controlled its own internal decisions, with Britain responsible for defense and external relations. Gairy's personality seemed to swell along with this clout—he was even referred to as a "wall-eyed Don Juan" due to his distinctive white suits. His appeal was based on a curious mixture of earnest charisma and quirkiness.

A *Washington Post* article described Gairy like this: "A colorful, flamboyantly dressed Caribbean legend who can be found each Saturday night tending bar and openly tickling the ladies at the Evening Palace, one of a number of entertainment establishments and hostelries he owns here." Gairy attributes the strength of his government to "my relationship with the divine."[18]

He was also fond of displaying religious symbols including those associated with voodoo. He would often talk about unexplained phenomena like UFOs, the Bermuda Triangle, psychic research, and the universality of God.[19] Gairy made sure his unique interests became significant issues among Grenadian officials, including at the United Nations.

In fact, during one meeting with President Jimmy Carter at the White House, Gairy was careful to raise these topics. Carter's Secretary of State Cyrus Vance and National Security Advisor Zbigniew Brzezinski were also present for what must have been a bizarre meeting. At one point, Gairy leaned toward the president and said, "I've introduced a resolution at the UN General Assembly," he began, " . . . calling for an international study of UFOs and related phenomena." The president listened intently, his brow furrowing. "Can we support such a resolution?" Gairy pressed. He recounted his recent address at a special meeting in Acapulco, Mexico, where he had shared tales of inexplicable events and UFO sightings, garnering support for his cause.

Secretary Cyrus Vance interjected, recalling the U.S. Air Force's past investigations into UFO sightings. "In 5% of cases, no explanation could be found," he admitted, his tone betraying a hint of polite uncertainty. The president nodded thoughtfully, considering Sir Eric's proposal. "If the report is declassified, we should share it with him," he instructed Ambassador Frank Ortiz, his voice resonating with a sense of openness to the unknown. Gairy's gaze hardened with determination. "An international study is crucial," he insisted, his belief in the existence of otherworldly phenomena unwavering. "There's more to this world than meets the eye."

Gairy's willingness to share his unique interests seemed boundless. He spoke passionately of convening an international assembly of philosophers, scientists, theologians, and political leaders to explore the elusive concept of God. Amid these heady topics, Gairy also wove in more practical matters. He expressed his desire for a U.S. military presence in Grenada, citing the strategic advantages of the island's location near South America. His vision painted a picture of collaboration and mutual benefit between nations.

Before parting ways, Sir Eric presented the president with copies of his speeches, as a gesture of goodwill. As he bid farewell, he expressed hope for a future meeting at the upcoming UN General Assembly in New York, a continuation of their enlightening discussions.

## THE "MONGOOSE GANG"

The "Mongoose Gang" originated in the 1950s when local health authorities, some of them under the supervision of Gairy himself, paid people to kill mongooses. The animals were thought of as pests on the island at the time. They had been introduced to target rats and poisonous snakes on the island's sugarcane plantations.

By the 1970s the Mongoose Gang had a new mission and was composed largely of thugs.[20] It had morphed into something similar to other Caribbean gangs like the Tonton Macoute of Haiti.[21] The Mongoose Gang served as Eric Gairy's muscle during the

1967 elections and were not fully disbanded until the New Jewel Movement's coup 12 years later. They acted like a secret police force reporting directly to Gairy.

The "unrelenting reign of terror" caused by the Mongoose Gang hung like an ever-present storm cloud over Grenada and anyone who dared to challenge Gairy's authority.[22] Their methods were brutal, using any means necessary, even murder, to silence dissent.

On Sunday, November 18, 1973, a young Grenadian lawyer named Maurice Bishop, who had been educated in England, would experience the ruthlessness of Gairy's Mongoose Gang firsthand. Bishop, a socialist, was subjected to vicious beating at the hands of the Mongoose Gang. As Maurice Bishop and fellow leaders of the New Jewel Movement traveled from Saint George's to Grenville in two cars for a meeting with local businessmen, their convoy was intercepted by members of the Mongoose Gang. Nine people from Bishop's entourage were arrested and subjected to beatings. In jail, the detainees were forced to shave their beards, which showed the intensity of the beatings, including Maurice Bishop's fractured jaw. These harrowing events came to be known in Grenada as Bloody Sunday.

Then on January 21, 1974, a Monday, Bishop led a group of protesters to confront the Gairy government again.[23] After a peaceful demonstration calling for higher wages and a general strike, the group made their way back home, but they suddenly faced an onslaught of stones and bottles coming from Gairy's henchmen in the Mongoose Gang.

Uniformed Grenadian security forces were then deployed. They used tear gas to quell the melee. Amid the chaos, Rupert Bishop, a popular community leader and businessman, also Maurice's father, was shot and killed while leading a group of women and children to safety. This event would become known as Bloody Monday.

Following the tragic events of Bloody Sunday and Bloody Monday, Maurice Bishop started to recognize the limitations of his party's influence among workers' unions and rural communities who were still loyal to Gairy. In response, he and his colleagues devised a new strategy. Instead of relying solely on propaganda and organizing anti-government demonstrations, they shifted their focus toward building grassroots groups for greater organizational strength.

Gairy's rule, though harsh, was seen as a stabilizing force by British interests in the Caribbean. Now-declassified documents from England's National Archives in London reported on by *Vice News* shed light on efforts by British intelligence to prevent opposition forces from upending Gairy's authority and the status quo.[24] Especially as London was getting ready to grant Grenada its full independence as part of the British Commonwealth, there were serious concerns that opposition forces would stage a coup on Independence Day at a time when crowds and celebrations offered the best opportunity for a distraction.

Once-secret files show us that military preparations were made just in case England needed to restore order and colonial rule. MI5 expressed worry about the New Jewel Movement, viewing it as an extremist group aiming to violently overthrow Gairy's government. MI5's surveillance extended into Grenada's trade unions and the NJM, with informants embedded within the movement. This scrutiny occurred despite acknowledgment that Gairy had a less-than-angelic reputation, with his Mongoose Gang noted for its ruthlessness and connections to criminal elements.

> Nevertheless, the files reveal that information from MI5 prompted the British military to prepare a full-scale invasion plan on the eve of Grenada's independence, "to restore law and order and constitutional government. This would involve a reversion to colonial rule," the

foreign secretary warned Conservative Prime Minister Edward Heath in late January 1974.

British concerns about the potential overthrow of Gairy by the NJM in Grenada reached the highest echelons of Parliament and even to 10 Downing Street.[25] On January 25, 1974, the foreign secretary briefed the prime minister on the deteriorating situation in Grenada, highlighting strikes, disruptions in public services, and violent demonstrations that had resulted in fatalities. Despite this turmoil, Mr. Gairy's government maintained control, buoyed by the security forces at its disposal, notably the police and the Mongoose Gang.

The foreign secretary, however, cautioned the prime minister that the situation might escalate beyond the government's control. In the worst-case scenario, the government might lose its grip, jeopardizing the transfer of sovereignty scheduled for February 7, 1974. This would pose a dilemma for the United Kingdom, potentially necessitating an invasion to restore "colonial rule."

On January 30, Britain's defense secretary called a meeting with military leaders to review a confidential document titled "Grenada: Policy on Intervention by HM Forces." The document outlined potential scenarios for intervention, including the need to restore order following a breakdown of the Gairy government. It detailed plans for how such an operation might be conducted, as analyzed by the Ministry of Defense.

According to *Vice News*, the documents also reveal British apprehension about deploying the 1st Battalion Parachute Regiment into Grenada, because the soldiers had been involved in their own "Bloody Sunday" massacre of peaceful protesters in Londonderry, Northern Ireland, in 1972.[26]

Interestingly, Whitehall had approved of Gairy's brutal crackdown but saw no need to add insult to injury. A secret memo from the foreign secretary to the prime minister in May 1973 warned of signs that a newly formed Black Power organization might replace the official opposition in Grenada.[27] The minister suggested it might be better for Gairy to handle such developments independently to avoid risking British involvement. The British invasion plan remained dormant as Gairy retained control during independence.

For the next few years Gairy, with the blessing of London, remained focused on putting down any opposition groups. He even pressured his allies for legislative approval for an Emergency Powers Act strengthening police powers and restricting the movement and free assembly of Grenada's citizens.

"We are now doubling the strength of our Police Force, we are getting in almost unlimited supplies of new and modern equipment . . . (the) Opposition referred to my recruiting criminals in a reserve force. . . . Does it not take steel to cut steel? . . . Indeed, hundreds have come and some of the toughest and roughest roughnecks have been recruited," Gairy once boasted.[28]

## THE NEW JEWEL MOVEMENT

During the late 1960s the English Caribbean had been hit by a wave of high unemployment, political turmoil, and civil unrest that affected almost every island. Free university education, offered by progressive governments, had also started to open doors for many in the working class who had previously been excluded from higher learning. This new class of academics contributed to growing protests against the status quo. There were demonstrations in Jamaica and Trinidad, fueled in part by the Black Power movement. On smaller islands like Saint Lucia, Saint Vincent, Antigua, and Dominica, grassroots movements also emerged, including what would become known as the New Jewel Movement on Grenada.

In 1972, the Joint Endeavor for Welfare, Education, and Liberation (JEWEL) was formally established with the help of Maurice Bishop. He had just returned to Grenada after several years of legal training in England. Upon his return, Bishop immediately engaged in left-wing domestic politics, supporting protesting nurses. He successfully defended the nurses from their employers' reprisals. Bishop also helped initiate the Movement for the Assemblies of the People (MAP) in 1972. MAP's leaders advocated for public assemblies as an alternative to the existing model of British-led parliamentary style of government. Bishop's group also sought to challenge the power of the prime minister directly. Despite being separate organizations at the time, JEWEL and MAP both proposed similar methods of restructuring Grenada's political and economic systems, leading to inevitable confrontation with the powers that be.

In the parish of St. David, the geographical base of the JEWEL movement, an English estate owner, with Gairy's approval and assistance, purchased land cutting off access to a local beach popular with the locals. The parish protesters called on Maurice Bishop for assistance. Bishop organized the protesters and led them to the beach, defying the police forces sent to protect the estate. The protesters tore down fences, allowing them to regain access to the land that had been shut off from the public in favor of private ownership. It was a small but significant victory.

In March 1973, the MAP and JEWEL organizations combined forces to form the New Jewel Movement. MAP had been focused on political reorganization and JEWEL on agricultural development. Now the two movements were combined, and for the first time Gairy was faced with a broadly based and well-organized opposition group with mass appeal and a Marxist political platform. The burgeoning opposition groups also included stevedores, farmers, shop owners, the Roman Catholic Church, and young Black radical socialists. A committee of 22 religious, union, and business leaders started to accuse Prime Minister Eric Gairy's government of fiscal irresponsibility and outright corruption.

Grenada had started to resemble a fascist state. Gairy's government was now almost completely free from England's influence. Gairy himself held multiple ministerial positions, including minister of external affairs, home affairs, national security, tourism, land and surveys, national resources, planning and development, and information. Between 1974 and December 1976, Gairy's party controlled 14 of the 15 seats in parliament. The lone opposition member was rarely in attendance. And he was encouraged to stay away.

After the elections in December 1976, the coalition of opposition parties continued to gain strength, but slowly, the gains due in part to growing resistance to Gairy's hardline tactics. Gairy's government now controlled only 9 of parliament's 15 seats. In that election, widespread electoral fraud charges were brought against the government.

However, during the entire duration of Gairy's second independence government, a period of 27 months, the parliament met for a total of just 18 days, a violation of the constitution, which mandated more. The formal structure of democracy barely existed.

Under pressure, Gairy agreed to set up an independent commission, which would include outsiders from Jamaica, to investigate the allegations of financial mismanagement. But the commission met only twice, and no official action or reports ever emerged from the meetings.

The events of Bloody Sunday and Bloody Monday had been just the beginning of an unprecedented period of violence in Grenada. The murder of Rupert Bishop and the imprisonment of the other NJM members helped to coalesce opposition to Gairy, culminating in an alliance between the NJM, the GNP, and the United People's Party.

While Gairy continued to try to consolidate his power and wealth, the Grenadian economy continued to falter. The island's basic infrastructure steadily fell apart. The road system was in disrepair. The medical system was ill-equipped and understaffed. The educational system was failing at all levels. However, Gairy's system of repression—policemen, paid auxiliaries, soldiers, the Mongoose Gang—expanded steadily.

The Grenadian government was also operating at a deficit. And to compensate for the deficit, taxes were dramatically increased again. By the late 1970s taxes accounted for 27% of GDP, but the deficit still continued to grow. The Gairy government also embarked on a "land reform" program. Under this program he purchased midsized estates either from those opposed to him or from his friends, the latter at inflated prices, and he then returned it, in smaller parcels, to his supporters. Many of these estates, though, were still maintained under state control.

Because of the physical deterioration of the society and increased repression, Gairy's government became increasingly isolated from its regional partners in the Caribbean. At this point, Gairy turned to Presidents Augusto Pinochet in Chile and Tachito Somoza in Nicaragua. Gairy struck a military agreement with Pinochet in 1977 that called for the training of Grenadians in Chile as well as arms transfers. It indicated the future course of the Grenadian government unless something changed at the top. While Somoza was facing his own problems, he still was able to commit his full support to Gairy.

## THE COUP

On March 12, 1979, Eric Gairy departed Grenada for the United Nations. He was traveling to New York to hold meetings on topics that included the much-anticipated UFO discussion Gairy had raised with President Carter two years earlier. The day after Gairy's departure, Maurice Bishop, at just 34 years old, along with the leaders of his New Jewel Movement, staged a predawn and nearly bloodless coup.

Within a few hours after the coup, the leader of the new People's Revolutionary Government took to the state-controlled radio waves to explain what had just happened.[29] "People of Grenada, this revolution is for work, for food, for decent housing and health services, and for a bright future for our children and great grandchildren. The benefits of the revolution will be given to everyone regardless of political opinion or which political party they support. Let us all unite as one. . . ."

An urgent and confidential CIA memo was sent to the White House that read:

> There are no reports of serious disturbances since the takeover in Grenada this morning of the national radio station by a group calling itself the new revolutionary government.
> 
> As of 1600 hrs. EST, however, conditions still have not stabilized sufficiently to permit a definitive evaluation of the situation. Maurice Bishop, the leader of the Marxist-Leninist opposition party—the New Jewel Movement—claims to be prime minister of the new government and has called for the extradition of prime minister Eric Gairy, who is visiting New York City.
> 
> Bishop says that the national defense forces and police, which number less than 500, have surrendered without a struggle. At least some former government officials are said to be under arrest. Gairy claims to have been in telephone contact with some of his ministers in

Grenada and says that only some 70-80 members of the NJM are involved in the uprising.

He added that the police have not surrendered as alleged by rebel radio but are not able to counterattack "because they have no ammunition." Gairy plans to ask the United States and United Kingdom for help but believes there is still a possibility of a countermove by his own supporters.

Prime Minister John Compton of nearby Saint Lucia, after contacting several Grenadian officials, feels like the takeover of the government by the NJM is a fact. Although he finds no evidence of external forces involved, he has called for the governments of the Caribbean to move quickly to "quarantine the new group allegedly in power.[30]

The United States provided temporary sanctuary for Gairy, but then, along with Canada and several Caribbean nations, acknowledged the legitimacy of Bishop's new People's Revolutionary Government in Grenada. The upheaval had apparently caught the State Department and most of the Carter administration off guard.[31]

U.S. apprehension heightened on April 6 when a Cuban airplane, reportedly experiencing "technical difficulties," unexpectedly landed in Grenada.[32] U.S. officials were alarmed because the plane was mysteriously able to take off again but left some passengers behind. Many believed the passengers were Cuban military advisors.

The NJM's leadership later claimed that the final decision to go forward with the coup was influenced by their belief that the Gairy regime was preparing to assassinate all the NJM's leadership. They also claimed remorse for the two lives that were lost during the coup. Bishop even extended an invitation to international media outlets to visit their approximately 80 detainees, held as political prisoners. The tour was to be organized and led by Bishop's wife, Angela.[33]

The NJM and the PRG quickly announced their plans for a foreign policy platform based on the principle of non-alignment. Grenada participated in the Sixth Summit of Non-Aligned Countries in Havana in September 1979.[34] A further radicalization of Grenada's foreign policy was evident when it voted with the Soviet Union at the UN General Assembly's debate on a resolution to condemn the USSR's invasion and occupation of Afghanistan. None of this served to enhance Grenada's relationship with the United States, which responded by increasing its pressure on Grenada, both rhetorically and by pressuring America's allies and international lending agencies against supporting Grenada.

The PRG also faced two immediate and urgent problems that arose from domestic pressures and impacted the foreign policy of the new regime. The first problem was the PRG needed to get Grenada's sluggish economy moving. The second was the perceived threat of a Gairy-led invasion of the island.

One of the things the new PRG would do to mitigate these concerns is leave Grenada's Governor General Sir Paul Scoon in place. During the coup, Scoon had been briefly detained by the People's Revolutionary Government, but he was later released with an apology. Scoon was Queen Elizabeth's representative on the island of Grenada, and while he had limited power, his position provided some level of continuity and stability both internally and externally. Scoon was generally against the Marxist-Leninist ideas of the government, but he was willing to quiet his opposition to retain his position.

Within one month of the coup, American Ambassador Frank Ortiz, who was based in Barbados, visited Grenada. According to a report from April 27, 1979, Ortiz's instructions consisted of ten main points. Nine of them were focused on reassuring Grenada that the United States was monitoring Gairy's activities closely. The final point was a warning for Grenada and the PRG. Ambassador Ortiz told Bishop directly that "it would not be in Grenada's best interests to seek assistance from a country such as Cuba to forestall such an attack,"[35] and the U.S. government would "view with displeasure any tendency on the part of Grenada to develop closer ties with Cuba."

Bishop and the other leaders of the PRG were incensed. In a public speech three days after the American ambassador's visit to Grenada, Bishop reiterated the objectives of Grenada's foreign policy in an address that was broadcast on Radio Free Grenada and has since become known as the "Nobody's Backyard" speech. Bishop pulled no punches.

"We do not recognize any right of the United States . . . to instruct us on whom we may develop relations with and who we may not," Bishop declared. He continued, "Grenada is a sovereign and independent country. . . . We are not in anybody's backyard, and we are definitely not for sale."

And then, in an act of defiance, Grenada established formal diplomatic relations with Cuba the next day. From that point onward, the steady deterioration of Grenada's relations with the United States was matched by increasingly closer linkages to Cuba.

One of Bishop's stated fundamental political objectives was to move Grenada away from the Westminster-type parliamentary system. The 1973 NJM Manifesto had dismissed it as colonial and repressive.[36] The PRG immediately suspended Grenada's constitution, and a committee of appointed ministers ruled using what they called "People's Laws."

While the ruling committee had a majority of NJM leaders, they formed alliances with business figures and the GNP. Non-NJM members were appointed to positions in the new Marxist government, but they had limited power. The balance of the real power remained with Maurice Bishop and his closest confidants in the NJM.

Under Bishop and the NJM, the PRG initially focused on populism and social justice rather than full-blown revolution. The PRG outwardly pushed for a self-sustaining economy, prioritizing agriculture and tourism development. But there were significant challenges, like falling commodity prices for its exports, rampant inflation, and natural disasters that complicated the PRG's plans. Bishop himself explained the problem this way: "The nature of the struggle we have undergone [is] not only to raise production and productivity, but to instill new values into our people."

The PRG had gained control by forcefully overthrowing the problematic but democratically elected government of Eric Gairy. And the fact that the PRG had made no attempt to legitimize their position through elections after three years made them vulnerable. Presumably, a new constitution would have been a prerequisite to national elections, but it was never ratified. The government faced criticism from other regional governments, not just the United States. Dissent simmered but was muted at home. Many would argue that this was a consequence of the intimidating presence of the People's Revolutionary Army, which was controlled by a radical militant named General Hudson Austin.

From the outset, Bishop and his cohorts sought to underscore their value to the Soviet Union. The Grenadian ambassador to Moscow wrote a memo to the Grenadian Foreign Minister, stressing the importance of demonstrating to the Soviets that Grenada's revolution was part of a global movement, rooted in the Great October Revolution of 1917.[37] The ambassador articulated: "For

Grenada to ascend to a position of increasing significance, we must be perceived as influencing regional affairs. We must establish ourselves as the authority on events in the English-speaking Caribbean and champion revolutionary activities and progressive developments in this region."

In pursuit of Grenada's regional aspirations, the Bishop government implemented an active initiative of convening biannual meetings with "progressive and revolutionary parties in the region." Bishop seemingly viewed these gatherings to persuade the Soviets of Grenada's pivotal role as their Eastern Caribbean proxy. Belize and Suriname emerged as particularly fertile grounds for strategic engagement. But these meetings were expensive, which prompted a request for additional financial assistance from the Soviets.

## CUBAN AND SOVIET INFLUENCE

Following Castro's playbook, the NJM initially formed a diverse coalition. While the radical left took the lead, they also welcomed noncommunist factions. Bishop shed light on this strategy during his "Line of March" speech on September 13, 1982, noting, "This was done to prevent imperialism from becoming overly alarmed."[38]

Bishop gradually sidelined the moderate voices within the government, mirroring events from two decades earlier in Cuba. Elections were indefinitely postponed, and dissent was swiftly suppressed, often through incarceration. Soon after the NJM's coup, Grenada's three newspapers were closed, including one that declared itself loyal to the NJM while also publishing an editorial stating they reserved the right to criticize the results of the revolution and Bishop's government.

Bishop implemented a range of surveillance tactics reminiscent of other totalitarian regimes. The Ministry of the Interior closely monitored Western diplomats, local opposition factions, and business figures, routinely infringing upon the privacy rights of both Grenadians and foreigners. Telephone lines were tapped, mail intercepted, and personal records scrutinized, including private bank accounts.

The People's Revolutionary Army assumed police duties, carrying out searches and detentions without warrants. Reports emerged of torture, physical assaults, arbitrary imprisonments, and psychological intimidation tactics, echoing the oppressive methods of the ousted Prime Minister Eric Gairy.

Opposition political parties were forced to disband or operate clandestinely, leading some leaders to flee the country. Independent churches were viewed as a threat to the NJM's authority. Under the guise of "People's Laws," Bishop and his inner circle wielded near-unlimited power, while a pervasive propaganda and indoctrination campaign solidified their control.

Mandatory political orientation classes were imposed on both children and adults, with ideological training targeting virtually every Grenadian, particularly within the military ranks. In many ways, Bishop replicated Castro's playbook from the early 1960s to consolidate his grip on power. Propaganda materials circulated by the New Jewel Movement proudly highlighted Grenada's close ties with Cuba and Nicaragua, with images featuring Daniel Ortega, Maurice Bishop, and Fidel Castro prominently displayed.

The governing New Jewel Movement, compelled by its Marxist-Leninist ideology, regarded religion as an enemy of the state and worked to undermine it. The various churches were at first neutral after the March 1979 revolution. But they moved into opposition as the undemocratic nature of the NJM became apparent. Despite a shortage of trained security personnel, an officer attached to the Ministry of the Interior, Michael Roberts, was assigned full-time to reporting on church activities. According to a State Department report, Roberts would later report that Grenada's churches were "the main political source of internal counter-revolution."[39]

Bishop Sydney Charles, head of the Roman Catholic Church in Grenada, was considered to be one of PRG's most powerful and vocal critics, as he was very popular among churchgoers. The Catholic Church started pushing back against some of the PRG's policies in 1980 and spoke openly about its concerns for the human rights of political detainees held at the Richmond Hill Prison. Government informants reported that "every Sunday at one church or another priests were heard to ask people to pray for the detainees whose rights have been denied."

Catholics, which made up more than half of Grenada's population, helped organize retreats and conferences at which "hostile statements were hurled against the Grenadian government over violations of human rights." Other traditional churches, including the Anglican Church, which was Grenada's second largest, took the same approach and pushed for new elections.

One of the areas of particular concern to the PRG was the effort of Bishop Charles to invigorate the youth organizations inside the Catholic Church and to bring them under his personal control. The PRG forced churches to distribute a booklet called "Marxism, Humanism and Christianity" to all priests to study. Bishop Charles said the church in Grenada was facing its greatest challenge, writing that "there are people who want to dictate to the Churches what to do . . . and CRUSH the Church."

The PRG's security officers had concluded it was clear that the Catholic Church was gearing up for confrontation with the government. In response, a plan was devised to increase government surveillance inside various churches and work with Cuba and Nicaragua on starting new "progressive" churches. Security officers recommended the removal of deeply religious teachers and administrators from schools and suggested replacing them with "progressive" teachers and administrators. The efforts to offset the influence of the church also called for increasing the amount of Marxist-Leninist literature in schools by September 1983 and opening Marxist-Leninist bookshops all over Grenada.

## OCEAN VENTURE '81

The Reagan administration, which had also started to probe Soviet intelligence-gathering capabilities in the Pacific with military exercises and covert operations, decided similar exercises would also be necessary in the Atlantic. According to a report by the *New York Times* published on August 1, 1981, there was an increasing focus at the Pentagon on the importance of preparing for a prolonged conventional war in Europe.[40] The official goal of these new war games was to show Moscow and its friends how NATO and Western navies had recently enhanced their capacity to safeguard commercial and military shipping lanes.

Exercise Ocean Venture '81 started in August that year and stretched into mid-September. At the time it was the "largest maritime military exercise since World War II." It utilized 120,000 personnel, 250 ships, and 1,000 aircraft from 14 different nations.

Anti-submarine warfare was also a focal point during the exercises off the Virginia Capes, which were followed by extensive exercises in the North Atlantic. This phase of the exercise included two aircraft carrier battle groups that engaged in simulated combat against each other before joining forces to facilitate an "opposed" Atlantic crossing. Troops from Britain, Canada, West Germany, the Netherlands, and Portugal joined the American forces.

The ability to reinforce United States and NATO troops in Europe was addressed in another phase of the exercise, during which an amphibious force moved from the eastern United States to the Mediterranean. Along the way, it conducted exercises with the Spanish navy and French air force. In the final phase, the U.S. Navy sailed into the Baltic Sea, where a destroyer squadron worked with Danish, German, and Dutch units. Pentagon officials correctly predicted the Soviet government would protest given their claims that that part of the world was the Soviet navy's domain. Similar to the significant involvement of the Army in Reforger (Reforger, a series of military exercises conducted by NATO during the Cold War which simulated the rapid deployment of U.S. forces to Europe to counter a Soviet threat), the Navy's operations occurred at a time when European political attitudes were hardening against the United States military's role and President Reagan's style of confronting the Soviets.[41]

In the South Atlantic, five Latin American navies participated alongside units from the Air Force's Strategic Air Command. NATO units also joined the exercise during this phase and collaborated with British and Dutch elements as well as units from the U.S. Army, Marine Corps, and Puerto Rico's National Guard. During this phase, the United States conducted a mock invasion of Vieques, Puerto Rico. A Ranger battalion and paratroopers were airlifted in to support attacks by Marine amphibious assault groups. For the purposes of the exercise, planners had code-named Vieques "Amber" and the surrounding islands the "Amberdines." The significance of the names was not lost on the Soviets, Cubans, or Maurice Bishop. They all saw the exercise as a thinly veiled threat.

Ocean Venture '81 "came as a thunderclap to the Soviets," according to Naval Secretary John Lehman, who wrote in his book *Oceans Ventured: Winning the Cold War at Sea* that Moscow had never seen such a NATO exercise on its northern doorstep. The Soviets were especially concerned about the possibility of being attacked during a U.S. military exercise. This fear stemmed from their own history, which involved using military exercises to conceal their own surprise invasions, as they did in Poland in 1981.

The specific focus on Grenada, or "Amber," during Ocean Venture '81 may have been the result of a plan floated by the CIA that summer, designed to undermine the political control of Maurice Bishop. The CIA operation was scuttled by the Senate Intelligence Committee, which heard proposals for intervention in July. One Republican member of the committee told the *Washington Post*, "Yes, there was an operation, and we all thought . . . that it [Grenada] was just a small island, and so the Cubans or the communists control it, so what?"[42] Senator Lloyd Bentsen reacted to the CIA's Grenada proposal by saying, "You've got to be kidding." Committee Chairman Barry Goldwater reportedly suggested that the CIA reconsider. Another committee member told the *Post* the CIA's proposal did not include any plans to overthrow Maurice Bishop's government. "We may cause a little economic trouble, a little publicity and [give] aid [to the opposition], but we don't overthrow governments," the unnamed senator added.

## NEW MILITARY ASSETS IN GRENADA

Both the Soviets and Cubans wasted no time in capitalizing on Grenada's potential.[43] Just a month after Bishop's rise to power, a significant shipment of arms from the Eastern bloc arrived from Havana. Among the contents were 3,400 rifles, 200 machine guns, 100 heavier weapons, and ammunition. Fidel Castro personally dispatched Cuban military advisors to oversee the organization and training of Grenada's military and internal security forces. Additionally, hundreds of young Grenadians were sent to Cuba for military instruction.

Highlighting the covert nature of much of this support, shipments of ammunition labeled "Cuban Economic Office" were discreetly sent to Grenada from Cuba. Furthermore, key Grenadian military figures, including the army chief of staff and both deputy secretaries of defense, received training in the USSR.

President Reagan's Assistant Secretary of Defense for Inter-American Affairs Nestor Sanchez, a former CIA officer, briefed members of Congress and the public about the gathering threat.[44] During a speech to Florida Republicans, Sanchez described how Cuba had built a battalion-sized military camp on Grenada that could supplement air and naval facilities already under construction on Grenada. Sanchez described military barracks, administration buildings, and a Soviet-style training ground with an obstacle course. He also explained how Cuban advisors and laborers were building new runways at Point Salines and deepwater port facilities. Sanchez said Grenada had become a "virtual surrogate" of Cuba.

At this same time, Cuba also started to receive more military aid from the Soviet Union. In 1981 Moscow exported a total of $600 million in military aid, and by 1982 that number had climbed to $1 billion. The shipments included Turya-class hydrofoil torpedo boats, MI-24 Hind assault helicopters, and even MiG-23 fighter jets. The uptick in Soviet military aid to Cuba spurred the National Security Council to authorize the CIA to take "unilateral paramilitary action against special Cuban targets." But that action was limited to Cuba, and attempts to expand operations to include Grenada ran into roadblocks.

Grenada had entered into five clandestine military agreements, three with the Soviet Union, one with Cuba, and another with North Korea.[45] The Soviet Union wanted to utilize Cuba as an intermediary to channel military, economic, and technical support to Grenada. This assistance encompassed Soviet and Cuban resources, including materials and equipment utilized in the construction of the Point Salines Airport. While purportedly designated for civilian purposes, the construction was largely undertaken by armed Cuban personnel, despite Grenada's significant unemployment rate.

There was also a Soviet plan to deploy SS-20 missiles to Grenada that factored into the White House's concerns. Under President Carter, the United States made a deal with the Soviets that called for the deployment of Pershing II missiles only if no arms reduction agreement was reached by 1983. After he took office, President Reagan adopted a "zero option" proposal, offering to cancel Pershing II deployment only if the Soviet Union started to dismantle its SS-20 program.

In response, Moscow proposed limiting SS-20 missile deployment to match the number of British and French missiles, if the United States canceled plans to send more missiles to Europe. But the United States' European allies rejected that idea, citing their vulnerability. Moscow's concerns were also growing over the Pershing II's accuracy and quick launch capabilities. Talks stalled. And Brezhnev warned of reciprocal deployments if the United States proceeded to place its Pershing missiles in West Germany, further escalating tensions.

Apart from the remote Soviet northeast, which could target Seattle, other potential sites for SS-20 deployment included Suriname, Nicaragua, Cuba, and Grenada. But the risk of a slow-developing, seaborne missile deployment to the Caribbean deterred Moscow, especially as the U.S. Navy intensified operations around the world.

The Soviets eventually decided to use their new Ilyushin Il-76 cargo aircraft to airlift the SS-20 missiles. The planes could carry 50 tons and had a range of 3,000 miles. That meant they could reach Grenada from the Soviet's West African airfields. From Grenada, the SS-20s could target a significant portion of the

United States, surpassing the capabilities of Pershing missiles in West Germany.

By late March 1982, it was evident that Grenada wouldn't be ready to host Soviet missiles for several months. This gave the Reagan administration a little time to adjust policies and prepare for potential crises. Initially, U.S. policy toward Grenada hadn't anticipated it becoming a missile base, but rather a center for subversion in the Caribbean and potentially South America. However, with the rejection of proposals to destabilize Grenada by the Senate, the focus shifted toward strengthening collective efforts among regional states.

During arms control talks, the Soviets suggested that if the United States deployed Pershing II missiles to West Germany, they would deploy missiles to "Cuba and other Central American countries." Despite this, Moscow publicly bolstered military strength in Cuba and Nicaragua while secretly preparing to deploy missiles to Grenada and other locations. Their plan for Grenada involved securing political allegiance, pre-positioning weapons, sending Cuban troops for security, and ultimately deploying SS-20 missiles once the airport was completed.

As construction on a new runway at Point Salines progressed, the urgency of the Grenada situation started to surpass that of the Cuban Missile Crisis. Unlike Cuba, where slow ships were used, the Soviets planned to use fast-flying aircraft for deployment. Additionally, the SS-20 missiles for Grenada came with their own mobile launchers, eliminating the need for fixed sites.

In March 1983, a Soviet survey team arrived at the small, 11-square-mile Grenadian dependency of Carriacou, inhabited by around 7,000 fishermen and farmers.[46] Their assessment led to plans for constructing an airfield, naval port, cement plant, and electric power generating plant on the island. Tyrell Bay, with its historic significance as a sheltered anchorage used by the

British fleet in the eighteenth century, was earmarked for development. As part of the package, Moscow offered a gift of 2,000 tons of steel. The pervasive presence of the Soviet bloc, including personnel from the Soviet Union, Cuba, East Germany, Libya, Czechoslovakia, Bulgaria, and North Korea, left little room for the pretense of Grenada's independence.

Maurice Bishop had been spooked by Ocean Venture '81 and the mock invasion of "Amber and the Amberdines," which had been prompted by an agreement Bishop made with the Soviets and Cubans allowing them to use a new airport already under construction. Bishop had become a cog in the wheel of the Cold War.

A formerly secret CIA document prepared for director William Casey explained in more detail the cache of Cuban military assets located on Grenada in 1982.[47] Cuba had delivered an estimated $40 million ($130 million today) worth of gear—including artillery, small arms, anti-aircraft armaments, and armored personnel carriers. In terms of manpower, the CIA estimated there were somewhere between 400 and 600 Cuban troops on the Island. There were also another 300 Cuban "construction workers" in Grenada, who were suspected to be there for military activities in addition to labor. The arrival of these workers raised suspicions because Grenada's unemployment rate was relatively high.

In August 1982, the largest single shipment of military equipment was delivered. By October 1983, Grenada would be able to boast that it had a military force larger than that of all its Eastern Caribbean counterparts combined, wielding an arsenal surpassing them in both men and military equipment. Ambitious designs were afoot to position Grenada as one of the world's foremost per capita military powers.

Fidel Castro's three main motivations were checking internal and external threats to the Bishop regime; establishing Grenada as a training ground for revolutionary-minded radical groups from neighboring islands; and building an operational base that would enable Cuba and the Soviet Union to influence geopolitics in the Caribbean and the Americas.

## THE NEW AIRPORT

The PRG's publicly stated desire to improve tourism revenue, which was genuine, also provided an opportunity that Fidel Castro and the Soviets could exploit—the planned airport construction at Point Salines, located on the far southwest portion of Grenada. The island's only existing runway at the Pearls Airport was too short to handle modern-day jet airliners, or Soviet-built military transport planes for that matter.

Ever since 1955, a new airport had been on the Grenadian government's wish list. Saint Lucia had experienced an almost 300% increase in tourism after it built a new 9,000-foot runway at Hewanorra in the mid-1970s. By 1980, there were at least 10 other airports in the region big enough to attract tourists from North America and Europe. Maurice Bishop and the PRG had first turned to the United States, Britain, and Canada for assistance to build the airport. But the United States refused, leery of the PRG's Marxist leanings.

The new airport's runway would need to be at least 9,000 feet long, but plans called for a runway that would be closer to 10,000 feet long. The existing airport at Pearls had a runway that was just 5,500 feet long, insufficient for anything bigger than turboprop planes holding less than 50 passengers. Also, the Pearl's location wedged between the island's mountainous terrain and the Atlantic Ocean provided little to no room for expansion. So the PRG's attention turned to the Point Salines Airport. And so did Castro's.

In 1981 Grenada organized a conference in Brussels, Belgium, seeking loans for their new airport venture,[48] but the United States pressured its European allies to stay away from the project.⁴⁹ U.S. allies did stay away. However, Layne Dredging, a Miami-based company, was hired to work on the inlet where the runway would be extended. Additionally, a British defense contractor, Plessy, was contracted to install navigation and communication systems.

Cuba, though, was more than willing to provide the most support for Grenada's commercial aviation ambitions, especially after the U.S. military started to augment its presence after Reagan's election. Additional support for airport construction came from Libya, Algeria, Syria, Iraq, and Venezuela. Once the loans and financial guarantees were secured, construction could begin with an anticipated date of completion set for March 1984, the fifth anniversary of the NJM's revolution.

The biggest portion of Cuba's contribution to airport construction came in the form of manpower. Some 300 workers were almost immediately shipped to Grenada, along with some construction supplies. Cuba developed a quarry and built the first rock-crushing plant and asphalt mixing facility on the island.

Once completed, Point Salines could have provided a stopover point for Cuban flights to Africa, an additional facility for Soviet long-range reconnaissance aircraft, and possibly a transshipment point for arms and supplies for Latin American insurgents and the Sandinistas. Had the Point Salines Airport been operational in April 1983, it could have offered an alternative refueling stop for the Libyan aircraft intercepted in Brazil, clandestinely transporting military supplies to Nicaragua.⁵⁰

Grenada's foreign minister told the *Washington Post* that his government "has no plans" to grant military landing rights.⁵¹ "To us, it is strictly a commercial facility, we have no agreements and no plans to use the airport for military purposes." That turned out to be a lie.

The United States, and especially President Reagan, believed there was a dual purpose for the new airport expansion project. The longer runway could facilitate Cuban and Soviet military expansion in the Caribbean. And a Cuban-Soviet naval base in Grenada could be used to harass U.S. shipping interests, especially oil tankers. On March 23, 1983, President Reagan delivered his nationally televised speech addressing the Strategic Defense Initiative, also known as the "Star Wars" program, during one of the hottest moments of the Cold War.

In addition to concerns about nuclear proliferation in Europe, Reagan also talked about a tiny island in the Windward chain most American had probably never heard of. "On the small island of Grenada . . . the Cubans with Soviet financing and backing are in the process of building an airfield with a 10,000 foot runway," the president noted. "Grenada doesn't even have an air force," he added. "More than half of all American oil imports now pass through the Caribbean. . . . The Soviet-Cuban militarization of Grenada . . . can only be seen as a power projection into the region." After Cuba and Nicaragua, Reagan was determined that no other country would be permitted to fall deeper into a Marxist-Leninist government easily influenced by the Soviets.

The Point Salines Airport project was a key issue for Maurice Bishop during an April 15, 1983, meeting with Soviet Foreign Minister Andrei Gromyko. Bishop's "Outline of Presentation" for this meeting emphasized the economic benefits of the project, but also included the revealing statement, "There is also the strategic factor which is well known!"

Around this same time, the People's Revolutionary Government in Grenada sent a message to the United Kingdom's Commonwealth secretary general in London, accusing the United States of "economic, military, and political aggression."[52] The letter was circulated around 10 Downing Street and was met with scorn and suspicion. Margaret Thatcher's private secretary for foreign and defense affairs, John Coles, wrote to the Commonwealth Office and instructed them to essentially ignore the PRG's concerns.

Coles wrote that Prime Minister Thatcher "expressed some surprise that the Commonwealth Secretary General would circulate such a message and believes we should ask why he thought it necessary to do so." The prime minister's office eventually decided that any further follow-up would be a waste of time.

## BISHOP IN WASHINGTON, THE EASTERN BLOC, AND HAVANA

Maurice Bishop, who had openly defied warnings about getting closer to Cuba from both the Carter and Reagan administrations, was starting to feel the pressure from the United States. Bishop wanted to have his cake (financial backing from the Cubans and Soviets) while eating it too (bringing in tourists and their dollars from the United States). But he was also starting to face mounting political pressure from inside the PRG and from his chief deputy, Bernard Coard, who was far less charismatic than Bishop, but far more ideological and a hardline Marxist.

To address both concerns, Bishop accepted an invitation from Secretary of State George Shultz and took a trip to the United States during the first week of June 1983. He wanted to engage in a "dialogue" with the Reagan administration and clarify what he characterized as misunderstandings between Grenada and the United States. But things didn't go well. The *New York Times* wrote this headline about the visit: "Caribbean Left-Wing Leader Received Coolly in Washington."

State Department officials were firm with Bishop. The Reagan administration would maintain a distant relationship with the

Grenadian prime minister and his unelected Marxist-Leninist regime. This was due mostly to Bishop's close ties with the Soviet Union and Cuba. But there were other factors as well, including allegations of ongoing human rights violations on the island. There were now about 100 political prisoners held by the PRG while Bishop was on his diplomatic mission to the United States in 1983. Few had been charged with crimes, and even fewer had gone to trial since the coup four years earlier. Among the jailed were the leaders of the nongovernment press.

On June 5, 1983, Maurice Bishop left Washington and went to New York where he delivered a speech at Hunter College, defending the Grenadian Revolution with fervor by comparing it to the American Revolution of 1776 and Lincoln's emancipation of the slaves. He talked about what he believed to be a continued economic subservience of the developing world to Western powers like the United States. Bishop talked about the overthrow of Salvador Allende's government in Chile, and of the brutal Contra interventions against the Sandinistas in Nicaragua. He accused Western nations of hypocrisy for refusing to condemn apartheid in South Africa. Bishop also called for the creation of a Palestinian state, and pledged his support for the PLO, stating, "The people of Palestine and their sole authentic representatives, the Palestine Liberation Organization, will always have the full support of the fraternal people of Grenada."

He also highlighted the rise of socialism in the Caribbean, citing Fidel Castro's revolution in Cuba and Michael Manley's socialist government in Jamaica. "We are one people from one Caribbean," Maurice Bishop declared at Hunter College, emphasizing unity and shared destiny.

He firmly rejected America's Monroe Doctrine and its notion of intervention in the region and repeated the same line he had delivered during the radio address that followed the U.S.

ambassador's visit and warning about Cuba in 1979. "Grenada ain't nobody's backyard, and ain't part of nobody's lake!" His words resonated, eliciting a rapturous response from the audience of college students, teachers, staff, and left-wing activists.

## A CRISIS ERUPTS

Maurice Bishop's attempts to mend relations with the United States backfired on multiple fronts. Not only did he further alienate Grenada from the United States, but he also deepened the rift within the NJM and PRG. Within the Central Committee of the party, a whisper campaign started painting Bishop as soft, "petit bourgeois" rather than a true "Marxist-Leninist."

Deputy Prime Minister Bernard Coard had languished in Bishop's shadow for four years following the overthrow of Eric Gairy's government. Coard was in secondary school when he first met Maurice Bishop. Both were early students of and devotees of left-wing political theories. That interest in socialism and communism laid the foundation for their friendship. In 1962 they cofounded the Grenada Assembly of Youth After Truth. Twice per month, the two would lead political debates in Saint George's Central Market.

Coard had moved to the United States to pursue studies in sociology and economics at Brandeis University. He would also join the Communist Party USA. In 1967, Coard moved to England and studied politics and economics at the University of Sussex. That same year, Coard met and married his wife, Phyllis, a Jamaican, who was a student as well. Coard also joined the Communist Party of Great Britain while there. In 1976, Coard returned to Grenada and joined the New Jewel Movement, reuniting with his boyhood friend Maurice Bishop. He also ran for and won a parliamentary seat in Saint George's.

But Coard had grown restless in the years since this first election, and he started to actively challenge the prime minister's supremacy behind the scenes. Coard had resigned from his positions on the Political Bureau and the Central Committee of the NJM in October 1982.

The roots of the Coard faction in the NJM go back to the early 1970s when Coard started his own group called the Organization of Revolutionary Education and Liberation. The OREL was a study group, not a political party, which Coard used to teach basic principles of Marxism. When the MAP and JEWEL fused into the NJM in 1973, Coard's group was absorbed as well, but its harder-line Marxist objectives were not emphasized as much as Coard would have liked.

Coard's clique remained more ideological than other factions in the NJM. Coard was also quite shrewd when it came to consolidating his political power. Even after resigning from leadership positions on the Central Committee, Coard managed to place his supporters in key positions within the PRG and the People's Revolutionary Army.

Maurice Bishop had been the Soviets' conduit to further expanding their power in the Caribbean, but Bernard Coard had emerged as an unwaveringly and more ideological pro-Soviet ally. Moscow had nurtured Coard discreetly from the outset, maintaining frequent communication with him ever since the New Jewel Movement rose to prominence.

In the autumn of 1982, apprehensive of Bishop's overtures to Washington, Moscow directed Bernard Coard to consolidate his position within the leadership. Undoubtedly, the guidance of the newly appointed Ambassador Gennadi Sazhenev, who had been dispatched to Grenada in April, played a pivotal role in this endeavor. The appointment of Sazhenev, a seasoned Kremlin operative in Latin America since the Cuban Missile Crisis, sent ripples of concern through the CIA and the White House, signaling the strategic significance the Kremlin attributed to Grenada.

Coard's scheming against Bishop continued for a year before it exploded into a full-blown leadership crisis, which happened shortly after Bishop's visit to the United States and seemed to be the catalyst for a hostile takeover of the PRG. The PRG's Central Committee called meetings for September 14–16, 1983, to address some of the members' waning confidence in Bishop. The mid-September meetings also came in the wake of two previous meetings where it was widely acknowledged that the NJM had "failed to transform itself" because it wasn't taking a "Leninist path." The Committee also recognized "the spreading of anti-communism within the country." However, no criticisms were leveled directly against Maurice Bishop, and no proposals for joint leadership were offered.

Liam James, a member of the Central Committee and Political Bureau, also a protégé of Bernard Coard's, claimed, "We are seeing the beginning of the disintegration of the party," and the blame for this was placed at the feet of the entire Central Committee. Once again, Bishop was not yet the direct target of the criticism. But the internal pressure was mounting, and Bishop's critics were getting bolder. Liam James declared, "What is needed is firm Leninism . . ." but "the fundamental problem is the quality of leadership . . . by Comrade Maurice Bishop."[53]

While James was willing to concede that Bishop had virtues, he nevertheless concluded that "today these strengths alone cannot put the party any further in this period. The qualities he lacks [are] . . . 1) A Leninist level of organization and discipline. 2) Great depth in ideological clarity. 3) Brilliance in strategy and tactics." James added, "These qualities . . . are essential for Marxist-Leninist leadership."

Leon Cornwall, Grenada's ambassador to the Soviet Union, continued the criticism, stating, "History has placed a great responsibility on our shoulders which we must seek to deal with in the correct and scientific way." Phyllis Coard was much blunter in her criticism of Maurice Bishop. She claimed that he was "disorganized" and "avoided responsibilities." Then she further asserted that "some comrades are scared to criticize him because he is hostile to criticism."

The Central Committee's overwhelming sentiment was a desire for the transformation of the NJM and the PRG into a true Marxist-Leninist government. And the only way to accomplish that was new leadership. James, who had initiated the discussion, brought the issue to a head by formally proposing a model of joint leadership with Bishop essentially responsible for working with the masses and in the international arena, and with Bernard Coard concentrating upon party development and ideology.

This proposal sparked further heated discussions with a vocal base of opposition to the dual-leadership model, which was also supportive of Maurice Bishop. Bishop's supporters believed that Grenada's difficulties were caused by economic factors beyond the control of Maurice Bishop or any prime minister. Phyllis Coard further emphasized that a dual-leadership government should be "not only for a short term but on a long-term basis."

Even though Bernard Coard was not present at these meetings, his interests were well represented. When the vote was taken on formalizing the joint leadership proposal, nine were in favor, only one opposed, and three members abstained. Significantly, on another vote to inform the public of the decision to install a joint-leadership government, nine were opposed with three abstentions. Bishop requested time to personally consider the resolution and suggested to the Committee that they begin meeting with Coard on that issue.

The Central Committee continued to meet and debate the leadership structure daily throughout September, but Bishop stayed away. He was finally persuaded by a Central Committee delegation of his supporters to attend a meeting on September 25. One of the primary reasons was that after a previous meeting, the balance of power had clearly shifted to Coard's faction. Coard also began attending Central Committee meetings and accused Bishop of "vacillating between the Marxist-Leninist trend and the petit bourgeois trend."

During this meeting, the question of the ideological direction of the party, as compared with Bishop's direction, became the focus of discussion and the grounds for the determination of Bishop's future role in the party. Liam James stated, "[O]ur whole approach to this question must be totally cold-blooded, honest and objective."[54]

At this meeting in particular, members outdid themselves with Marxist rhetorical excesses. All the "proper" words and phrases were employed. Indeed, linguistic skill appeared almost to be an end in itself. As though to increase the drama of the moment, and possibly to impress their colleagues as well, Coard's faction consistently argued that the masses should not be involved and should not be informed of the joint-leadership proposal. As James himself declared, "[J]oint leadership is an internal party matter and is not to be brought to the masses."

On Monday, September 26, 1983, Maurice Bishop and his delegation embarked on a scheduled two-week journey to Hungary and Czechoslovakia to negotiate a new deal for electrical power generators. Departing from the island's modest airport in Pearls, necessitated a layover and aircraft change in a neighboring country, with Cuba serving as the stopover for this trip.

During his visit to Eastern Europe, Bishop apparently experienced a change of heart. Consulting with his closest advisors, he recognized that entering a power-sharing arrangement with Bernard Coard would be a grave error, potentially spelling the demise of his leadership.

On their way back to Grenada, Bishop's delegation made another stop in Cuba. Arriving in Havana on the evening of Thursday, October 6, Bishop engaged in discussions with Fidel Castro over the next 36 hours. Meanwhile, a member of Bishop's personal security detail purportedly contacted Grenada and conveyed Bishop's reversal regarding accepting a joint-leadership role, ominously warning of potential repercussions: "[B]lood will flow!"

Meanwhile, during the early morning hours of October 6, there was an unexpected development—a Cuban vessel named *Vietnam Heroico* had eased into Point Salines. The cargo ship delivered more Cuban "workers" onto Grenadian soil.[55] For many Grenadians, the memory of the recent political upheaval at home and in neighboring countries, particularly the rise of Cuban influence in the Caribbean, fueled their apprehensions about the Cuban ship's arrival.

As news of the *Vietnam Heroico*'s arrival spread like wildfire across the island, Bernard Coard and members of his faction worried that the ship's arrival was part of a new clandestine operation orchestrated by Bishop and Castro to neutralize Coard's challenge to his authority. Despite denials from Bishop regarding discussions with Castro on internal party matters during his final Cuba trip, the rumors persisted. Castro himself would later state that Bishop had not broached the subject with him, suggesting that such a conversation would likely have been awkward for Bishop.

Upon the delegation's return to Grenada on the morning of Saturday, October 8, 1983, only one member of the PRG leadership was there to greet Bishop and his entourage. During the 45-minute journey from Pearls to Saint George's, Bishop confirmed that he intended to reject the joint-leadership proposal at the upcoming NJM Central Committee and Political Bureau meetings that were scheduled for October 12.

Upon arriving at his residence, Bishop discovered that his neighbors, Deputy Prime Minister Bernard Coard and his wife, Phyllis, had vacated their home, opting to spend the night elsewhere.

## BISHOP'S ARREST AND ASSASSINATION

On October 13, the People's Revolutionary Army, under the command of General Hudson Austin, placed Prime Minister Maurice Bishop and several of his supporters under house arrest, in coordination with the People's Revolutionary Army and the radical Marxist faction of the NJM led by Deputy Prime Minister Bernard Coard. The next morning, an announcer for Radio Free Grenada attempted to reassure the listening public. "Everything is calm so far," the voice said. There were no reports of widespread violence—yet.

But reports coming from the Caribbean Broadcasting Corporation, based in Barbados, were telling a much different story. There was ongoing turmoil in Grenada following the coup. Reports on CBC radio also talked about the growing rift within the military's ranks, with some of the soldiers and officers pledging allegiance to Bishop while others stood behind Deputy Prime Minister Bernard Coard.

During an interview with a Grenadian newspaper, General Hudson Austin later claimed that Maurice Bishop was placed under house arrest due to a circulating rumor.[56] Supposedly, Bernard Coard and his wife, Phyllis, were plotting to kill Bishop. Austin explained that he and the security forces were acting on the direction of certain members of the NJM who believed that both Bishop and Coard should be confined to their homes for their own safety. This move would enable the security forces, then under the leadership of a pro-Coard ally, to investigate the origin of the rumor. However, Austin noted that Coard was allowed freedom of movement while Bishop remained confined to the prime minister's residence, with his phone lines cut. Austin, previously known for his support of Bishop, highlighted the disparity in treatment.

Protesters poured into the streets of Saint George's after the PRA's security forces arrested Bishop and confined him to his house. In response to the demonstrators calling for Bishop's release, Coard said, "[T]hey could stay in the street for weeks, after a while they are bound to get tired and hungry and want peace." The protests lasted for almost a week.

On October 19, a large crowd of pro-Bishop supporters gathered once again at the prime minister's residence and physically overwhelmed the soldiers guarding him, allowing Bishop to regain his freedom. After being freed, Bishop embraced his supporters and then confronted the lieutenant in charge of the soldiers who had been keeping him under house arrest. Bishop declared that his people had come for him, and so he was leaving.

The plan was to take the prime minister to Saint George's Market Square, where he would address the growing mass of supporters demanding his release. Bishop was anticipated to publicly denounce Coard and his associates and reclaim control of the revolution in Grenada. While on his way from the prime minister's residence to Saint George's Market Square, however, one of Bishop's aides convinced him to go to Fort Rupert first, which had become the command center for the Revolutionary Military Council. Upon reaching the PRA's Operations Room, Bishop purportedly proclaimed that the revolution would persist, albeit without the presence of Bernard Coard.

Two of Bishop's confidants engaged in a tense phone call with some of Coard's associates, who proposed negotiations to resolve the NJM's internal leadership crisis. The offer was swiftly rebuffed, and Coard's allies were told to surrender at the nearest police precinct.

Bernard Coard and the members of the Central Committee aligned with him, along with factions of the military, huddled at Fort Frederick. Led by a 25-year-old officer, these troops took three armored vehicles to Fort Rupert. Upon reaching their destination, gunfire erupted between the troops and those stationed at Fort Rupert. Bishop was quickly apprehended and then marched into the main yard of the fort, where he and six of his allies were lined up against a wall and subjected to a hail of machine gun fire. Outside the fort dozens of Bishop's supporters were wounded and 13 were killed, during a gunfight with Coard's security forces and those loyal to Bishop.

## THE FALLOUT

More chaos came in the wake of the murder of Maurice Bishop and his supporters. General Hudson Austin appointed himself in control of the PRA and the Grenadian government. A 16-member military council led by General Hudson Austin declared martial law and took control, brushing Bernard Coard aside. Radio Free Grenada carried a statement from the RMC saying it had dissolved the People's Revolutionary Government, dismissed the cabinet, and taken over "full executive and legislative powers." The broadcast said nothing about Bernard Coard.

The radio broadcast also warned of Austin's orders for an "all day, all night" curfew and said any violators would be shot on sight. It said only workers in "essential services" could obtain passes to move about the island.

A statement released by the RMC further stated, "Any attempt at foreign aggression will be resisted by the People's Revolutionary Armed Forces to the last man." The RMC also called "upon all countries to respect the sovereignty and territorial integrity of Grenada."

One of the complications that General Austin and Coard failed to take into consideration was the relatively large population of Americans on the island, many of them attending and working at St. George's University School of Medicine.

According to foreign journalists who arrived on the island to cover Bishop's assassination, Austin and his RMC had also ordered all airports closed.

Dr. Robert Jordan, a member of the St. George's faculty, described the situation this way: "[T]here were a few little boys with big guns just across the street in . . . Grand Anse and lots of Cuban workers and a few PRA next to our True Blue campus. They never ventured on our campuses (except in a few planned meetings . . .). In reality we could move about rather easily . . . , especially at night," said Dr. Jordan.[57]

But others say they faced harrowing experiences, including deep fear about being taken hostage, the university's two campuses being locked down under the government's "shoot to kill" curfew, and encounters with armed soldiers, according to the *New York Times*.[58]

Fidel Castro's government in Cuba released an official statement saying they would hold three days of mourning in honor of Bishop and the other slain officials. Flags on all state buildings would fly at half-staff. "No doctrine, principle or proclaimed revolutionary position and no internal split justifies such brutal procedures as the physical elimination of Bishop and the renowned group of honest and dignified leaders killed yesterday," the declaration, given to reporters at the Cuban Foreign Ministry, said.

The Cubans insisted that they had no part in the coup. In Moscow, TASS, the official state news agency, reported on Bishop's murder, saying the military council had pledged to "uphold the cause of the revolution," Reuters reported.[59]

Sir Paul Scoon, Queen Elizabeth's governor general and last remaining legitimate government official in Grenada, was again briefly placed under house arrest, along with his wife and his staff at the governor general's mansion. During the curfew period, Governor General Scoon was permitted to meet with foreign diplomats and engaged in discussions with the new military junta about forming a civilian government. He was also permitted to receive international calls from leaders in the Caribbean and England. On October 22, Queen Elizabeth II's assistant private secretary called. Scoon reassured him that both he and his wife were in "good form."

He was also able to use secret diplomatic channels to ask the United Kingdom, the United States, and other concerned Caribbean nations to intervene to restore peace and order to the island. Scoon sent an urgent cable to Prime Minister Tom Adams of Barbados that read:

> Dear Prime Minister,
>
> You are aware that there is a vacuum of power in Grenada following the killing of the prime minister and subsequent serious violations of human rights and bloodshed. I am, therefore, seriously concerned over the lack of internal security in Grenada. Consequently I am requesting your help to assist me in [stabilizing] this grave and dangerous situation. It is my desire that a peace-keeping force should be established in Grenada to facilitate a rapid return to peace and tranquility and also

a return to democratic rule. In this connection I am also seeking assistance from the United States, from Jamaica, and from the Organisation of Eastern Caribbean States through its current chairman, the Hon. Eugenia Charles, in the spirit of the treaty establishing that organisation to which my country is a signatory.[60]

CHAPTER 6

# Contingency Plans

*"The president [Reagan] was far too results-oriented for the careful tastes of some State Department types."*
—Constantine Menges, National Security Council staff member, in his book *Inside the National Security Council*

## THE NATIONAL SECURITY COUNCIL

Constantine Menges wrote in his book *Inside the National Security Council* that on Monday, October 10, 1983, he was "filled with a nervous yet pleasurable excitement." That was the day he attended his first regular senior staff meeting of the National Security Council.

These meetings, Menges wrote, were set for every morning at 7:30 a.m. in the Situation Room located in the White House basement. These senior NSC staff meetings were attended by National Security Advisor William Clark; Bud McFarlane, his deputy; Admiral John Poindexter; and the individuals responsible for various geographic parts of the world. There are other senior staffers there to cover topics like international economics, politics, military flashpoints, Congress, and the media.

Most of the attendees arrived at 7:00 a.m. and began by reading reports. NSC staffers poured over the CIA's National Intelligence Daily, overnight diplomatic and intelligence cables, and various items sent by the State Department and the Pentagon. They would also take a "quick look" at the daily press and the White House news summary.

At 7:30 each senior NSC staffer would give a two- to three-minute summary of the key events and issues in their respective areas. The goal was to limit those events to issues that might require imminent executive action from the president.

William Clark briefed the president one-on-one on national security issues for at least a half hour every morning. Menges recalled that if an issue was "hot," Clark usually asked the senior staff members with expertise or knowledge on that issue to participate. In those cases, the president would often have a direct conversation with the staff member.

Menges wrote that these opportunities also gave him as a "staff member a personal sense of the president's perceptions on the issue, which helped when it came time to write the background and decision memos." Menges would find this out for the first time 12 days later. "President Reagan was pleasant and easy to talk with," Menges observed. Throughout the course of his presidency, President Reagan and his top advisors held over 350 National Security Council meetings. Reagan chaired most of these meetings where his team debated and shaped U.S. foreign policy.

On his second day at the NSC, October 11, 1983, Menges went to the State Department to have lunch with Jim Michael, the principal deputy assistant secretary for Latin America. Menges noted that as he entered the building, he "felt curious 'vibes.'" He claims that people working in the Latin American bureau were unhappy that he had moved from the CIA, where he had worked closely with Director Bill Casey for two years, to the National Security Council. Menges writes that he was in "wholehearted agreement" with President Reagan, which was a problem for the State Department because "many of them seemed to believe their calling was to save Ronald Reagan from himself." The president was far too results-oriented for the careful tastes of some State Department types.

"Their main approach to foreign affairs was that the United States should make 'agreements' with nations that presented problems. That was not Ronald Reagan's style. He believed we should measure our foreign policy by whether or not our strategic and democratic interests were advancing or retreating."

At lunch, Michael told Menges about the State Department's latest proposal, which was intended to help obtain congressional approval for funding the Contras, the armed democratic resistance in Nicaragua. The State Department wanted a Republican congressman to publicly state that if Mexico and the three other Latin American countries acting as mediators determined that Nicaragua and its Sandinista government stopped fomenting Marxist-Leninist revolutions in neighboring countries, the United States would end its support for the Contras.

"That stunned me." Menges wrote. "It was about as incompetent a proposal as I'd yet heard come out of State."

"Jim," Menges asked in a calm voice, "what do you think would happen next?'

"I think," Michael replied, "this would pass the House and the Senate."

Menges agreed, but then said, "If this became U.S. law, what would happen in Central America?"

Menges pointed out that Mexico had been supporting the communist government in Nicaragua since 1979, both politically and with hundreds of millions of dollars in economic assistance. The State Department's plan was an affront to President Reagan's core philosophy because it allowed the Sandinistas to ignore the 1979 Organization of American States requirement that Nicaragua become a genuine democracy and hold elections.

There was another huge problem with the plan. At that time, only the United States had the intel resources to keep track of the Sandinistas' clandestine activities. The whole process by which they provided training, weapons, money, and other support to terrorist and communist fighters was highly secret and "officially denied." So the United States wasn't likely to share what it knew with others.

Mexico and other countries in Latin America lacked the political will and the means to monitor the Sandinistas' operations, which were done with the full technical aid of Cuba and the Soviets.

Menges, like his boss National Security Advisor William Clark, knew that Reagan would not allow the United States to relegate its foreign policy to other countries. Any proposed compromise with Congress should specify that only our president would make the final judgment about whether the Sandinistas were continuing subversive aggression against their neighbors.

Menges wrote that "Michael looked as if I had just spoiled his lunch. Grimacing, he said, 'But I've already discussed this compromise with Ollie North, and he agrees with it.'" Menges remarked that Oliver North was in a separate unit of the National Security Council, involved with U.S. arms transfers and military aid, not with strategic policy.

The day after his lunch at the State Department, Menges had a meeting with Bill Clark, and as they were finishing up, Menges told Clark about State's proposal involving Mexico and a GOP congressman to be named later.

"What do you think about it?" Clark asked Menges in his signature quiet voice.

"In short, it would be a major mistake," Menges responded.

Clark then said, "I agree, it contradicts the president's policy. Let's send State a memo immediately letting them know this approach is not acceptable to the president."

Menges writes that he felt Clark needed to know that Michael had said Ollie North agreed with State's plan.

In response, Clark then said, "Constantine, *you* are the senior person for Latin America."

At Clark's direction, Menges wrote "a short but pointed memo to State," which he says "stopped for a time their misguided effort at a self-destructive compromise with Congress."

It was now October 12—the same day Bernard Coard and General Hudson Austin had staged their coup against Maurice Bishop in Grenada. The new government, which called itself the Revolutionary Military Council, had Bishop and several of his key cabinet allies under house arrest.

Grenada was in Menges's purview, and he had been monitoring the events closely ever since the initial coup led by Bishop and the New Jewel Movement in March 1979. The 110,000 Grenadians and about 1,000 Americans were now at the mercy of a small Marxist-Leninist clique that seemed like it was determined to establish a totalitarian dictatorship by any means necessary. By 1981, the Reagan administration, according to Menges, "had definitive information that the Bishop regime was acting in classic dictatorial fashion."

Under the cover of darkness, Soviet and Cuban ships often unloaded military equipment. On October 6, the Cuban vessel *Vietnam Heroico* had landed with an undisclosed number of Cuban workers, presumably to join others already at work on the runway at Point Salines. Then, on October 13, other Cuban vessels had delivered a cargo of arms for transit to an undisclosed location in the interior. The presence of a well-armed force of Cubans complicated planning. Menges, a former CIA intelligence officer, said Cuban guards lined the routes from the port to the PRA's clandestine camps, ensuring that none of the locals learned what was being transported.

As Grenada fell deeper and deeper into a Marxist-Leninist dictatorship, fear quickly spread through nearby Caribbean democracies. These predominantly Black, English-speaking nations watched as Cuban, Soviet, East German, Bulgarian, and Libyan operatives infiltrated Grenada, indoctrinating and training students and radicals who would return to their island nations to spread the revolution.

These leaders also knew that since their security forces numbered in the tens or low hundreds, a trained and disciplined force of 50 to 100 people acting with the benefit of surprise might be enough to stage a successful radical coup. Grenada had been accepted as a member in the OECS in the hope that doing so might moderate its foreign activities and pull it in a democratic direction, but that never happened.

Now, in October 1983, Menges said he grew increasingly concerned that the Americans at St. George's University Medical School could be caught in the crossfire as "thousands of newly armed, radicalized Grenadians in the revolutionary police, army, and militia forces picked sides." He claims that NJM leaders had threatened to use the American medical students as hostages a few years earlier.

But this developing crisis, Menges believed, could also "present an excellent chance to restore democracy to Grenada while assuring the safety of our citizens." He wrote that he immediately asked all the foreign policy agencies to provide their latest facts on Grenada. At the Thursday, October 13, meeting of the NSC's senior staff, Menges offered a short presentation on Grenada. It included intel on Cubans and Soviet bloc countries and noted the concerns being raised by the friendly Caribbean democracies.

Maurice Bishop had just returned from his trips to the United States, Eastern Europe, and Cuba, where he had spent a significant amount of time with Castro. There were questions about a potential power struggle between Havana and Moscow for control of Grenada. Castro had invested a lot of money and personal capital in mentoring Bishop, but Bishop was now making overtures to the United States. That was a problem in both Havana and Moscow.

After the meeting, Menges returned to his office and drafted a short plan designed to protect U.S. citizens and restore democracy to Grenada. Menges was the first to call for a "collective security force," including democratic Caribbean countries. He planned to go over the plan with Bill Clark at the next NSC staff meeting the following day. Menges wouldn't get the chance.

Clark called "an unusual" afternoon NSC staff meeting in the Roosevelt Room. For several hours rumors had been circulating that had nothing to do with foreign policy. At the meeting Clark, "in his direct and quiet way," told the NSC staff that he would accept the president's nomination to become the next secretary of the interior.

Menges wrote that "we were all surprised and sad." And without Clark, "the National Security Council would never be the same." Menges also wrote that he talked to Bill Casey about Clark's replacement, "and I told him I thought Jeane Kirkpatrick would bring creative vision and in-depth knowledge of foreign policy issues.

Secretary of State George Shultz reportedly wanted Chief of Staff James Baker III to replace Clark at the top of NSC. "It was rumored that at the last minute Weinberger and Casey talked the president out of naming Baker, who had no foreign policy experience. The press speculated about possible appointees: Undersecretary of State Lawrence Eagleburger and Robert McFarlane were mentioned," Menges wrote. By Sunday, October 16, Robert "Bud" McFarlane had emerged as the consensus choice. The formal announcement was made the following day.

McFarlane moved up from deputy to NSC advisor. "He immediately asked the senior staff members for a brief outline of the key issues in our area and informed us that he would continue the daily 7:30 a.m. meetings." Menges confessed that he "was not too happy with McFarlane's appointment." Both men had worked closely together while Menges was working at the CIA on Cuba and other hostile countries. McFarlane "had always followed the State Department approach."

Menges thought McFarlane would most likely fire him from the NSC, based on their history. But he continued to work on his Grenada plan anyway. Menges would also meet privately with a senior Defense Department official to talk about the plan with him.

The unnamed Pentagon official told Menges his "plan has no chance whatsoever. . . . McFarlane doesn't like you. He thinks you're too Reaganite. If you mention this to him, you'll give him the pretext to remove you from the NSC before you even get a chance to do any of the good work I know you can accomplish there. This is a waste of time. Take my advice. Don't do anything about Grenada, and don't mention this plan to McFarlane or Poindexter."

"I know this is risky for me," Menges replied, "and I know the chances are slim that we will do it." But he continued and laid out the important reasons for action: Protect U.S. citizens, aid the Grenadian people, curb the communist threat to neighboring democracies, and boost political morale in Central America and the Caribbean. Additionally, he feared the Soviets might deploy nuclear-armed aircraft or submarines in Grenada to deter the United States from deploying medium-range missiles in Europe.

The Soviets had threatened an "analogous deployment." Under the 1962 Kennedy-Khrushchev agreement, placing nuclear weapons in Cuba risked a major crisis, while Nicaragua was too valuable for destabilizing Central America. But Grenada, with its deepwater port and new runway, was perfect for Soviet nuclear forces. If the United States backed down in Europe, the Soviets could offer to remove their "temporary" nuclear weapons from Grenada.

Menges also asked his friend at the Pentagon to discreetly dig up the 1981 reports from the military exercise "Operation Amber in the Amberdines." The DOD official reiterated his opinion that there was no chance that the Reagan administration would use force, and if he told his plan to McFarlane, Menges would soon find himself out of the NSC.

Simultaneously on October 12, Langhorne "Tony" Motley, the assistant secretary of state for inter-American affairs, reached out to the Joint Chiefs of Staff to advise them that they might need to put together a military operation to rescue Americans on short notice.[1]

The next morning McFarlane presided over his first senior staff meeting. When Menges's turn came, he told him he viewed the situation in Grenada as one that required the protection of U.S. citizens and offered the opportunity to restore democracy. He said he had written a plan to accomplish this, had discussed it informally with a Defense Department colleague, and planned to discuss it today with Bill Middendorf, the U.S. ambassador to the Organization of American States and with the State Department.

Menges wrote that McFarlane looked at him "with a quizzical expression." He wondered if the new NSC advisor had fully understood what he was suggesting. "Well," said McFarlane, "that's okay." He then called on the next staff person. At least he hadn't said that I should stop thinking along those lines, which was a pleasant surprise, nor had he told me not to discuss the idea further.

Later that day, Menges met with William J. Middendorf II, a seasoned diplomat with extensive experience in previous Republican administrations. Their acquaintance dated back to the 1980 Reagan campaign, where Middendorf had chaired an advisory group in which Menges had participated. Middendorf, known for his energy and staunch support of Reagan's foreign policies, held prestigious positions in the Department of State and had a keen interest in Latin American affairs.

In Menges's office at the Old Executive Office Building, adjacent to the White House, they delved into the Latin American landscape before focusing on Grenada. Menges sought Middendorf's insights on the potential reactions of Organization of American States (OAS) members to military action in Grenada, with or without the support of other Caribbean nations.

Unlike some of his counterparts, Middendorf responded with enthusiasm and optimism. Menges noticed a spark in his eyes as Middendorf voiced his support for the idea, emphasizing its significance for freedom. Before departing, Middendorf offered a word of caution, advising Menges not to set his expectations too high despite the favorable reception. "It's a great idea," he affirmed, "but if I were you, I wouldn't get my hopes up."

Next, Menges contacted a trusted foreign service officer at the State Department, seeking an update from the Latin American bureau. The officer reported that Ambassador Milan Bish, a Reagan appointee in Barbados, had sent urgent cables highlighting the deep concerns of Caribbean democratic leaders, but little action had been taken. Additionally, the U.S. ambassador in Jamaica relayed that Prime Minister Seaga was very worried and planned to meet with six Eastern Caribbean prime ministers.

Menges also met with Bill Doherty from the AFL-CIO, who had previously led the American Institute for Free Labor, an organization that had trained over 350,000 democratic union leaders across Latin America. Doherty, familiar with several Grenadian labor leaders targeted by the communist government, informed Menges that democratic union leaders throughout the Caribbean feared that the RMC's coup could lead to serious bloodshed. Both communist factions in Grenada were notoriously ruthless, and Doherty anticipated that the free trade unions of all Caribbean countries would soon issue a resolution condemning both communist groups in Grenada.

Menges noted that Doherty reminded him of their shared concerns from a year ago about Suriname's military dictatorship growing closer to Cuba. This worry centered on Osvaldo Cardenas, a Cuban secret agent who had helped Bishop seize power in Grenada and appeared in June 1982 as the new Cuban ambassador in Suriname.

Doherty recalled that in October 1982, Castro, Bishop, and Suriname's brutal dictator Desi Bouterse forged an alliance following Bishop's visit to Suriname. During this visit, Bishop advised Bouterse on dealing with democratic political and labor leaders protesting the regime's communist ties, saying, "Either you eliminate them, or they will eliminate you."

In December 1982, Desi Bouterse carried out a brutal crackdown. More than a dozen prominent pro-democracy figures, including lawyers, journalists, and a university professor, were rounded up and executed at a colonial fortress in the capital city of Paramaribo.

On Wednesday, October 19, 1983, the State Department held a meeting to explore what it would look like if it should become necessary to conduct a "quick in and out" military rescue of U.S. citizens in Grenada, with or without the consent of the Revolutionary Military Council.

The meeting included representatives from the Joint Chiefs of Staff and the CIA, and Menges wrote that he learned of this meeting from his close friends at the State Department, even though the Latin American bureau had "forgotten" to tell anyone from the NSC. During the fall and winter of 1981, State Department Under Secretary Al Haig had started to exclude key members of the NSC staff from interagency meetings. The practice, Menges concluded, was continuing with the new leadership.

As noted earlier in the book, on Wednesday, October 19, the situation in Grenada took a dark turn. Initially, reports indicated that a large crowd supporting Prime Minister Bishop managed to free him and four cabinet ministers who had been arrested. They then gathered at Fort Rupert, overlooking the harbor. However, the Revolutionary Military Council, catching Bishop and his followers by surprise, lined them up against a wall and executed them by firing squad. Troops then turned their weapons on the crowd, resulting in approximately 50 deaths. The Revolutionary Military Council imposed a 24-hour shoot-on-sight curfew.

Throughout the evening, Menges worked diligently to prepare three concise overviews. The first was a factual summary of the tragic events. The second comprised responses gathered over recent days from various Caribbean governments, trade unions, political parties, and religious groups, all denouncing the bloodshed and urging preventive action. The third described pro-democratic leadership and institutions that could facilitate the restoration of democracy.

Menges urged Bud McFarlane and John Poindexter to convene a Crisis Pre-Planning Group (CPPG). While the State Department typically hosted such meetings, the severity of the situation warranted an exception in this case. If the national security advisor deemed a situation potentially requiring presidential action involving force or the threat of force, they could initiate the CPPG at the sub-cabinet level, as was now the case.

McFarlane and Poindexter agreed to convene the CPPG the following day. Menges then reached out to Bill Middendorf via secure phone, inviting him to the CPPG meeting focused on Grenada. Additionally, he spoke with Bill Casey about other matters, refraining from mentioning the Grenada plan to avoid raising premature expectations, especially as Casey was about to embark on a trip.

At 9:00 a.m. on Thursday, October 20, the Crisis Pre-Planning Group meeting on Grenada convened in room 208 of the Old Executive Office Building. John Poindexter, seated at one end of the long wooden table, puffed on his pipe. Admission to room

208 was by invitation only, and it served as the White House's new crisis facility, equipped with state-of-the-art electronic gadgets, computers, visual displays, and a combination lock on the door. This was Menges's first time working in the new crisis center.

The meeting started with a briefing on the latest developments, highlighting the presence of the Cuban weapons transport ship, the *Vietnam Heroico*, in Saint George's harbor. Discussions then turned to the military and logistical requirements for landing troops to rescue and evacuate U.S. citizens.

The Revolutionary Military Council's total strength was estimated at about 4,000, supplemented by approximately 600 armed Cuban construction workers, many of whom had prior military training. In contrast, Castro's armed forces numbered 230,000, with the capability to airlift 5,000 to 10,000 troops to Grenada within days.

Menges emphasized the critical need for secrecy, stressing two essential reasons: "to prevent Castro from preemptively moving in more Cuban troops" and "to keep the American medical students from being removed to hidden locations." Despite some media and the U.S.-based medical school administrator later downplaying the threat, CPPG members recognized the real danger. They feared the students might face tighter military control and be declared hostages to thwart any counteraction.

After discussing the feasibility of a swift rescue operation, Menges proposed his bold plan: a multinational force not only to rescue citizens but also to restore democracy and permanently eliminate the communist threat. "If we carry out a quick in-and-out rescue," Menges warned, "but leave the communist regime in place, it will become even more hostile."

Silence greeted Menges's proposal at first, until Middendorf and Fred Ikle voiced support, suggesting the plan could get international backing from regional allies. They endorsed the idea. A State Department official proposed negotiating with General

Hudson Austin, but Menges dismissed the idea, citing Austin's recent violent actions. "I think," Menges said, "his killing 50 people yesterday told us what kind of person he is."

Poindexter concluded the meeting, announcing a cabinet-level NSC meeting at 6:00 p.m. Menges's next task was to draft a background memo for the vice president, who would chair the first NSC meeting on the issue. He also prepared the agenda and briefed key personnel, with assistance from Oliver North, who had started to show increasing interest in Grenada.

North, however, remained skeptical, citing past instances of inaction. He predicted opposition from the State Department and the Joint Chiefs of Staff. Menges anticipated opposition from figures like James Baker, Vice President Bush, and Secretary of State Shultz, who tended to lean toward nonintervention.

At nearly 6:00 p.m., the participants, including Vice President Bush, Secretary Weinberger, and others, convened in the Situation Room at the White House. As the meeting unfolded, Menges witnessed a gradual shift within the NSC group toward action, with discussions focusing on the availability of military forces and planning a successful rescue with minimal casualties.

Secretary Shultz arrived late. He had just finished briefing Senator Jesse Helms on the 1962 Kennedy-Khrushchev accords on Cuba. The State Department emphasized Caribbean democratic leaders' desire for action and their fear of bloodshed in Grenada.

Menges presented an overview of democratic leaders and groups, a presentation he had prepared in advance, as the discussion shifted from the rescue plan to the plan to restore democracy. He highlighted the potential for an interim government leading to free and fair elections.

There were a few more minutes of discussion, and then the one-hour meeting ended. The first suggested presidential decision was to prepare for possible military action by redirecting navy ships, which were transporting a Marine unit for force rotation in Lebanon, toward Grenada. All government leaders were to maintain their announced schedules. Any leak, or even active speculation, could jeopardize the mission and the lives of the American students.

Menges arrived at his office early on Friday, October 21, to review the latest information before his 7:30 a.m. meeting with Bud McFarlane. He informed the national security advisor that the State Department was preparing a detailed plan to be reviewed at a noon Restricted Interagency Group meeting.

"Fine," said McFarlane, "but we also need to have a CPPG meeting in room 208 late this afternoon to prepare for tomorrow morning's NSC meeting." The noon meeting at the State Department, led by Assistant Secretary Tony Motley, lasted for two hours with increasing intensity. Motley and his staff had prepared the political aspects of the rescue plan and the establishment of an interim government. Each representative from Defense, CIA, NSC, and State had a few ideas and suggestions to add.

Meanwhile, Caribbean democratic leaders from Jamaica, Barbados, Dominica, Saint Lucia, Saint Vincent, Montserrat, and Saint Christopher-Nevis were meeting in Barbados. They agreed that military intervention was necessary and legal under customary international law and the 1981 OECS treaty. Hundreds of American medical students were surrounded by hostile forces, and many citizens from these Caribbean countries were also trapped by the 24-hour shoot-to-kill curfew. Jamaica and Barbados, as the largest countries, were willing to provide substantial military forces. The smaller island nations could offer only token contributions, some numbering in the tens or hundreds.

President Reagan's closest advisors had to consider the balance of regional military power. The Grenadian People's Revolutionary Army totaled 4,000 troops, but the Cuban military boasted 230,000 troops, including about 200 jet fighters, fast torpedo boats, and even two submarines.

Caribbean leaders were alarmed about what could come their way, having seen the Ford and Carter administrations stand by while Fidel Castro sent 20,000 Cuban troops to aid communist factions in Angola and Mozambique in 1975, and another 15,000 troops to support a pro-Soviet military group in Ethiopia in 1977. Since 1979, thousands of Cuban troops, secret police, and operatives had propped up dictatorships in Nicaragua and Bishop's dictatorship in Grenada. The leaders felt vulnerable, knowing that Cuba, the Soviets, and Libya were training some of their citizens to disrupt life on their islands. For example, in 1980, the Cuban ambassador to Jamaica was caught supplying weapons and ammunition to radical terrorists during the national election campaign.

The Soviet Union provided $4 billion annually to Cuba, a third of its gross national product, including tens of thousands of tons of weapons. Caribbean leaders saw this as Moscow backing and encouraging Castro's aggression in Africa and Latin America. These leaders hesitated to suggest military action in Grenada, an ally of Cuba, unless they were certain of U.S. participation. If the United States were unwilling to join them, they could only protest the violence in Grenada to avoid further hostility from Cuba or Grenada's new communist regime.

In the U.S. government, some were hesitant to act unilaterally. Menges believed joint security action was preferable for political and strategic reasons, but if Caribbean countries were too afraid to ask for help, the United States had the right to act alone to protect its citizens. Ambassador Milan Bish could tell Caribbean leaders that the probability of U.S. military action would be much higher if they requested it collectively.

Poindexter chaired the late Friday afternoon CPPG meeting in room 208. The State Department had revised its preliminary action plan, and copies were distributed to the attendees. The discussion shifted from whether they would act to how the operation could be accomplished with minimal casualties and speed to avoid Cuban or Soviet counterattack. Menges also felt they had to prepare for possible harassment or more serious actions by Soviet allies like East Germany against West Berlin, North Korea against South Korea, or terrorist attacks backed by Libya or Syria targeting U.S. assets.

The previous day, Poindexter had said the most secure means would be used to order U.S. ships to change course from Lebanon toward Grenada. Nevertheless, ABC News learned about this and broadcast it.

That evening, Ollie North and Menges worked together for four-and-a-half hours, writing the background and decision memoranda for the next morning's secret NSC meeting. Early in the evening, Poindexter reviewed their first draft and made a few minor revisions. Then the Grenada memoranda were sent to the president, Shultz, and McFarlane, who were traveling to play golf in Georgia.

## A HOSTAGE CRISIS IN AUGUSTA, GEORGIA

Around 5:00 a.m. on October 22, 1983, Secretary of State George Shultz and newly appointed National Security Advisor Bud McFarlane were standing outside the president and first lady's bedroom room inside the Eisenhower Cabin. An urgent situation demanded attention.

Knock, knock, knock . . .

Secretary Shultz had already been awake for about two hours and fifteen minutes. The State Department had sent Shultz a cable from the Organization of Eastern Caribbean States. The OECS, which the United States had helped start just two years before, was asking for assistance to restore democracy and order in Grenada.

President Reagan was not a big golfer, but the White House had planned the two-day working vacation in Augusta, Georgia, anyway after an invitation from Secretary of State George Shultz, who was a member of the club. It would be Reagan's first visit to the prestigious Augusta National Country Club, a favorite retreat of President Dwight Eisenhower. Eisenhower loved the club so much that they built a cottage named after him on the grounds.

During this trip, President Reagan and the First Lady, Secretary of State George Shultz and his wife, former New Jersey Senator Nicholas Brady along with his wife, and Treasury Secretary Donald Regan and his wife were all staying at the iconic Eisenhower Cottage. Reagan had considered canceling the trip due to the recent developing events in Grenada, but a decision was made to proceed to ensure that everything looked normal to the public. In reality, the situation was anything but normal.

Before everyone left Washington, D.C., President Reagan had held a nationally televised news conference on Friday, October 21, and was asked about the long-planned trip.[2] One reporter raised the fact that the club appeared to be lacking black members and asked about the perceived hypocrisy of Reagan's decision to play the course after just signing new legislation establishing Martin Luther King Jr.'s birthday as a national holiday.

President Reagan responded, "I don't know anything about the membership, but I know there is nothing in the bylaws of that club that advocates for any discrimination of any kind." The president mentioned that he had seen Black golfers play in the Masters on television and then said, "I'm invited to go down there as a guest. . . . I think I've covered all I know about it."

The following question was about President Reagan's recent announcement that the man whom many would consider his closest friend in his administration, William "Judge" Clark, was leaving his position as the national security advisor to become the next secretary of the interior. A reporter commented that Clark's nomination "shocked just about everyone except [Reagan] and Judge Clark." And then the reporter asked if the move came at Clark's request.

After Reagan complimented Clark for his service as Reagan's chief of staff when Reagan was governor of California, and for his work on the California Supreme Court, Reagan confirmed that Clark, a fourth-generation rancher, had initiated the move. Reagan's first secretary of the interior, James Watt, had resigned on October 9. Watt had a history of making controversial statements and was a constant target of left-wing environmentalists. The last straw came when Watt described a panel reviewing his coal-leasing policies as having "every kind of mixture—I have a black, I have a woman, two Jews and a cripple."[3]

The change would have a profound impact on the rest of the Reagan presidency. In the short term, it meant that McFarlane and Shultz would, in effect, be running point on Grenada, as they were closest to the president at the precise time he had to make a "go" or "no go" decision.

The American response to the military intervention proposed by the OECS was the main topic of the conversation in Augusta, and in Washington. Shultz advocated for something big and overwhelming. Some might call it shock and awe. There were about 1,000 Americans in Grenada, most of them attending or working at St. George's Medical College, which had two campuses located near the Point Salines Airport. Shultz emphasized his concern that the hostile takeover of the PRG and the murder of Maurice Bishop led by Bernard Coard and the MRC would put Americans on the island in grave danger. But he certainly wasn't alone in thinking that way. "The entire Grenada operation was driven by the State Department," Shultz would later boast in his memoirs.

Reagan certainly didn't want a repeat of the Iran hostage crisis. Predawn phone calls were organized on a secure line with Vice President Bush and Defense Secretary Caspar Weinberger. Reagan, wearing a robe and slippers, along with Shultz and McFarlane, joined the calls from the Eisenhower Cottage. Shultz continued to urge for robust military action, while Weinberger pressed for caution. The secretary of defense wanted more time and intel. "You never had a day when the secretary of state and the secretary of defense weren't at each other's throats," Reagan's then–Chief of Staff James Baker III would tell a presidential historian.[4] At the time he was talking about Al Haig, but the theme would carry over to George Shultz's time as well. The vice president also wanted to wait. Bush, the former CIA director under President Ford, believed that the United States could enlist more support from other Spanish-speaking countries in the region like Venezuela.

After the first round of calls briefing the key players, an emergency Saturday meeting of the National Security Council was scheduled for 9:00 a.m., with the president and his entourage calling in by secure phones from Augusta National Country Club. The meeting attendees in D.C. were told to arrive inconspicuously and use various entrances to the White House. No one wanted to raise the suspicions of the press corps, many of whom were already starting to smell a story brewing.

Constantine Menges, the NSC's point man for Latin American affairs, was already at the White House prepping for the meeting. The tense mood was bolstered by the OECS's unanimous request for U.S. military participation to restore order to Grenada. Intelligence reports at the time also indicated that Cuba did not appear to be sending additional military assets to the island. Menges was working alongside Marine Lieutenant Colonel and White House liaison Oliver North, who was focused on military affairs and coordination inside the NSC. North and Menges divided up the meeting prep work. Menges would handle the political and strategic issues, and North would be responsible for briefing the Joint Chiefs of Staff.

By this point, it was already clear that President Reagan was inclined to act militarily. Shultz continued pushing Reagan toward increasing the size of the operation, even before it was fully developed by the Joint Chiefs. And Shultz had the commander in chief's ear.

After everyone arrived, the meeting was moved from the White House Situation Room to room 208 in what is now called the Eisenhower Executive Office building, then the Old Executive Office Building. This is the same room where, in 1941, Secretary of State Cordell Hull received a phone call from President Roosevelt describing an unconfirmed report that the Japanese had attacked Pearl Harbor.

Not only were American lives in jeopardy in Grenada, but other countries were also asking for American military support. Democratic, English-speaking Caribbean countries like Jamaica and Barbados were also willing to provide military force as part of a joint operation with the United States.

The emergency NSC Special Situations Group meeting was chaired by Vice President Bush. It began with an overview and an update of the current situation in Grenada and where things stood in the planning process. The State Department's representatives then informed everyone about the request for military assistance from the OECS and the State Department's consultations with other friendly governments. The unanimous request from the OECS included a new dimension and meant that the operation now had to be augmented. In addition to rescuing Americans, the mission now included "restoring an orderly government to Grenada."

Constantine Menges wrote, "There were animated discussions about just how many Soviet-Bloc, Cuban, and Libyan hostile personnel were in Grenada. Views differed as to the combat capabilities of the Grenadian and Cuban forces."

The Special Situations Group also discussed how different U.S. ambassadors would handle Moscow, Havana, and other hostile governments with citizens in Grenada. They decided that any captured noncombat personnel would be treated justly and returned as soon as possible.

Vice President Bush asked President Reagan for his thoughts. From a secure remote phone at Augusta National, Reagan said, "Well, if we've got to go in there, we might as well do all that needs to be done."

Ultimately, they decided that by early Tuesday, October 25, the United States would be ready to invade Grenada, rescue Americans, and restore order—all while suffering few, if any, casualties.

A thick binder with a detailed hour-by-hour plan was circulated to everyone at the meeting. There was also a short discussion of the War Powers Resolution, which requires the president to get approval of Congress if he intends to deploy U.S. troops in combat for more than 60 days. There was little question that U.S. combat forces would be in and out in just a couple of days, and the Caribbean troops could provide internal security as the interim government was set up.

The president was also advised that according to Article 51 of the UN Charter and Article 5 of the Rio Treaty, the State Department should inform the UN Security Council members of the operation and the reasoning for it. And since Grenada was still part of the British Commonwealth, the United States should also get the assistance and/or approval of the United Kingdom.

President Reagan had authorized the operation, but many details were still being worked out, and diplomatic solutions were still on the table. The Joint Chiefs of Staff had already been consulting with Admiral Wesley McDonald, the commander in chief of Atlantic Command, for more than a week, even before Bishop's assassination, about how to protect and evacuate Americans from Grenada if things continued to deteriorate. They had to account for six different scenarios, everything from commercial airlines being allowed in to a *coup de main*—a rapid and overwhelming military takeover that ends after a single blow. There was a consensus among the Joint Chiefs that a "well-executed display of U.S. military prowess would convey U.S. determination to protect its vital interests."

General John Vessey, chairman of the Joint Chiefs of Staff, had also contacted Army Major General Richard A. Scholtes, the commander of the newly formed Joint Special Operations Command, to ask for his thoughts about the invasion. By this point, plans for two different versions of the operation were under consideration. Both called for 1,800 troops. The Atlantic Command's initial plan assigned the assault to the 22nd Marine Amphibious Unit (MAU), which would receive air support from Navy jets on the USS *Independence*. Under normal circumstances the Marines' 22nd MAU would have been more than adequate for the operation. An alternate JSOC plan had Army Rangers leading the way, with Navy SEALs and Army Delta Force operators providing specialized recon and evacuation support. The option would mean the Marines would be used as reserves, except for their helicopters. Some Marine choppers would be needed to transport the SEALs and other Special Operators to and from their objectives; others would provide additional airborne firepower. The initial assault would be followed by the Army's 82nd Airborne Division, designated to serve as a mop-up and occupation force until a new government was restored.

Weinberger's reservations were evident during a meeting at the Pentagon on Saturday, where he conveyed his concerns to the

Joint Chiefs, emphasizing the inadequacy of actionable intelligence. Notably, the military planners faced a significant challenge due to the lack of reliable maps. The only available map was a wall-sized enlargement derived from a tourist map, outdated and incomplete, as it predated the construction of the Point Salines airport. The newly added runway was merely penciled in, exacerbating the situation. Compounding these issues, the map's scale was inaccurately calibrated by 1 kilometer, a critical oversight that remained undetected until it was too late.

Weinberger was more hesitant than Shultz, but since it appeared that the president favored the invasion, he also pressed the Joint Chiefs to double the size of the force. "I always had in mind that one of the major problems with our attempt to rescue our hostages in Iran in 1979 was that we sent too few helicopters," Weinberger later wrote.

Around the same time Reagan, Shultz, and McFarlane were making their calls to national security advisors in Washington, Admiral McDonald was convening his own meeting in Norfolk. The key players from all the different branches were mostly unfamiliar with one another, adding an additional undercurrent of tension to the war-planning meeting. Strict secrecy rules imposed by the Joint Chiefs forbade printed materials, forcing all military planning to take place via secure phones or in person. At one point, they ran out of secure phone lines, compelling some planners to scramble off base for suitable pay phones.

Admiral McDonald, a 1946 graduate of the U.S. Naval Academy and an early jet fighter pilot, had a storied career. He led the first strike against North Vietnam after the Gulf of Tonkin incident. By 1983, he commanded the U.S. Atlantic Command, the U.S. Atlantic Fleet, and NATO's Allied Atlantic Command. But despite his extensive knowledge of Navy and Marine combat procedures, he was less familiar with the Air Force and Army, and even less familiar with the Joint Special Operations Command, which was just three years old.

McDonald began the meeting by reviewing the two available options and then opened it up for discussion. The Army representatives pushed for JSOC troops with Rangers, SEALs, and Delta Force operators as the primary assault force, and then the 82nd Airborne would parachute in, stressing their readiness in as little as 18 hours.

Brigadier General Robert Patterson, in charge of the Air Force's Military Airlift Command, hadn't been given sufficient notice to make it to Norfolk. His planes would be crucial for flying the 82nd Airborne and other JSOC units from their U.S. bases to the battlefield. The Air Force would also provide AC-130 Spectre gunships, which would play a critical role in the early stages of the invasion.

A Marine general confidently asserted that the 22nd Marine Amphibious Unit could handle the mission, emphasizing their proximity. They were already en route to Grenada as a precautionary move after Bishop's assassination. However, the conspicuous absence of any 22nd MAU representative at the meeting, like the absence of General Patterson, underscored the fragmented nature of the planning for that option.

After some more consultation Admiral McDonald chose the JSOC option. The military brass in attendance also reached a consensus on the operation's timing. The operation was set to formally start at 0230. JSOC's warriors were trained and equipped to fight in darkness, and McDonald wanted to exploit this advantage.

After the meeting, McDonald called Joint Chiefs Chairman General Vessey to discuss the next steps. Two years before Pearl Harbor, Vessey lied about his age and enlisted in the Minnesota National Guard at 16. By 21, he was a first sergeant who had seen heavy combat in North Africa and was among the first troops to invade Europe. He received a battlefield commission after the 34th Infantry Division entered the beachhead in Anzio, Italy, during World War II. He earned his bachelor's degree while serving, and then the Distinguished Service Cross for his service in Vietnam, where he and his artillery battalion had repelled a larger force of Vietnamese fighters.

Vessey had just returned to the Pentagon from the critical meeting where President Reagan had green-lit the invasion of Grenada. He also conveyed to McDonald his support for using the JSOC invasion force to lead the charge, backed by the 82nd Airborne and the Marines.

At around 1:00 p.m. on Saturday, it was cool and overcast on the golf course in Augusta. The president and his foursome were playing the sixteenth hole, a par 3 nicknamed "Rosebud," known to demand precision off the tee and featuring a prominent pond and a green sloping notably from right to left. It was also where this round of golf would end. Outside the gates, a local man named Charlie Harris had been surveying the situation.

Harris was well acquainted with the grounds of Augusta National. Through high school, he had worked concessions at the Masters. He would also sneak in to scavenge for balls in a pond behind the club's cottages. Harris was nicknamed "Smiley" because he never smiled and wore a trench coat that could conceal a sawed-off shotgun. He was a former lineman, linebacker, and fullback for the semipro Augusta Eagles until he was 38. Football, car wrecks, and bar fights had ruptured his spleen, torn up his knees, given him scars, and broken his nose six times.

Harris had stopped his jacked-up blue Dodge pickup truck on Washington Road, walked to the front, and locked its hubs, activating the truck's four-wheel drive. Charlie Harris had been told the president was at the golf course. Earlier in the day, he'd driven past the club with his sister, Harriet. They recognized one of the Richmond County Sheriff's deputies and asked him, "Mitch, who you got in there?"

"The president's here to play golf," the deputy said.

After that short but informative morning conversation with the deputy, Harris went home and poured himself a drink. He had recently heard reports that U.S. Steel was about to lay off thousands of workers because it was losing business to foreign-made steel. Harris himself was out of work for the first time in 30 years, and he later said he felt bad for all those steelworkers. That's when he remembered what the deputy had said about the president.

"Why don't I just ride up there and see him?" Harris thought to himself as he finished his drink.

His father, a Navy vet and retired Augusta police detective had recently died. Harris coped with his father's death by drinking—a lot. His marriage was also falling apart. He was, by all accounts, a desperate man.

As the president and his group putted out on the sixteenth green, 45-year-old Charlie Harris crashed his truck through Augusta National's gate 3, which was locked. He drove the truck, with a half-empty bottle of tequila in it, toward the pro shop. There, he says, he saw Ronald Reagan.

"I never had any idea of shooting the president. If I'd wanted to kill him, I'd have driven up to him and done it. I just wanted to talk to him. I was protesting our government giving our jobs to foreign people."

"It wasn't to hurt anybody; it was just to get where I needed to get."

He parked the truck, took out his .38, and walked a club chauffeur toward the golf shop at gunpoint. There he let the chauffeur go. And Harris said, "I told him, 'If you look behind my seat in the truck, there's a bottle of tequila, and I'd be pleased if you drank it all.'"

In the golf shop, Harris held six people hostage—four club employees and two White House staffers, one of whom he quickly released and sent to tell the president he wanted to talk.

A golf-shop clerk later told *Golf Digest* that when he saw Harris come in, "He was very agitated and kept saying, 'They don't think I mean business.'"⁵

"I think he [Harris] was stunned he got that far. You could tell he'd been drinking. He said, 'I've lost my job, and I've lost my family, and my daddy's gone, and I want to talk to the president.'"

As the hours passed, Harris started letting some of the hostages leave. He observed helicopters descending on the lush grass behind the clubhouse, black-suited commandos, and sharpshooters set up near the putting green. An authorized history of Augusta National says that Harris held a pistol to the head of a club professional and threatened to shoot off his fingers one at a time if the president wasn't brought to see him.

Among the hostages was Lanny Wiles, who was an advance man for the White House. Wiles told ESPN, "Harris told the remaining hostages his single demand: 'I want to see that son of a bitch on the golf course.'" Harris also pointed his revolver at Wiles, pressing it between his eyes. Wiles commented later, "If you've never been on the wrong end of a .38, it looks about the size of a water pitcher." Wiles told Harris that he didn't want to die.

Reagan made at least two phone calls to the golf shop; some witnesses recalled more. The first call was monitored by the news media. The president said, "This is the president of the United States. This is Ronald Reagan. I understand you want to talk to me. . . . If you are hearing me, won't you tell me what you want?"

Harris thought it could be a taped recording of the president. He hung up without speaking but shouted to the Secret Service agents and police outside, "I'll give you my gun when he shows his face through that door. I've risked my life here. I'm not going to hurt anybody. I just want to talk to the man."

After some time passed, the phone rang a second time, and Wiles answered. "Stand by for Rawhide" (Reagan's Secret Service code name), said the voice on the other end, patchy on a giant early mobile phone. The president called in and attempted to defuse the situation. Wiles said he handed Harris the phone, but Harris couldn't hear the president due to a poor connection and tore the phone off the wall.

By 4:20, two hours in, the president had left the grounds at Augusta National, while the authorities tried to coax Charlie Harris out. The golf shop's TV showed news footage of Reagan leaving the club, trailed by a car filled with Secret Service agents carrying Uzis and wearing boat shoes.

Wiles says he then distracted Harris by talking about drinking. "I don't know about you," Wiles told Harris, "but I could use a stiff drink." Harris then told Wiles to go find them a bottle. Wiles left and found a Secret Service agent instead.

By this point, Harris's ex-wife and mother had arrived to try to convince him to surrender. Some food was also sent into the pro shop, and during that moment, there was a flurry of confusion and the last of the hostages managed to escape.

Harris told *Golf Digest* some years later, "With Reagan gone, I put my gun down and figured I might as well take my punishment." Harris would serve five years in prison for his hostage stunt at Augusta National, and while in prison he found religion and devoted his life to Jesus Christ. He went on to live a full life after his release.

As for President Reagan, it was decided that the group would spend the night in Georgia before flying back to Washington,

D.C., early in the morning. This was done in part to maintain the appearance of normalcy.

After the NSC SSG meeting wrapped up in room 208 of the Old Executive Office Building, Constantine Menges was drafting a memo for McFarlane to send to the president as well as a National Security Defense Directive that would become the official order, required for the Departments of State and Defense and the CIA to begin what would soon be known as Operation Urgent Fury. Drafts of those documents were passed between Ollie North and John Poindexter, an experienced naval officer who had just assumed his new role at the White House as the deputy national security advisor. Menges wrote that he "felt an enormous sense of satisfaction" about the decision.

Menges also pointed out the importance of keeping the operation a secret until it had begun. Late in the afternoon on Saturday, the NSC had received a report that General Hudson Austin wanted to talk to the United States, and the Revolutionary Military Council was going to open the airport and allow commercial planes to land. Poindexter, normally stoic, replied with a jest to the news and said mockingly, "Constantine, tell the State Department to inform Grenada that we will send some people to talk, and that they will arrive early next week."

Just before 5:00 p.m., based on Reagan's decision, the NSC issued an execution order to McDonald and the other branch commands involved. McDonald would then depart Norfolk for Washington, D.C., to meet with General Vessey. They would have just two-and-a-half days to plan the operation. The clock was ticking, and the tension was palpable as they moved closer to executing the high-stakes mission.

## THE MARINE BARRACKS BOMBING IN BEIRUT

Lebanon was already deep in the grip of violence when tragedy struck the U.S. Marines stationed there on October 23, 1983. Hezbollah-linked militants carried out a devastating attack with a truck bomb containing half a kiloton of explosives, detonated at the Marine barracks at Beirut International Airport.

Witnesses saw the truck circle the parking lot to gain speed and, traveling an estimated 60 miles per hour, crash through a barbed wire barrier, go between two sandbagged sentry posts, run through a gate and an iron fence, go over a sewer pipe that had been placed as an obstacle, and hit a four-foot-wide passenger entryway into the lobby of the building with precision.

Because of its speed and mass, the truck was now powerfully wedged into the lobby of the barracks, where its cargo of explosives detonated. The explosion killed 220 Marines and 21 other U.S. service members.

Marine Corps Commandant General Paul Kelley later described the horrific event as the delivery of a 5,000-pound bomb hurtling at 60 miles per hour, a cataclysmic event that unfolded in a mere six seconds. He underscored the tragic irony that the security measures, meticulously calibrated to combat prevalent threats like artillery, rockets, and small arms, had been effective until that fateful moment. For 13 months, not a single Marine, sailor, or soldier under the building's protection had fallen victim to such dangers.

However, Kelley acknowledged the glaring inadequacy of these measures against the unprecedented "kamikaze" attack. Despite exhaustive investigations, no intelligence had forewarned of this novel form of terrorist onslaught.

The president spent more than two hours discussing the Beirut bombing in person with Shultz and McFarlane and by phone with General Kelley before departing Augusta for Washington, D.C. It was pouring down rain Sunday morning when Marine One touched down at the White House just before 9:00 a.m. As President Reagan entered the West Wing, he greeted Secretary Weinberger by saying, "Remind me never to go away again."

Prior to this latest attack, five Marines had already died in three separate incidents. A suicide bomber had struck the U.S. Embassy in April, killing 63 people, including 52 Lebanese and American Embassy employees. In response to these escalating threats, McFarlane had successfully persuaded President Reagan to respond forcefully. The president ultimately authorized the USS *New Jersey* to retaliate with a significant bombardment. According to former Secretary of State Colin Powell, once the naval attack began, the Shiites had assumed that America had taken sides against them. Since they had no way to attack the battleship, they targeted the Marines at the airport.[6]

A year earlier, and at the Lebanese government's request, the United Nations had assembled a multinational force (MNF) to help restore order in Lebanon. Within the Reagan administration, there were significant disagreements regarding the extent of U.S. involvement. The Joint Chiefs had proposed various options, including deploying up to 63,000 U.S. troops to Lebanon to disarm Shiite militias and enforce the peace in regions that were controlled by Syria and Israel. However, President Reagan had opted for a more limited mission, one that wouldn't require congressional approval. He authorized the deployment of around 1,800 Marines, who joined forces with troops from France, Italy, and Britain. Reagan asserted that the Marines' mission was to serve as a peacekeeping force at agreed-upon locations, but they were not to engage in combat.[7]

Following the withdrawal of the Palestine Liberation Organization from Beirut in August 1982, the UN troops returned to their ships offshore. But chaos followed a short time later. The assassination of Lebanese President Bashir Gemayel and the massacre of Palestinian refugees by militias connected to the Maronite Christian Phalange Party led to immediate international support for a second MNF deployment. This is when the intention and scope of U.S. forces started to get murky.

Shortly after the U.S. troops returned to Lebanese territory, Reagan contended that they would now "assist the Lebanese Armed Forces in carrying out their responsibility for ensuring the departure of PLO leaders, officers, and combatants in Beirut from Lebanese territory," and "facilitate the restoration of the sovereignty and authority of the Lebanese Government over the Beirut area."[8] He added, "In no case will our troops stay longer than 30 days."

Secretary of Defense Caspar Weinberger's statement appeared contradictory, as he expressed the need for a multinational force until certain conditions were met, but also emphasized that it was not an open-ended commitment. In his memoir, he wrote that he strongly objected to the deployment, citing the lack of a defined mission for the MNF.[9]

The mission was even more complicated and harder to define after the bombing of the U.S. Marine barracks in Beirut. President Reagan would now have to decide how to proceed in Lebanon, while also having to navigate the crisis in Grenada. Chairman of the Joint Chiefs General John Vessey remarked that retaliating against the terrorists who bombed the Marine barracks would be beneath the dignity of the United States.

Admiral McDonald, accompanied by General Scholtes, had also flown to Washington Sunday morning to brief the Joint Chiefs. The news of the bombing of the Marine barracks at Beirut

International Airport had preceded their arrival. At the Pentagon, McDonald reviewed his notes with Scholtes. In the JCS conference room, known as "The Tank," McDonald presented key targets and the timeline of events.

Marine Corps Commandant General Paul Kelley then asked if he could speak. He implored McDonald and Vessey to give the Marines a larger role in the operation. "The Marines must land on the island of Grenada, or you will have destroyed the Marine Corps," Kelley stated emphatically. Scholtes, who was seated behind the principals, was taken aback by Kelley's statement. While Scholtes had envisioned the Marines as a floating reserve, he was even more surprised when Vessey signed off on Kelley's request.

The decision-making process was likely influenced by both emotion and tactical calculations. Shultz and Weinberger had previously advocated dispatching a more robust force than McDonald's initial recommendation. Vessey, who had a close relationship with Weinberger, may have already received the secretary's directive to increase the force. Additionally, intelligence indicated that the People's Revolutionary Armed Forces were mobilizing, suggesting a need for a more substantial landing force.

Under the revised plan, McDonald proposed an amphibious landing by the Marines on the beaches at Grand Anse, while the Rangers seized the airfields at Pearls and Point Salines, and special operations forces targeted key locations. Vessey pressed McDonald to keep the operation as simple as possible. To illustrate his point, he drew a line across the island north of Saint George's. North of this boundary, the Marines would operate, while south of it would be the domain of the Joint Special Operations Command. McDonald accepted this suggestion and incorporated it into the operational plan.

During the initial discussions on Grenada, President Reagan actively engaged with the NSC staff, demonstrating what Menges describes as a genial yet effective demeanor. The president sought honest viewpoints on the operation. Despite the somber backdrop of the Beirut terror attack, Reagan remained sensible and energetic, meticulously weighing the implications of Beirut for the Grenada decision.

Meanwhile, Under Secretary Lawrence Eagleburger, known for being Henry Kissinger's right-hand man during the first half of the 1970s, started playing a larger role in the Grenada planning. He and Menges were waiting in Bud McFarlane's office with the other members of the NSC, focusing specifically on Lebanon, and met with the president.

Recognizing the need to bolster international support, Menges proposed three additional tasks once Reagan reaffirmed the decision on Grenada. First, he believed it was imperative to persuade friendly nations in Latin America and Europe of the necessity and correctness of the action. Given potential condemnation from countries like Mexico and certain European Social Democrats, Menges stressed the importance of State Department assistance in elucidating the details of internal repression and external subversion emanating from Grenada.

Furthermore, Menges suggested that either Eagleburger or Fred Ikle oversee the deployment of government film crews alongside the troops. These crews would document the liberation of political prisons, conduct interviews with democratic leaders held captive, and reveal the clandestine military installations in Grenada. Menges emphasized the likelihood of communist propaganda distorting the truth, underscoring the importance of countering such falsehoods with factual evidence.

Second, Menges emphasized the importance of what he termed "the humane deinstitutionalization of the communist dictatorship." This entailed instructing all combat forces to ensure proper treatment for all prisoners and former Grenadian officials, including the secret police and military. It was crucial to guarantee their safety from torture or physical abuse by vengeful Grenadians.

Additionally, the U.S. military needed to implement a system for photographing, fingerprinting, and interrogating all prisoners from the communist regime. This would facilitate the identification of key leaders and differentiate them from most rank-and-file members, enabling the release of the latter at the earliest opportunity.

Only the top communist leaders should be detained, and they should be afforded a fair trial using the legal procedures customary in the former British colonies of the Eastern Caribbean. It was imperative to demonstrate to individuals associated with communist regimes worldwide, such as those in Nicaragua, Angola, and Afghanistan, that defeat would not result in abuse, torture, or prolonged imprisonment. Grenada could serve as a positive example of reconciliation following liberation from communist dictatorship.

Third, Menges proposed ensuring that the interim government of Grenada comprise respected individuals genuinely committed to democracy. Allowing the replacement of a communist dictatorship with an anti-communist one would constitute a significant error. Menges noted that Eagleburger offered little response, and Motley appeared to struggle to grasp the concept of "humane deinstitutionalization of the dictatorship."

Once they went back inside the Situation Room with the president, another State Department official explained that their diplomatic efforts to get American and British citizens off the island had failed. One State Department official said they "kept turning over every stone to get 100% assurance [that they could safely evacuate everyone], but we could not get it. That's when the decision to take action was made."

An intelligence report, surreptitiously provided by a CIA case officer embedded within the American delegation, revealed the distress of medical students on the island, urgently expressing their fear and desire to evacuate.[10] Reagan, recognizing the gravity of the situation, read the report aloud during a Sunday afternoon meeting on Grenada in the Situation Room, ensuring that all present were informed of the imminent danger faced by the students.

Simultaneously, reports from the Defense Intelligence Agency indicated alarming developments at the Richmond Hill Prison in Saint George's, with Grenadian security forces allegedly instructed to execute all prisoners in the event of invasion. Unconfirmed accounts also surfaced suggesting the execution of British citizens and other foreign nationals.

As tensions escalated, dissatisfaction with the oppressive Grenadian regime spread, with reports of militia members failing to report to their assigned units. Christopher Lehman, a special assistant for national security affairs, recalled Reagan's decisive response: "There are Americans there, and they are in danger. We are going!" With Reagan's directive, American troops were committed to overt combat for the first time since the Vietnam War. Intelligence from the Joint Chiefs of Staff indicated the Revolutionary Military Council had made preparations to mobilize popular resistance against a foreign invasion.

Amid the escalating crisis, leaks regarding the diversion of U.S. naval assets to Grenada emerged, prompting concern within the White House. Acting Press Secretary Larry Speakes highlighted the disturbing nature of these leaks, attributing them to sources with potential ties to the CIA. General Vessey, concerned about the operation's risks, requested a private meeting with Reagan and top-ranking representatives from each government agency. During this meeting, the potential dangers for special operations forces and the political risks for the president in case of failure were candidly discussed.

Following extensive discussions with President Reagan and the National Security Council, preparations for the operation continued late into the evening, as key personnel awaited further directives outside the Situation Room. Menges wrote that Oliver North was still pessimistic about the operation and thought it would get canceled out of concern that it would be perceived as retaliation for the Beirut bombing.

News of leaks regarding the diversion of the USS *Independence* battle group and the 22nd Marine Amphibious Unit, originally destined for Lebanon, began to circulate. Acting White House Press Secretary Larry Speakes deemed these leaks as "the most disturbing element" of the Grenada invasion. In a memo addressed to Chief of Staff James Baker, Speakes recounted an encounter with correspondent Bill Plante, who inquired about the aircraft carrier's change of plans on October 23.[11] Plante hinted that his information came from individuals associated with or formerly part of the CIA.

Similarly, Bob Schieffer, CBS's State Department correspondent, approached the National Security Council with a similar inquiry. These inquiries underscored the alarming breach of security surrounding the Grenada operation, prompting heightened concern within the White House.

On that Sunday, Major General Norman Schwarzkopf was busy cleaning the weekend's catch by a lake near his headquarters at Fort Stewart, Georgia. With a bounty of bass at his disposal, he couldn't resist the opportunity to treat his family to a promised feast of beer-battered fish. He was breading the fish, shaking it in a paper bag, when the phone rang. It was the director of operations at Forces Command at Fort McPherson, near Atlanta, Georgia, General Dick Graves.

"What have you got lined up for the next few weeks?" General Graves asked.

"What's this all about?" General Schwarzkopf replied.

"You're being considered for a very important mission, and the Pentagon asked me to find out your plans," Graves responded.

General Schwarzkopf informed Graves that he had planned to be on base for the next few weeks.

Graves said, "Okay. I'll call you back around six o'clock."

Schwarzkopf wrote in his book, *It Doesn't Take a Hero*, that he "felt both curious and anxious" about the call. The previous day had seen the brutal bombing of the U.S. Marine barracks in Beirut by terrorists, leaving him with the inkling that a swift military retaliation might be in the cards. He says he tried to get his mind back on cooking, but now that was impossible. Instead of a relaxed dinner, Schwarzkopf now had to eat quickly so he could start to pack. At exactly six o'clock the phone rang.

"How quickly can you get up here to Atlanta?" General Graves asked. Schwarzkopf needed just a few hours. "All right. You're going on a military operation. You'll be away for about three weeks," General Graves said.

Since his home phone was not secure, Schwarzkopf didn't ask any follow-up questions. He laid out both his summer and winter uniforms and then drove to Fort Stewart so he could find out the details of the operation from Graves over a secure phone. Schwarzkopf wrote that he could barely hear Graves because the connection on the secure phone was awful. But he was able to determine that he would be going to Grenada.

He met with the assistant commanders of 24th Mechanized Infantry to inform them of his mission. Schwarzkopf then drove back home and threw his summer battle dress uniforms into his duffle bag and put his winter uniforms away. At nine o'clock a car pulled up to take Schwarzkopf to the airfield. He kissed his children good-bye and took his wife, Brenda, by the hands. The general remembered that she looked scared.

"Are you going to be in any danger?" the general's wife asked quietly.

"I'm not going to Beirut," Schwarzkopf said, "but I can't tell you any more than that."

She then kissed him good-bye.

His leadership would prove invaluable over the next few days.

A team of Navy SEALs along with Air Force combat controllers were air-dropped from C-130s into the ocean about three dozen miles off the southeast coast of Grenada, with specially outfitted 18-foot Boston Whalers, to perform reconnaissance on the coastal areas around Point Salines. But the mission was doomed, even before it started.

The intelligence reporting was so deficient that Air Force planners failed to realize that Grenada doesn't observe daylight savings time. In addition, because of its geographical location, Grenada is one hour ahead of the Eastern Time Zone, so the sun sets about an hour before it sets on the East Coast of the United States. And for some reason, perhaps because of the expanded role of the State Department in the operation, the SEALs' plans were drawn up using the wrong local time instead of Zulu, also known as Greenwich Mean Time, which is standard operating procedure. The drop was originally supposed to happen at 4 p.m. EST, but it got pushed back two hours. Thunderstorms were already developing in the area; the seas were building at six to eight feet, and now the SEALs would be dropping into total darkness.

Master Chief Johnny Walker, leading the jump in the first C-130, anticipated a routine drop into calm seas and light winds. But as he leapt into the stormy skies, the reality shattered expectations. Hit by a gust, he plummeted into the raging waves, struggling against his inflated parachute dragging him underwater. In a desperate fight for survival, he cut himself free and swam toward where his boat should have been, only to find it sunk. Walker's version of the story is recounted in Orr Kelly's book *Never Fight Fair: Navy SEALs' Stories of Combat and Adventure*.[12]

Amid the chaos, the USS *Sprague* sent out a recovery boat, but Walker, unable to locate his team or the rescue vessel, resolved to swim to the frigate. Clinging to a cargo net, he and another SEAL finally found refuge onboard, discovering that they were among the last to be rescued. Tragically, four SEALs, seasoned professionals with official Navy roles unrelated to their actual clandestine work, were lost: Hull Technician 1st Class Stephen L. Morris, 31, of South Plainfield, New Jersey; Senior Chief Engineman Robert R. Schamberger, 42, of Oakland, New Jersey; Machinist Mate 1st Class Kenneth J. Butcher, 31, of West Islip, New York; and Quartermaster 1st Class Kevin E. Lundberg, 32, of Kodiak, Alaska.

Shortly after Operation Urgent Fury, Kenneth Butcher's widow went to Grenada, hoping that her husband had survived. During an interview she claims she heard about a "fisherman who said he saw four guys in wetsuits come out of the water, and then two days later he saw four bodies being thrown into the water. So, we would like to think they made it, 'cause there was a boat smashed up on the beach. We would like to think the four of them got in that boat, made it to shore, got someplace, and were captured. And they're, you know, gonna come back."[13]

Captain Robert A. Gormly, the SEAL Team Six commander, monitored the ill-fated drop by radio from the United States. He never learned exactly what went wrong. "I can only surmise that the four men couldn't get rid of their parachute canopies, were dragged through the water facedown and drowned," he wrote in his 1998 autobiography.

Undeterred by setbacks, the surviving SEALs and combat controllers embarked once more on the *Sprague*'s Boston Whaler, braving rough seas for the journey to Grenada. Despite plans to deploy a Zodiac upon nearing the shore, the need never arose.

Approaching within 30 miles of Grenada, they encountered what appeared to be a Grenadian patrol boat, forcing the SEALs to alter their plans, reduce their speed, and divert course. However, the small Whaler was taking on water after an engine stalled, forcing them to return to the *Sprague*.

They made another attempt the following night. The *Sprague* repositioned closer to shore as the recon party set out once more. They encountered yet another suspected patrol boat. Again, engine troubles plagued their efforts, leaving them adrift as the invasion hour drew near. Eventually, they were rescued at dawn without the crucial intelligence they tried so hard to get. Without firm intel on a good location for an amphibious landing site, the entire force would have to be flown in by plane or helicopter. Plus, Operation Urgent Fury had already claimed its first lives—and it hadn't officially started yet.

### Monday, October 24

Early on Monday, October 24, the NSC gathered for another CPPG meeting, finding solace in the fact that although the students remained surrounded, their situation remained unchanged. The prospects for rescue operations still appeared feasible. Menges wrote that when it came to highly sensitive information about the operation, sometimes ignorance was bliss for NSC staffers. Many staffers preferred to remain in the dark when it came to information outside of their direct responsibility to avoid being the source of an unauthorized leak to the media.

Constantine Menges's direct responsibility on that Monday was to join the NSC's legal counsel on an Operation Urgent Fury briefing for Attorney General William French Smith. National Security Advisor Bud McFarlane wanted to give the attorney general a heads-up and to make sure he agreed with the NSC's interpretation of the War Powers Act. Menges said he found himself struck by the grandeur of the attorney general's office during their meeting, noting its impressive wooden decor and size. Secretary Weinberger and General Vessey had determined that a small circle, including McFarlane and Shultz, should be privy to the evolving military plans in advance.

Schwarzkopf arrived at Norfolk early Monday morning. Admiral McDonald had called a meeting to bring all the key players together for the first time. Vice Admiral Joseph Metcalf III, the three-star commander of the Navy's Second Fleet, was also at the 7:30 a.m. meeting at Pier 25. One day before, Admiral Metcalf had a surprise visitor show up behind his house on base. It was McDonald's chief of staff, who said his boss had been calling all over looking for Metcalf. "You better get yourself over to the compound because you're it," the guest told Metcalf. He had been selected to lead the all-service task force that would invade Grenada.

Metcalf's combat assignment did not come as quite the same surprise to him that it was to Schwarzkopf. He and McDonald knew each other well; Metcalf served under McDonald's command. The Second Fleet's main responsibility was the western Atlantic from the North Pole to the Caribbean. One of Metcalf's Second Fleet roles was to also serve as the commander of an established multiservice unit known as Joint Task Force 120 that could be activated in times of crisis to execute emergency military and rescue missions.

Metcalf's staff had been monitoring Grenada's political turmoil for a week. He was aware that McDonald's command was working on a secret intervention plan—just in case. Metcalf was not yet personally involved in Urgent Fury, though he could have been. "My rationale was that I wanted to avoid being wedded to, or emotionally identified with, the development of a particular plan," Metcalf later wrote in a chapter for a textbook on military decision-making.

Metcalf was the son of a wealthy wool manufacturing family in Holyoke, Massachusetts. Still, he joined the Navy in 1946 at the age of 19 instead of the family business. After a year, he won an appointment to the U.S. Naval Academy. He was commissioned an ensign in 1951 as the Korean War was settling into a stalemate. He rose to command positions during the Vietnam War, and by 1975 he was commanding the Navy forces covering Saigon when South Vietnam fell. He was described by his peers as a "rock-hard, salt-stained, dyed-in-the-wool Surface Warrior." His personal credo was adopted from a famous quote by Admiral Chester Nimitz, "When you are in command, *command!*"

On Sunday, October 23, Metcalf got his orders to take command of Task Force 120 and invade Grenada by dawn the next Tuesday. He got a quick briefing on the invasion plan from Atlantic Command. In general, he liked what he heard about the Marines being involved and the Marines and the Army having clearly defined areas of operation. He was much less enthusiastic about the involvement of Special Forces, but he accepted that was a decision that had been made at the Joint Chiefs level. His overriding concern was time.

Schwarzkopf wrote that he got a reception that made him feel "about as welcome as a case of the mumps." When he landed in Atlanta the night before to meet General Graves at the small Army terminal at Charlie Brown Airport, Schwarzkopf recalled that his "briefing was sketchy." He heard something about the government of Grenada being overthrown in a military coup and hundreds of American medical students were being held captive. He was told, "The Navy is preparing to launch a major operation . . . and a lot of Army forces are going to be involved." Graves briefed Schwarzkopf about how the special operations units and one or perhaps two Ranger battalions would be going in along with the 82nd Airborne. "Washington wants to make sure that the Navy uses them correctly," Graves said.

"Hold it," Schwarzkopf shot back, "It doesn't sound as if I'm exactly going to be welcome."

"As a matter of fact, you're not," said Graves, whose name, according to Schwarzkopf, matched his gloomy presence as he winced and said, "[T]he Navy doesn't like the fact that you're being sent. "But," Graves added, holding up a finger, "you have the support of the highest people in Washington. If the Navy gives you a hard time, just let us know and we'll get it straightened out."

Schwarzkopf admitted that he had heard of Grenada but couldn't find it on a map. Schwarzkopf and Metcalf were an odd couple in every sense. At six-foot-three and more than 230 pounds, the Army general was nicknamed "The Bear." He towered over the shorter and leaner Navy admiral.

Metcalf wanted to level things with Schwarzkopf, so to speak, by turning their initial conversation into a cross-examination. Then, just to be sure he got the message, McDonald took Schwarzkopf aside for a preemptive attitude adjustment. Schwarzkopf wrote in his memoir that Metcalf immediately started firing off questions in a sharp New England accent about what he expected to contribute to the operation. Then Admiral McDonald arrived, and everyone went to a briefing room.

After being greeted with mild hostility by Metcalf, and while everyone was getting settled, Admiral McDonald walked up to Schwarzkopf and said, "Now, for chrissakes, try and be helpful, won't you? We've got a tough job to do, and we don't need the Army giving us a hard time."

Schwarzkopf replied, "Sir, I'm here to help in any way I can. I served two years at Pacific Command under Admiral Weisner and Admiral Long, and I understand how the Navy works. I have no intention of being disruptive." A couple of other Army generals were present—Major General Edward Trobaugh, commander of the 82nd Airborne, and Major General Dick Scholtes, JSOC commander; but Schwarzkopf said Admiral McDonald singled him out.

The invasion was scheduled for two o'clock the following morning, just 19 hours away from that moment. This would be the Pentagon brass's final planning conference. At the end of the long table was a copy of a large tourist map of the island. Grenada, which looks like a football and spans approximately 10 miles from east to west and 25 miles from north to south, has a few sandy beaches, but most of the coast is dominated by rugged, mountainous jungle that rises abruptly from the sea.

Admiral McDonald started by cautioning everyone, "Before we get into the operational plan, everyone should bear in mind that we won't have to carry it out." Diplomatic efforts were still underway, and McDonald believed there was still a chance the RMC would cave under pressure and allow the State Department to evacuate the Americans on Grenada. Across the conference table, a representative from the State Department nodded in concurrence with the admiral's assessment.

Representatives from the CIA also attended this meeting. General Scholtes reported the loss of the SEALs who were sent on the recon mission to the coast near Point Salines earlier that morning. Some of the commanders, including General Scholtes, now wanted to consider postponing the operation for 24 hours so a suitable amphibious landing spot could be found. It was also still unclear, at this point, in what condition they'd find the runway at the Point Salines Airport. Based on his experience, General

Scholtes knew it would be much safer for the Air Force's transport planes, carrying the Rangers and 82nd Airborne, to land and off-load the troops. The weather conditions around Grenada had already proved how dangerous jumping into the battle could be.

The State Department representative protested loudly and called the RMC a "third rate, lightly armed and poorly trained adversary." He also added that such a delay might unnerve the governments participating in the Caribbean Peacekeeping Force.

Admiral McDonald was also firmly against the idea, and he left little to no room for negotiation. "I can't believe what I'm hearing around this table. All you're going to face is a bunch of Grenadians. They're going to fall apart the minute they see our combat power. Why are we making such a big deal of this?"

The Grenadian army consisted of as many as 2,000 active duty troops and a few thousand more in reserve. But the military commanders responsible for executing the operation were assured, "When the Grenadian army sees that we're Americans, they'll give up." Some of the commanders pressed for more information about the roughly 800 Cuban construction workers at Point Salines—who had had military training and were armed. "Don't worry," said the briefers again.

The plan called for the Army Rangers to drive to the Cuban compound and announce, "We are here to reinstall the legitimate government of Grenada. You will not be hurt. Please stay here while we get this thing over with." A thought kept running through Schwarzkopf's mind. "How do we know the Cubans aren't going to fight?"

Metcalf later recalled hearing very optimistic intelligence estimates predicting that the mission would be "a piece of cake." He also wrote that his own subordinates were "extremely confident" and exuded "a distinct air of bravado." But Metcalf had his own doubts, as did the other combat commanders. Trobaugh, the 82nd Airborne commander, was stunned by the absence of more formal briefings with specific intelligence, logistics, and other info. The meeting was instead described as a "freewheeling discussion." Trobaugh worried that the plan was too big, given the footprint of the initial incursion force, the rapidly approaching deadline, and the obvious remaining gaps of coordination between the branches that still needed to be bridged.

McDonald refused to delay the operation for another day, but he ultimately postponed H-hour from 2:00 a.m. to 5:00 a.m. so the SEALs could attempt to take another look at Point Salines. The operational plan was also expanded once again to allow for a bigger role for the members of the military operation.

But the additional changes and the delay required the special operations forces and Rangers to land at dawn instead of in the dark as had been planned. One of JSOC's massive tactical advantages, fighting in the dark, had been mitigated because of a lack of intel. And that's if everything progressed according to plan.

The next thing Schwarzkopf knew, he found himself on an airplane bound for Barbados, accompanied by the rest of the task force. The aircraft was filled with personnel, all bracing themselves for what lay ahead. Touching down in Barbados in the midafternoon, it was evident that news of potential U.S. military action had spread. The airport was abuzz with press activity. Admiral Metcalf instructed everyone to remain on the airplane while they awaited helicopters to ferry them to their ships off the coast of Grenada. After a brief wait, two large Navy helicopters arrived, and they promptly boarded, setting off toward the sea.

Observing his fellow officers during the journey, Schwarzkopf noted a palpable sense of disbelief that they were en route to combat. Many harbored skepticism about the likelihood of engaging in combat. After an hour or so, a small vessel emerged on the horizon. It was the USS *Guam*, designated as Admiral Metcalf's flagship for the operation. As they approached, Schwarzkopf dispatched one of his officers to procure seasickness pills.

By late afternoon, they had descended below deck to freshen up for dinner. In the admiral's mess, adorned with a single long table covered in a pristine white tablecloth, they began their meal with a bowl of soup, followed by turkey as the main course. And then Admiral Metcalf's chief of staff entered the mess and said matter-of-factly, "It's a go." There was a stunned silence. "It's a go," he repeated. "We're going. H-hour has been bumped back one hour—it's a go at 0500. Everyone sat for a moment in disbelief, poking at their food.

As they started to leave the room one by one, Schwarzkopf recalled finding himself alone, his thoughts swirling contemplating the gravity of the impending mission. With no immediate tasks to attend to, he lingered, finishing his meal and attempting to process the weight of the situation. Eventually, he made his way upstairs to the command center and stood behind Metcalf on the bridge. There, he watched as directives poured in from Norfolk and Marine commanders, each issuing their terse last-minute orders to their units.

Schwarzkopf looked out into the darkness enveloping the *Guam*'s flight deck, and he suddenly realized that within a day, American forces would be engaged in war. Schwarzkopf was having second thoughts about whether the United States should be sending troops to Grenada. Were they committed to another war that the American public wouldn't support? He had to remind himself that he'd thought this all through when he'd come home from Vietnam and decided to remain in the military. His job was not to question the judgment of our leaders or the wisdom of our mission. His duty was to help make sure it got carried out with a minimum loss of American lives. He said a prayer and went back below deck to get some rest.

Later that afternoon, McFarlane asked Menges to update the public briefing materials and ensure that the national security advisor and the president were equipped with all the information they would need to address congressional leaders and the media. Menges felt apprehensive about the potential for bipartisan backlash from Capitol Hill leadership, who would be briefed that night. It would only take one member of Congress to derail the Grenada operation by leaking information to the media.

President Reagan convened two additional meetings with the Joint Chiefs. During these meetings, each member of the Joint Chiefs reiterated their views on the operation, unanimously agreeing that while resorting to force was not ideal, the circumstances on the island left no alternative but to rescue the medical students. The JCS assured the president that the operation would be successful.

Around 7:30 that night, McFarlane, Poindexter, North, and Menges convened for a final review in the Situation Room. McFarlane relayed the reactions of congressional leaders briefed earlier: Speaker Tip O'Neill and House Majority Whip James Wright expressed understanding and support, while Senate Democratic Majority Leader Robert Byrd opposed the action and Senate Republican Leader Howard Baker deemed it "bad politics." House Republican Leader Robert Michel was notably supportive.

McFarlane expressed surprise at Baker's lack of support and O'Neill's tacit approval. Contemplating how to garner public support, McFarlane stressed the importance of truthfulness about the need to rescue the students and emphasized the positive outcomes of restoring democracy and ending communist rule. He then assigned several team members to brief members of the House and Senate Foreign Relations Committees that night.

Later that evening, the JCS reconvened with the president in the upstairs residential area of the White House, this time joined by the majority and minority leaders of the House and Senate. General Vessey briefed the congressional leaders on the final plan, and although some appeared uneasy about the operation, no one offered any alternative.

After the congressional leaders left, President Reagan posed two questions to General Vessey.[14] First, he inquired about the critical decision times for executing and potentially calling off the operation if necessary. Vessey explained that if the landings were to proceed as scheduled, he would need to contact the Pentagon immediately after their meeting and provide the prearranged code word. However, the president retained the authority to call off the operation until just a few hours before the landings.

Regarding the second question: "How did the General plan to spend his final hours before the first landings on Grenada?" Vessey outlined his plan for the final hours before the first landings in Grenada. He stated that once he sent the message to the Pentagon to proceed, he intended to go home and get some rest. Vessey emphasized that the mission had been entrusted to the operational commander, who possessed the necessary forces and had the full support of the secretary of defense, the president, and the Joint Chiefs of Staff. If additional assistance were required, the operational commander would request it. Otherwise, there was little the president or Vessey could do until the troops had landed, unless the president decided to call off the operation. In response, President Reagan indicated that he would also retire for the night and await the first reports in the morning.

There was a sense among the JCS and the administration that, despite the incredibly short timeline, they had crossed every *t* and dotted every *i*. But the commander in chief had decided to intentionally ignore one key and very personal detail of the operation. And he would eventually have to apologize profusely for doing so.

CHAPTER 7

# The Special Relationship

*"This is democracy and our island, and the very worst thing for democracy would be if we failed now."*

—U.K. Prime Minister Margaret Thatcher, while speaking to President Ronald Reagan about the Falkland Islands, May 31, 1982

## THATCHER'S 1967 U.S. TRIP

On February 23, 1967, a 41-year-old Margaret Thatcher landed in the United States as a guest of the State Department. She was participating in an international exchange program and was still a relatively unknown member of Parliament. But anyone with a discerning eye for talent could see she was a star ready to rise in the Conservative Party. Thatcher would travel America for six full weeks, stopping briefly in several major cities. Her husband, Denis Thatcher, accompanied her while paying his own way.

MP Thatcher's itinerary had her crisscrossing America at a feverish pace.[1] After spending a few days in Washington meeting with movers and shakers, she would depart by train and head to Wilmington, Delaware, then fly to Miami and Atlanta. Next was a stop in Houston, and then on to San Francisco followed by Los Angeles. After a day in Los Angeles, she took off for Omaha, Nebraska, before she went to Chicago. From Chicago she went to Boston. And then from Boston to New York, from which she would eventually depart and head back home to London. Her stops were marked by meetings with American leaders and politicians.

She did all of this while the United States was in the throes of significant social and political upheaval. The Vietnam War continued to escalate, with protests becoming increasingly vocal and widespread. Martin Luther King Jr. led antiwar demonstrations, emphasizing the conflict's moral implications. The space race was also in full swing, as NASA worked toward the goal of landing a man on the moon. The Beatles had just released their sonically saturated and groundbreaking album *Sgt. Pepper's Lonely Hearts Club Band*, which quickly became a soundtrack of the counterculture movement. Meanwhile, *Bonnie and Clyde* had just premiered in movie theaters, shocking audiences with its graphic violence and antiestablishment themes. The streets were about to be buzzing with the energy of the Summer of Love. Thousands of young people flocked to San Francisco, embracing the ideals of peace, free love, and happiness.

Thatcher was traveling to San Francisco for different reasons. She visited the Kaiser Foundation Hospital, a local high school, KQED-TV, and the University of California at Berkeley. There, she met with professors and held scholarly discussions on the ins and outs of the New Deal and the Marshall Plan, public finance, taxation, Keynesian economics, and government interventionism.

The trip had a great impact on her. Most importantly it reinforced her belief in free-market principles and entrepreneurism. Her journey left her with an abiding sense of the energy fueled by the openness of the people she met in the United States and her cohorts on her trip. Her admiration for America's politics were now evident. A report from a State Department official in San Francisco stated that Thatcher "was very enthusiastic about her visit to the Bay Area. . . . She was one of the most enthusiastic grantees the program officer has had the pleasure of working with."

Newly elected Governor Reagan's California was thriving. And while he and "Maggie" Thatcher wouldn't meet until 1975, the seeds of their deep political friendship were sown during Thatcher's 1967 visit—especially over the four days she spent in California.

Governor Reagan was fully immersed in his duties as the freshly inaugurated leader of California. Having taken office just two months prior, Reagan was already making headlines as a conservative reformer. He focused on shrinking the state's budget by cutting California's bloated welfare programs, advocating for stricter requirements and reduced benefits to combat what he saw as systemic abuse.

Reagan's commitment to law and order also saw him take a tough stance against the burgeoning student protests at universities like UC Berkeley. He famously clashed with the university administration and student body, deploying the National Guard to quell demonstrations and restore order, which garnered national attention and solidified his reputation as a firm, no-nonsense governor. It is hard to imagine that Thatcher did not read about the governor's efforts in the *San Francisco Chronicle* or the *Los Angeles Times* while she visited the state or saw him in a television news report or two.

Amid these political activities, Reagan maintained a charismatic public presence. He leveraged his Hollywood background to connect with voters, often appearing on television and at public events, where he articulated his vision for California's future with his signature blend of charm and conviction.

One time Reagan was talking about the campus protesters with the media and described them this way: "I was picketed by some youngsters a couple of days ago who had signs that said, 'make love not war.' The trouble is they didn't look like they were capable of doing either. This fella that was doing the talking, he had a haircut like Tarzan, he walked like Jane and smelled like Cheetah."

## THE FIRST MEETING

Margaret Thatcher and Ronald Reagan likely met for the first time in July 1972 when Reagan, then the governor of California, visited Europe as an emissary of President Richard Nixon. Nixon initially harbored suspicions that Governor Reagan might challenge him for the Republican nomination, but instead Reagan threw his full support behind Nixon and campaigned on his behalf. Reagan had clearly impressed Nixon and earned his respect. Governor Ronald Reagan had run for reelection in California and secured a decisive victory two years earlier, reinforcing his popularity and political influence. During his second term, and before Watergate, Nixon frequently called upon Reagan to represent America on the global stage.

Reagan's first significant diplomatic mission took place in October 1971, when Nixon sent Reagan and the First Lady of California, Nancy, on a tour of several key Asian allies: Japan, Thailand, Singapore, South Korea, and Taiwan. The primary objective of the tour was to reassure these nations about the stability of their alliances with the United States in the face of Nixon's upcoming historic meeting with Communist China. There were widespread concerns among America's Asian allies about the potential implications of this diplomatic rapprochement with China on their security and bilateral relations with the United States. Reagan's task was to convey Nixon's commitment to maintaining strong ties and support for these nations, despite the new diplomatic developments.

In a 2014 article published in *New Criterion*, Henry Kissinger said he regularly briefed Governor Reagan on international developments at President Nixon's request.[2] Kissinger once recalled a particularly memorable moment during the 1973 Yom Kippur War. The United States faced a delicate situation: It needed to resupply Israel's military without provoking the Arab nations that had not yet entered the conflict. During one briefing, Kissinger shared this dilemma with Reagan.

Reagan's response was both witty and insightful: "I have a suggestion," Reagan told Kissinger, "Tell them you will replace all the planes that the Egyptians said they have shot down." This clever idea would have effectively tripled the Israeli Air Force, as the Egyptian Air Force at that time had a notorious reputation for claiming they shot down far more planes than they had actually had.

Kissinger had also fostered a relationship with Thatcher that started when he was the national security advisor. His wife had just met Thatcher, and Kissinger recalled her saying to him, "You have to meet Margaret Thatcher." Prime Minister Edward Heath was a friend of Kissinger's, but he believed Heath would be suspicious if Kissinger requested to meet with Thatcher, who was then the U.K. Education Minister. Heath was a firm believer that United States–United Kingdom contact should operate under the protocols of the Special Relationship, and a meeting between the White House national security advisor and the U.K. education secretary would be highly unusual.

So instead, he had his personal contacts in England arrange for a private dinner. Later, when she became leader of the opposition, Kissinger recalled one of the first things she said to him was, "I'm not going to fight for the middle. I'm going to fight for my convictions and let the middle worry about itself," adding, "If this goes on, then everybody fights for the middle. We will destroy democracy because leaders will become indistinguishable. And it would be far preferable if each side stated its views clearly and then let the people decide, rather than have a confused mélange of ideas."

On the Reagans' 1972 trip to Europe, Prime Minister Edward Heath hosted a luncheon at 10 Downing Street for the American delegation and other select guests. The Thatcher Archives contain a copy of the menu from this luncheon, meaning Thatcher was most likely there and saved the menu as a memento. Reagan's visit to London was part of a broader European tour aimed at strengthening transatlantic relations. As they gathered around the table in the historic residence of the British prime minister, the atmosphere was a blend of formality and camaraderie. The menu featured a selection of refined dishes, reflecting the importance of the occasion and the distinguished guests present.

Reagan's and Thatcher's formal political partnership began just a few years later, when Thatcher became the leader of the Conservative Party in 1975. Their first one-to-one meeting came in April 1975, at the House of Commons. Reagan was 65 and Thatcher was 50. Thatcher's star was beginning to shine in the world of British politics, and she was now the formidable leader of the opposition. But for many, it was still hard to imagine that she could become Britain's first female prime minister. Reagan was now the former governor of California. His ascension to the White House was by no means a certainty.

Despite the age gap, Reagan and Thatcher bonded instantly. A Reuters article said they were completing each other's sentences by the end of a 90-minute meeting that was supposed to have lasted only for 15.[3] They discovered they had both found validation for their convictions in the works of Friedrich Hayek, at that time a long-forgotten theorist even among conservatives.

Afterward, Reagan wrote a thank you letter to Thatcher on April 30, the same day the U.S. Embassy fell in Saigon and Admiral Joseph Metcalf commanded the Navy fleet off the coast nearby.[4] Reagan opened his letter by writing that he chose "a dark day" to write a belated thank you letter for her recent hospitality in London. Reagan continued, "for . . . somehow the shadows seem to have lengthened as news of Saigon's surrender has just arrived."

Reagan wrote that he and Mrs. Reagan hoped that Thatcher would accept some upcoming speaking engagements in

California, so they could "repay the hospitality." Reagan closed his letter with, "Please know, you have an enthusiastic supporter out here in the 'colonies.'"

They met again in November 1978 at the House of Commons, by which time Reagan had run unsuccessfully for the Republican nomination against the sitting president, Gerald Ford, but his Republican convention concession speech four years earlier had elevated him into contention for the 1980 GOP nomination.

The day after Thatcher's conservatives secured a victory in the 1979 elections, a British newspaper, the *Guardian*, wrote:

> Mrs. Thatcher evokes powerful devotion and equally powerful antipathy. But her place in history is booked already. By luck—but also by the spunk to stand— she came to the head of a traumatised, humiliated party. Putting that party together again was no mean achievement: moulding it to her own image over four years in the wilderness showed grit and fire and the feat—luck or no—of becoming Britain's first woman Prime Minister is one, whatever the sisters may say, that can only change perceptions of what women can aspire to throughout the democratic West. What ever else she is. Mrs. Thatcher is not the Statutory Woman.
>
> But of course the Conservatives did not fight and win this poll on a feminist liberation ticket. After almost a full Parliament of dour, struggling Labour Government they offered a policy sea change. For the State read the individual. "Substantial" tax cuts. Something done about unions. A blend of traditional Conservative values plus a strong pitch to those simply bored by the long, slow thrash against National economic decline.[5]

## THE FALKLANDS: A TEST OF RESOLVE

After Reagan's inauguration, and due in part to his initial focus on the U.S. economy, there was relatively little direct interaction between the president and the prime minister. But by 1982, the world's simmering geopolitical hotspots festered and grew, and their shared values once again drawing them together. The bond between Prime Minister Margaret Thatcher and President Ronald Reagan was obvious, and often hailed as the "gold standard" of what the Special Relationship between the United States and the United Kingdom could be. However, this dynamic wasn't always harmonious, particularly during the 1982 Falklands War between Argentina and Britain in the South Atlantic.

In early April 1982, six hundred Argentine troops boldly invaded and claimed possession of the Falkland Islands, a British territory located off the southern tip of South America. The 57 Royal Marines stationed there were forced to surrender. Control of the Falklands, along with South Georgia and the South Sandwich Islands, had long been contested. Argentina, which calls them las Islas Malvinas, claimed the islands citing their proximity to Argentina and the legacy of Spanish colonial rule in the early 1800s. Britain believed, and still does, that sovereignty should be decided by self-determination and the islanders themselves who were expressing a strong desire to remain under British rule.

Secretary of State Al Haig had asked for and been given permission to try to negotiate a settlement between the Argentines and the British. Haig traveled to London and Buenos Aires and sent secret cables back to Washington. President Reagan, reacting to Haig's reports on the British position, wrote to the secretary that he "makes clear how difficult it will be to foster a compromise that gives Maggie enough to carry on and at the same time meets the test of 'equity' with our Latin neighbors."

Under Thatcher's leadership, the United Kingdom launched a massive military expedition in response to the Argentine invasion. It was a massive logistical undertaking for the British Armed Forces. It took the task force nearly a month to sail from England, south through the North Atlantic Ocean, across the equator, and all the way down to the Falklands, located off the southern tip of South America. For the British, the mission's justification hinged on retaking the Falkland Islands and restoring the status quo. An April 6 analysis from the Department of State's Bureau of Intelligence and Research predicted that "the effectiveness of the fleet, far from its maintenance bases, will rapidly deteriorate after its arrival on station. [Thatcher's] damaged leadership could not survive a futile 'voyage to nowhere.'"

"The Prime Minister has the bit in her teeth," Haig reported to President Reagan on April 9, following the Argentine attack on the islands. "She is clearly prepared to use force. Though she admits her preference for a diplomatic solution, she is rigid in her insistence on a return to the status quo ante, and indeed seemingly determined that any solution involves some retribution." Haig continued, "It is clear that they had not thought much about diplomatic possibilities. They will now, but whether they become more imaginative or instead recoil will depend on the political situation and what I hear in Argentina."

The documents reveal that, initially, U.S. support for Britain was discussed quite openly between the two nations. During her first meeting with Haig on April 8, Thatcher "expressed appreciation" for U.S. cooperation in intelligence matters and in the use of a U.S. military base on Ascension Island, which is located halfway between Africa and South America in the South Atlantic. But it was clear she wanted more from the United States.

Argentina was mired in economic stagnation, and President Leopoldo Galtieri's military campaign was designed to rally support from large sectors of Argentine society. But U.S. observers foresaw serious problems ahead for him. Top-secret State Department intelligence analysis reported: "[Galtieri] wants to hold on to the Army's top slot through 1984 and perhaps the presidency through 1987. The Argentine leader may have been excessively shortsighted, however. The popular emotion that welcomed the invasion will subside. Galtieri's problem is that he has so excited the Argentine people that he has left himself little room for maneuver. He must show something for the invasion, or else he will be swept aside in ignominy."[6]

A few weeks later at the White House, the National Security Council gathered with President Reagan, Secretary of State Haig, Defense Secretary Weinberger, UN Ambassador Jeane Kirkpatrick, Counselor Ed Meese, and a few other high-ranking officials from the CIA and the administration. They were there to discuss what they were calling the "South Atlantic Crisis." Deputy National Security Advisor Bud McFarlane opened the meeting with a sobering observation: The Falkland conflict had reached a critical point, and it was time for the United States to get more involved. McFarlane turned to Admiral Inman, the CIA's deputy director, for an intelligence briefing. He was followed by Secretary Haig, who provided a diplomatic and political update.

Inman explained that the British forces, focused on neutralizing the airfield at Port Stanley, faced challenges due to the 8,000-miles distance they had to travel and weather conditions in the Falklands. While a large-scale landing wasn't imminent, the British were preparing for a prolonged military conflict. Concerns were raised about Soviet satellite capabilities and the potential for Argentine air strikes.

Secretary Haig then delved into the diplomatic intricacies a little deeper, painting a picture of two sides teetering on the edge of warfare. On the political front, support for Prime Minister

Thatcher remained robust in the United Kingdom, but President Galtieri faced narrowing support in Argentina. Haig's attempts to broker a deal while shuttling between London and Buenos Aires were stalling. His deal was a nonstarter for Thatcher because it would eventually give sovereignty to Argentina, although with British supervision and required support from the islanders. Haig's overtures were also being rejected by Argentina, which baffled Haig.

With the risk of escalation looming, diplomacy remained a distant option, but pressure was building to support Britain both domestically and internationally. Balancing these interests was delicate for the White House. They knew they needed to engage with Argentina to safeguard American interests in the region. That included protecting their relationship with Argentine intelligence officers who were collaborating with the CIA to support Contra insurgents in Nicaragua. This cooperation gave the Argentines a false sense of confidence. Prior to launching their invasion of the Falklands, they believed their assistance with the Contras might earn them a policy of noninterference from the United States.

Thatcher clearly understood the complexities and pitfalls of Haig's negotiated resolution, and she didn't like what the United States was offering either. On April 29, Thatcher wrote a letter to Reagan:

Dear Ron,

The Cabinet considered Al Haig's current proposals on the Falkland Islands for the first time this morning. We were all very grateful for his tireless efforts.

The prime minister went on to explain that she told her advisors that Argentina had not responded to Haig's proposals within the given deadline, signaling rejection. The cabinet saw this as the end of peace efforts and expected full public support from the United States. Thatcher then wrote:

> You will remember that when we spoke on the telephone on 17 April, about the earlier proposals which we worked out in London . . . , you told me that in your view we had been as accommodating as we could have been and it would not be reasonable to ask us to go further. Against that background, you will not be surprised to know that the Cabinet saw fundamental difficulties from Britain's point of view in Al's latest proposals which we regard Argentina as having now rejected. These difficulties lay in the essential areas where the latest proposals differed from the 12 April proposals. It was, of course, just these areas which Francis [Pym] discussed so thoroughly with Al in Washington last week.
>
> One stage in the effort to settle this crisis has now ended. It seems to me essential that, as we enter the next stage, the U.S. and Britain should be seen to be unequivocally on the same side, staunchly upholding those values on which the Western way of life depends.
>
> Warm personal regards,
> Margaret[7]

The next day, President Reagan replied to the British prime minister to confirm that Argentina had rejected Haig's plan and to explain his "views on where matters stand and how the United States will proceed." The president wrote:

Dear Maggie,

I am sure you agree that it is essential now to make clear to the world that every effort was made to achieve a fair and peaceful solution, and that the Argentine Government was offered a choice between such a solution and further hostilities. We will therefore make public a general account of the efforts we have made. While we will describe the U.S. proposal in broad terms, we will not release it because of the difficulty that might cause you. I recognize that while you see fundamental difficulties in the proposal, you have not rejected it. We will leave no doubt that Her Majesty's Government worked with us in good faith and was left with no choice but to proceed with military action based on the right of self-defense.[8]

Reagan also complimented Thatcher for her commitment to peace and her preparedness for military action. He told her it would be vital to maintain avenues for negotiation to prevent prolonged instability. Reagan then wrote:

There can be no doubt about our full support for you and the principles of international law and order you are defending. You can count on that support in whatever forum this issue is debated. You can also count on our sympathetic consideration of requests for assistance. We will also announce that Argentina's refusal to withdraw its invasion force and to negotiate in good faith have made it necessary for the United States to adopt a new posture toward Buenos Aires. Al Haig will be in touch with Francis Pym concerning the specific measures we will take.

We will of course want to stay in very close touch in the days and weeks ahead. I remain convinced that our combined efforts can yield a just settlement which will strengthen the principles for which we stand, and I can only hope for the least amount of bloodshed before that goal is reached.

Thatcher wanted a wingman, and Reagan was offering "sympathetic consideration of requests for assistance." During the April 30 meeting of the NSC, Secretary Haig called the president's letter a measured response to "a brittle note from the Prime Minister." Haig said he believed Thatcher's letter had been a reaction to false press reports that claimed the United States was controlling British forces by having them slow down their operations.

K. T. McFarland, who was working at the Pentagon at the time, said during an interview for this book, "Everyone [in the administration] thought, 'Oh, really?' I mean, we're going to support the Brits, right? And they gave Al Haig about a week to see if he could do any more negotiating Henry Kissinger style, but he was not able to."

By this point Reagan had all but given up on supporting Haig's proposal. And a decision was made to try to kick the plan over to the United Nations to get them to lead the peace talks. The White House meeting room was charged with tension. President Reagan convened with his top advisors, each grappling with the delicate balance between diplomacy and military action. Secretary Haig began the discussion, distributing copies of a revised press statement for the NSC principals to review. McFarlane asked for comments. Secretary Weinberger immediately brought up evacuation plans, noting the challenges they would face if the environment turned hostile. The USS *Eisenhower*, stationed in Tunis, would take at least 15 days to reach the South Atlantic, Weinberger advised.

Ed Meese raised concerns about protecting the U.S. Embassy. Weinberger responded bluntly: Sensitive materials had already been removed, but the safety of American diplomatic personnel and staff was now in the hands of the Marines there to protect them. Admiral Inman inquired about the specifics of the U.S. military aid that would be offered to the United Kingdom. Weinberger anticipated requests for more fuel and ground support at Ascension Island, possibly even specialized ammunition.

National Security Advisor William Clark, who was on the phone, highlighted a crucial distinction between "lawful" and "unlawful" use of force, urging caution in the press statement's wording. Weinberger asked if their actions were communicated to the Argentines. Haig confirmed that their ambassador had briefed President Galtieri, although Galtieri's autonomy was now questionable. Ambassador Kirkpatrick assured that room that the United Nations was keenly interested in Haig's proposal. She believed the Argentines, reluctant to face war, would eventually be forced to accept a UN initiative, to save face.

Haig noted his previous reluctance to involve the United Nations but now agreed that it was a last resort option. He emphasized that while the British needed to avoid concessions that would topple Thatcher, the Argentines were hoping to delay the hostilities until weather conditions worsened and favored them.

The discussions shifted to the specifics of economic and other sanctions against Argentina. Reagan then asked about the impact providing military support to the United Kingdom would have on America's role as a mediator. Haig insisted the Argentines needed to understand U.S. resolve, while Weinberger stressed the importance of U.S. credibility. Admiral Inman mentioned previously damaging press leaks that included details about U.S. intelligence capabilities, which led to a change in Argentine ciphers, complicating the ability to monitor the specifics of what the Argentines were doing.

As the meeting wrapped up, Ambassador Kirkpatrick again speculated that the Argentines would want to avoid war through a face-saving measure. Haig cautioned that without firm Argentine concessions on sovereignty, the British would act decisively. Reagan closed the meeting, approving the decision pivot, while he attempted to stay optimistic about the idea of the United Nations finally averting a war between the United Kingdom and Argentina.

The British forces arrived in the Falklands on May 2. The assault started when the Royal Air Force launched an opening attack on Port Stanley Airport using Vulcan bombers. The bombing raid covered close to 8,000 nautical miles round trip. These became known as the Black Buck Raids and were the longest-ranged bombing raids in history at that time.

The British bombers departed from Ascension Island, situated near the equator and in the heart of the Atlantic. The Vulcans, primarily designed for medium-range European missions, faced a daunting challenge. To accomplish their objectives, the planes needed to be refueled multiple times while in flight. The RAF's tanker planes required midair refueling as well. The process required a total of eleven tanker planes to support the mission of just two Vulcans.

Shortly after the bombing raids started, a British submarine torpedoed an Argentine vessel, leading to its sinking and the death of more than 300 sailors. Two days later the Argentinians would strike back—sinking the HMS *Sheffield* with a missile. It was the first British warship lost in action since World War II. Twenty crew members died.

A week later another infantry brigade boarded the requisitioned Queen Elizabeth II and sailed toward the conflict. When they arrived on May 21, the units of 3 Commando Brigade successfully executed landings that were mostly unopposed.

However, the Royal Navy continued to suffer from Argentine air attacks in what became known as the Battle of San Carlos. Three Royal Navy ships were sunk in the space of four days. After the invasion, the British started to gain the upper hand on the Argentines, having secured key battle victories on the ground.

Documents from the British government's archives reveal Thatcher's deep frustration with her closest ally and "political soulmate" in Washington and how Reagan had handled the situation. A memo from one of Thatcher's aides documented a midnight phone call Reagan made to Mrs. Thatcher on May 31, 1982. During this call, British troops were closing in on Port Stanley, the capital of the Falkland Islands. Reagan, acting on the advice of his advisors including Secretary of State Al Haig, who considered Britain's desire to retain sovereignty over the Falklands an outdated form of colonialism, tried to persuade the prime minister to compromise one more time. "The best chance for peace was before complete Argentine humiliation," Reagan told Thatcher. "As the U.K. now has the upper hand, it should strike a deal now," rather than act in a way that would further harden Argentine feelings.

"Britain had not lost precious lives in battle and sent an enormous task force to hand over the queen's islands to a contact group," Thatcher told the president. She had now rejected the president's request three times, becoming more emphatic each time. She included a pointed reminder that Britain had been forced to "act alone, with no outside help," in recovering the Falklands, a reference to Reagan's refusal to allow the United States to be drawn directly into the conflict on the British side.

"Just supposing Alaska was invaded," Thatcher said to Reagan.[9]

"No, no, although, Margaret, I have to say I don't quite think Alaska is a similar situation," Reagan responded.

"More or less so," Thatcher snapped back. "I didn't lose some of my best ships and some of my finest lives, to leave quietly under a ceasefire without the Argentines withdrawing," she said firmly.

"Oh. Oh, Margaret, that is part of this, as I understand it." Reagan said softly.

"Ron, I'm not handing over . . . I'm not handing over the island now," insisted Thatcher.

"Your impressive military advance could maybe change the diplomatic options. . . . Incidentally, I want to congratulate you on what you and your young men are doing down there. You've taken major risks and you've demonstrated to the whole world that unprovoked aggression does not pay."

"Well, not yet, but we're halfway to that," replied Thatcher, then correcting herself, saying, "We're not yet halfway, but a third of the way."

"Yes, yes you are," said Reagan.

And then he tried to move on quickly back to the ceasefire deal. "Argentina might turn it down," he conceded, but "I think an effort to show we're all still willing to seek a settlement . . . would undercut the effort of . . . the leftists in South America who are actively seeking to exploit the crisis. Now, I'm thinking about this plan."

Thatcher butted in, saying, "This is democracy and our island, and the very worst thing for democracy would be if we failed now." According to the once secret memo, the call ended with Mrs. Thatcher explaining to Reagan that the only acceptable outcome was for Argentina to surrender and agree to withdraw from the islands without negotiation.

At this same time, Thatcher was also firing off terse cables to French President François Mitterrand. Argentina had used French-made Exocet missiles to sink several British naval ships during the war. British military leaders were warning the prime minister that a successful strike on one of Britain's aircraft carriers could lead to defeat and force them to surrender the Falklands.

According to Mitterrand, Thatcher demanded that he hand over secret codes that could disable the Exocet missiles. And if he refused, she threatened to launch a nuclear attack on Buenos Aires.[10] Mitterrand is quoted as saying: "Happily, I gave in. Otherwise, I assure you, that lady's iron finger would have pushed the button."

Another diplomatic cable, this one from Sir Nicholas Henderson, Britain's ambassador in Washington during the Falklands War, railed against UN Ambassador Jeane Kirkpatrick, who had advocated for compromise. The cable described Kirkpatrick as "more fool than fascist," and added, "She appears to be one of America's most reliable own-goal scorers: tactless, wrong-headed, . . . and ineffective."

As the situation intensified in the Falklands, and Thatcher's recalcitrance was established, Reagan pivoted and started to actively support the British Armed Forces in a more substantial way.

Henry Kissinger recalled that during the middle of the Falklands crisis, he had lunch at the Foreign Office in London. They had assembled a group of former top diplomats, and he was invited. The U.K. foreign secretary at that moment was Francis Pym, and the group discussed several ideas for a compromise with the Argentines.

Later Kissinger was invited to tea with Thatcher, and he asked her about the prospect of compromising. Kissinger described Thatcher as "irate." And she said, "You, my old friend, would dare to use the word compromise here." In fact, he said, Thatcher "was so irate that I didn't even tell her where I had gotten all these ideas." One can imagine the former secretary of state, who would soon resign, may have talked to Secretary Haig about his proposal.

Kissinger then understood, "[I]t was absolutely clear that you could not touch British territory while she was Prime Minister."

The Falklands War eventually ended on June 14, 1982, when Argentine forces surrendered to British troops in Port Stanley, the capital of the Falkland Islands. After intense fighting that included land, sea, and air battles, the British successfully reclaimed control of the islands. The conflict lasted 10 weeks, and 255 British and 649 Argentine military personnel would die in the conflict. The Argentine defeat led to the fall of the ruling military junta, paving the way for the country's democratization. In the United Kingdom, the victory bolstered the Conservative government, securing their reelection the following year.

## LEBANON: DIVERGING PATHS

That summer, there was another flashpoint demanding both Thatcher's and Reagan's attention. On June 6, 1982, the Israeli Defense Forces breached the Lebanese border, initiating Operation Peace for Galilee with the goal of eradicating Soviet-backed Palestinian Liberation Organization militants who were entrenched in southern Lebanon.

The invasion came during a period of substantial turnover within the foreign policy communities of both London and Washington. Although his resignation would not come for another couple of weeks, Al Haig was a lame duck. Reagan's administration and Thatcher's government were both keenly aware of the potentially devastating consequences of the rapidly deteriorating Middle East crisis. Their concerns were heightened as Israel advanced toward Beirut and the involvement of Syrian forces looked likely.

The key players in the Reagan administration disagreed on how to handle Israel's invasion of Lebanon. Secretary of State Haig believed the United States should go easy on Israel and avoid publicly pressuring the Israelis to withdraw unless the United States was also willing to apply the same pressure on the PLO and Syria in this highly asymmetrical conflict. In contrast, Secretary of Defense Weinberger, Vice President Bush, and National Security Advisor William Clark argued for an immediate Israeli pullback and suggested sanctions if Israel didn't comply, as Syria's support was viewed as the linchpin of their peace plan.

President Reagan wanted to get the stalled Middle East peace process moving again, so he made some key changes in his staff. George Shultz, a former business executive, was now the secretary of state. The president also named his deputy national security advisor, Robert McFarlane, to replace Philip Habib as his chief Mideast negotiator.

Reagan announced the change as he said goodbye to Lebanese President Amin Gemayel, who was visiting the White House, and had been calling for a new and urgent U.S. drive to bring about the withdrawal of Israeli, Syrian, and Palestine Liberation Organization troops from Lebanon in time to rescue U.S. credibility and stave off a major new outbreak of fighting.[11]

McFarlane then departed for major Mideast capitals to explore the next steps in the Lebanese problem and the broader regional peace process. Perhaps the most important stop on his trip was Damascus. Syrian President Hafez al-Assad had refused to withdraw his forces from Lebanon and rejected a proposed visit by Habib, thus eroding Habib's usefulness as a negotiator with Syria. Assad's attitude was a factor in the decision to promote McFarlane. Habib himself reportedly was convinced that he had worn out his welcome in several Mideast capitals. The State Department also believed that Assad would like McFarlane, a former Marine officer, who had earned a reputation for being honest, blunt, and fair.

McFarlane's selection also led to rampant speculation, perhaps originating from the recently departed Al Haig, that the NSC, which was really starting to flex its muscle in Central America and push harder against the Soviets for arms control negotiations, was edging out the State Department in the day-to-day direction of these critical areas of foreign policy. White House officials said the new Secretary of State George Shultz was aware that the appointment of McFarlane would lead to rumors about the State Department's relegation in policymaking and diplomacy, but he wasn't concerned. This concern was outweighed by Shultz's good personal relations with McFarlane, his view that the deputy national security affairs advisor was well versed in the Reagan administration's Mideast policy, and Shultz's belief that McFarlane's position at the White House "carries a political message" in the region that would be useful.

McFarlane was somehow supposed to also continue as William Clark's deputy national security advisor. But a White House official told reporters at the time that McFarlane's full attention for an unlimited and indefinite period would be paid to the Mideast. McFarlane was not a Mideast expert, but he had significant experience including time working on the staff of the Joint Chiefs of Staff during the height of the Vietnam War. He also served as a military assistant to Henry Kissinger while he was the national security advisor. Haig had brought McFarlane with him to the State Department, where McFarlane undertook mostly unpublicized missions for Haig to Israel, Pakistan, Saudi Arabia, Oman, and Egypt, according to associates at the National Security Council.

In announcing McFarlane's appointment, Reagan said, "[T]he United States remains firmly committed to the earliest possible resolution of the conflict in Lebanon." Reagan also promised the United States' "energy and perseverance" in aiding Lebanon and said that "Lebanon can count on our support."

In response, the Lebanese president read a prepared statement that said he continued to "be confident that the major problems still confronting us in Lebanon and the Middle East can best be addressed and resolved by full cooperation with our Arab community and our American friends." He said the United States and Lebanon "will intensify their consultations until the expected results are achieved." Reporters were told that the next step, as seen by McFarlane, was to try harder with a new team to pursue "an intensified dialogue," involving shifts in emphasis rather than any fundamental change in U.S. concepts or strategy.

Hostilities escalated on June 9 when the IDF destroyed Syrian missile batteries in the Beqaa Valley, raising fears of a wider conflict. President Reagan sent envoy Philip Habib to demand a ceasefire from Israel. While the IDF halted its advance in the Beqaa, it continued moving toward West Beirut, which was controlled by the PLO.

Reagan decided at that point to support the Lebanese government's attempts to reclaim West Beirut and then negotiate for the withdrawal of both Israeli and Syrian forces. On June 15, Reagan wrote to Margaret Thatcher and stressed that Lebanon's "independence and unity must be preserved, and its government's authority must be strengthened." He closed his letter by writing, "We will have to be closely in touch concerning humanitarian relief and a formula for peacekeeping forces which will be essential to ensure rapid Israeli withdrawal."[12]

By July, the PLO agreed to leave Beirut, but only if the MNF could guarantee the protection of Palestinian civilians displaced by the conflict. Despite Weinberger's strenuous objections, Reagan agreed to deploy the Marines as part of a multinational force along with French and Italian troops. By that point, the multinational peacekeeping force in Lebanon included 1,200 U.S. Marines.

The Palestinian withdrawal began on August 21, but it was challenging to find a single Arab nation to accept the PLO fighters, resulting in their dispersal across multiple countries. Initially, Israel intensified attacks on Beirut and refused to let the MNF operate until the PLO had fully left. The PLO eventually completed its withdrawal by September. Although the MNF was meant to stay for 30 days, Weinberger announced the Marines would leave on September 10.

But four days later, Lebanese President-elect Bashir Gemayel, who was supported by Israel, was assassinated in a bombing attack at his headquarters. The Reagan White House issued a statement calling the attack on Gemayel "cowardly."[13] The IDF quickly moved into West Beirut, and by the middle of September they were accused of allowing Maronite Lebanese militia to enter refugee camps and massacre Palestinian civilians. The massacre caused international outrage, prompting Reagan to deploy Marines as part of a new MNF. By that point, the multinational peacekeeping force in Lebanon included 1,200 U.S. troops.

As discussed in an earlier chapter, on April 18, 1983, a suicide bomber targeted the U.S. Embassy in Beirut. The devastating explosion killed 63 people, including 17 Americans. President Reagan, sitting at a desk in a camel hair sport jacket, read a prepared statement for a radio address that was also filmed. Reagan said:

> We don't know yet who bears responsibility for this terrible deed. What we do know is that the terrorists who planned and carried out this cynical and cowardly attack have failed in their purpose. They mistakenly believe that if they're cruel enough and violent enough, they will weaken American resolve and deter us from our effort to help build a lasting and secure peace in the Middle East. Well, if they think that, they don't know

too much about America. As a free people, we've never allowed intimidation to stop us from doing what we know to be right. The best way for us to show our love and respect for our fellow countrymen who died in Beirut this week is to carry on with their task, to press harder than ever with our peacemaking efforts, and that's exactly what we're doing.[14]

Congress almost immediately took up a debate about additional aid for Lebanon amid growing tensions. But the House and Senate wanted to include a requirement for congressional approval for any expanded U.S. military role. After the embassy bombing, on April 19, Republican Senator Barry Goldwater of Arizona said, "I think it's high time we bring the boys home."[15] For the multinational peacekeeping force, the bombing was a grim reminder of the perilous environment they operated in, as factions within Lebanon became increasingly hostile to foreign presence. This violent act foreshadowed the complex and deadly challenges that lay ahead for the MNF.

In May 1983, a glimmer of hope emerged with the signing of the Israeli-Lebanese agreement on the withdrawal of Israeli forces. The agreement, brokered under intense diplomatic efforts, aimed to pave the way for a more stable Lebanon. However, this hope was quickly dashed by Syrian opposition, which rendered the agreement ineffective. Syria's strategic interests in Lebanon meant that any progress toward stability without its involvement was unacceptable. As a result, the withdrawal plan stalled, leaving the situation in Lebanon as precarious as ever.

Over the summer of 1983, the fragile peace was shattered as fighting intensified between various factions, including the Lebanese army, Druze militias, and Shiite groups. The MNF, initially deployed to stabilize and support, found itself increasingly embroiled in the conflict. Skirmishes and hostilities drew the peacekeepers into the fray, challenging their mission and stretching their resources thin. The volatile mix of political and sectarian strife turned Lebanon into a battleground where alliances shifted constantly.

Then another suicide bomber struck on October 23, 1983, unleashing a devastating attack on the U.S. Marine Corps barracks in Beirut, Lebanon, killing 241 U.S. military personnel, including 220 Marines, 18 sailors, and 3 soldiers. Moments later, another suicide bomber targeted French forces, killing 58 paratroopers. The blasts not only took the lives of these brave servicemen but also claimed the lives of six innocent Lebanese civilians The prospect of peace in the Mideast now seemed more distant than ever.

As soon as she got word of the bombing, Prime Minister Thatcher sent a confidential telegram to President Reagan at the White House:[16]

> Am horrified at the news of the barbarous attack on your marines in Lebanon. Please accept the deepest sympathy of all of us here for you and for the families of the victims.
>
> They gave their lives for peace. I was distressed to hear of the incident on the golf course. As usual, of course, you responded magnificently.

After receiving her condolences in the form of an urgent and confidential letter, President Reagan wrote back to Thatcher:

Dear Margaret:

There is no doubt that the perpetrators of the latest bombings in Beirut have attempted once more to undermine our collective will and sense of purpose as we work to support the legitimate government of Lebanon in its efforts to secure a more stable and peaceful future.

Despite our sorrow at the great loss of life, I want to assure you that the United States remains firmly committed to our joint search for peace and stability in Lebanon. The United States will not be dissuaded by acts of violence committed by those who are seeking to prevent Lebanese political reconciliation and the restoration of Lebanese sovereignty over territory at present controlled by foreign forces.

Our common goals are still unattainable; we believe that we can achieve them if we stand united and work closely together in the face of these new provocations.

I believe that our foreign ministers should meet to discuss matters concerning the MNF. I have asked Secretary Shultz to call his counterparts in the MNF governments to see if a meeting time and place can be arranged promptly.

Sincerely,
Ron[17]

## LATE SEPTEMBER IN WASHINGTON, D.C.

Toward the end of September 1983, a month before the bombing at the Marine barracks, Prime Minister Margaret Thatcher met with President Reagan for a working visit in Washington. At their dual public press events, their shared respect and mutual affirmation was quite apparent.

The *New York Times* reported that Thatcher was "not assured at all" that President Reagan planned any new actions to reduce the United States deficit.[18] The prime minister had just spent a full day with the president, senior administration officials, members of the Senate Foreign Relations Committee, and the chairman of the Federal Reserve Board, Paul Volcker. Thatcher said that the administration appeared to have "a different view" about the effects of the deficit than she did. She said she had made it clear she felt the high deficit was keeping interest rates up and hampering economic growth. What was remarkable about the news conference was the ability of Reagan and Thatcher to not only talk about what they agreed on, but also be open about what they disagreed on.

Thatcher also told reporters that she found it "disappointing and discouraging" that Soviet leaders had rejected President Reagan's latest proposals to break the deadlock in talks on medium-range missiles in Europe. "It takes two to negotiate, and the President has constantly put forward detailed proposals to the Soviet Union," she said, adding that the latest Soviet rejection "should not be the end of the negotiations." Thatcher reiterated her stance that if no agreement was reached in the Geneva arms talks, the United States should move forward with the planned deployment of Pershing II and cruise missiles in Europe in December.

But during that same news conference she also said that she had urged the United States not to restore military aid to Argentina. She said talks with Argentina over the future of the Falkland Islands were "absolutely wrong," given Argentina's refusal to accept a formal end to hostilities with Britain.

And when it came to the Middle East, she added that Britain was "not prepared to make indefinite commitments" to the multinational force there while Syrian, Palestinian, and Israeli forces worked out the terms of their withdrawal. "We cannot stay there indefinitely," Thatcher said, "and I think the people of the United States have taken a similar view.

At this point there were still disagreements inside the White House about how to proceed in Lebanon. Officials from the Reagan administration had also recently suggested that the multinational force might have to remain until all foreign forces were withdrawn from Lebanon.

Thatcher wrote about the late September meeting in her book *The Downing Street Years*.[19] She and Reagan talked about the thriving American economy, now growing faster and with less inflation than when he had taken office, despite lingering deficit concerns. Thatcher remembered that Reagan quipped, "[N]ow that [Reaganomics] is working, how come they don't call it Reaganomics anymore?"

The pair talked about how the Soviets were on the defensive, facing the upcoming deployment of NATO's intermediate-range nuclear weapons and the fallout from the Korean Airliner incident. She praised Reagan's UN speech after the Korean Airliner incident, agreeing that arms control negotiations should continue despite the outrage. Reagan argued that the Soviets were paranoid about their security, possibly feeling genuinely threatened by the West, and questioned the control dynamics within the Soviet Union. He believed the Soviets were negotiating due to the U.S. defense buildup and that their economic struggles limited their military spending. The task, he said, was to convince Moscow that negotiation was their only viable option. He recalled a cartoon where Brezhnev lamented, "I liked the arms race better when we were the only ones in it," which now seemed prophetic.

Thatcher also seized the opportunity to explain Britain's opposition to including the British and French independent nuclear deterrents in U.S.-Soviet arms talks, a stance previously supported by the Americans. She argued that the Soviet insistence on including the British and French deterrents was a tactic to distract from American proposals for deep cuts in strategic nuclear weapons. She reiterated that Britain's deterrent, constituting a mere 2.5% of the Soviet arsenal, was an irreducible minimum. Reagan seemed to appreciate her point, which reassured Thatcher. She also reassured him about the timetable for deploying Cruise and Pershing missiles in Europe, despite delays in the Bundestag debate. Reagan, confident in Chancellor Kohl but wary of his advisors, believed the Soviets aimed to prevent deployment.

Their discussion then turned to the broader strategy toward the Soviet Union. Thatcher, having consulted experts at a Chequers Seminar at her official country residence, emphasized the importance of accurately assessing the Soviet system and leadership. Reflecting on their partnership, Thatcher noted that while she and Reagan shared a strategic vision, their approaches differed. Reagan grasped the big picture, leaving tactical details to others, while Thatcher focused on day-to-day management to keep events under control. This difference underscored their complementary strengths.

During a discussion that morning and over lunch, Reagan shared his optimism about Central America, noting that the government in El Salvador, supported by the United States against communist insurgents, was gaining ground, depriving the American media of their nightly guerrilla stories.

Thatcher raised the contentious issue of the United States resuming arms supplies to Argentina, stressing that such a move would be incomprehensible to Britain after the hostility in the Falklands. Reagan acknowledged her concerns but noted that pressure would mount for resuming arms supplies if a civilian regime emerged in Buenos Aires.

Part of Reagan's diary entry from that day also focused on the visit.[20] Reagan wrote that he and Thatcher began with an hour-long discussion focused primarily on the Soviets and the potential paths to rekindling a productive relationship. Reagan reflected on the current state of U.S.-U.K. relations, noting that "they had never been stronger." Reagan also wrote about the "light-hearted ceremony" he attended that day with the Olympic hockey team and the Washington Capitals on a makeshift plastic ice rink. "They asked me to hit a puck and believe it or not I scored a goal."

Thatcher later wrote that she felt like her meetings and speeches were well received, but she would soon realize that not everything she was trying to communicate to the president had been fully understood.

## FURY AND FRIENDSHIP

At the White House, contingency planning for Grenada was in high gear. So was work on the response to the bombing in Beirut.

Chris Lehman, during a joint interview for this book conducted with Ed Meese, recalled that pivotal morning when the president called his team down to the Situation Room for an urgent meeting.[21] "Lebanon, Lebanon," Lehman thought, "what's going to happen now?" To everyone's surprise, President Reagan began, "I called you down here this morning because at 6 a.m., elements of the 82nd Airborne enveloped Grenada."

Confusion swept through the room. One congressman in the meeting, bewildered, whispered, "Where the hell's Grenada?" Lehman, seated among the officials, said he could feel the gravity of the moment. After the president's announcement, Secretary of Defense Cap Weinberger stepped up with a map to brief the room on the unfolding situation. He outlined the deployment of 10,000 troops to the tiny island. Lehman said the congressman, incredulous, questioned the necessity of such a large force for such a small target. Weinberger, ever composed, delivered his response with a mix of stern practicality and understated rebuke: "Because I'd rather have too many than too few."

As Edwin Meese recounted, "[T]he most interesting event" of that day took place during a White House meeting with congressional leadership. They had to be discreet, sneaking Tip O'Neill and Howard Baker into the Treasury Department and through a hidden passage to avoid detection. Christopher Lehman chimed in to highlight the logistical finesse required: "If you brought Tip O'Neill or Howard Baker in a limo through West Executive Avenue, Sam Donaldson would be all over it. This was critical, given that we were just 6, 10, 12 hours before the operation."

As the meeting wrapped up, National Security Director Robert McFarlane asked the room, "How are we going to sell this to the American public?"

Constantine Menges responded, "By telling the truth about the need to rescue our students and by stressing the positive results that will come from the restoration of democracy and the ending of a communist dictatorship."

During this tense time, Meese said the White House attempted to contact 10 Downing Street. Meese remembered, "Ronald Reagan had called Margaret Thatcher to tell her what was going on. She was not available for some reason; she was away from Number 10 Downing Street for something."

In the middle of the meeting in the White House residence, Thatcher returned Reagan's call. Reagan and Meese stepped out to take the call in private. Meese vividly recalled the one-sided conversation. "Well, Margaret, it's this way. Yes, Margaret. No, Margaret. Yes, Margaret. Sorry, Margaret, but we have to do it," Meese said he heard Reagan say. The exchange underscored the weight of the decision and the close, albeit strained, collaboration between the two leaders in that critical moment.

That evening, President Reagan, in a letter to Prime Minister Margaret Thatcher, expressed his deep concern over the recent political turmoil in Grenada. The violence and the ascension of a blood-stained regime had rattled the democratic nations of the English-speaking Caribbean, raising fears for the welfare of both Grenada's citizens and the nationals of allied countries. The Organization of Eastern Caribbean States had unanimously decided to pursue a collective security effort to restore peace and order and had formally requested U.S. support.

Reagan informed Thatcher of his serious consideration of the OECS's request. He had dispatched Ambassador Francis McNeil to Bridgetown to discuss the situation with Prime Minister Adams and other Caribbean leaders. The ambassador reported that forces from various island nations had already assembled in Barbados. The United States firmly endorsed the political objectives of the proposed OECS operation: to restore order and security, enable the formation of a provisional government, and hold early elections. Reagan emphasized the potential role of Her Majesty's governor general in Grenada, the only remaining legitimate authority on the island, in designating a new provisional government.

Reagan shared his belief that free and fair elections were essential for reestablishing a truly democratic government. He noted that the Caribbean states intended to request an emergency meeting of the Permanent Council of the Organization of American States to seek endorsement for their collective security effort. He assured Thatcher that he would keep her informed of any U.S. involvement in the proposed security force and any political or diplomatic efforts. Reagan concluded by expressing his confidence in Thatcher's advice and support on this critical issue.

But the wheels of Operation Urgent Fury were already in motion. McFarlane assigned some of the staff members from the National Security Council to meet with high-ranking members of Congress to let them know they would participate in a CIA-led briefing the next day.

John Poindexter, McFarlane's deputy, in a rare personal exchange with Constantine Menges, said, "Well, Constantine, your initiative worked. Tomorrow we'll see the results." Menges says he then went back to the crisis management center in room 208 of the Old Executive Office building for one more update. Later he went to Ollie North's office and said he found North asleep on the couch. North had hunkered down in his office for the night, ready to wake and respond to the operation, with H-hour just a few hours away.

Menges covered North with his overcoat, and then called the Situation Room to let them know where they could find North in the interim.

# PART THREE

CHAPTER 8

# Operation Urgent Fury

*"The hills 300 meters north of the runway came alive with anti-aircraft fire. I counted eight sources of heavy red tracer, .50 caliber, and an estimated 80–100 sources of green tracers, AK-47 fire."*

—Maj. James Roper, AC-130 Spectre pilot in Operation Urgent Fury

## OCTOBER 25, 1983: H-HOUR

Operation Urgent Fury (OUF) kicked off late at night just before October 25, 1983. The plan called for dual strikes with an H-hour of 0500. But all the active alert troops had already been given their orders at their bases days before.

Army Private Mike Parnell's unit (Bravo Company, 325th Airborne Infantry Regiment, 2nd Battalion) was already on alert status. It was part of the 82nd Airborne's Rapid Deployment Force. During an interview for this book, Parnell explained that he had known nothing preemptively about OUF. Until they brought out the maps, he admitted he had thought Grenada was in Spain. He recalled, "When the call came down it was fast moving. Not much time to cover specifics, but it was explained in an overview where we were going and why. It really centered on restoring order after the government there collapsed and protecting the Americans who lived and studied on the island. For me personally, that was enough."

Parnell has just turned 18. His enlistment a year earlier had required a parental release. It is very likely that he was the youngest soldier to see action in Grenada. "At the time, I believed strongly in the ideals of being American. Obviously, there's much more to the story both politically and strategically. I'm not a politician, I'm a soldier. I did what needed to be done," Parnell said.

Almost nothing would go as expected. The 1st and 2nd Battalions from the Army's 75th Ranger Regiment, followed by elite elements from the 82nd Airborne, planned on dropping into, or preferably landing at, the still-under-construction Point Salines Airport on the south end of the island. They would then spread out to rescue American medical students and staff at St. George's University's True Blue campus nearby.

Meanwhile, 400 Marines, pushed into a larger role by Commandant General John Kelley's impassioned plea after the Beirut bombing, would secure Pearls Airport and the port town of Grenville in the north, arriving by helicopter from the assault ship *Guam*, then just five miles from Grenada.

Operation Urgent Fury would provide a baptism by fire for the Army's new UH-60 Black Hawk helicopters. A significant leap forward from the aging UH-1 Hueys of Vietnam, these advanced machines boasted a potent combination of muscle and resilience. Black Hawks could transport a full squad of operators, offering a significant force multiplier compared with their predecessors. They weren't just about muscle, though. These birds could handle high altitudes and adverse weather, ensuring mission flexibility regardless of the conditions. Redundant flight controls meant the Black Hawk could keep flying even if one side of the cockpit were damaged. Self-sealing fuel tanks minimized the risk of fiery explosions from ground fire, and armored seats offered a crucial layer of protection for the troops inside. This emphasis on survivability was no accident. The Black Hawks were designed with a specific threat in mind—the Soviet-made ZU-23 anti-aircraft guns, the very same weapons Grenada had deployed for its own defense.

Nine brand-new Black Hawk helicopters waited on the tarmac at Fort Campbell, Kentucky, to carry teams of Delta Force or SEALs to their objectives in Grenada. They were designated Chalks One through Nine—a throwback to World War II when paratroopers would have their flight numbers written on their backs with chalk during Operation Overlord. The first six Chalks were filled with Delta Force operators, veterans hardened by covert warfare. The last three belonged to the SEALs.

The Black Hawks would soon be loaded onto three massive C-5A Galaxy transport planes. The plan was to fly from Fort Campbell to Pope Air Force Base in North Carolina and pick up about 100 additional special operators. By nightfall, all three C-5s were airborne, heading south toward a staging area in Barbados at Grantley Adams Airport.

Unfortunately, the Air Force's timetable for reassembling the Black Hawks in Barbados proved overly optimistic, throwing the carefully choreographed schedule into disarray.

In the aftermath of President Carter's failed Iranian hostage rescue Operation Eagle Claw, President Reagan ordered the creation of an elite task force. The 160th Special Operations Aviation Regiment was established in 1981. Its objective was to forge a first-class night-fighting helicopter unit that could strike and deliver special operators with surgical precision and never again leave American lives hanging in the balance. The Army's "Night Stalkers" were handpicked from the 101st Airborne's best. Their use of new night vision technology gave them an advantage in the darkness and provided an opportunity for air dominance. Their motto—"Night Stalkers Don't Quit"—was etched in the heart of every one of their missions.

By the time they were tapped for Operation Urgent Fury, TF-160 had already conducted several dangerous missions, but their training proved to be just as, if not more, dangerous than what they were about to encounter.

Official records indicate that between March 20 and October 4, 1983, sixteen TF-160 aviators and crewmembers were killed in training accidents. They also lost a total of four aircraft. This was a particularly deadly period due to the unit's early high-risk training, which involved long-range, low-level, blacked-out map-of-the-earth, close-formation flying at night with first-generation night vision goggles.

According to one member of TF-160, Chief Warrant Officer C. Scott Atkins—call sign "FLIR Mullet"—who was interviewed for this book, the number of training deaths was higher than reported. He recalled that 21 of his fellow Night Stalkers were killed during the unit's first year of existence. Still, on the way to Operation Urgent, Atkins recalled feeling "immortal."

Atkins was a Black Hawk helicopter pilot and would be tasked with transporting Navy SEALs and Delta Force commandos into combat. TF-160 would soon fly three critical and ultimately deadly missions on the first day of OUF. Objective one: Extract Governor General Paul Scoon, his wife, and his staff from his residence with a team of SEALs and Delta Force Operators. Objective two: Insert a team of SEALS at Beausejour to disable the television and radio tower. Objective three: Insert a team of special operators at Richmond Hill Prison, where it was believed dozens, if not hundreds, of political prisoners were being held.

Atkins was onboard one of the C5 transport planes flying from Pope Airfield in North Carolina to Barbados. "The lights were dimmed, and everyone was quiet. It was serene," he recalled. "All the men were resting, some were sleeping."

Captain Keith Lucas, who was also part of TF-160 and Atkins's company commander came over and sat down next to him. Atkins recalled that both men "knew it was about to get crazy unloading their birds from the C-5s and "spinning up for

Grenada." As the two pilots sat there on the darkened plane, both were "deep in thought and saying very little."

Atkins said Lucas then turned to him, and said, "I feel some will not be returning home."

At that point, Atkins said it was clear to him that Cpt. Lucas had more information than he did about their mission. And Cpt. Lucas was trying to say something that he was just not able to fully express.

"I could tell he was aware of the real danger, and I could sense his concern for the men under his leadership, including me," Atkins said.

"I said a prayer, which he listened to, too. He remained very motivated but deep in thought. It was the last time we spoke."

When the three C-5s landed in Barbados between 2:50 and 3:30 a.m. the clock was already working against them. Ground crews from TF-160 scrambled to reassemble the UH-60s and get them mission-ready. Despite working at a dead sprint, the birds didn't lift off until 5:30 a.m. By then, the sun was already rising over the island.

The delay cost them dearly. By the time the Black Hawks lifted into the sky for the forty-five-minute flight to Grenada, the main assault was already underway.

Atkins said, "I remember the 110-mile flight across the water in daylight, flying over the beach of Grenada and seeing a beautiful island and initially seeing Grenadians, waving at us. I thought we were being greeted as conquering heroes."

The raw beauty of Grenada's tropical paradise was broken almost as soon they flew deeper into enemy territory. The element of surprise was gone.

Radio presenters repeatedly read the same prepared script. A female voice would come on the radio and say, "You should report to the militia bases immediately. Why? Because we are under attack." A male voice would then follow, "Defend our homeland, we shall win, we shall beat them back, we shall bury them in the sea. They have to get a beating." The female voice would then say, "... foreign troops began landing in our country. Our armed forces are engaging them in fierce battle. All doctors, nurses, and medical staff report to the hospital immediately." Then the male voice: "We shall beat them back. Militia come out now. Together with the People's Revolutionary Army we will save our country!" The female voice then followed again, "The Revolutionary Military Council was calling on all friendly countries to condemn this act of aggression and immediately come to Grenada's aid." Songs like Peter Tosh "Stand Up for Grenada" and Bob Marley's "Get Up, Stand Up" were played in the background while the script was read. Soon after that, Grenadian soldiers and Cuban construction workers started to break out weapons, anticipating an attack.[1]

Havana's state news media reported that Cuba's "glorious combatants" were "at this moment immolating themselves for the homeland, wrapped in the Cuban flag." That was the order Havana had given to the detachment of more than 700 Cuban "soldier-bricklayers" building an airport in Grenada, according to the *Miami Herald*.[2] A U.S. military unit monitoring radio traffic intercepted a transmission from Havana, ordering the Cubans to "fight to the last man," according to Chris Simmons, then an Army lieutenant who landed in Grenada on the first day of combat.[3]

The first Marine helicopters lifted off the *Guam*'s darkened deck at approximately 5:15 a.m. under a moonless sky in a driving rainstorm. Pilots navigated through inky darkness with limited visibility. Radio silence rules complicated coordination further.

The landing zone, marked as an old racetrack south of Pearls Airport, turned out to be surrounded by towering palm trees and large grazing cows, surprising pilots. They had to improvise and find a new landing zone. The first helicopter finally touched down at 5:20, encountering minimal resistance initially but running behind schedule.

As dawn broke, anti-aircraft fire briefly lit up the sky before Marine Sea Cobra gunships silenced two 12 mm guns that started firing on the Marines. The hasty unloading of Marines and gear from their helicopters led to mishaps: A jeep overturned in marshy ground, and two others became entangled during off-loading, leading to broken bones and more damaged or lost gear. But, of course, the Marines pressed on.

Around the same time, another company of Marines landed at Grenville and were greeted as liberators by civilians eager to express their displeasure with the new military regime. Locals helped identify disguised soldiers, located hidden weapons, and even loaned vehicles for transporting captured arms.

The two Ranger battalions were already inbound, flying nonstop from Hunter Army Airfield near Savannah, Georgia, to Grenada on 16 C-130 transports. They had taken off the night before around 10:00 p.m. Five of the transports were specialized "Combat Talon" models, and the remaining eleven were standard and packed with troops and equipment. The operation planned for three phases of transport arrivals. The first two would consist of the 1st and 2nd Ranger Battalions, and the third phase was inbound from Fort Bragg and contained the operators and planners responsible for the JSOC missions.

Three AC-130H Spectre gunships, armed with an array of large-caliber guns and high incendiary ammo, were part of this aerial entourage, tasked with providing cover for the unarmed transport planes. The Spectres were flying in from Hurlburt Field in the Florida panhandle. The complex airlift plan, which required precision timing and navigational skills, faced an immediate setback when an engine fire forced one AC-130H crew to return to base to switch planes.

The preferred plan was for a company of Rangers to land onto the airfield at Point Salines under the cover of darkness, clear obstacles, and suppress the resistance. The plan was modeled on the 1976 Israeli commando raid at Entebbe Airport. However, the two prior unsuccessful SEAL recon missions had left the ground situation uncertain.

Earlier in the morning, under the cover of darkness, Major Michael Couvillon piloted his AC-130H for a pass over the Point Salines runway at an altitude of 9,000 feet. He poked his plane below the cloud cover momentarily to get a look at the runway. His infrared detectors revealed three construction vehicles and scattered obstacles blocking the tarmac. Major Couvillon relayed the news to the rest of the squadron, leading commanders to decide on a low-altitude jump from 500 feet for the first wave of Rangers, despite the still surface winds and increased risk of landing injuries.

The planes in the first phase of the airdrop assembled themselves about a minute apart for their low-level approach to the airfield. The Grenadians and Cubans knew Point Salines would be a prime invasion target, but they were expecting an amphibious assault, not a parachute drop, and had fortified the beach to the south of the east-west runway. Aircraft guns were positioned on the hills north of the runway.

The two lead aircraft, carrying the newly designated runway clearing teams, sped up and separated themselves from the others, hoping to complete their work in time for all the USAF transports to land on the runway. They encountered thunderstorms as they approached the island's coast from the northwest, and in the final minutes before the now-delayed H-hour, about 20 miles out, the transport plane that was supposed to lead the way had a navigational equipment failure. The pilot was unable to make the necessary airdrop calculations to ensure that the Rangers on board his plane wouldn't be dropped in the ocean. The aircraft's jumpmaster made a hand motion across his throat to signal "no jump," and they had to readjust again, delaying the operation by another thirty minutes to reorganize the drop sequence. They would now be jumping as the sun was rising.

A decision was made for the third plane to now be the first in the first group to drop, since the two lead planes were flying extremely close to one another in heavy clouds, and having the second plane now go first would be too risky considering the first plane's problems with its navigational computer. The paratroopers who had just become the tip of the spear included one platoon of about two dozen Rangers along with 1st Battalion Commander Lieutenant Colonel Wesley Taylor. The others were part of the Tactical Operations Center (TOC) team. They oversaw communications and intelligence and directed supporting fire, supported by Air Force combat air controllers.

The TOC team formed the brain trust of the mission. But most of the muscle for the initial assault force was on the first two planes that just had to abort their drops. As they neared landfall, the two Air Force jumpmasters moved through the plane, inspecting each man's parachute. They then stationed themselves at the two rear exit doors, where a red light glowed ominously.

"Stand up!" the jumpmasters shouted. The men struggled to gain their footing under an enormous load of weapons and gear. Each Ranger had two parachutes, a main and reserve, that together weighed about 35 pounds. They also carried ammunition and water in pouches and belts that added another 25 pounds. But the heaviest weight of all was in their rucksacks, crammed with more battle gear.

When the jumpmasters opened the doors, gusts of warm, humid tropical air swept into the fuselage. "Hook up!" the jumpmasters shouted in loud and deliberate fashion. The Rangers attached the static lines of their parachutes to an overhead cable that ran the length of the cargo bay. "Drop zone coming up," the jumpmasters warned.

The pilot looked intently through his night vision glasses, searching for the landing zone. About a mile out, he was momentarily blinded by a searchlight that swept across the aircraft's canopy and then locked onto the cockpit. The first Ranger in line on both sides of the cargo bay stood in the open doorway, poised to jump. "Green light!" the plane's navigator called out over the radio.

Just after 5:30 a.m., the jumpmasters shouted, "Go, go, go!"[4] Green parachutes blossomed under the sunlight that was just starting to filter through the heavy clouds in the early morning sky. But as soon as the Rangers jumped, tracer bullets from anti-aircraft machine guns and small arms started streaking across the sky around the falling paratroopers.

## URGENT FURY AT THE WHITE HOUSE

Soon after the first Rangers dropped in on Point Salines, Constantine Menges was in his office compiling a concise situation report, summarizing the battle's progress and the political reactions from hostile governments like Cuba, Nicaragua, and the Soviet Union, alongside the initial responses from friendly nations. He then made his way to the White House.

The State Department had invited Prime Minister Eugenia Charles of Dominica, chairperson of the Organization of Eastern Caribbean States, to join President Reagan for a televised statement, and if she were up for it, a news conference with the press corps. Prime Minister Charles had signed and transmitted the formal request for U.S. assistance following Governor General Paul Scoon's plea for help. An Air Force plane had flown Mrs. Charles from the Caribbean early that morning, and Menges greeted her upon her arrival at the White House. They chatted briefly, and he informed her of the plan to join President Reagan, Secretary Shultz, and Robert McFarlane in the Oval Office for coffee and juice. He also mentioned that the public announcement with President Reagan would take place at 9:00 a.m. and encouraged her to speak with members of Congress and the media about the Grenada operation from her perspective as a Caribbean leader.

Menges described Prime Minister Charles as an "intelligent, dignified, and exceptionally articulate woman," often likened to a "Caribbean Jeane Kirkpatrick," a high compliment given Kirkpatrick's esteemed reputation among Reagan administration officials. Despite her predawn flight, Charles was energetic and optimistic, believing the Grenada operation would save many lives and restore peace and democracy. As they made their way from the White House basement to the Oval Office, Menges, still new to the NSC and equipped with a temporary White House ID, asked a Secret Service guard for directions. The guard, initially surprised and reluctant, responded promptly when Menges mentioned that Prime Minister Charles had a meeting with the president.

Upon entering the Oval Office, Menges noted the warm, inviting atmosphere: "[A] fire crackled in the fireplace, and the early morning light filtered through the large windows," he wrote.[5] Secretary Shultz and Bud McFarlane stood to greet Mrs. Charles, while a steward brought in coffee and orange juice. President Reagan warmly welcomed Prime Minister Charles, escorting her to one of the armchairs and ensuring she was comfortable before taking his seat. Menges, seated nearby, said he felt a profound sense of appreciation for being part of this historic moment as they prepared for the significant announcements and discussions that lay ahead.

Prime Minister Charles began by expressing her gratitude to President Reagan for his intervention and the authorization of

Operation Urgent Fury. She vividly described how the situation had spiraled out of control since the overthrow of Eric Gairy's dictatorship. She emphasized that the faction responsible for Maurice Bishop's assassination included some of the most extreme and dangerous communists in the region. Menges later remembered that moment as he sat in the Oval Office, being struck by the "absolute rightness of the decision the president had made."

President Reagan responded thoughtfully, underscoring the democratic values and the mutual aspiration for peace shared between the OECS and the United States. He outlined his planned public announcement and extended an invitation to Prime Minister Charles to join him at the White House press room for a news conference later that morning. Charles agreed without hesitation, eagerly stating her desire to speak directly to the American people, ensuring they understood "the truth about the situation in Grenada."

At one point, Prime Minister Charles said, "I have heard that the White House press corps is very assertive. Is that true?" Menges wrote that he and everyone else "ducked the question," as they didn't want to spook her. They knew that the press corps, given the previous adamant denials from Deputy Press Secretary Larry Speakes about the existence of the operation a few days before, would be particularly aggressive. This was their first chance to ask the president questions after Operation Urgent Fury was confirmed, after it had first been denied. Menges had never witnessed a presidential news conference in person, but he knew what to expect. To prepare, he spent about 10 minutes playing the role of devil's advocate, diplomatically posing the toughest and most hostile questions he could think of to Charles.

Shortly afterward, he received the latest draft of the president's imminent announcement regarding Operation Urgent Fury. Menges was surprised to find that the State Department had removed the phrase "to restore democracy" from the mission's stated purposes. He believed it was crucial for the president to publicly affirm this goal, emphasizing that their intention was to establish a genuine democracy in Grenada, not just replace one dictatorship with another. Menges insisted on reinstating the phrase and successfully persuaded the State Department to agree.

## THE FIRST DROP ON POINT SALINES

The C-130 that had just dropped the first load of Rangers into Grenada banked right hard and dropped below 100 feet toward the ocean to avoid the unexpected incoming heavy anti-aircraft gunfire.

The pilot of the plane that dropped the second batch of Rangers compared the gunfire to the annual Fourth of July fireworks display in Washington, D.C. The pilots of two other transport planes in the first wave twice attempted to drop their Rangers but were driven away, one of them taking direct hits from small caliber rounds. The pilot radioed to the rest of the first wave to break off their approach. The aborted drop required another reshuffling of the drop sequence.

For the next 15 minutes, the first group of Rangers were alone on the ground facing a hostile force larger and more powerful than anyone had expected. They scrambled for cover, ducking behind any cover they could find on or near the runway. The two transport planes that had had to break off from the initial airdrop radioed back to ask for assistance. "Need help to get in," one of the pilots said firmly. Another followed with "We need the gunships." At this point, the AC-130 Spectre gunships circling nearby were called in to suppress the anti-aircraft artillery (AAA), which included two Grenadian-manned 23 mm anti-aircraft guns positioned on a hill near the village of Frequente, northeast of the runway.

But there was another massive problem. All the radios that the Ranger TOC members had brought with them were broken, destroyed in the drop. One of the TOC officers, Major James Roper, described the scene in the book *Ghostriders*, by William Walter: "The hills 300 meters north of the runway came alive with AAA fire. I counted eight sources of heavy red tracer, .50 caliber, and an estimated 80-100 sources of green tracers, AK-47 fire."[6] There was another large gun active behind the hills, Roper explained. "The fire was directed at the aircraft and jumpers and several rounds zinged close overhead as I sprawled in the grass."

The AC-130, now cleared to engage, opened fire on one of the AAA installations, silencing the gun. The high-explosive incendiary rounds started a fire inside the building nearby. Then the gunship targeted some of the smaller anti-aircraft guns near the east end of the runway, which was close to St. George's University's True Blue campus.

Lieutenant Colonel Wesley Taylor, commander of the 1st Ranger Battalion, set up his command post with his TOC staff just off the runway.[7] The rest of the Rangers took up a defensive position on high ground north of the runway and west of the control tower. They were in a hornet's nest with bullets whizzing over their heads.

The north end of the runway was fortified by Cuban construction workers armed with AK-47s, heavy machine guns, recoilless rifles, and mortars. On October 22, Castro had ordered these "workers," most of whom had served in the Cuban military earlier in their careers, to prepare for combat, instructing them to "vigorously defend" their positions as if they were on Cuban soil. He intended to show the Americans the determination of Cuban forces in protecting communist territory.

The Cubans were positioned northeast of the runway, near Grand Anse Bay. Their defenses were based in a barracks compound just north of the airport terminal, known as the Old Camp, and a newer headquarters compound under construction to the northeast, near a village that the Americans dubbed Little Havana. One day before the invasion, Fidel Castro had sent one of his trusted military commanders, Colonel Pedro Tortolo, and a Communist Party operative, named Carlos Diaz, to Grenada. They arrived on a plane loaded with weapons. Their job was to organize the "soldier-bricklayers" for a fierce resistance.

Other PRA soldiers guarded the gates around the True Blue campus of the medical school at the eastern end of the runway or were stationed at the Great House, a plantation-era building west of the terminal used by Cuban engineers. While the Grenadians at Point Salines opened fire as soon as they spotted American planes, the Cubans initially held back under their leaders' orders.

The first platoon of Rangers from Bravo Company crawled into a drainage ditch on the north side of the runway; to duck under enemy fire, they crawled through the ditch until they got to their assembly area. From there, they moved up a hill to establish a 360-degree defensive position, ready to clear the Cuban work camp once the rest of their company arrived.

Lieutenant Colonel Wesley Taylor, meanwhile, set up his command center about a mile to the east in a roofless concrete structure on the south side of the runway. With opposition temporarily subdued thanks to the presence of the Spectre gunships, Taylor ordered his men to begin clearing the runway. In two-man teams, they removed the vehicles, barrels, wire fences, and other obstacles from the taxiways and runways.

One of the Spectre gunships approached the runway and spotted the 23 mm anti-aircraft gun firing from Frequente, northeast of the airstrip. With pinpoint accuracy, the gunship unleashed two bursts of cannon fire, silencing the Grenadian-manned gun. These ZU-23 anti-aircraft guns had a range of one-and-a-half miles, and the Spectres engaged them at the very edge of their capabilities, relying on their advanced airborne targeting systems.

The Spectre gunship, designed for close air support, interdiction, and force protection, proved its mettle. Its onboard sensors and computer-assisted targeting allowed it to precisely hit enemy positions while staying out of the effective range of ground-based defenses. This engagement demonstrated the gunship's lethal efficiency, turning the tide in favor of the Rangers on the ground.

The presence of anti-aircraft guns at Salines was an unwelcome surprise. "They weren't supposed to be there," Taylor later remarked. Intelligence briefings had indicated no anti-aircraft threats, based on a Defense Intelligence Agency analysis of satellite images taken nine days before the invasion. The analysis noted twenty-four mobile AA guns in Grenadian inventory, but none was supposed to be deployed at that time, according to DIA analysts.

By the morning of the invasion, however, these guns had been moved under the cover of darkness and strategically positioned around the island. Although the CIA had reported the presence of these guns to Washington, the crucial information had never reached the Rangers, leaving them vulnerable to the unexpected resistance. The first Rangers on the ground were outnumbered more than 15 to 1 by armed Cuban and Grenadians at that point, and the Marines were fifteen miles away on the other side of the island. Reinforcements were on the way, but they were desperately needed right then, at that moment. The fighting was intense. A second C-130 transport finally conducted its drop just before 6:00 a.m., twenty-two minutes after Taylor's plane. At that point, there were about eighty Rangers in the group, but they were still outnumbered.

Within half an hour after the second drop, the orbiting Spectres managed to silence about three-quarters of the hundred or so Grenadians firing at the Americans from the ground. The Spectre gunships, typically not tasked with engaging anti-aircraft guns, had already knocked out five artillery positions near the airport. This was crucial, as the Grenadian defensive plan called for a battery of six more Soviet double-barreled 23 mm AAA guns to be positioned around the Point Salines runway. Thankfully for the Americans, several of these guns remained silent because the militia gunners never reported for duty.

As the Spectres dominated the skies like dragons spitting fire down on the enemy, the Rangers advanced, clearing obstacles and securing the airstrip. The Spectres' success in silencing the enemy guns allowed the Rangers to establish a foothold on the island and clear the way for the subsequent phases of Operation Urgent Fury. But Point Salines wasn't the only theater in Grenada where the Spectres and their guns would be needed, and heavily involved.

With sun still rising in the sky, the squadron of nine Black Hawks skimmed over the waves at an altitude of 500 feet. The pilots of TF-160, the SEALs and Delta commandos had been forced to sacrifice their night vision advantage—the sun now exposing them as silhouettes in the early morning sky. The aircrews test-fired their M60 machine guns as they readied their assault. As they flew along the eastern coast of Grenada, they spotted the Marines who had secured Pearls Airport. The Black Hawks then banked south toward the capital of Saint George's. Below, the firefight between Army Rangers and the PRA and Cuban soldiers raged on at Point Salines. As the formation of nine TF-160 Black Hawks closed in, the arial convoy split up. Two peeled away early, turning south toward the Governor-General's mansion. Five aircraft pressed on toward Richmond Hill Prison, the hardest target on the island. The final pair broke off in trail, angling toward the Beausejour radio station. Each team now had its heading. The island was beneath them, and their fight was about to begin.

## RESCUING THE GOVERNOR GENERAL

Governor General Paul Scoon woke on D-day, October 25, to the concussive sound of whirling rotors from two Black Hawk helicopters hovering over his home. Two dozen Navy SEALs were gearing up to insert themselves into the Government House compound. One of the Black Hawks also carried two CIA agents and a State Department official. They were there to get Scoon's signature on an official document formalizing his request for the assistance of the United States and the OECS—while the operation was already underway.

But before they were able to land, their helicopter pilot had to pull away from the mansion to avoid opposing ground fire from uniformed Grenadians in the PRA. That repositioning exposed the Black Hawk to anti-aircraft fire coming from two PRA outposts in the capital city of Saint George's. One round ripped through the cockpit floor and tore a softball-sized chunk of flesh out of the air mission commander's left leg, knocking him into shock. The other pilot took control of the Black Hawk and headed out to sea to seek medical help for the wounded pilot—with the CIA officers, State Department official, and SEAL team commander still on board. The Black Hawk landed hard, without permission, on the flight deck of the USS *Guam*, Metcalf's flagship. The aircraft's radio was inoperative, and the engines would not shut down. Deck crews used fire hoses to douse the runaway turbines with seawater.

Meanwhile, at the governor general's mansion, 22 Navy SEALs and Delta operators fast-roped to the ground without their commander, Captain Robert A. Gormly, the head of the newly minted SEAL Team 6. In the rush of their disembarkation, the SEALs' satellite radios had somehow fallen out of their helicopter, leaving them without long-range communication and cut off from command.

As gunfire erupted outside, Governor General Scoon, his wife, and their nine-person retinue had fled to the mansion's cellar. Hearing the SEALs' American voices shouting from above, Scoon ordered his staff to reveal themselves, and the SEALs swiftly took charge of Scoon's entourage and cleared the mansion room by room for any hidden threats.

The group of PRA fighters, who had initially retreated during the SEALs' landing, regrouped behind a tree line and resumed firing. The team had planned for a helicopter extraction within forty-five minutes, but the heavy enemy resistance and lack of communication with their commander thwarted those plans. Without the ability to call in AC-130 gunships for air support, they were forced to adapt.

A rifle-fired grenade then exploded in one of the vacant rooms of the mansion, and small arms fire directed at the house intensified. Some of the SEALs and Delta operators took up defensive positions in and around the building, preparing for a prolonged standoff. The others moved Scoon's family and staff to a dining room upstairs, where they were better shielded from the relentless gunfire. But their ammo would only last so long.

While the mansion raid devolved into an all-out siege, Captain Robert Gormly, commander of SEAL Team 6, flew from the USS *Guam* to a Special Forces command post at Point Salines Airport. There, he finally established contact with the embattled SEALs at Government House, who were six miles away and equipped with limited-range handheld radios.

Grenadian infantry approached from the northwest, while a turreted armored personnel carrier advanced from the southeast. Captain Gormly's radioman relayed their pleas for air support through an Army Delta Force radioman nearby, who fortunately had used a Vietnam-era backpack radio to coordinate with the gunships. There were also reports that Captain Gormly would eventually get the phone number to the governor general's mansion and then call his SEALs to establish contact.

An Air Force AC-130 Spectre arrived over the mansion around 10:15 a.m., using a combination of its 20 mm and 40 mm cannons to hold off the advancing PRA soldiers. Another Spectre soon joined the fight, and together they thwarted the assault, but they would soon start running low on fuel. The SEALs and Delta Commandos held off the PRA soldiers for the rest of the night and were eventually relieved when two Black Hawks returned to carry them to Port Salines in the morning.

## THE FIGHT FOR RADIO FREE GRENADA

Chalk Nine, which was piloted by CW3 Scott Atkins and CW3 Ernest Armentrout, veered off from the rest of the Black Hawks. The SEALs on board had been tasked with taking out Radio Free Grenada's high-power transmitter, which had been supplied as a gift from Fidel Castro after Maurice Bishop orchestrated his coup against Eric Gairy. Lieutenant Donald "Kim" Erskine, a seasoned SEAL leader, felt a wave of apprehension wash over him as his chopper approached the landing zone.[8] The intel he had—a single satellite photo and a tourist map—was inadequate. In addition to the weak intel, six of the twelve men with him were last-minute replacements, and he barely knew their names. (Erskine's story is recounted in the books *Navy SEALs: Their Untold Story*, by Dick Couch and William Doyle,[9] and *The U.S. Invasion of Grenada: Legacy of a Flawed Victory*, by Philip Kukielski.)

Lieutenant Erskine had already been awake for two days, drawing back on his BUD/S (Basic Underwater Demolition/SEAL) training. He and the others assigned to the mission were continuously revising their assault plan as the mission was modified in Washington and Norfolk right up until the last minute. Originally, Erskine's SEALs were supposed to team up with the Army Rangers and secure the American medical students along with the airport at Point Salines. But as the overarching objective shifted from rescuing Americans to regime change, Erskine's platoon was relegated to what he considered an "afterthought" mission: securing and disabling Radio Free Grenada.

Lieutenant Erskine was standing in a packed Black Hawk as the harsh morning sunlight broke through the chopper's windows and open door. Their final approach came from the southwest. The Black Hawk flew over a mountain and down a canyon and found the transmitter in an open field near the coastal village of Beausejour. Farm equipment blocked the area in front of the station originally selected for their landing zone, so the Black Hawk flew to a meadow behind the building. As the aircraft got close to the ground, it started taking a massive amount of small arms fire from the PRA soldiers defending the area. And the gunfire was coming from close range, directly under Chalk Nine's rotor blades.

"Suddenly there were "tracers everywhere," Scott Atkins recalled. "I remember members of Seal Team panicking." Our orders were that we had to have an 80 percent attrition before we could abort the mission." This meant that eight of the eleven people on Chalk Nine, or one of the pilots, had to be killed or severely wounded before they could pull out.

While he was dodging bullets, Atkins said he was also trying to avoid the radio tower's guy wires. At times, the tower itself was just fifty feet away from his Blackhawk's rotor blades.

Atkins said Lt. Erskine told him to abort the mission.

Erskine shouted at Atkins, "GET THE HELL OUT OF HERE, IT'S TOO HOT!"

"There was a lot of screaming, at the time I assumed people were being shot," Atkins said.

"WHAT THE HELL IS GOING ON?" Atkins asked.

Erskine shouted back, "ARE YOU READY TO BE THE FIRST ONE DEAD? YOU'RE GONNA GET SHOT IF YOU DON'T LEAVE!"

"At first, I thought he was talking about shooting me," Atkins recalled. Atkins said he went back and forth with the SEALs, arguing for about two minutes. "It was chaos in that LZ."

We finally convinced Erskine that we weren't leaving unless eight of the SEALs were dead, or one of the pilots was dead.

Around that same time, the door gunner fired off several bursts lasting a total of forty-five seconds. It was just enough time for the SEALs to jump off the helicopter and run fifty yards from the landing zone to a concrete-block building next to the tower.

Erskine and his SEALs wasted no time securing the building. They methodically cleared the eight rooms inside, encountering minimal resistance. It appeared the Grenadians responsible for the initial gunfire had already fled. With the radio station building now under their control, Erskine took a moment to assess the situation. Their mission, like many others in the operation, had gotten off to a rough start. Nevertheless, they had achieved their immediate objective.

Erskine then focused on securing the rest of the isolated facility. He deployed his team strategically, with some members establishing positions on the east and west ends of the building and others setting up an ambush along a road that ran north-south past the building toward the capital. Erskine also planned a potential escape route for his team, which would require them to scale three fences to get to a beach on the island's western side. It wasn't ideal, but it was their only option. From there, they could swim out to sea where naval and air support would be patrolling. Hopefully, it wouldn't come to that.

Erskine's orders were to briefly hold the station until CIA operatives arrived by helicopter from the governor's residence with Governor General Paul Scoon. After Scoon signed the backdated document requesting foreign intervention, he was supposed to fly to the Radio Free Grenada transmission tower and broadcast an appeal for his countrymen to lay down their arms. That plan quickly unraveled when SEAL Team 6 faced heavy resistance and had to evacuate to the *Guam*.

There was another problem: The SEALs' taking of the transmission tower had zero impact on the government-run station's ability to broadcast. Radio Free Grenada continued to transmit its pro-coup propaganda message from another studio near Grand Anse Beach just south of Saint George's. They had a backup 10-kilowatt transmitter.

Erskine also soon discovered that he, too, was unable to contact his superiors. The encrypted satellite radios the SEALs carried weren't working. The frequencies and codes had apparently been changed overnight without their knowledge. Erskine could receive calls on his backup field radio, but he was unable to successfully transmit because of his radio's limited range.

The SEALs assigned to guard the road then stopped a station wagon carrying civilians: a mother, a father, three kids, and a dog. Erskine ordered his SEALs to take the family into custody to keep them from spreading word about the ongoing invasion.

Around 9 a.m., uniformed Grenadian militiamen started approaching the radio station riding in a Soviet-made truck accompanied by other civilian vehicles. Erskine called out to the caravan, ordering them to stop. Following the rules of engagement he had been issued, he identified himself and demanded that the approaching PRA soldiers throw down their weapons. A brief standoff ensued. Then one of the Grenadian soldiers opened fire. The SEALs responded with a salvo of gunfire that lasted only fifteen seconds, but it left all the Grenadian soldiers either killed or wounded. Their truck was also destroyed, and a large column of smoke rose through the air, letting everyone nearby know exactly where they were. Erskine ordered his medical corpsman to tend to the wounded enemy survivors while the other SEALs separated out the dead.

The radio transmitter building had now turned into a field hospital. The concrete walls were splattered with blood, and the wounded PRA soldiers were wailing in pain and fear. Erskine decided to let the civilian family go—the American presence at the station was no longer a secret.

News of the fighting at the radio transmitter site had reached the Grenadian military leadership at Fort Frederick by around 8 a.m., and the enemy commanders sent a detachment that included some of the PRA's best-trained soldiers. Their mission was to launch a counterattack on the SEALs at the transmission tower. The PRA platoon traveled in a Soviet-made armored personnel carrier. They stopped on a ridge 500 yards short of the station to plan their counterattack and start shelling the SEALs with mortars.

Erskine was on the roof of the station trying to get his backup radio to work when one of his men called up to him, "Get down here! Guys are coming from everywhere!" Erskine soon found himself and his platoon in a firefight, outnumbered and unable to call for help. His team had nothing to match the firepower of the PRA BTR-60 armored personnel carrier's 14.5 mm heavy machine gun.

"I'm dead. There's no way out of this," Erskine remembered thinking. He gathered himself and ordered his men to take cover inside the transmission building, but the walls were rapidly being blown apart. One of the SEALs on the roof fired a rocket-propelled grenade toward the Grenadians, but it was a glancing blow.

The blast failed to destroy the BTR-60, but it did manage to jam the gun turret, which gave the SEALs a momentary reprieve. Erskine ordered his men to abandon the building. One by one, they dove out of a doorway, continuing to face a barrage of small arms fire. Erskine remembers hearing a repeated and distinctive "snap" sound of AK-47 gunfire as the enemy's bullets passed all around him.

The SEALs had no option now other than to escape, which meant they had to recross the open field where they had landed to get to safety. They ran in groups, periodically dropping to the ground to avoid getting shot. Erskine remembers being knocked from his feet several times by bullets. The first bullet shattered his canteen; another sliced the heel off his boot. Then he felt a searing and tremendous pain in his arm. A bullet had struck his right elbow and forced him to drop his weapon.

Erskine used one of his kneepads to make a tourniquet and pressed on in pursuit of safety. Somehow, all the SEALs survived the fifty-yard trek over open ground until they reached a high fence topped by barbed wire. Erskine pulled wire cutters from his pocket, and another SEAL cut a hole in the fence. Yet another team member held their pursuers at bay with a rifle-mounted grenade launcher.

Erskine used a brief pause in the fighting to count his men. He was one short. Erskine looked back and saw the platoon's radio operator still in the open. He had been wounded while dragging the unit's satellite radio. "Shoot the radio and run!" Erskine shouted. The operator destroyed the radio's classified electronic components with a round from a 9 mm pistol and joined the others.

Fortunately, the Grenadian soldiers were stalking them cautiously after suffering their own casualties in the firefight. Once the SEALs cleared the chain-link fence, they plunged into dense, jungle-like vegetation, their movements now masked by the thick foliage. They had to cross a neck-deep, fast-running river and then follow a narrow path to a secluded beach on Beausejour Bay. There they shed some of their heavier weapons and equipment and started swimming in pairs parallel to the shore. Erskine was still dealing with intense pain from the gunshot wound to his elbow. The adrenaline in his veins did little to dull the pain.

As night fell, the team found themselves effectively split into two groups. Grenadian soldiers prowled the area, their search inching dangerously close to the SEALs hidden in the dense growth of the jungle. As the sun started to set, Erskine sent three SEALs to swim toward a nearby fishing village to procure boats. The remaining SEALs dug in and held their breath as MH-6 Little Bird helicopters started skimming overhead close to their concealed positions. Later, the rumble of Navy A-7 jets overhead signaled a new threat, as the radio station and its vicinity became the target of airstrikes, adding urgency to the SEALs' desperate escape plan.

One of the SEALs turned to Erskine: "Sir, maybe it's time to get the hell out of here." Erskine nodded grimly, his gaze sweeping over the rugged terrain surrounding them. He led his group of SEALs to a rocky outcropping that offered the men a direct escape route from the cliffs to the churning waters below. With adrenaline coursing through their veins, they braced themselves for the perilous plunge.

As they hit the water, the SEALs found themselves battling against the relentless pull of the ocean currents, struggling to stay together amid the darkness and the tumultuous surf. In the inky blackness of the night, their unity became their lifeline, a fragile thread binding them together against the unforgiving elements.

## THE ASSAULT ON RICHMOND HILL PRISON

The assault on Richmond Hill Prison unfolded with unexpected ferocity, surpassing the challenges faced during the raid on Radio Free Grenada. The morning sun cast a golden hue over the tiled rooftops of the picturesque port city. The serenity of the moment was shattered by the sound of the approaching Black Hawks and a storm of gunfire erupting from below as Grenadian-manned anti-aircraft guns awoke and unleashed a barrage of tracer rounds into the sky. The Black Hawks, lacking a gunship escort, relied solely on their side-mounted machine guns for defense against the onslaught of AAA fire.

The Delta operatives had anticipated minimal resistance and forgone heavy protective gear due to the stifling tropical heat. Armed with carbine rifles and pistols, they braced themselves for the chaotic descent into the heart of the conflict zone. With no accompanying air support allocated for the prison raid, the Delta fighters knew they were venturing into hostile territory with limited reinforcements.

The original plan called for the helicopters to rally at a traffic circle in the city center before splitting off to conduct their missions. However, the unexpected barrage of anti-aircraft fire disrupted the carefully laid strategy. The SEAL and Delta operators' initial attempt to breach the prison was thwarted by the relentless onslaught of enemy fire. During the chaos, one of the pilots sustained a gunshot wound to his right arm, and a door gunner was hit in the leg. With their aircraft compromised and their mission in jeopardy, all eight helicopters retreated to the safety of the sea to regroup.

Two of the helicopters headed to assist with the raid at the governor general's mansion. The remaining six charted a new course through a narrow valley toward Richmond Hill Prison, perched atop a north-south ridge southeast of the city core. As the prison came into view, the lead aircraft faced a barrage of fire from four anti-aircraft guns strategically positioned to defend the PRA's stronghold at Fort Frederick. In darkness, these World War II–era weapons would have posed little threat. However, in broad daylight, the Cuban-trained Grenadian gunners unleashed a formidable defense.

With relentless fire from two four-barrel 12.7 mm guns and two twin-barrel 23 mm guns, along with AK-47s wielded by approximately 40 Grenadian soldiers stationed at the prison, the helicopters were engulfed in a ferocious firefight. In response, the Black Hawk door gunners unleashed salvos from their M60 machine guns, while Delta operators joined the fray with their M4 carbines, targeting the anti-aircraft gun crews.

"They were ready for us," said Chief Warrant Officer Dave Bramel. "We stabilized to fast rope, but never executed. I looked down—there was a Cuban with an AK, just shredding my aircraft."

The team hovered for seconds—five, maybe ten. But Bramel waved it off. "Don't go, don't go." They circled. Came back in. This time, the defenders were even more dug in. The same Cuban gunner was still there, still firing. Bramel took a round to the leg. His foot slipped off the pedal. Behind him, Major Larry Sloan was hit in the back. The round would've gone through Bramel's head if Sloan hadn't been there. One of the operators leaned out and dropped the Cuban with a burst of return fire.

No one got out. The aircraft pulled away—damaged, bleeding, empty.

"The fire was unbelievable," Bramel recalled. "I called it in, said, 'I'm gone,' and I broke away."

As the Chief Warrant officer Bramel and the other Black Hawks veered off, an anti-aircraft round detonated inside the cockpits of one of the other helicopters, instantly killing the pilot, Captain Keith Lucas. The other pilot, Chief Warrant Officer Paul Price, though wounded in the explosion, managed to wrest control of the helicopter, which now trailed thick black smoke as it veered southward, away from the prison toward Point Salines, where there were a runway and Rangers on the ground.

The crippled chopper struggled to maintain airspeed and altitude as it flew over the Grenadian military compound at Frequente. The soldiers in the compound opened fire from the ground below. With each hit, the helicopter's stability further deteriorated until it rolled over and plummeted to the earth, crashing about three miles south of the capital on Amber Belair Hill.

The impact was devastating. It tore the tail rotor from the aircraft and sent its four main rotor blades spiraling through the air. The Black Hawk careened violently and flipped over once more before erupting into flames. Three of the soldiers on board were dead, the rest were severely wounded, by either enemy fire or the brutal force of the crash. But they managed to flee the wreckage as the enemy moved in.

A 12.7 mm round pierced another helicopter through the floor and struck a radio carried by Major Terry Boykin, a Delta Force operations officer who had fervently sought permission to join the combat mission. The impact of the round sent debris flying, tearing through Boykin's armpit and into his chest and shoulder, narrowly avoiding a major artery, and the force of the blast splintered a bone in Boykin's left arm. His teammates quickly bandaged his chest and injected morphine into his thigh. The pilot and two other Delta operators onboard also sustained injuries. Remarkably, the helicopter endured a total of fifty-four rounds, each one leaving its mark on the aircraft's battered exterior.

The Black Hawk pilot, with adrenaline-fueled urgency, steered the aircraft away from the prison, setting a course out to sea in search of a Navy vessel equipped to handle the injured. Four other Black Hawks, also carrying wounded, followed suit, despite the Army pilots lacking training or clearance for landing on Navy ships.

Ignoring attempts to dissuade it, one of the Black Hawks circled the USS *Guam*, prompting the ship's "air boss" to rush out in protest. However, the sight of the wounded and the severity of their condition prompted a swift change in attitude, leading to authorization for other Black Hawks to follow suit. Some chose to land on the USS *Moosbrugger*, a destroyer serving as the primary search and rescue ship in the aircraft carrier group. Major Terry Boykin, one of the more seriously wounded, was promptly shuttled by Marine helicopter to the *Guam* for urgent surgery. Yet despite their escape from immediate danger, their ordeal was far from over.

Back at the Amber Belair Hill Black Hawk crash site, the scene was grim. The door gunner's foot hung precariously by a sliver of skin, severed by a round of artillery. Others writhed in agony, blinded by hydraulic fluid that sprayed from ruptured lines inside the chopper. Amid the chaos, one Delta operator, already wounded in the leg, found himself trapped beneath the wreckage, his pelvis crushed by the impact of the crash.

Three of the survivors pooled their strength to lift the fuselage just high enough to free the trapped operator from the wreckage. Perched atop a plateau surrounded by sheer cliffs cascading down to the island's jagged coastline, the crash site offered no suitable terrain for another Army Black Hawk to safely land. But they would still try.

Chief Warrant Officer Scott Atkins and the flight crew aboard Chalk 9 were headed to the airport at Port Salinas to regroup after the assault on the radio tower. Atkins admitted that he had felt "overwhelmed during the initial gunfight." But his day was far from over.

"Point Salinas was not yet taken as we circled back to land," Atkins recalled.

After just one hour of the battle, Atkins was flying one of the two remaining TF-160 Black Hawks that were still able to fight. The other one had been tasked with medivac'ing the wounded back to an offshore naval hospital.

"I remember seeing a black smoke cloud on the hill and wondering who was shot down," Atkins said. He would soon find out it was coming from the wreckage of the Black Hawk that was piloted by his company commander Captain Lucas, and Chief Warrant Officer Price. All the officers and NCOs were called together. One of the commanding officers on the ground at the Airport looked to Atkins and said, "Yours is the only aircraft we got. We need you to try and move down towards the beach and rescue the survivors." Atkins then linked up with a team of a dozen Rangers. The young captain, who was in command of the Ranger platoon, boarded Adtkin's helicopter with his men shaking in fear. "This is a suicide mission," said the Captain. "He broke down in tears," Atkins recalled. "Captain, why don't you hop out of the aircraft—we're going to take off without you."

He and the other members of the platoon felt like everyone was safer without a panicking officer on board. Next, they were making their way to a small inlet, just south of the crash site near where they would soon face heavy anti-aircraft and small arms fire.

Atkins's Black Hawk, loaded with Rangers, set down on a tiny rocky island just off the coast near Amber Belair Hill. They stayed there for one or two minutes to assess the situation.

They realized they would have to insert the platoon of Rangers at the bottom of a cliff that was fifteen to twenty feet high. It seemed like an impossible task, but the Rangers all agreed they were up for the challenge.

Almost as soon as they took off, the treeline on the cliff erupted. Atkins radioed back to headquarters, "WE'RE TAKING GUNFIRE, AND IT'S HEAVY!" His Black Hawk then banked sharply to avoid the incoming rounds. And that's when Atkins remembered hearing over the radio, "SOMEBODY FELL OUT! WE CAN'T GO! WE LOST SOMEONE!" One of the Rangers had fallen out of the cabin door.

Around this time, three MH-6 Little Bird helicopters were approaching the crash site. They were responding to the radio calls. Each Little Bird was equipped with 2.75-inch rockets, which were about to be set loose on the enemy. Atkins's Black Hawk descended down to the water line to pick up the Ranger in the water. After several attempts, Atkins recalled, hearing "We got him, we got him!" At this point, the tail of the Black Hawk was partially submerged in the ocean. The rotor chop created a vortex of water that engulfed Atkins's helicopter, making it hard for the Little Birds to see where their aircraft was. As they ascended from the water line, Atkins said he looked over his shoulder and suddenly saw more than a thousand white-hot flechettes from the 2.75-inch rockets headed towards his aircraft. He said they looked like shooting stars streaming in his direction. Suddenly everything seemed like it was in slow motion as the flechettes approached. Instead of striking the Black Hawk, the projectiles miraculously passed through both of the open cabin doors.

Atkins said they made a total of five attempts to insert the Rangers at Amber Belair Hill, but the enemy's defenses made it impossible. So they were forced to return to the runway at Port Salines.

A desperate Mayday call finally reached the ears of vigilant Navy radio operators offshore. Responding swiftly, a Navy Sea King helicopter from the USS *Independence* was dispatched to locate the downed Army copter. It didn't take long to find the wreckage, the telltale plume of thick black smoke billowing upward from the dense jungle growth, a somber beacon of tragedy less than a mile east of the Point Salines runway.

The Sea King was not designed to conduct a contested environment combat rescue. The Navy version was painted bright white and used primarily for anti-submarine warfare patrols. Pilots affectionately compared it to a flying pickup truck or recreational vehicle. M16 rifles carried by two Marine volunteers from the *Independence* were the helicopter's only weapons.

The Sea King's pilots were much more familiar with conducting combat search and rescue operations over open ocean, but in this case, saving the lives of the downed Delta operators superseded protocol. The Sea King made a quick reconnaissance pass over the crash site. Two camouflaged fighters emerged from the jungle, and the pilots heard a radio call for help on their ultrahigh frequency (UHF) radios.

The voice called out for help and said there were five or six crash survivors who were badly wounded and needed to be flown to a hospital. The Sea King's pilot radioed back and told the survivors to make their way down to the shoreline at the base of the cliffs below the crash site. There, rescuers could extract the survivors while also ducking under the reach of the nearby anti-aircraft guns.

The Sea King banked and flew out over the ocean, where the pilots waited for permission from command to execute the daring rescue. The rescue was initially denied, and the pilot was told not to fly any closer than 3,000 yards, a little more than a mile and a half, from the island. While Admiral Metcalf was commanding the entire operation, the *Independence* had not been cleared to conduct air operations over the Army's designated zones on the southern half of the island. The pilot heard another desperate radio call. The crash survivors had made it down to the shoreline, but one needed immediate evacuation. The Sea King's pilot,

Commander Harvey Fielding, relayed this dire news back to the fleet and said emphatically, "If I can't go in, you need to get somebody else. We'll lose this guy otherwise. I know where they are. I've already been in there."

"OK, cleared to go," said a voice over the radio.

On the shoreline, there was just five feet of clearance on either side of the Sea King's sixty-foot-diameter main rotor blades. Moreover, the pilot would have to make a difficult downwind approach to land with its cabin door facing the shore.

As the Sea King helicopter touched down, it found itself precariously balanced in three feet of water, with one landing wheel planted firmly on the sandy beach while the other dipped into the lapping surf. Undeterred by the challenging conditions, the Delta fighters waded into the chest-deep waters, determined to reach the aircraft door and aid their wounded comrades.

With a sense of urgency pervading the air, the Sea King's cabin crew leaped into action, plunging into the water to assist in hoisting the wounded aboard the already crowded helicopter. Despite the swiftness of their efforts, it took a grueling ten minutes to load the passengers and their equipment onto the aircraft, which was already burdened with a crew of six. The additional weight of the survivors and their gear, totaling roughly a ton, strained the aircraft to its limits.

A crewman began to relay a report on the condition of each passenger. Yet impatience gnawed at the pilot, who was eager to take flight. He abruptly cut short the crewman's verbal report before learning that eleven men, not the expected six, had been taken aboard. With the aircraft struggling under the weight, compounded by the stifling heat and humidity, its aerodynamics started to falter.

Complicating matters further, the wind dictated a sharp left turn to escape the cove. Fielding improvised, guiding the helicopter along the water's edge until sufficient forward momentum could be generated for lift-off. Despite efforts to lighten the load by dumping fuel, the process was terrifying and slow.

With the aircraft barely skimming above the wave tops, Fielding issued a tense warning to the passengers to brace themselves for the possibility of reentry into the water. Desperate for a solution, he resorted to a counterintuitive maneuver known as "milking the throttle," briefly sacrificing altitude to boost the RPMs and sustain lift.

In a heart-stopping moment, a radio transmission crackled through: "You're on fire!" Fielding's initial alarm gave way to skepticism as he quickly discerned the true nature of the warning. The rotor wash was pulling up droplets of seawater, which, upon contact with the engine heat, turned to steam, creating the illusion of smoke. With relief flooding through him, Fielding steered the helicopter onward, navigating through the tumultuous skies to safety.

## MRS. CHARLES MEETS THE PRESS

By midmorning, the press corps had figured out what was going on. And according to Constantine Menges, they were very angry. Part of that anger stemmed from the fact that only yesterday, in answer to a direct question about the possibility of such action, Deputy NSC Advisor Admiral John Poindexter had told the press that it was "preposterous" to suggest that the United States would invade a tiny island in the Caribbean.

Further, the administration had decided that until the fighting ended, there would be no media presence with the forces in Grenada, and obviously no members of the media had been asked to make the trip. Suddenly, the television lights were on. The president and Prime Minister Charles were announced as television reporters delivered live breaking news reports. Mrs. Charles walked in first, followed by the president. They both walked to the podium, and the president spoke first.

"Ladies and gentlemen," Reagan began, "on Sunday, October 23rd, the United States received an urgent, formal request from the five member nations of the Organization of Eastern Caribbean States to assist in a joint effort to restore order and democracy on the island of Grenada." His words echoed with the weight of responsibility as he delved into the details of the multinational effort, emphasizing the imperative to protect innocent lives and to stem the tide of chaos unleashed by the brutal seizure of power in Grenada.

"We have taken this decisive action for three reasons," the president declared, his gaze piercing through the gathered crowd. "First, to protect innocent lives, including up to a thousand Americans, whose personal safety is my paramount concern. Second, to forestall further chaos. And third, to assist in the restoration of conditions of law and order and of governmental institutions to the island of Grenada."

The third reason was the one Menges had fought to keep in the speech. Reagan also painted a vivid picture of the violence and bloodshed inflicted upon the innocent people of Grenada by a ruthless cabal of power-hungry individuals, whom the president referred to as "leftist thugs." "Let there be no misunderstanding," President Reagan asserted, his voice carrying a note of solemn resolve. "This collective action has been forced on us by events that have no precedent in the eastern Caribbean and no place in any civilized society. American lives are at stake."

The president emphasized the unanimous call for assistance from neighboring states including Barbados and Jamaica, a testament to the shared commitment to restore democracy and uphold the principles of justice and freedom. After the president finished his opening statement, he moved to his right, placed his left hand on the arm of Mrs. Charles, and welcomed her to address the room. "We, as part of the Organization of East Caribbean States, realizing that we are, of course, one region—we belong to each other, are kith and kin," Prime Minister Charles affirmed, her voice firm and tinged with a sense of solemn duty.

Mrs. Charles continued, "It is true that we have managed to live with the [Maurice Bishop] regime since March of 1979. And we felt quite clearly, and we had good reason to believe that the regime was seeing it our way and was on the way to having elections. And we think this is the reason why himself and his Cabinet were destroyed, because he realized that the pressure we put on him to have elections was worthwhile, was right, and he'd begun to see that the democratic institutions must be put in place in any of these small countries."

Mrs. Charles also talked about the importance of a "small island state, a poor island state" like Grenada, having democratic institutions. "Grenadians had never been given the chance to choose for themselves the country that they want. And, therefore, it is necessary for us to see to it that they have the opportunity to do so," she stated. "To do this, we have to isolate the persons who have committed the acts that they did last week, in killing off most of the Cabinet. And we have to ensure that, in fact, an interim government of persons of, not political greed, but persons who are good administrators and who are Grenadians who can run the country for a few months for the pure purpose of putting the country back on the democratic status, so that elections can take place as soon as possible."

The press corps then started peppering the president with questions as if Mrs. Charles weren't there. One reporter asked, "Mr. President, did you have information that the Soviets and the Cubans were behind this takeover of Grenada? Did the Joint

Chiefs tell you that yesterday afternoon?" The prime minister, confident and resolute, didn't hesitate. She looked over her right shoulder to inform President Reagan that she was ready to handle that question.

Charles asked Reagan, "Want me to answer this?" but it was more of a suggestion than a question. Reagan nodded and smiled and yielded to Mrs. Charles. "Yes, we do have this information," Mrs. Charles stated. "I can't give you all the details because of the safety of people concerned." But Prime Minister Charles added, "In the two weeks before the assassination took place," they were greatly concerned about "the movements between the Soviet Embassies and known activists and the activists returning to Grenada, obviously a conduit between some of these Russians and some of these Grenadians."

Another reporter shouted at the podium, "Mr. President, can you tell us, are all the Americans safe, sir? And how long will the American forces be on the ground there? What is their role?"

"I could—well, we don't know how long that will be," President Reagan responded, his tone measured yet resolute. He continued, "We want to be out as quickly as possible, because our purpose in being there is only for them to enable—to take over their own affairs. As far as we know, the citizens are safe." His words offered hope, but his assessment was perhaps premature.

The next round of reporter questions kept probing the military situation on the ground. The president explained, "We've secured both the airports, and the landings have been completed." It was technically true, but he did not mention that the fighting was still intense. Reagan added a hint of caution to his assessment: "We are yielding to the influence of General Vessey in that we don't think in these early hours of that landing that we should be on the horn asking the commanders to stop and give us detailed reports."

Another reporter shouted, "With what's happening in Lebanon, are we spread too thin, Mr. President?" The president's response was swift: "No; we're not spread too thin," he declared, his voice steady amid the storm of uncertainty. He then wrapped up his remarks, informing the press corps that he and Mrs. Charles would be leaving and Assistant Secretary of State Tony Motley would stick around to answer some follow-up questions.

Deputy Press Secretary Larry Speakes then stepped in, signaling an end to the news conference with the president and Prime Minister Charles. Motley took the podium and, along with Speakes, handled mostly hostile questions for the next half hour.

Bud McFarlane and John Poindexter had been giving background briefings to the media and called Constantine Menges to the Situation Room. They told him that the president would be giving a nationally televised speech on Lebanon and Grenada that evening. They discussed themes for that speech for about half an hour. Menges was instructed to write the Grenada portion. In one hour, he had come up with a ten-page draft, which he gave to Poindexter.

## ABOARD THE *GUAM*

From the bridge of the *Guam*, General Schwarzkopf wrote that he "could see the parachutes coming down and the green tracers of anti-aircraft fire reaching up past them at Point Salines. The general recalled hearing reports that "the Cuban construction workers were not only heavily armed but dug in: they occupied sandbag bunkers on the hills all along the airfield. At first, we got only fragmentary reports, but it was clear that this was no cakewalk. People were getting killed."

"It was total chaos and confusion." Those on the *Guam* watched as the Army helicopters limped back from Grenada. Two crashed into the ocean. Others set down hard on the *Guam*'s flight deck, "full of holes and leaking hydraulic fluid all over." As the chaos was unfolding, Schwarzkopf watched as Admiral Metcalf received a message from the Navy's controller in Washington telling him he should not refuel Army helicopters, "because the funds-transfer arrangements with the Army had not yet been worked out." Metcalf read the message and handed it back to his chief of staff. "This is bullshit. Give them fuel," he said.

Fort Frederick had been identified as the headquarters for the Revolutionary Military Council and the PRA. "I want to bomb it," Metcalf told Schwarzkopf. "What do you advise?"

Schwarzkopf remembered thinking it was "a tough call because the fort was close to town, and we were under orders to minimize property damage and civilian casualties."

"Bomb it," Schwarzkopf said.

## LITTLE HAVANA

"Rangers, be hard. We'll be taking some ground-to-air fire," Lieutenant Colonel Ralph Hagler, the 2nd Battalion commander, said just before leading his men out the door of their C-130. The 2nd Battalion paratroopers also dropped at 500 feet, but without their reserve chutes, since there wasn't enough hang time to deploy them anyway. The C-130 pilots took evasive action as soon as they dropped their paratroopers. Once they started to climb after the drop, the pilots had to bank hard and fast, while dropping chaff and flares, in case there were any anti-aircraft missiles on the ground.

In the middle of the mass jump, some of the Black Hawks from the aborted prison raid unexpectedly started to land on the runway. They gathered in the western section of the drop zone where the surrounding high ground sheltered them from anti-aircraft guns. Some newly arriving Rangers landed almost on top of the Black Hawks as aircrew members worked on repairs.

The planes carrying the remainder of Lieutenant Colonel Taylor's 1st Battalion Rangers were now intermingled with the second element of five planes carrying Lieutenant Colonel Hagler's 2nd Battalion. Somehow, logistics officer Captain José Ventura managed to land on his feet in the stiff 20-knot gusts. Captain Ventura then immediately dropped to the ground, as the battle continued in the background. He looked around and saw Rangers everywhere standing and gathering up their chutes, acting like they were on a training exercise.

Ventura shouted, "What the hell are you doing?!" Leave that stuff. Get down. Can't you see they are firing?" He ordered the men to move off the runway toward berms that would offer them cover while they assessed the situation. Ventura saw Cubans with AK-47s scurrying around the high ground, but he told his men to fire only if fired upon. He also noticed some Rangers he didn't recognize. "What unit?" he asked. "1-75," they responded.

"God damn it, get your ass over to the far end of the runway. That's where you're supposed to be!" He was stunned when seven other 1st Battalion Rangers nearer to him rose and also moved away. "I realized: Oh my God, you know, we're intermingled here."

As the full force of nearly 500 Rangers descended from the skies, they swiftly organized themselves to secure the perimeter around the runway from all sides. According to the original battle plan, Taylor's 1st Battalion was tasked with securing the area extending from a lagoon to the True Blue medical campus on the eastern half of the airport, while Hagler's 2nd Battalion was to secure the other end, stretching from the lagoon to the ocean. Their primary objective, however, was to complete the clearance of the runway. To aid in this endeavor, two heavy equipment operators from the 82nd Airborne were hastily recruited. Despite their lack of experience, they commandeered Cuban construction vehicles to remove obstacles from the runway.

By 7:30 a.m., just 15 minutes after the conclusion of the mass airdrop, the runway was declared secure. Fixed-wing aircraft were promptly given clearance to land. Among the first transports to touch down were four C-130s carrying Delta Force's A Squadron and Charlie Company of the Ranger 1st Battalion. Additionally, eight light helicopters, outfitted for either troop transport or armed support, were brought in for air support. But they encountered formidable air defenses around the capital, and the attack helicopters were forced to return to Salines within 10 minutes.

General Scholtes, the JSOC commander, wasted no time upon his arrival in Grenada setting up headquarters at the airport terminal to oversee ongoing missions. Despite the urgent need for medical attention for Delta Force casualties, Scholtes made the difficult decision to cancel the 2nd Ranger Battalion's planned secondary attack on the Calivigny training complex, recognizing the strain on his engaged Rangers. Similarly, a secondary SEAL mission to seize Grenada's electric plant was also abandoned considering the unfolding circumstances.

As the runway clearance progressed, another squad of Rangers ventured into the northern hills behind the terminal buildings, where the old Cuban camp was situated. The camp consisted of twenty-two prefabricated Soviet-style barracks, each housing up to forty men. A three-man team from Bravo Company of the 1st Ranger Battalion moved in to assault a defensive position just outside the camp. They stealthily dispatched 2 Cuban guards, then moved into the camp and forced the surrender of twenty-eight others. According to Fidel Castro, it was at this moment that combat between Cuba and the United States officially started.

Subsequently, a platoon from Bravo Company navigated a trail from the runway to the heart of the compound, progressing through the camp from west to east under the cover of snipers and heavy machine guns. The unmatched military proficiency of the Rangers quickly overwhelmed the Cuban workers, prompting them to surrender en masse, abandoning their weapons and equipment. Some of the Cubans managed to get away and seek asylum in the Soviet Union's embassy, including Castro's top commander in Grenada, Colonel Pedro Tortolo.[10] A joke would soon start to circulate around Havana that the colonel had suffered a "combat injury"—a broken thumb from ringing the doorbell at the Soviet mission. Communist Party operative Carlos Diaz was killed in the fighting and was honored as a hero for fighting for Cuba's honor.

Initially, about 275 prisoners were detained and later handed over to the 2nd Battalion. Captain Ventura, a battalion staff officer, immediately started interrogating the captured Cubans in Spanish. Ventura gleaned that most had been on the island for about 14 months, with some recent arrivals. While they had received rifle training from Cuban military advisors, many feigned ignorance when it came to using their weapons. Moreover, it was revealed that several AK-47s were brand new, and their sights had yet to be calibrated.

When questioned about their firing despite orders not to do so, one worker explained the challenge of managing individuals with a penchant for violence, expressing difficulty in controlling those eager to engage with the Americans. His frank admission shed light on the complexities within the Cuban contingent. "Well, we have our problems, too," one worker responded. "We've got those guys who are gung-ho, more or less, who want to kill Americans, and we can't control them. They were running and shooting," the man said in Spanish.

In the heat of the battle surrounding the runway, distinguishing between Grenadians and Cubans proved challenging. Many Cuban construction workers, along with most Grenadian militia members, were attired in civilian clothing. Moreover, the olive-green uniforms worn by regular PRA soldiers were provided by Cuba. While Grenadians generally had darker skin tones compared with Cubans, a diverse range of skin colors was observed in both groups.

Language was a potential identifier, with native tongues serving as a distinguishing factor between Cubans and Grenadians. However, this distinction did little to assist in identifying the deceased. Following the conflict, American transports evacuated sixty-eight bodies from Grenada for repatriation to Cuba. Yet Havana recognized only twenty-four of these casualties as Cuban nationals, rejecting the remaining bodies as Grenadian. Consequently, the bodies deemed Grenadian were returned to their homeland.

As the remaining Cubans from the old camp retreated toward the Cuban headquarters compound at Calliste, northeast of Point Salines, the Rangers continued their mission in the designated area they had dubbed "Little Havana" on their maps.

With their attention now turned to the eastern end of the runway, where the medical school campus was situated, Alpha Company of the 1st Ranger Battalion regrouped at an assembly point nearby. Major John Abizaid, commanding Alpha Company, swiftly organized his troops. One platoon was dispatched to maneuver south of the runway along the shoreline toward the True Blue campus, while the other two platoons were tasked with fully clearing and securing the northern side of the eastern end of the runway.

Amid the hustle of preparations, Private Brian C. Ivers arrived at the assembly area just as the units were departing for their assigned missions. His astonishment peaked as he witnessed a white flatbed dump truck charging toward them from the still-contested eastern end of the runway. Reacting swiftly, twenty-year-old Mark Yamane, a machine gunner, bravely halted the civilian vehicle by stepping out in front of it. Two Grenadian men, armed with AK-47s, surrendered upon Yamane's orders and were taken prisoner without further resistance.

As Yamane secured the truck, radio operator Specialist Fourth Class Blair Donaldson and several others proceeded north from the runway along a road leading to a designated rally point for the 1st Platoon. However, they soon found themselves under fire from the ridgeline to the north, forcing them to take cover. Donaldson attempted to relocate the truck to a safer position but encountered a Grenadian soldier blocking his path. Amid the exchange of fire, both Donaldson and Yamane were wounded. Despite Donaldson's efforts to save him, Yamane succumbed to his injuries during the relentless battle for control of the eastern end of the airport.

"The fighting was at least as intense as any of the fights I was in Vietnam. And I saw two years over there," Taylor later recalled. Taylor was ordered to send his men across the airfield and take the high ground on the other side as fast as he could. One determined Ranger took charge of Yamane's still-hot M60 and provided crucial covering fire for the advancing Rangers. Simultaneously, an Air Force AC-130 gunship unleashed its 40 mm cannon, targeting a house that contained the source of the enemy fire that had killed Yamane.

As the Rangers pressed forward, additional covering fire from machine guns and mortars fortified their defensive positions on the runway. Despite the intense barrage, two more platoons from Alpha Company embarked on the perilous journey across the runway. Tragically, Tony Davis, a machine gunner with the 1st Platoon, fell victim to enemy fire, sustaining a severe neck injury that would leave him paralyzed. In an act of selfless bravery, Paul

Bell risked his life to rescue Davis from the exposed runway, earning him a Bronze Star with a V for valor.

Once safely across the runway, Spanish-speaking Rangers attempted to negotiate with concealed Cubans, only to be met with hostility and gunfire. In a bold move, Major Abizaid's company improvised armored support by commandeering a Cuban bulldozer and using it as a makeshift tank, a tactic famously depicted by John Wayne in the 1944 film *The Fighting Seabees*. With the bulldozer shielding them from enemy fire, the Rangers pressed on with their assault.

Donaldson and his comrades pushed forward, passing the demolished Grenadian home that had triggered the fatal counterfire. Inside, they encountered Grenadian soldiers, one of whom had lost a leg in the exchange. Despite their losses, the Grenadians welcomed the arrival of the Americans, expressing gratitude for their medical assistance. Upon reaching the hilltop, the Rangers seized a formidable 12.7 mm anti-aircraft gun, intending to turn it against the retreating Cubans. However, their efforts were thwarted by the weapon's complex Soviet controls.

By this point, the airfield was secure enough to land the partly emptied C-130s that had flown the Rangers to Grenada. After dropping their paratroopers, these twelve planes had headed to Barbados to refuel. Now they began landing at Point Salines to off-load their vehicles and remaining men. Among the new arrivals was a five-man jeep gun crew from Alpha Company of the 1st Battalion led by Sergeant Randy E. Cline, a twenty-eight-year-old former police officer.

The jeep team's mission was to secure a road junction on the northeast side of the runway, about a mile past the True Blue campus. Like all the Rangers, Cline was issued a photocopy of a British-made topographic map of the island that had no road names or longitude and latitude grid lines. The jeep missed a turn and proceeded past the assigned road junction, winding up on a dusty road leading east from the airport toward the village of Ruth Howard. Realizing their mistake, Cline's team backtracked and ran into a PRA ambush. The machine-gun jeep was wrecked by a shoulder-launched RPG. The ensuing firefight was detailed in a 2015 Facebook post by Joe Muccia, an Urgent Fury historian who has interviewed more than 300 Grenada veterans. According to Muccia's account, three of the five Rangers were killed in the initial salvo of Grenadian fire: Cline and Privates First Class Russell Robinson and Marlin Maynard. The other two Rangers managed to exit the jeep. Sergeant Mark Rademacher ordered Private Timothy Romick to go for help while he provided covering fire. Rademacher and at least one Grenadian soldier were killed in the ensuing exchange of fire. Romick was also hit multiple times but managed to crawl away. He armed himself with an abandoned Soviet-made light machine gun and made his way back to friendly lines near the True Blue campus. There he yelled for help by calling out a mash-up of prearranged passwords: "Black Tape, Crusade, Tear-drop, One-three!" He survived.

As Alpha Company pressed on with their firefight on the east end of the runway, Bravo Company began their advance westward. Positioned atop a vantage point, Bravo Company's Rangers peered down at the fortified stronghold of Cuban resistance known as Little Havana. Situated just over a mile north of the Point Salines terminal, the compound encompassed the Cuban mission headquarters and newly constructed barracks, overseen by Cuban military advisors who had assumed command of the construction workers. Defensive positions on the surrounding hills were manned by these advisors and workers.

The compound, roughly the size of a football field, was effectively encircled by elements of Bravo Company from the 1st Battalion. Sniper fire from the Rangers inflicted casualties on the Cubans inside, with some targets taken out from distances exceeding half a mile.

Meanwhile, the arrival of fresh troops from the 2nd Battalion signaled a new resolve to confront the entrenched enemy. Two Rangers on motorcycles raced toward Little Havana, unaware of the peril awaiting them. Both were wounded and stranded in a precarious no-man's-land between opposing forces. Quickly-thinking Ranger snipers from the 1st Battalion provided cover for the stranded soldiers until rescue could be organized.

Bravo Company assumed control of the overwatch positions around Little Havana, replacing Alpha Company. With a determination to neutralize the compound and retrieve the wounded, a direct message was broadcast in Spanish via bullhorn, demanding surrender within fifteen minutes. In response, 175 encircled Cubans, including twenty-three wounded, surrendered. These prisoners, along with the two injured Ranger motorcyclists, were evacuated. The remaining holdouts in Little Havana were left for the 82nd Airborne Division to handle as they joined the offensive the following day.

The unexpected arrival of the 300-strong Caribbean Peacekeeping Force brought some initial logistical challenges, but the peacekeeping force ultimately provided a solution for managing the influx of prisoners. Tasked with guarding the Cuban and Grenadian detainees, the Caribbean peacekeepers efficiently transported them away in captured Cuban trucks, establishing a temporary detention camp at the old Cuban camp near the runway.

With the prisoners secured, attention turned to reaching the American medical school students at True Blue. This critical mission was entrusted to the 2nd Platoon of Alpha Company, who set out to navigate the chain-link fenced compound consisting of five barracks-style dormitories housing the first-year students, who were new to the island.

The facility at True Blue also boasted amenities such as a lecture hall, a cafeteria, and a basketball court. When the Rangers arrived, they encountered minimal resistance from the Grenadian soldiers guarding the campus gates. It took the 2nd Platoon another ninety minutes to fully secure the campus and ensure the safety of the 138 students.

The soldiers' arrival outside the dormitories was met with relief by the students, who had been confined by the round-the-clock curfew for days. They cheered upon hearing that they were going home. Despite being only in the early stages of their medical studies, the students were enlisted by the Rangers to assist in treating casualties. Makeshift treatment centers were established, utilizing the school library for Americans and the lecture hall for Cubans and Grenadians. The basketball court was repurposed as a landing pad for helicopters evacuating the seriously wounded to the *Guam*, while the laboratory served as a temporary morgue.

While grateful for the Rangers' protection, the students revealed unsettling news—they were only a fraction of the medical students on the island. Over 200 others resided at the main campus on Grand Anse Beach, with an additional 200 living off campus in various homes.

The oversight regarding the multiple campuses came to light when the Defense Intelligence Agency stumbled upon photos of the Grand Anse campus. These images were brought to the DIA's attention by a National Security Agency employee who had a relative attending the school. Despite the intelligence package reaching General Scholtes's JSOC and Admiral McDonald's Atlantic Command, no action was taken at that time to secure the Grand Anse campus or account for the off-campus students.

Schwarzkopf wrote in his memoir that the news of the second campus and students living among the Grenadian population came as "the biggest shock of the day."

By noon, Schwarzkopf and Metcalf had concluded that Grenadian anti-aircraft defenses posed a significant obstacle to Special Ops forces securing Saint George's. They realized that taking the city would require a different approach. Schwarzkopf proposed redirecting the Marines' amphibious assault force, which was stationed off the coast near Grenville and Pearls, to land north of Saint George's.

Meanwhile, the Rangers at True Blue used the island's functioning phone lines to contact the Grand Anse campus for directions. Metcalf coordinated the repositioning of the 22nd MAU's ships and dispatched a SEAL team to assess the feasibility of a beach landing. Within a couple of hours, the SEALs confirmed that a landing was possible and scheduled it for later in the afternoon.

Later, Metcalf and Schwarzkopf convened to assess the day's objectives. Despite securing the airfields and isolating the island, the RMC still held government buildings, Governor General Scoon and SEAL Team 6 remained surrounded, and most of the American students were still captive. The commanders recognized that the initial *coup de main* had largely failed.

Metcalf and Schwarzkopf recognized that the Army and Marines would need to advance overland to rescue the students and capture Saint George's. Schwarzkopf recalled that Metcalf then admitted his limited knowledge of ground operations and asked Schwarzkopf to devise the plans for the following day. The Navy admiral and Army general, diametrically different from each other in almost every sense of the word, except their commitment to the mission, discussed the details of sending Marines to stage an assault on the northwestern side of the island in a classic envelopment maneuver. "Of course," Schwarzkopf agreed, and he immediately convened with his planners to develop the strategic and tactical plans for the upcoming operations.

## AN AFTERNOON UNDER SIEGE

By midday, the two AC-130 gunships providing firepower from the sky had to leave the fight at the governor general's residence to refuel. SEAL Team 6 commander Captain Robert Gormly urgently requested additional forces to relieve the besieged mansion. Gormly had taken a chopper to the Point Salines Airport, where he was now able to communicate with Admiral Metcalf's staff on the *Guam*.

Metcalf had just ordered the attack on Fort Frederick, the command post where the PRA was directing the counterattacks on Scoon's mansion. The fort, defended by Soviet-made ZU-23 anti-aircraft guns, was in close proximity to civilian buildings, so Metcalf decided not to use Navy ships or jets. Metcalf's first choice was two Marine Cobra attack helicopters. They attacked the fort in tandem, one making a pass while the other distracted the defenders.

On their fifth attack run, one Cobra was hit by three anti-aircraft rounds, crippling both engines and severely injuring the pilot, Captain Timothy Howard. The copilot, Captain Jeb Seagle, was knocked unconscious. Despite his wounds, Howard managed to land his chopper with a semi-controlled hard landing on a playing field in Saint George's. On the ground, Seagle slowly regained consciousness and dragged Howard from the burning wreckage.

The other Cobra provided covering fire, but it was also hit by anti-aircraft fire, killing both pilots, Captain Pat Giguere and Lieutenant Jeffrey Scharver. The aircraft crashed into the sea just outside Saint George's harbor. The unexpectedly stout resistance coming from Saint George persuaded Metcalf to unleash Navy A-7 Corsairs from the USS *Independence* to bomb Fort Frederick. But no one knew at the time that an additional colonial fort neighboring Fort Frederick served as a civilian mental hospital.

While labeled as Fort Matthew on maps, locals referred to it as the General Mental Home, or colloquially as the "Crazy House." Unlike typical medical facilities, there was no red cross marking on the roof. Instead, the exterior walls prominently displayed the flag of the Grenadian revolutionary government and military—a large red dot on a white background. Subsequent investigations revealed that on D-day, weapons were discharged from within the hospital premises, as well as from two anti-aircraft guns situated just 50 yards away.

The A7s dropped a 500-pound bomb on this target, and twenty-one patients were killed. Other uninjured mental patients were set loose to wander the streets of the capital. Aboard the *Guam*, the unintended effects of the bombing were not known until days later. The only immediately apparent result of the air strike was a cessation of radio traffic coming from Fort Frederick. "In hindsight the battle was won right there," Metcalf later recalled. "From that time on, everything was local action." Metcalf personally learned that the hospital had been hit when he visited the island two days later, but the mistaken attack was not publicly confirmed by Washington until Halloween.

The situation at Government House was tense, and everyone's safety remained an open question. Admiral Metcalf and General Schwarzkopf devised a plan to alleviate the pressure on Paul Scoon and those besieged with him, including SEAL Team 6. Two rifle companies from the 22nd Marine Amphibious Unit were tasked with executing a landing operation. Golf Company, stationed aboard the USS *Manitowoc*, would assault a narrow beach at Grand Mal Bay using amphibious landing craft. Tanks and jeeps from the USS *Fort Snelling* would follow suit once the beachhead was secured. Additionally, Fox Company, already positioned near Pearls Airport, would be transported across the island by Marine helicopters to reinforce the amphibious force.

At approximately 3:30 p.m., a contingent of thirty Grenadian soldiers, accompanied by an Eastern Bloc armored personnel carrier (APC), was observed advancing from the vicinity of Bishop's former residence nearby. The SEAL team's radio operator's batteries were dwindling, so he resorted to using Scoon's house phone to urgently call for assistance, utilizing a long-distance calling card. Thanks to the firepower of an AC-130 Spectre gunship, they successfully thwarted the advancing soldiers by neutralizing the APC and subsequently igniting the former residence of the prime minister, which was being utilized as a staging area for attacks on the U.S. forces.

As night descended upon the shoreline, the Marine amphibious force commenced their unopposed landing north of Saint George's. Golf Company established a landing zone for the imminent arrival of Fox Company via helicopter. Despite these efforts, concerns loomed aboard the USS *Guam* that the Marines dispatched to rescue the besieged SEALs might arrive too late.

An AC-130 used its 40 mm cannon to again beat back a group of fifteen to twenty Grenadian soldiers who had moved close to the mansion. Lady Esmai Scoon broke down and began to cry. Then, around midnight, the Roman Catholic bishop on the island telephoned Scoon to offer his prayers and support. The couple's courage was restored by his call—and by the AC-130 gunship that remained overhead.

Admiral Metcalf, who had been working 36 hours straight, got ready to knock off for the night. But as he turned to leave the command center, a call came in from Atlantic Command in Norfolk. "What's your enemy body count for today?" an officer wanted to know.

Schwarzkopf looked at Metcalf darkly. "We need to stay away from this body-count business. It caused terrible trouble in

Vietnam, and it'll cause terrible trouble here. Let's just concentrate on accomplishing the mission.

"You're right," Metcalf said, and so instructed his staff before leaving.

Later that night, the first SEALs who had escaped the melee at the Radio Free Grenada transmission tower were recovered. The USS *Caron*, patrolling offshore, spotted their strobe lights in the water and turned to investigate; it was the three SEALs who had been sent to acquire the fishing boats. A rescue boat was launched by the destroyer to retrieve the exhausted trio in the commandeered boat.

## *October 26, 1983*

As dawn illuminated the morning of October 26, the military outlook improved significantly. Throughout the night, two Marine infantry companies, accompanied by thirteen amtracs (amphibious tractors) and five tanks, advanced southward along a narrow road leading to the capital, encountering minimal resistance. By daybreak, they had reached Paul Scoon's residence. The newly arrived Marines joined forces with the twenty-two-man SEAL team and rescued the group of eleven civilians who were accompanying Scoon.

Shortly before 9 a.m., Scoon and his wife were airlifted offshore to the USS *Guam*, arriving in time to enjoy a hearty breakfast and tea in Metcalf's mess. Later, the couple traveled by helicopter to Point Salines, where an ad hoc headquarters had been set up by Caribbean forces working alongside U.S. troops. There, Scoon was handed four identical typed letters, initially drafted in Barbados, calling for U.S. and OECS intervention. Each letter was backdated to October 24 and addressed to Reagan and the leaders of Barbados, Jamaica, and the OECS nations.

After freeing Scoon and securing his safety, Golf Company from the 22nd Marine MAU received orders to head south toward Fort Frederick, the main Grenadian military base where intense fighting had occurred earlier. When daylight came, the Grenadian resistance quickly crumbled, and their leaders disappeared into the city. The Marines didn't realize it then, but the sight of tanks rolling through the streets scared off the Grenadian forces.

Reflecting on the situation, Admiral Metcalf remarked, "If I had known then what I know now, I would have landed five tanks off Point Salines, and that would have done it." The absence of preparation to confront armored vehicles left the Grenadian forces vulnerable, as the mere presence of tanks instilled fear among the populace, facilitating the swift dissolution of resistance.

Around noon, Golf Company set off toward Fort Frederick. Along the way, they encountered two abandoned armored cars, a silent testament to the unexpected surrender of the PRA. When they reached the colonial-era fort, they saw several men fleeing from the walls, and the Marines advanced without encountering resistance.

By 5:00 p.m., Golf Company entered the deserted underground command post of Fort Frederick. A captured PRA staff officer revealed that Cuban advisors had been present at the fort until that morning. Although no Cubans were found when the Marines arrived, they discovered ample evidence of Soviet influence on the island, including a large cache of weapons and ammunition, military maps, and documents outlining Grenada's secret military relationship with the Soviet Bloc.

Schwarzkopf used the information from the captured maps to plan the remainder of the ground campaign, ensuring that every military location on the map was reached and neutralized. What was initially planned as a one-day unconventional *coup de main* turned into a conventional war, taking seven more days to officially conclude.

## THE RESCUE

The combined efforts of the 82nd Airborne and Rangers at Point Salines faced a formidable challenge in rescuing the students at the St. George's Medical School Grand Anse campus. Despite ample troop numbers, including reinforcements that had landed the previous day, progress was stymied by reports of a significant enemy presence. While the 82nd Airborne continued to consolidate its units, pressure mounted from higher command levels to expedite the rescue mission. The tension within the command center escalated as demands for action intensified from Washington via Atlantic Command.

As the plan for the student rescue unfolded, Schwarzkopf wrote in his memoir that he had clashed with the colonel who was in charge of an entire Marine landing brigade and it's helicopters. "We don't fly Army soldiers in Marine helicopters," the colonel stated firmly.

"Colonel, we've got a mission to rescue these students now," Schwarzkopf replied, emphasizing the urgency of the situation. "Your Marines are occupied in Grenville, and your helicopters are right here. The quickest way to get the job done is to utilize these helicopters."

The colonel remained steadfast. "If we have to do it, I want to use my Marines. They'll be the ones to rescue the hostages," he insisted.

"But that'll take at least twenty-four hours," Schwarzkopf countered, his tone growing more forceful. "We don't have that kind of time."

The standoff intensified until Schwarzkopf issued a direct order: "This is an order from me, a major general, to you, a colonel. If you disobey, I'll ensure you're court-martialed."

After a brief exchange with his subordinates, the colonel relented. "Well, all right. I guess we'll do it."

With the decision made, preparations for the raid commenced swiftly. General Trobaugh coordinated with the soldiers, while instructions were relayed to the students via shortwave radio and over the phone. One of the medical students was able to relay a message to the *Guam*, thanks to his ham radio. Another American on the island simply called the Point Salines Airport terminal and was able to speak directly to the U.S. military. The students, staff, and other evacuees were advised to wear white armbands, cover their windows with mattresses, and wait for the helicopters to show up.

The evacuation count surged to 233, prompting a pre-assault bombardment of suspected enemy positions. Army mortars and howitzers, Navy A-7 jets, and an Air Force AC-130 gunship launched the assault around 4:00 p.m. The AC-130 targeted the Carifta Cottages, which housed Cuban engineers and supervisors near the medical school campus. Navy A-7s targeted a former hotel, known as the Police Training College, northeast of the campus.

The AC-130 devastated the cottages with its 20 mm gun, while a Navy A-7 conducted bombing and strafing runs on the police training building. Grenadian anti-aircraft gunfire briefly engaged the gunship before being silenced. However, concerns arose about the naval gunfire potentially endangering the student-occupied building. Metcalf swiftly reversed the order to fire, preventing a catastrophic mistake. "We almost blew away the students with naval guns," the *Guam*'s chief of staff later told a Marine historian. But he added that he had been amazed by Metcalf's ability to improvise a joint operation on short notice by "grabbing all concerned by the short hairs."

Nine CH-46 Sea Knight helicopters, carrying the Rangers, flew in, landing on the pristine white sand beach in groups of three. One of the students watched the approach in awe, comparing it to the famous "Ride of the Valkyries" helicopter assault scene in the movie *Apocalypse Now*. The pilots scrambled for suitable landing spots, some touching down farther up or down the beach than originally intended. As some of the Rangers jumped into waist-deep water, the rotors of one Sea Knight clipped a palm tree. The pilot shut the engine down, and the aircrew and Rangers abandoned the stricken helicopter on the beach. The other eight CH-46s took off undamaged.

Alpha and Bravo Companies from the 2nd Battalion quickly established a defensive position around the campus, while Charlie Company directed the students to assemble in the gym. "U.S. soldiers! Friend or foe?" shouted the Rangers. "Friend!" the students replied. The Rangers led the students outside in groups to the beach to await the arrival of their rescue helicopters.

The Sea Stallions, larger helicopters, were now on their way to pick up the students and other evacuees. The crew chief of the disabled Sea Knight ran back to his aircraft to take a second look at the damage. After a quick inspection, he reported to the pilot. "I think we can fly it," he said. The pilot and two crew members returned to the copter. It shook violently on takeoff but managed to stagger back to safety at Point Salines.

The Sea Stallions landed on the beach one at a time, picking up about fifty students at a time in over five successive flights. Due to the last-minute additions, one aircraft carried 60-plus passengers on one flight, well over its maximum load. A total of 233 civilians were flown from Grand Anse to Point Salines. Once all civilians were safely evacuated, the Rangers signaled the Sea Knights to come pick them up with a yellow smoke grenade. The plan was to extract them in three flights, with about fifty Rangers on each flight.

However, as the Sea Knights began extracting the Rangers, heavier resistance was encountered. As many as seven mortar rounds exploded nearby during the extractions. On the second landing, another Sea Knight clipped a palm tree, rendering it unflyable. In the final extraction scramble, eleven Rangers were left behind. They were briefed to evade and escape, but fearful of friendly fire, they opted to paddle out to sea toward Navy ships.

Eventually, they were spotted and picked up by the destroyer USS *Caron*. Meanwhile, Dr. Robert Jordan, an assistant professor of anatomy at the medical school, along with two companions, decided to shelter in place during the evacuation. They emerged to a deserted campus and eventually made their way to safety.

The successful evacuation came at the cost of one CH-46 wrecked, another damaged, and five Rangers wounded. None of the students was injured, but they were very frightened. After securing the safety of the students, the Rangers who had evacuated the students returned to defensive positions near the guarded compound, where they were greeted with cheers by the civilians.

The evacuation of the Grand Anse campus was a completely improvised operation that had no prior planning by the Pentagon. The successful operation received high praise from top-level officials during a press briefing at the Pentagon. Meanwhile, in the United States, the first transport plane carrying students and staff from the True Blue campus landed at Charleston Air Force Base, where they were met with relief and gratitude.

At the Air Force Base in Charleston, American students recounted their ordeal of being held captive by Grenadian soldiers after the United States landed in Grenada. "The Cubans were definitely out to get us," said one of the students, who was among those evacuated. Marines provided protection as the students were walked to safety. "We were grateful to see U.S. troops," remarked another student. However, the media chose to highlight one student who seemed unhappy about the evacuation.

Stewart Rasch, a twenty-five-year-old from the Bronx, New York, expressed his dissent to reporters, stating, "The people in Grenada were very much in support of the action, but I was not. We are meddling in others' business and overstepping our authorities as powers of peace."[11] He decided to leave the island out of fear of being taken hostage by fleeing Grenadian forces.

Student Bill Riffley recounted a harrowing experience of waking up amid chaos. "We woke up right in the middle of World War III. It was scary," he described. Later that day, their house was invaded by the People's Revolutionary Army, with around thirty Grenadians armed with AK-47s. Seeking refuge, Riffley's group fled to a friend's house at the bottom of the hill, enduring a terrifying night amid relentless bombings. Military trucks passing by prompted their decision to leave, fearing Cuban snipers, and they sought shelter several blocks away. He said there was a bad feeling between the Cubans on the island and the American students. "They didn't like us, and we didn't like them. We wanted to get the hell out of there and call the Marines and have them blow up that hill."

John Doyle said he had attempted to negotiate with the Grenadian soldiers for their release, highlighting the medical students' desire to save lives. After being held for three hours, they were finally allowed to leave. Some of the American students on this flight said Marines had reached them just before noon on Thursday and walked them from two to four miles to the airport, forming a "human shield" around them, although they had taken no fire.

Richard Cascio of Birmingham, Michigan, described a terrifying assault by invading troops near their house. "It was the loudest thing I ever heard," he recounted. Lasting about fifteen to twenty minutes, the assault had been followed by intense mortar fire for three to four hours. Cascio and others had been forced to lie on the floor, fearful of being hit by their friendly gunfire if their location were unknown.

Joseph DiLiberta, hailing from Worcester, Massachusetts, emphasized the necessity and protective intent of the invasion, stating, "I don't see how anybody can criticize that invasion, and I can't even call it an invasion. It was for our protection." Describing their precarious situation, DiLiberta recounted how they had sought refuge in their rooms, fortifying themselves against potential danger. "We were lying face down . . . with pillows over our heads and blankets on the floor," he explained.

The sudden appearance of Marines heightened their anxiety, unsure of their identities at first. "We weren't sure they were ours," DiLiberta admitted, as they had been instructed to freeze with rifles pointed at them. Ordered to evacuate, DiLiberta's group had been led single file through a column of Marines to a waiting helicopter on the beach. Urged to move quickly and leave behind any luggage, they had obeyed without hesitation, running toward safety.

June, DiLiberta's wife, expressed gratitude toward the Marines, acknowledging their protective stance as they had run toward the helicopter. "They gave us a wall," she recounted, highlighting the Marines' efforts to shield the students from harm.

As night fell, Schwarzkopf revisited the resistance he had faced earlier that day over the use of Marine helicopters to fly Army Rangers. Finishing his orders, he contemplated his lack of formal authority. "Here are your plans," he said to Metcalf in his office, then recounted the incident that afternoon. "I'm more than happy to run your ground campaign, but I've got to have some authority," he concluded. Metcalf responded quietly, "I can fix that."

He called in the entire senior staff and declared, "As of now, Schwarzkopf is the deputy commander of this task force. He is my second-in-command. In my absence, he is in charge, and when he gives an order, you should consider that that order comes from me." Schwarzkopf was gratified to see Metcalf act swiftly and decisively on his behalf.

*October 27, 1983*
The following morning, the Marines finished sweeping the high ground above Saint George's and encircled the town. Meanwhile, the 82nd Airborne—which now had six battalions on the ground—had finally taken over from the Rangers and begun working its way north and east from the air base. Metcalf and Schwarzkopf flew into Point Salines to visit Army headquarters around noon. They had just sat down for a briefing when the *Guam* relayed an urgent message from Atlantic Command: The joint Chiefs of Staff wanted them to take the Calivigny barracks by the end of the day.

Calivigny was a garrison situated on a peninsula about five miles east of the air base; intelligence sources reported it to be a Cuban-run terrorist training camp. Schwarzkopf wrote that they had been planning to secure it in the final phase of Operation Urgent Fury. The 82nd Airborne was headed in that direction, too, but was moving very slowly because it was clearing out each pocket of enemy resistance as it was discovered. Schwarzkopf and Metcalf sent a message back to Atlantic Command that said something like, *The 82nd Airborne is moving that way and should take the Calivigny barracks by the end of the day tomorrow.*

But Atlantic Command responded, in effect, *Absolutely not.* They wanted the Calivigny barracks taken out by that night. Someone at the Pentagon ordered another helicopter assault. The task force was instructed to bomb the Calivigny barracks for almost an hour with air strikes and naval gunfire until finally the Rangers went in. The operation was a disaster.

Metcalf and Schwarzkopf were aware of Calivigny's political importance, but they were surprised by the tactical military decision dictated from the Joint Chiefs on such a tight deadline. Until then, orders had mainly come from Admiral McDonald's CINCLANT command in Norfolk, with little interference from their Pentagon bosses.

Schwarzkopf was furious. "That's the stupidest goddamn order I've ever heard," he told Metcalf. It didn't seem like something Vessey would approve of. Metcalf instructed his staff to confirm the directive.

The reply from Norfolk confirmed it: "JCS has ordered you to take Calivigny barracks before dark." At noon, Metcalf relayed the order to the 82nd commander for execution.

General Trobaugh's own 82nd troops were advancing on Calivigny, but they wouldn't reach it before dark. Facing the tight deadline, Trobaugh turned to the Rangers for the attack. The Rangers had more helicopter assault experience and were familiar with the target. Although they were awaiting airlift back to the United States, Metcalf decided to keep them under Trobaugh's command. Colonel James Scott, an 82nd Brigade commander and former Ranger battalion commander, was assigned tactical command of the assault to smooth over any issues. He delegated tactical control back to Hagler, the Ranger 2nd Battalion commander, once the attack began.

A plan was quickly drafted to assault the camp with Hagler's reinforced Ranger battalion transported on Army Black Hawks. They were briefed that the camp might contain a battalion of Grenadian troops, over 300 Cubans, sixty Soviet advisors, and up to 6 ZU-23 anti-aircraft guns, making it a highly hazardous daylight assault.

Only two of the nine Task Force 160s Black Hawks were still operational, so the airlift was assigned to newly arrived

Army Black Hawks from the 82nd Airborne's Combat Aviation Battalion. These pilots were less experienced, which added to the apprehension about the mission. "Guys, we don't know what's out there. Just remember that your primary job is to fly the aircraft until it won't fly anymore. Concentrate on that," advised Lieutenant Colonel Robert N. Seigle, the helicopter battalion commander.

The assault was to be preceded by an intense fifteen-minute Army-Navy barrage starting at 4:00 p.m. Three 82nd Airborne batteries at Point Salines fired 500 shells at Calivigny to initiate the bombardment. The Rangers boarded their Black Hawk helicopters and flew toward the Calivigny peninsula. Smoke rose from the burning barracks in the distance. Most of the artillery rounds had missed their targets, but two had nailed the objective. This time, there would be minimal anti-aircraft fire as the Rangers approached.

Navy A-7 Corsairs and an AC-130 Spectre joined forces in an aerial bombardment, demolishing most of the buildings and igniting two 1,000-gallon oil drums. The Spectre gunship also launched two 105 mm rounds into each of the fifteen to twenty corrugated-roof buildings, triggering a secondary explosion in one of them, indicating it may have been an ammunition or fuel storage facility.

With the path cleared, the Rangers arrived in four flights of four Black Hawks per flight, each Black Hawk carrying fifteen soldiers. Flying low at over 100 knots, the helicopters encountered unexpected challenges due to faulty aerial maps. They reached their designated landing zone sooner and faster than anticipated, partly obscured by thick black smoke from the burning oil drums. To swiftly reduce speed, the pilots flared their helicopters nose-up.

Suddenly, enemy rounds hit the lead Black Hawk. Alarms blared as one of the helicopter's hydraulic lines was severed, causing it to collide with another chopper. A third Black Hawk swooped to avoid hitting the other two, forcing it to land in a ditch, resulting in a damaged tail rotor. After things settled down for a moment, the pilot tried to take off, unaware of the damaged tail rotor. The Black Hawk spun out of control and crashed into the others.

Three brave soldiers lost their lives in the tragic incident: Specialist Kevin Lannon, Sergeant Stephen Eric Slater, and Specialist Philip Sebastian Grenier. Three more Rangers suffered severe injuries, one of whom was left permanently paralyzed. The landing zone turned into a scene of mass casualties, with survivors sprinting away from the devastation to carry out their mission.

Sergeant Stephen Trujillo, a Ranger medic, was ordered to return to the crash site to provide aid to the wounded. Despite the danger, he embarked on a search for trapped survivors. However, his efforts were interrupted by a secondary explosion that threw him away from the wreckage, causing burns to his skin and clothes.

Trujillo then heard cries for help and located First Lieutenant Will Eskridge, trapped in mud near a smoking Black Hawk. Trujillo quickly administered first aid, applying a tourniquet to Eskridge's injured leg and starting an IV. Another medic, Sergeant Gerry Eric Holt, joined in the rescue effort, while additional medical personnel arrived to assist.

Among the rescued was Staff Sergeant Bill Sears, who was found near death in the wreckage. Trujillo and his fellow medics played a crucial role in keeping Sears alive until further medical help arrived. Trujillo's bravery and lifesaving actions earned him a Silver Star, while Holt was awarded a Bronze Star with a Combat V for his role in the rescue efforts.

Lannon, also a medic, was posthumously awarded the Bronze Star for his selfless actions in providing lifesaving care during the initial days of the conflict. His dedication was evident as he had gone AWOL from advanced medical training to rejoin his battalion for the mission in Grenada.

Slater, who was part of Lannon's squad, tragically lost his life alongside his comrade during the same incident.

Back on the USS *Guam*, Schwarzkopf rushed to the hospital bay and witnessed the return of the wounded from the disastrous raid. The scene was grim, with blood splattered everywhere from grievous wounds. As a Ranger lieutenant who had lost his leg attempted to rise and salute upon seeing the general, Schwarzkopf gently restrained him with a comforting touch. "Sir, how did my troops do?" asked the lieutenant anxiously. "Did we accomplish our mission?"

Schwarzkopf reassured him, expressing pride in their performance. The lieutenant smiled and echoed their motto: "Rangers lead the way, hoo-ah!" Yet, as Schwarzkopf walked away, he couldn't shake the feeling that they had been chasing ghosts—there had been no enemy to be found. This realization haunted him as he ascended back to the bridge, filled with anger and questions about which "son of a bitch" had ordered the attack on the Calivigny barracks in the first place.

CHAPTER 9

# A Nation with Global Responsibilities

*"Vietnam syndrome and the Brezhnev Doctrine perished in Grenada, replaced with a renewed American spirit that robustly confronted the Soviet Union and its proxies around the world."*

—Former U.S. Ambassador to Venezuela Otto Reich,
*Wall Street Journal*, October 24, 2018

## OCTOBER 27, 1983

The fighting in Grenada had mostly stopped by Thursday, although U.S. troops would see sporadic hostilities over the next several days and combat would not officially end for almost another week. At the White House and inside the National Security Council, there were still pressing matters to attend to, including urgent diplomatic concerns that needed to be addressed with London.

After the rescue, Constantine Menges was in the White House watching the live television coverage of the students' return. He was apprehensive, knowing that some of these students would be liberals who might minimize the danger they'd been in and denounce the whole operation. So as he sat in the White House and watched the first few students come down the stairs from the plane, he knew the media would search for critics. Menges and his colleagues knew that if the media found even 1, 2, or 3 among the 800 students who had been rescued, the haters would be featured on every network news program, and they'd have their 15 minutes of fame.

As the first students reached the ground, instead of walking over to the bank of microphones and press people, they stopped. Menges recalled that he watched with "amazement and happiness as one student knelt and kissed the ground." He recalled another student who said simply, "I support President Reagan's move.... He really did save our lives." Menges wrote in his memoir that he "felt pride in the fact that President Reagan had acted with courage, that his entire administration had performed correctly, competently, and with real teamwork."

Meanwhile, officials in Whitehall were incensed by the lack of detailed advance notice from the United States regarding its intention to invade Grenada. In an unprecedented move, they at first scrambled to prevent the impending U.S. military intervention, even going as far as publicly criticizing it after it occurred. But despite the well-known British opposition to the invasion, declassified files reveal that ministers and officials refrained from outright condemning the U.S. action. Instead, they opted to withhold explicit criticism and hoped for the successful operation once Reagan gave the go-ahead.

On October 24, prior to the invasion, Reagan sent a cable to Thatcher at 7:15 p.m. London time, expressing his serious consideration of going into Grenada to rescue the Americans and restore law and order. This communication to 10 Downing Street followed the request from the Organization of Eastern Caribbean States. Before Thatcher could respond, Reagan sent another message around 11 p.m. London time, confirming his decision to proceed with Operation Urgent Fury.

Thatcher replied to both messages shortly after midnight on October 25, expressing strong concern. She emphasized that the only justifiable reason for intervention would be to protect the safety of U.S. and British citizens, a justification that she didn't believe applied in this case. Furthermore, she warned of the perception of meddling in the internal affairs of an independent nation, which could have a negative impact on foreign relations in the context of the Cold War. Thatcher urged Reagan to reconsider, and she reinforced her arguments in a subsequent phone call on a secure line.

Despite Thatcher's efforts, Reagan remained resolute. A final message from him at 7:45 a.m. on October 25 confirmed the U.S. decision to proceed with the invasion, and the hour had passed for him to call it off. At 9:40 a.m. London time, U.S. troops had landed in Grenada.

Thatcher found herself in an incredibly challenging position, needing to navigate both the criticism inside the United Kingdom and what now appeared to be a strained relationship with her best political friend, President Ronald Reagan. Britain's credibility as a trusted ally of the Reagan administration and a key player in the Caribbean region came into question. Anti-American sentiments surged within the United Kingdom as public scrutiny intensified over perceived American strategic interests. Doubts arose regarding the reliability of the Reagan administration, particularly concerning the planned deployment of U.S. cruise missiles on British soil.

President Reagan picked up the phone and tried to mollify Thatcher, his closest international ally, by employing his renowned charm. "If I were there, Margaret, I'd throw my hat in the door before I came in," Reagan said with a hint of guilt in his voice. Thatcher responded, "There's no need to do that," her curt answer signaling her discontent.

The president then tried to explain the rationale behind the United States' decision not to disclose the invasion plans in advance, citing concerns about potential leaks. He reassured Thatcher of the meticulous precautions that were taken to safeguard the operation, emphasizing the need for secrecy. Thatcher, drawing parallels with her own experiences during the Falklands conflict, expressed understanding, acknowledging the complexities of sensitive military operations.

As their 10-minute dialogue neared its end, Thatcher mentioned her need to return to a contentious debate that was taking place in the House of Commons. The timing of Operation Urgent Fury wasn't the best for Thatcher, considering that she had to appear before the House of Commons the next day, the day members of Parliament get to question the prime minister publicly. Reagan, appearing relieved, urged her on with a spirited, "Go get 'em. Eat 'em alive." Thatcher bid farewell tersely and hung up.

These recordings, unearthed from the White House Situation Room, offer a rare glimpse into Reagan's interactions. Author William Doyle, who uncovered the tapes, described them as providing invaluable insights into presidential decision-making during turbulent times.

According to senior Thatcher aides and U.K. Foreign Office sources cited by the *Washington Post* a few days after the invasion: "That judgment was reached at a lengthy meeting of senior U.K. Cabinet ministers" on October 26 not to participate in Operation Urgent Fury, "after assessing reports from Grenada and other Caribbean countries as well as weighing the potential consequences of British intervention."

According to the *Washington Post*:

> That Cabinet group, including Defense Secretary Michael Heseltine and Foreign Secretary Sir Geoffrey Howe—concluded from intelligence reports that the situation in Grenada was "tense but calm" and seemed to be stabilizing. The risks to the 200 British citizens there did not appear to be great. Both of those conditions would surely change for the worse if an invasion took place, the ministers agreed.
> 
> On the political front, they were concerned about the impact of such a move at a particularly sensitive moment in relations among the western allies, with the

controversial deployment of medium-range nuclear missiles about to begin in Britain and elsewhere. They were especially mindful that morning because of the massive antimissile demonstrations in London and elsewhere.

On this last point, one source said, "our worst fears were very quickly confirmed" by the denunciations of the United States throughout Europe and the renewed call in Britain for greater control of American nuclear weapons based here.

But most important, the government decided not to participate in the operation because its disapproval of the regime was not considered sufficient grounds for stretching international law and using military force to oust it.

"A change of government is not in itself sufficient reason to justify invasion by one country of another," Howe asserted in Parliament ... responding to charges that Britain had showed a failure of fortitude in not joining the U.S. operation and, alternatively, a lack of influence with the Reagan administration in not being able to prevent it.

The prime minister's supporters contend that surprise [in London] and in Washington over the British choice of restraint is based on the mistaken assumption that because of the Falklands conflict, "Thatcher spends her time waiting to go to war and that she would find it impossible to disagree with President Reagan on a matter like this.

"That view is seriously wrong on both counts," one source insisted.

Britain's role in the Grenada affair has also been confused, these sources say, by the notion that it must retain some responsibility for its troubled former colony, especially since the island's head of state, like Britain's, is Queen Elizabeth II and the monarch appoints a governor general there. The governor general, however, is chosen by Grenadians, and Britain plays no part in any aspect of the island's administration.

Beyond their membership in the Commonwealth and the legacy of language and history, Britain has no special link to Grenada. British sources said that for reasons of geography and the presence of 1,000 of its citizens, the United States was far closer to the island in its sensitivity to the menace posed by the deposed government of Maurice Bishop and the now ousted revolutionary council that executed him.

For that reason, while declining to assist in the invasion, the Thatcher government decided not to condemn the United States for its intervention as other American allies in Europe did. Instead, Howe told Parliament that the American action was a "matter of regret" and attributed the U.S. move to differing "perceptions" of the proper course of action.

"We do not agree with the Americans on every issue," Howe said to choruses of derision from opposition critics, "any more than they always agree with us—nor are we expected to do so."

By neither supporting the American invasion nor assailing it, [Thatcher's] government left itself wide open for a criticism that runs directly counter to the [prime minister's] hard-earned reputation for, as her campaign the spring before called it, "the resolute approach." Her aides argued that it was not the position that was weak—it was straightforward and grounded in firm principles of respect for sovereignty—but the lackluster way it was presented.

This was the result of several separate misfortunes for Thatcher. The Foreign Office had received its first word the Friday night before the invasion that the Organization of Eastern Caribbean States was considering a military intervention in Grenada and preparing to ask for help in carrying it out. But the seriousness of that notification was apparently underestimated because it was not rendered "formally." . . .

As events in the region unfolded over the weekend, British officials regarded the decision by CARICOM, the organization of Commonwealth countries in the Caribbean, to impose economic and political sanctions against Grenada as the prevailing trend rather than the military option. They also accepted the Reagan administration's promises that it would consult London before taking any conclusive steps.

Both of the beliefs proved incorrect.

In a press conference on Tuesday, Secretary of State George P. Shultz revealed that President Reagan made a tentative decision to invade on Sunday evening, but no word to that effect was sent to the British for another 24 hours— only a short time before the final go-ahead was given.

So by the time that the Cabinet met Monday morning, the British case was essentially irrelevant as the U.S. military gears were [already] in-motion. It was this failure to "stay in touch" with London, as had been promised, that was particularly annoying and embarrassing to Thatcher.

Moreover, Howe looked foolish when his assertion to Parliament on Monday that the United States had no intention of invading Grenada was dramatically contradicted a few hours later. This highlighted the government's ineffectual appearance.

"Howe's dilemma was to demonstrate our differences with the Reagan administration without lambasting it, and that made matters worse," one source observed.

A senior government official said that Howe made all these points of grievance forcefully in a meeting with Shultz in Paris [when the two met in the days after the operation in Grenada had concluded] and received the secretary's apologies.

A bipartisan committee of the House of Commons later released a report criticizing Prime Minister Margaret Thatcher's government for its handling of the Grenada crisis. The report indicated that the United States deliberately withheld information about its invasion plans from Britain. The committee, led by prominent Tory backbencher Sir Anthony Kershaw, accused Foreign Secretary Howe of being sluggish in responding to the events leading up to the invasion. It suggested that British officials were slow to recognize the danger signals in the Caribbean and failed to consider the attitudes of Commonwealth countries in the region, such as Barbados's desire for British involvement in any intervention.

The report highlighted that during the critical weekend of October 22 and 23, 1983, the British government did not take any action to consult Caribbean political leaders or deter their support for an invasion. Additionally, it noted that even the State Department was ill-informed about President Reagan's plans, limiting its ability to inform Britain.

While the committee did not explicitly criticize American actions or endorse Mrs. Thatcher's decision to abstain from the operation, it remarked that the United States did not intend for the United Kingdom to play an active role in the military intervention. One Conservative minister and committee member described the American approach as extraordinary treatment of a valued ally. However, an amendment condemning the invasion and supporting British nonintervention proposed by a member of the Labour opposition was defeated by Tory members.

## THE GLOBAL RESPONSE

The UN General Assembly overwhelmingly passed a resolution condemning the "armed intervention" in Grenada, with 108 countries voting in favor, 9 against, and 27 abstaining. Thirteen countries were absent from the vote, further highlighting the isolation of the United States from its allies. The resolution, proposed by Nicaragua and Zimbabwe, received support from a broad spectrum of nations, including Australia, France, NATO members, and several American allies such as Egypt, Jordan, and Pakistan. Most of Latin America also voted in favor.

In a notable display of solidarity, only Israel and El Salvador, alongside the United States and the six Caribbean countries involved in the invasion, voted against the resolution. Countries like Japan, West Germany, and Canada, while abstaining from the vote, publicly expressed opposition to the U.S. intervention.

"The United States is proud to have participated in the liberation of the people of Grenada," UN Ambassador Jeane Kirkpatrick told the assembly after the vote, "and we are proud to have voted against a resolution that deplored this positive and constructive achievement."[1]

This vote echoed the condemnation of the Soviet invasion of Afghanistan in January 1980, with 104 countries voting against it. Ironically, the Grenadian government under Maurice Bishop had opposed this condemnation, aligning itself with the Soviet bloc, a fact previously emphasized by the Reagan administration to highlight the Grenadian-Soviet alliance. Diplomats remarked that the significance of the vote on Grenada was comparable to the anti-Soviet vote in 1980, underlining the international community's stance against unilateral military interventions.

The Soviet Union strongly condemned the United States for its invasion of Grenada, accusing it of attempting to intimidate "freedom-loving" people in Latin America. According to TASS, the official news agency, the Kremlin denounced the invasion as a "criminal" act aimed at imposing Washington's preferred government in Grenada and instilling fear in other Latin American nations. Despite condemning the invasion, the Soviet Union did not threaten retaliation but instead emphasized the responsibility of the Reagan administration for the consequences of its actions. Western observers in Moscow speculated that the Soviet Union would utilize the invasion to bolster anti-American propaganda, especially with NATO's impending missile deployment in Europe.

While acknowledging logistical challenges, observers suggested that Cuba might respond militarily given its proximity to Grenada. Meanwhile, Grenada's ambassador to the Soviet Union expressed confidence in their military capabilities, citing support in the form of Soviet, Czech, and North Korean equipment. TASS labeled Reagan's actions as hypocritical and condemned the perceived notion of the United States imposing its order on independent nations, dismissing it as "international brigandage and banditry."

In Havana, Fidel Castro and the rest of the Cuban Politburo personally greeted each of the 57 wounded Cuban fighters as they emerged from their plane. Castro put off any public remarks until the rest of the Cubans, including the dead and the evicted diplomats, arrived on other flights over the following days. A national day of mourning ceremony was eventually held in Havana's Plaza de la Revolution. Caskets with the bodies of the 24 Cubans who died in Grenada were put on display for an event witnessed by millions of Cubans either in person or on live television. Castro launched into a 90-minute speech in which he recounted how Havana's relationship with Grenada had come to such a sudden and inglorious end. Somewhat surprisingly, he blamed the Coard faction for recklessly provoking the United States' response.

"In our view," Castro declared, "[Bernard] Coard's group effectively destroyed the revolution and opened the door to imperialist aggression." At various points he derisively referred to the Coard faction as "the Pol Pot group," "hyenas," and "extremists drunk on political theory." He mourned his friend Maurice Bishop as a "noble, modest and unselfish leader" whose only fault was "excessive tolerance and trust." Predictably, he also accused the Reagan administration of using the Fort Rupert assassinations as a pretext to intervene and then telling "nineteen lies" to justify its actions. He then enumerated them in succession as the crowd cheered "Lie!" to each American assertion. "The United States did not achieve any victory at all—not political or military or moral. If anything, it was a Pyrrhic military victory and a profound moral defeat," Castro declared.

The speech made no acknowledgment of Cuban fault in its handling of the Grenada crisis, but Castro later publicly scolded his Grenadian diplomats for failing to detect the developing leadership struggle. Castro also blamed his military advisors for failing to adequately defend the national honor. The two senior Cuban officials in Grenada at the time of Operation Urgent Fury were publicly shamed for not "fight[ing] to the last man" as ordered and were forced to drop out of sight in disgrace, according to Western diplomats.

Neither Julian Torres Rizo, the Cuban ambassador to Grenada then, nor Colonel Pedro Tortolo, who was sent to Grenada shortly before the invasion to shore up the defenses of the nearly 800 Cubans who were working on the Point Salines airfield on the island, were seen at any official Cuban state functions in the following months. Diplomats reported that Oscar Osvaldo Cardenas, a former Cuban ambassador to Suriname, and other officials faced repercussions due to their roles in the Grenada turmoil. Cardenas is said to have been reassigned to a low-level position in the Ministry of the Interior. Additionally, Ambassador Torres Rizo and Colonel Tortolo, who were notably absent from several key events attended by President Castro and other senior officials, were believed to have been assigned to obscure posts. While rumors of house arrest were dismissed by most diplomats, it's clear that Torres Rizo and Tortolo were sidelined. Tortolo reportedly became deputy director of a military school, while Torres Rizo assumed a technical role in the Foreign Ministry.

Grenada, under Prime Minister Maurice Bishop, had cultivated close ties with Cuba. However, Cuba was blindsided by the power struggle within Grenada's leadership that led to Bishop's death and the rise of General Hudson Austin's revolutionary council. Some speculated that Torres Rizo may have hesitated to report negative developments to Castro regarding his friend Maurice Bishop, while others suggest that accurate reporting may have been hindered within the Cuban government. Castro, caught off guard by the events in Grenada, dispatched Colonel Tortolo and diplomat Carlos Diaz to assess the situation. Diaz was killed, while Tortolo (as mentioned earlier in the book) sought refuge in the Soviet Embassy following the U.S. invasion.

After the Grenada debacle, Suriname, a Cuban ally, distanced itself from Cuba, prompting the recall of Cuban diplomats.

## THE MEDIA

Later, Admiral Metcalf flew to Barbados to meet with representatives from the Organization of Eastern Caribbean States and discuss the transition of power and security in Grenada after the U.S. troops started to pull out. He also held a press conference and faced the media for the first time since the invasion started. Like the press corps in Washington, the media in Barbados were angry because they'd been blocked from getting a firsthand, real-time look at Urgent Fury.

Reporters had been told that they would get to Grenada after the initial wave of the invasion, but those plans were scrapped because "chaos had reigned" on that day. But on day two, a couple of reporters who were already on the island had succeeded in getting flown out to the *Guam*. When Schwarzkopf saw two civilians sprint across the flight deck and leap into a helicopter as the U.S. prepared to launch the raid on Grand Anse, he remembered running down to the deck and told them, "Get off. You're interfering with a military operation."

Metcalf then ordered the captain of the *Guam* to see that the reporters stayed off the flight deck. Those two reporters were then held for the rest of the afternoon in the officers' wardroom "drinking coffee and eating sweet rolls," according to the general.

At his news conference in Barbados, Metcalf said this about the media blackout: "The buck stops with me. If you want to argue with somebody about it, you've got to argue with me, not the DOD, not anybody else but me." One of the reporters at the news conference had been aboard a boat that had been turned away by a Navy jet. "Admiral, what would have happened if we hadn't turned around?" the reporter asked. Metcalf snapped back, "We would have blown your ass right out of the water!" growling.

Within a couple of days, the military would begin running three C-130 media flights a day from Barbados. The number of visiting journalists swelled to more than 100 a day for the next five days before interest began to trail off. Metcalf's personal assessment was that despite their complaints about their belated arrival, the press had done a "more than adequate" job of ferreting out what went on in their absence. He noted that the press learned about the bombing of the mental hospital before he did. The hospital bombing could have become a My Lai–like incident, but Metcalf was grateful that reporters on the scene uncovered "the full circumstances of the bombing."

Senator Robert Byrd of West Virginia, the Democratic minority leader, complained about the "censored news reports," saying they only provided "little bits of information."[2] Senator Paul Sarbanes, a Democrat from Maryland, was most worried about how the invasion treated the free press. He was concerned that this, along with other government efforts to control information, might mean that "the only sources of information are official sources." Edward Joyce, who was the president of CBS News, later testified in Congress that in Grenada, "there was a shift from military censorship to political censorship."

White House Chief of Staff James Baker III, when asked about the media blackout, hailed the success of the Grenada invasion, suggesting that he would adopt a similar policy for any future military operations under the Reagan administration. According to a report from the *Los Angeles Times*, Baker expressed satisfaction with the decision to withhold information from the White House press office until just before the invasion began on October 25. He emphasized the importance of maintaining secrecy surrounding the operation until it was underway.

However, Baker did express one reservation about the handling of the media during the invasion. He noted that reporters were not allowed onto the island until two days after the operation began, despite initial plans to admit them the day after the initial landing. Baker attributed this delay to the military's control over the situation.

While the news blackout received criticism from news organizations, Baker claimed that a majority of the American people supported the policy. Deputy White House Press Secretary Larry Speakes, who was forced to acknowledge concerns about his own credibility, agreed with the necessity of secrecy but expressed regret about being kept in the dark regarding the invasion plans. Despite Speakes's expectation of being informed in advance of similar actions in the future, Baker indicated a firm commitment to the Grenada model, asserting that he would defend the policy against any challenges.

In 1984, Lesley Stahl produced an in-depth report for CBS, aiming to highlight the contradictions between President Reagan's words and actions. The report, which aired during the presidential campaign, featured Reagan speaking at events like the Special Olympics and places such as a nursing home, juxtaposed with Stahl's narration detailing Reagan's cuts to funding for children with disabilities and his opposition to public health funding.

However, despite the critical content of the report, the White House's reaction surprised Stahl. Following the broadcast, Dick Darman, a White House official, called to praise her work, referring to it as a "great piece." Stahl, taken aback, questioned Darman about the content of the report, to which he responded, "Nobody heard what you said." Darman's explanation resonated deeply with Stahl, highlighting the power of visuals over spoken words in television journalism.

Stahl's report, though critical, had been accompanied by upbeat visuals, ultimately overshadowing the message conveyed by her narration. This anecdote, often referred to as "Lesley's Parable," became emblematic of the Reagan era. It underscored the notion that compelling visuals and soaring rhetoric could shape public perception more effectively than the dominant media's spin on current events.

The "Mastermind" sketch from the 1986 season of *Saturday Night Live* offers a satirical take on President Ronald Reagan, highlighting the complex public perception of his administration.[3] This sketch featured Phil Hartman as Reagan, portraying him as a bumbling, amiable figure in public but a shrewd, calculating mastermind behind closed doors.

This comedic depiction was particularly resonant because it played on the dual perceptions of Reagan. Publicly, Reagan was often seen as a genial, somewhat detached figure. However, critics and insiders noted that Reagan was far more involved and astute than his public persona suggested. As the sketch cleverly juxtaposes, Reagan's seemingly simple demeanor masked a keen political acumen and a hands-on approach to governance. The sketch's cultural significance lies in its ability to encapsulate this dichotomy. By depicting Reagan as both a kindly grandfather and a tactical genius, *SNL* underscored the multifaceted nature of the American president.

Former officials from Reagan's administration, such as Secretary of State George Shultz, have attested to Reagan's behind-the-scenes decisiveness and strategic thinking, which aligned more with the "mastermind" portrayal than his public image. Shultz noted that Reagan had a clear vision and was deeply involved in key decisions, a contrast to the more laid-back persona he often projected.

Author H. W. Brands, the historian and professor who wrote *Reagan: The Life*, a biography about Reagan, in 2015, was asked by PBS about the "Mastermind" sketch, and said it "overstated something that had a kernel of truth to it," but added, Reagan "didn't pretend to be the master of everything that happened in his administration. In fact, he often held himself out as a contrast to Jimmy Carter, who really was that micromanager in the Oval Office, and who had a very unsuccessful presidency."[4]

Brand went on to say, "Reagan focused on a couple of things." Following Grenada, there was a conscious effort by the Reagan administration to work with the corporate media and Hollywood to soften some of the hurt feelings experienced after Operation

Urgent Fury. Part of that effort included working with the producers of the 1986 film *Top Gun*, according to K. T. McFarland. Film crews were given never-before-granted access to the USS *Enterprise*. So it wasn't a coincidence that *Top Gun* reflected the values of Reaganism, a period marked by the restoration of American self-confidence after the traumas of the previous decades, such as the Vietnam War, the Watergate scandal, and the Iran hostage crisis. Reagan's administration emphasized patriotism, military strength, and traditional values, which are evident in *Top Gun*.

The movie's cultural impact aligns with the Reagan-era emphasis on traditional American values, making *Top Gun* a significant reflection of the period's spirit. Maverick's story represents America's recovery from past difficulties and its renewed confidence and optimism for the future. John Semcken, a real estate developer and former Navy fighter pilot, served as a technical advisor for *Top Gun*.[5] Initially reluctant, Semcken was tasked with teaching Hollywood actors to convincingly portray fighter pilots. He advised Tom Cruise on how to simulate pulling g-forces (the force of gravity on acceleration during takeoff) by tightening muscles. Semcken took pride in his contributions, and *Top Gun* significantly boosted Navy recruitment. Movie theaters even hosted recruiters to capitalize on the film's impact. According to Commander Ronald Flanders, many current senior Navy pilots cite the film as their inspiration for pursuing naval aviation.

## THATCHER AND LEBANON

On the evening of October 27, 1983, President Reagan spoke to the nation in a prime-time address and explained why the invasion of Grenada and the presence of Marines in Lebanon were both critically important for the interests of the United States. Reagan said that even though these events happened in different places, they were both connected—and that connection was the Soviet Union. The Reagan administration was now facing a lot of criticism from Congress, so it had to defend its actions.

Reagan firmly believed the Soviet Union and its friends had tried to capitalize on the slightest sign of American weakness in the past. So Reagan framed both issues, Lebanon and Grenada, as part of a bigger struggle between East and West. The United States had a responsibility to stop the Soviets, or the followers of their Marxist-Leninist ideology, from tilting the balance of power toward communism. Throughout the speech Reagan was measured in his words and approach, knowing he faced a lot of skepticism.

During his speech, Reagan delivered a stark portrayal of Grenada, stating, "Grenada, we were told, was a friendly island paradise for tourism. Well, it wasn't. It was a Soviet-Cuban colony being readied as a major military bastion to export terror and undermine democracy." He continued, "We got there just in time," echoing sentiments from his aides, who had asserted that the intervention prevented "another Angola," referring to the presence of 25,000 Cuban troops in the African nation.

As for Lebanon, Reagan emphasized the necessity for the continued presence of Marines. He stated, "The Marines must remain there not only to facilitate stability and to police the withdrawal of foreign troops . . . but also to offset the growing Soviet-supported Syrian power in the region." Reagan underscored the importance of the United States and its allies in Lebanon, asserting that their presence was crucial to preventing the Syrian-backed forces from toppling the government of President Amin Gemayel. He warned Israel's supporters in Congress that the withdrawal of Marines would not only jeopardize America's vital interests but also undermine Israel's security. Reagan cautioned that such an outcome would be "a devastating blow" to the peace process and could result in the Middle East being incorporated into the Soviet bloc.

The Reagan administration had recently stated that as soon as they identified the culprits behind the Beirut explosion, the United States would retaliate. President Reagan even told a group of White House visitors, "I think the evidence that I have is sufficient that this last horrendous act involved Iranian terrorists and they were facilitated in their entry and in the provision of the munitions by the Syrians." During his speech, he reiterated, "Those who directed this atrocity must be dealt justice. They will be."

Despite the stern tone, the underlying intent of the speech appeared to be firmness without belligerence. This approach comes amid concerns from many allies, including his closet foreign ally, Margaret Thatcher, regarding Reagan's swift actions in Grenada. President Reagan seemed to aim for a stance of resolve in Lebanon, hoping to convey to the Syrians and other stakeholders that it was in their interest to support the Lebanese national reconciliation talks. He emphasized the potential military strength of the United States by alluding to the battleship *New Jersey*, armed with 16-inch guns, stationed offshore and ready to intervene, if necessary, particularly in the Chouf Mountains near Beirut.

Reagan also reaffirmed his commitment to the peace initiative his administration had announced the previous September, and to a United Nations Security Council Resolution adopted in 1967. This resolution advocated for Israeli withdrawal from parts of Gaza, the West Bank, and the Golan Heights, an interpretation endorsed by the United States.

In December, Reagan stated that the Marines were in Beirut to "demonstrate the strength of our commitment to peace in the Middle East. . . . Their presence is making it possible for reason to triumph over the forces of violence, hatred, and intimidation." Nine days later, he told the nation: "Once internal stability is established and withdrawal of all foreign forces is assured, the Marines will leave." Finally, on February 4, 1984, Reagan stated,

"We'll be sending one signal to terrorists everywhere: If we're to be secure in our homes and in the world, we must stand together against those who threaten us."

Despite her embarrassment and anger over Grenada, Margaret Thatcher had gracefully put aside her frustration with her political soulmate and provided critical advice to President Reagan. Thatcher argued against responding to the bombings of the Marine barracks in Beirut with military action and a response that included a reference to her experiences in Northern Ireland. She conveyed her apprehension about the proposed retaliatory action, stating, "I am frankly apprehensive about the retaliatory action you propose." Thatcher emphasized the importance of targeting specific perpetrators, drawing on her own experiences: "We have had many outrages in Northern Ireland and over one thousand deaths to our forces there, but we have always concentrated on hunting out those criminals directly responsible, avoiding wider retaliatory acts."[6]

Reagan ultimately ordered the Marines to "redeploy" to their ships offshore on February 7, which was a full withdrawal achieved in just three weeks. Although the Marine's mission in Lebanon was not clearly defined and consequently not achieved, Reagan's decision to withdraw the Marines from Lebanon limited America's further involvement in foreign policy disasters, saving money, lives, and time. And it was certainly based, at least in part, on the advice he received from Margaret Thatcher.

## GRENADA'S INDEPENDENCE

The principal focus of military operations shifted to rounding up PRA and NJM leaders, uncovering arms caches, and extending the military control to the entire island. The American forces were assisted in all these efforts by Grenadians who provided them with actionable intelligence information. Bernard Coard, the leader of the coup, and his wife, Phyllis, were captured by Marines, who were tipped to their location by Grenadians. The Coards and four friends were found hiding in a private home on the eastern outskirts of the capital on Saturday morning, October 29, 1983. The fugitives were induced to surrender when an anti-tank weapon was pointed at the house. Coard was the last to emerge and kept saying, "I'm not responsible, I'm not responsible" according to the Marine gunnery sergeant who demanded the surrender.

The next afternoon, General Austin, the head of the military council, and two PRA lieutenant colonels were captured by 82nd paratroopers in a private home in the expatriate enclave at Westerhall Point. The Austin group and the Coards were flown separately to the *Guam*, where they were held in cells and the men were interrogated by Americans. After eight days, the prisoners were taken to Richmond Hill Prison to face civil criminal charges for the murder of Bishop and 10 of his supporters at Fort Rupert on October 19.

The Coards and Austin were among 14 people who were eventually convicted of murder and sentenced to death by hanging. Additionally, 3 other defendants were found guilty of manslaughter and received prison sentences ranging from 30 to 45 years. One individual was acquitted of all charges. The verdict was reached by a 12-member jury following just three hours of deliberation after a seven-month trial. Acting Chief Justice Denis Byron delivered the sentences in a packed courtroom, which included over 100 spectators, in a solemn atmosphere.

On Wednesday, November 2, 1983, Admiral Metcalf officially declared that hostilities had ceased. The next day, Schwarzkopf and Metcalf climbed aboard Metcalf's airplane in Barbados and flew back to Norfolk, where a cheering crowd and a Navy band greeted them at the airfield. Metcalf and Schwarzkopf shook hands with each other and said a warm good-bye, and then Schwarzkopf hopped into another airplane that flew him back to Georgia.

As he landed at the Fort Stewart airstrip, he recalled being "astounded to spot another crowd of people waiting, fifty or sixty people cheered and waved American flags." He also saw his family and was "moved almost to tears." He said he'd come home from combat twice before, but he'd never received "a warm welcome like this."

Schwarzkopf admitted his own emotions about the operation were complicated. He wrote that he "was proud that we'd gotten the job done and elated that the American public . . . had come out in support of its troops. At the same time," he wrote, "we had lost more lives than we needed to, and the brief war had revealed a lot of shortcomings—an abysmal lack of accurate intelligence, major deficiencies in communications, flare-ups of interservice rivalry, interference by higher headquarters in battlefield decisions, our alienation of the press, and more."

He found solace in the fact that these shortcomings were identified in after-action reports, and the U.S. military had abandoned the practice of glossing over issues, as we had done during Vietnam. For him, this was the most compelling evidence of the military's transformation.

Governor General Paul Scoon took significant political actions, including expelling Soviet bloc diplomats, authorizing arrests of the Coard clique, and reinstating Westminster-style rule on the island. Scoon appointed a nine-member Advisory Council to serve as an interim administration, taking steps toward restoring stability and governance on the island.

Determined to chart his own political course, Scoon was guided by the queen, Grenada's constitution, the tradition of the Commonwealth, the Eastern Caribbean community, and his personal knowledge of the island's political landscape. By signing the intervention request and assuming governance in Grenada,

Scoon effectively displaced the military junta and brought an end to the revolutionary period. With his signature, he asserted that a "vacuum of authority" existed in Grenada, thereby enabling him to take executive action on behalf of his nation. "The Governor General must remain impartial and is expected to transcend politics," Scoon asserted in his autobiography.

Paul Scoon, the son of a butcher, who was born in a fishing village on Grenada's western coast in the heart of spice and cocoa country in 1935, had played an intricately critical, albeit almost microscopic, role in maintaining law and order in the West during pivotal moments in the Cold War. And for all the derision colonialism gets, Scoon proved to be an ideal example of what can go right in times of crisis in the British Commonwealth. Like many British subjects in Commonwealth countries, he went to college in England, earning a degree in education from the University of Leeds. He went on to obtain a master's degree from the University of Toronto.

Scoon returned to Grenada to teach high school, where he liked to quote Shakespeare and Chaucer in his commanding voice. And now he was making plans for Grenada's first democratic elections in five years, which were eventually held on December 3, 1984, leading to the formation of a parliamentary government under the leadership of a new prime minister. Former Prime Minister Eric Gairy and his GULP tried but failed to win back power.

## ABLE ARCHER

Operation Able Archer, conducted in November 1983 by the United States and its NATO allies, had profound implications as it inadvertently made the Russians believe that a nuclear strike on their territory was imminent. When intelligence about the Soviet reaction reached the Tory government, Prime Minister Margaret

Thatcher took decisive action, instructing her officials to lobby the Americans to prevent such misunderstandings in the future.

The documents obtained by Peter Burt, director of the Nuclear Information Service (NIS), shed light on this critical moment in history. They underscore how the Cold War era was marked by perilous brinkmanship, with the world teetering on the edge of a nuclear catastrophe. Able Archer simulated a scenario where NATO forces defended against Warsaw Pact countries' aggression, escalating into a conflict involving chemical and nuclear weapons. This exercise, involving 40,000 troops and coordinated by encrypted communications, was so realistic that it triggered genuine alarm in the Soviet Union.

Various U.K. air bases, including RAF Greenham Common and RAF Brize Norton, participated in the exercise, which remained shrouded in secrecy for years. Former Australian intelligence official Paul Dibb even suggested that Able Archer posed a greater threat than the Cuban Missile Crisis had in October 1962.

The exercise occurred amid heightened tensions following incidents like the downing of a Korean Airlines Boeing 747 by the Russians and Reagan's "evil empire" speech. As Able Archer unfolded, the Soviets reacted by placing aircraft and missiles on high alert, believing it could be a prelude to a NATO attack. Classified documents revealed how close the Soviets came to treating Able Archer as a genuine threat. Thatcher, alarmed by these revelations, urged her officials to address Soviet misapprehensions. She advocated for transparency in NATO's exercise activities, aiming to prevent future misunderstandings.

Thatcher's efforts led to discussions with the United States, proposing that NATO inform the Soviet Union routinely about exercise activities involving nuclear simulations. Even before Mikhail Gorbachev ascended to leadership in the old Soviet Union, Mrs.

Thatcher recognized him as "a man one could do business with," a sentiment echoed by her ideological ally, Ronald Reagan.

Their diplomatic engagement began in earnest when Gorbachev visited the United Kingdom in 1984, amid expectations that he would become the USSR's next leader. Mrs. Thatcher saw an opportunity to cultivate personal rapport with him and to foster improved relations with the Soviet Union. During Gorbachev's visit, Mrs. Thatcher extended a warm welcome, even rolling out the red carpet for him at Chequers, her country residence. At the time, Gorbachev held the position of Number 2 in the Soviet Communist Party hierarchy.

The interactions between Thatcher and Gorbachev continued to deepen, with Mrs. Thatcher praising Gorbachev's visit as one of the most successful ever by a major world leader during President Konstantin Chernenko's funeral in 1985. This sentiment underscored her commitment to building constructive relations with the new Soviet leadership. Thatcher's engagement with Gorbachev was remarkable in its frequency and depth. She held more meetings with him than any other British prime minister had with a Soviet leader, surpassing even the wartime alliance between Winston Churchill and Joseph Stalin, whom Churchill famously referred to as his "wartime ally."

Reagan's determination matched Thatcher's to confront the Soviet Union on the world stage, as evident in his negotiations with Soviet leader Mikhail Gorbachev. The Reykjavík Summit in 1986 stands as a significant moment in this regard, where Reagan and Gorbachev engaged in intense discussions about nuclear disarmament. Despite the summit ending without a formal agreement, it showed Reagan's resolve and paved the way for further negotiations and signaled a shift toward a more cooperative relationship between the two superpowers.

During his visit to Berlin in 1987, Reagan delivered his famous "Mr. Gorbachev, tear down this wall!" speech at the Brandenburg Gate. This speech, advocating for the dismantling of the Berlin Wall that divided East and West Germany, captured the spirit of freedom and defiance against totalitarianism. However, crafting this historic address wasn't without its challenges. Secretary of State George Shultz initially sought to remove the phrase "tear down this wall" from Reagan's speech, fearing that it would escalate tensions and derail diplomatic efforts. Yet Reagan remained steadfast in his conviction, insisting that the message of liberty must be boldly proclaimed.

Ultimately, Reagan's unwavering commitment to freedom, coupled with his willingness to engage in dialogue with the Soviet leadership, helped set the stage for the eventual collapse of the Iron Curtain and the peaceful conclusion of the Cold War. His successes were possible because of his commitment to his ideals. But it's easy to see how so many of Ronald Reagan's Cold War wins would not have been possible without the friendship, counsel, and grace of the Iron Lady, Prime Minister Margaret Thatcher.

## DON'T GO WOBBLY ON ME

Thatcher's time as prime minister outlasted Ronald Reagan's presidency, and after Reagan left office, the Special Relationship would never be the same.

President Ronald Reagan, just a month shy of his seventy-eighth birthday, gave his last televised speech from the Oval Office to close out the first two-term presidency since Dwight D. Eisenhower's. "My friends, we did it," he said, asserting that his political "revolution" had changed the nation and the world.[7]

Reagan considered the economic recovery of the 1980s and the renewal of American morale after the Vietnam War as the two "greatest triumphs" of his presidency. "America is respected again in the world and looked to for leadership," he remarked.

Reflecting on his departure, Reagan stated, "Parting is such sweet sorrow. The sweet part is California, the ranch, and freedom. The sorrow? Goodbyes and leaving this beautiful place." He emphasized, "Once you begin a great movement, there's no telling where it will end. We meant to change a nation and instead changed a world. From Grenada to the Washington and Moscow summits, from the recession of 1981–1982 to the expansion that began in late 1982 and continues to this day, we've made a difference."

Constantine Menges wrote in his 1988 book *Inside the National Security Council* that "[Vice President] George Bush has far better instincts, judgments, and experience on key foreign policy issues than do the 1988 group of Democratic presidential candidates. During Grenada, Bush was superb; and I believe that with a competent staff of experts from outside the career services, his own sensible instincts could lead to an effective foreign policy."

The Reagan administration's foreign policy record, while not perfect, marked a significant improvement over U.S. performance in the previous decade. During Reagan's tenure, an American program aimed at encouraging democracy abroad was institutionalized without coercing friendly governments. As a result, more than 250 million people lived in countries that transitioned peacefully from dictatorship to democracy. Notably, no new pro-Soviet regimes came to power during this period.

The "Powell Doctrine," credited to Colin Powell, who served as Ronald Reagan's national security advisor at the end of Reagan's second term, was really the Reagan Doctrine. These were the questions that K. T. McFarland, who worked in the Pentagon during Urgent Fury, told me during an interview for this book that Ronald Reagan asked his administration before Operation Urgent Fury: *Is a vital national security interest threatened? Have the risks and costs been fully and frankly analyzed? Do we have a clear attainable objective? In other words—can the United States win?*

In his book *My American Journey*, Powell wrote about an exchange he had with Madeleine Albright in 1993. It underscores the principle of having clear political objectives before committing military forces. Albright, then secretary of state, challenged Powell by asking, "What's the point of having this superb military that you're always talking about if we can't use it?" Powell's reaction was one of extreme frustration, feeling she viewed American GIs as "toy soldiers to be moved around on some global chessboard."

This tension encapsulated a broader debate within the Clinton administration, which later employed NATO peacekeepers in the Balkans similarly to how the Bush and Obama administrations utilized U.S. forces in the Global War on Terror.

Grenada though, was liberated and became democratic. During the first 6 years of the Reagan administration, 10 Latin American countries, with a combined population of 240 million people, returned to democracy. Also, more than 400,000 resistance fighters were actively working to replace 7 pro-Soviet dictatorships. The Strategic Defense Initiative was launched, military strength was enhanced, and political pressures for indiscriminate U.S.-Soviet arms control and unilateral freezes were resisted. This created the potential for a reciprocal, realistic strategic arms reduction agreement with the USSR.

In 2018, former Assistant Secretary of State Otto Reich wrote that the "Vietnam syndrome and the Brezhnev Doctrine perished in Grenada," and they were "replaced with a renewed American spirit that robustly confronted the Soviet Union and its proxies around the world."[8] The liberation of Grenada—the first instance of American military force being used to roll back a communist government—marked a significant shift in the U.S. posture following the "malaise" of the Carter years. This decisive action showcased President Reagan's resolve to reassert the U.S. role as the world's premier defender of freedom, reinvigorating American confidence and influence on the global stage.

Many Americans don't realize that the collapse of the Berlin Wall and the fall of international communism were not inevitable. These events needed strong leadership, courage, and vision from a president who aimed to restore America's influence. October 25 is celebrated as Grenada's Thanksgiving Day.

Throughout Reagan's presidency, there were no serious direct political or military confrontations with the Soviet Union. This was partly because the administration prudently assisted friendly countries and movements in achieving their own goals of resisting Soviet indirect aggression. This approach avoided the mistakes of inaction or the belief that only U.S. combat forces or military threats could be effective.

After the election of 1988, the Special Relationship was now between Thatcher and George H. W. Bush. And one of the problems to carry over from the Reagan presidency was the Middle East. Only now, Iraq had joined Iran as a center of concern.

At the end of the Iran-Iraq War that lasted from September 1980 to August 1988, which was winding down as the Reagan presidency was ending, Iraq emerged intact but deeply indebted, owing around $37 billion to Gulf nation creditors. Iraqi President Saddam Hussein wanted his war debts forgiven by the UAE and Kuwait, arguing that the loans were payments for Iraq's protection of the Arabian Peninsula from Iranian expansion. When these appeals went unanswered, the Gulf states' refusal to cancel the war debts contributed to Saddam's decision to threaten Iraq's wealthy but militarily weak neighbor, Kuwait.

Saddam Hussein threatened to go to war over the Warbah and Bubiyan Islands, crucial for Iraq's port access. Historical disputes over these islands and the broader border with Kuwait resurfaced, exacerbated by Iraq's economic crisis and accusations against Kuwait for oil theft and overproduction. Relations between Iraq and the United States deteriorated rapidly.

In August 1990, President Bush telephoned Margaret Thatcher from Kennebunkport, Maine. The two leaders talked about a UN Security Council resolution that would enable the enforcement of a shipping embargo to block Iraqi ships from the Persian Gulf in response to Iraqi President Saddam Hussein's increasingly hostile actions toward his Gulf neighbors including Kuwait.

Although the United States was aware of Saddam Hussein's threats to Kuwait, it did not foresee the rapid Iraqi military incursion into Kuwait that began on August 2, 1990. Iraqi Republican Guard units swiftly moved toward Kuwait City, while Iraqi Special Forces secured critical sites including the Warbah and Bubiyan Islands, Kuwaiti oil fields, and the palaces of the emir and crown prince. Despite some resistance, Kuwaiti defenses were quickly overrun. Members of the Kuwaiti royal family fled to Saudi Arabia, seeking international support. On August 28, 1990, Iraq declared Kuwait its nineteenth province, further escalating the crisis.

Thatcher insisted that it was "no time to go wobbly" and that information from secret sources must be published to expose anyone who was against taking a hardline stance against Saddam Hussein's regime. President Bush agreed.

The U.S.-led coalition and Operation Desert Storm were launched early on January 16, 1991, followed by a ground offensive the next month, swiftly liberating Kuwait and driving Iraqi forces back, in the Gulf War (now also known as the First Gulf War). The United Nations imposed ceasefire conditions, sanctions, and reparations on Iraq, and subsequent UN resolutions aimed to dismantle Iraq's chemical and biological weapons capabilities. Internal unrest in Iraq was brutally suppressed by Saddam Hussein's regime, and Saddam Hussein remained president until the next U.S. invasion of Iraq in the Iraq War (also known as the Second Gulf War), which began on March 20, 2003.

## THE EULOGY

The relationship between Ronald Reagan and Margaret Thatcher was marked by a profound and mutual admiration, akin to a love story of deep friendship and political camaraderie. Thatcher once called Reagan "the second most important man in my life."

Reagan, too, cherished their bond, referring to Thatcher as "a staunch ally, my political soul mate, a great visionary and a dear, dear friend" during a public speech in 1994. Their friendship, which began in 1975, was built on shared ideologies and mutual support. They relied on each other for emotional and political backing, creating a dynamic duo on the world stage.

Their bond extended beyond politics; it was rooted in a shared vision of leadership and freedom. Thatcher saw Reagan as an American Winston Churchill, and Reagan admired her resolute nature. Their first meeting in 1975 set the tone for a partnership that would endure through their respective terms as leaders. Reagan often reminisced about their initial encounter, noting that they instantly recognized their shared values.

Thatcher's support for Reagan was unwavering, demonstrated during his first Economic Summit held in Ottawa, Ontario, Canada, on July 19–21, 1981, where she stood by him as he recovered from the gunshot wound he had received in the assassination attempt by John Hinckley Jr. on March 30, 1981. She also defended him against European leaders' criticism after his strong anti-communism speech to the British Parliament in 1982, affirming their joint commitment to freedom and democracy.

Their relationship epitomized a period of strong transatlantic alliance, with both leaders complementing each other's strengths.

As Reagan noted in 1988, Thatcher often bore the brunt of criticism on America's behalf, underscoring the depth of their partnership. This unique and steadfast alliance between Reagan and Thatcher not only shaped their respective countries but also left a lasting impact on global politics.

Margaret Thatcher's eulogy for Ronald Reagan was a heartfelt tribute to a leader she described as "a great president, a great American, and a great man" and "a dear friend." She emphasized Reagan's optimism and cheerful presence, which she believed helped him accomplish daunting tasks with a lightness of spirit.

Thatcher highlighted Reagan's goals of mending America's spirit, restoring the strength of the free world, and freeing those under communist regimes. She praised his ability to inspire optimism, stating, "His politics had a freshness and optimism that won converts from every class and every nation."

Reagan's humor, she noted, served a purpose beyond mere amusement. In a crisis, his jokes reassured the world, showcasing his "grace under pressure," as evidenced by his remark after surviving the Hinckley assassination attempt: "Whatever time I've got left now belongs to the Big Fella Upstairs."

Thatcher credited Reagan with transforming America's economy and inspiring faith in the mission of freedom. She lauded his strategic clarity during the Cold War, particularly his candid but constructive approach with Soviet leader Mikhail Gorbachev: "Let me tell you why we distrust you."

Reagan's firmness, yet nuanced understanding of Soviet realities, enabled him to resist expansion while fostering relationships when opportunities arose. Thatcher remarked on his ability to embody and express American patriotism genuinely, saying he could "say 'God Bless America' with equal fervor in public and in private."

Reagan's achievements, she argued, were deeply rooted in his private happiness, particularly his relationship with his wife, Nancy, whom he credited with saving his soul. As Reagan faced the challenges of illness in his final years, Thatcher found solace in the belief that "the Big Fella Upstairs never forgets those who remember Him."

Thatcher concluded by reflecting on the lasting impact of Reagan's example, suggesting it served as a beacon for future generations. She called for gratitude for a life that accomplished much for humanity, capturing the essence of Reagan's legacy in both public achievement and personal virtue.

Thatcher also mentioned Nancy Reagan, who called Thatcher "Ronald Reagan's political soul mate," saying:

> On that we have the plain testimony of a loving and grateful husband: "Nancy came along and saved my soul." We share her grief today. But we also share her pride—and the grief and pride of Ronnie's children.
>
> For the final years of his life, Ronnie's mind was clouded by illness. That cloud has now lifted. He is himself again—more himself than at any time on this Earth for we may be sure that the Big Fella Upstairs never forgets those who remember Him. And as the last journey of this faithful pilgrim took him beyond the sunset, and as heaven's morning broke, I like to think, in the words of Bunyan, that "all the trumpets sounded on the other side."
>
> We here still move in twilight. But we have one beacon to guide us that Ronald Reagan never had. We have his example. Let us give thanks today for a life that achieved so much for all of God's children.

# Epilogue

In October of 1983, Grenada was under the thumb of a brutal Marxist regime, which had just assassinated Maurice Bishop—the leader of a slightly-less brutal Marxist regime—during a bloody coup.

The U.S. government feared, with good reason, that the Soviet and Cuban-backed People's Revolutionary Government (PRG) would harm American citizens living on the island amidst a politically unstable situation, leading President Ronald Reagan to approve the invasion to rescue them.

At the time, approximately 1,000 American civilians were in Grenada. Most of these civilians were medical students at St. George's University School of Medicine, as well as faculty and their families.

Operation Urgent Fury took place from October 25 to November 2, 1983, and while the fighting only lasted four days, the combat was intense, and American soldiers died in the fighting.

After the American victory, rescue of American citizens, and liberation of the Grenadian people, the Grenadian government declared October 26th as a day of thanksgiving, recognizing the role that the United States played in stopping the chaos and providing stability after years of unrest. Schools, businesses, and government offices are closed for the day to allow citizens to participate in the observance.

Their freedom, and ours, would not be possible without the men who laid down their lives fighting tyranny on that tiny island in the Caribbean.

The victory also sent a clear message to the Soviets and Cubans. The United States, under President Reagan, was no longer willing to tolerate the spread of Marxism and Communism in the Western Hemisphere.

Let us recognize the 19 men who were killed during Operation Urgent Fury defending freedom everywhere. All honor to their names.

## U.S. ARMY

Specialist 4 Mark Yamane: 1st Battalion, 75th Rangers

Private First Class Russell Robinson: 1st Battalion, 75th Rangers

Private First Class Marlin Maynard: 1st Battalion, 75th Rangers

Sergeant Mark Rademacher: 1st Battalion, 75th Rangers

Sergeant Randy Cline: 1st Battalion, 75th Rangers

Specialist 4 Philip Grenier: 2nd Battalion, 75th Rangers

Sergeant Kevin Lannon: 2nd Battalion, 75th Rangers

Sergeant Stephen Slater: 2nd Battalion, 75th Rangers

Sergeant Sean P. Luketina: 82nd Airborne Division

Staff Sergeant Gary Epps: 82nd Airborne Division

Captain Michael Ritz: 82nd Airborne Division

Private First Class Dinesh Rajbhandary: 82nd Airborne

Captain Keith Lucas: 160th Special Operations Aviation Regiment

## U.S. NAVY—SEAL TEAM 6

Petty Officer 1st Class Kenneth J. Butcher

Petty Officer 1st Class Kevin E. Lundberg

Senior Chief Engineman Robert R. Schamberger

Petty Officer 1st Class Stephen L. Morris

## U.S. MARINE CORPS

First Lieutenant Jeffery Scharver: AH-1 pilot

Captain Jeb Seagle: AH-1 pilot

APPENDIX A

# President Ronald Reagan's "Evil Empire" Speech to the National Association of Evangelicals

## March 8, 1983

Those of you in the National Association of Evangelicals are known for your spiritual and humanitarian work. And I would be especially remiss if I didn't discharge right now one personal debt of gratitude. Thank you for your prayers. Nancy and I have felt their presence many times in many ways. And believe me, for us they've made all the difference.

The other day in the East Room of the White House at a meeting there, someone asked me whether I was aware of all the people out there who were praying for the President. And I had to say, "Yes, I am. I've felt it. I believe in intercessionary prayer."

But I couldn't help but say to that questioner after he'd asked the question that—or at least say to them that if sometimes when he was praying he got a busy signal, it was just me in there ahead of him.

I think I understand how Abraham Lincoln felt when he said, "I have been driven many times to my knees by the overwhelming conviction that I had nowhere else to go."

From the joy and the good feeling of this conference, I go to a political reception.

Now, I don't know why, but that bit of scheduling reminds me of a story—which I'll share with you.

An evangelical minister and a politician arrived at Heaven's gate one day together. And St. Peter, after doing all the necessary formalities, took them in hand to show them where their quarters would be. And he took them to a small, single room with a bed, a chair, and a table and said this was for the clergyman. And the politician was a little worried about what might be in store for him. And he couldn't believe it then when St. Peter stopped in front of a beautiful mansion with lovely grounds, many servants, and told him that these would be his quarters.

And he couldn't help but ask, he said, "But wait, how—there's something wrong—how do I get this mansion while that good and holy man only gets a single room?" And St. Peter said, "You have to understand how things are up here. We've got thousands and thousands of clergy. You're the first politician who ever made it."

But I don't want to contribute to a stereotype.

So, I tell you there are a great many God-fearing, dedicated, noble men and women in public life, present company included. And yes, we need your help to keep us ever mindful of the ideas and the principles that brought us into the public arena in the first place. The basis of those ideals and principles is a commitment to freedom and personal liberty that, itself, is grounded in the much deeper realization that freedom prospers only where the blessings of God are avidly sought and humbly accepted.

The American experiment in democracy rests on this insight. Its discovery was the great triumph of our Founding Fathers, voiced by William Penn when he said, "If we will not be governed by God, we must be governed by tyrants."

Explaining the inalienable rights of men, Jefferson said, "The God who gave us life, gave us liberty at the same time."

And it was George Washington who said that "of all the dispositions and habits which lead to political prosperity, religion and morality are indispensable supports."

And finally, that shrewdest of all observers of American democracy, Alexis de Tocqueville, put it eloquently after he had gone on a search for the secret of America's greatness and genius—and he said, "Not until I went into the churches of America and heard her pulpits aflame with righteousness did I understand the greatness and the genius of America. America is good. And if America ever ceases to be good, America will cease to be great."

Well, I'm pleased to be here today with you who are keeping America great by keeping her good. Only through your work and prayers and those of millions of others can we hope to survive this perilous century and keep alive this experiment in liberty—this last, best hope of man.

I want you to know that this administration is motivated by a political philosophy that sees the greatness of America in you, her people, and in your families, churches, neighborhoods, communities—the institutions that foster and nourish values like concern for others and respect for the rule of law under God.

Now, I don't have to tell you that this puts us in opposition to, or at least out of step with, a prevailing attitude of many who have turned to a modern-day secularism, discarding the tried and time-tested values upon which our very civilization is based. No matter how well intentioned, their value system is radically different from that of most Americans. And while they proclaim that they're freeing us from superstitions of the past, they've taken upon themselves the job of superintending us by government rule and regulation. Sometimes their voices are louder than ours, but they are not yet a majority.

An example of that vocal superiority is evident in a controversy now going on in Washington. And since I'm involved, I've been waiting to hear from the parents of young America. How far are they willing to go in giving to government their prerogatives as parents?

Let me state the case as briefly and simply as I can. An organization of citizens, sincerely motivated and deeply concerned about the increase in illegitimate births and abortions involving girls well below the age of consent, sometime ago established a nationwide network of clinics to offer help to these girls and, hopefully, alleviate this situation. Now, again, let me say, I do not fault their intent. However, in their well-intentioned effort, these clinics have decided to provide advice and birth control drugs and devices to underage girls without the knowledge of their parents.

For some years now, the federal government has helped with funds to subsidize these clinics. In providing for this, the Congress decreed that every effort would be made to maximize parental participation. Nevertheless, the drugs and devices are prescribed without getting parental consent or giving notification after they've done so. Girls termed "sexually active"—and that has replaced the word "promiscuous"—are given this help in order to prevent illegitimate birth or abortion.

Well, we have ordered clinics receiving federal funds to notify the parents such help has been given. One of the nation's leading newspapers has created the term "squeal rule" in editorializing against us for doing this, and we're being criticized for violating the privacy of young people. A judge has recently granted an injunction against an enforcement of our rule. I've watched TV panel shows discuss this issue, seen columnists pontificating on our error, but no one seems to mention morality as playing a part in the subject of sex.

Is all of Judeo-Christian tradition wrong? Are we to believe that something so sacred can be looked upon as a purely physical thing with no potential for emotional and psychological harm? And isn't it the parents' right to give counsel and advice to keep their children from making mistakes that may affect their entire lives?

Many of us in government would like to know what parents think about this intrusion in their family by government. We're going to fight in the courts. The right of parents and the rights of family take precedence over those of Washington-based bureaucrats and social engineers.

But the fight against parental notification is really only one example of many attempts to water down traditional values and even abrogate the original terms of American democracy. Freedom prospers when religion is vibrant and the rule of law under God is acknowledged. When our Founding Fathers passed the First Amendment, they sought to protect churches from government interference. They never intended to construct a wall of hostility between government and the concept of religious belief itself.

The evidence of this permeates our history and our government. The Declaration of Independence mentions the Supreme Being no less than four times. "In God We Trust" is engraved on our coinage. The Supreme Court opens its proceedings with a religious invocation. And the members of Congress open their sessions with a prayer. I just happen to believe the schoolchildren of the United States are entitled to the same privileges as Supreme Court Justices and Congressmen.

Last year, I sent the Congress a constitutional amendment to restore prayer to public schools. Already this session, there's growing bipartisan support for the amendment, and I am calling on the Congress to act speedily to pass it and to let our children pray.

Perhaps some of you read recently about the Lubbock school case, where a judge actually ruled that it was unconstitutional for a school district to give equal treatment to religious and non-religious student groups, even when the group meetings were being held during the students' own time. The First Amendment never intended to require government to discriminate against religious speech.

Senators Denton and Hatfield have proposed legislation in the Congress on the whole question of prohibiting discrimination against religious forms of student speech. Such legislation could go far to restore freedom of religious speech for public school students. And I hope the Congress considers these bills quickly. And with your help, I think it's possible we could also get the constitutional amendment through the Congress this year.

More than a decade ago, a Supreme Court decision literally wiped off the books of 50 States statutes protecting the rights of unborn children. Abortion on demand now takes the lives of up to one and a half million unborn children a year. Human life legislation ending this tragedy will some day pass the Congress, and you and I must never rest until it does. Unless and until it can be proven that the unborn child is not a living entity, then its right to life, liberty, and the pursuit of happiness must be protected.

You may remember that when abortion on demand began, many, and, indeed, I'm sure many of you, warned that the practice would lead to a decline in respect for human life, that the philosophical premises used to justify abortion on demand would ultimately be used to justify other attacks on the sacredness of human life—infanticide or mercy killing. Tragically enough, those warnings proved all too true. Only last year a court permitted the death by starvation of a handicapped infant.

I have directed the Health and Human Services Department to make clear to every health care facility in the United States that the Rehabilitation Act of 1973 protects all handicapped persons against discrimination based on handicaps, including infants. And we have taken the further step of requiring that each and every recipient of Federal funds who provides health care services to infants must post and keep posted in a conspicuous place a notice stating that "discriminatory failure to feed and care for handicapped infants in this facility is prohibited by Federal law." It also lists a 24-hour, toll-free number so that nurses and others may report violations in time to save the infant's life.

In addition, recent legislation introduced in the Congress by Representative Henry Hyde of Illinois not only increases restrictions on publicly financed abortions, it also addresses this whole problem of infanticide. I urge the Congress to begin hearings and to adopt legislation that will protect the right of life to all children, including the disabled or handicapped.

Now, I'm sure that you must get discouraged at times, but you've done better than you know, perhaps. There's a great spiritual awakening in America, a renewal of the traditional values that have been the bedrock of America's goodness and greatness.

One recent survey by a Washington-based research council concluded that Americans were far more religious than the people of other nations; 95 percent of those surveyed expressed a belief in God and a huge majority believed the Ten Commandments had real meaning in their lives. And another study has found that an overwhelming majority of Americans disapprove of adultery, teenage sex, pornography, abortion, and hard drugs. And this same study showed a deep reverence for the importance of family ties and religious belief.

I think the items that we've discussed here today must be a key part of the Nation's political agenda. For the first time the Congress is openly and seriously debating and dealing with the prayer and abortion issues—and that's enormous progress right there. I repeat: America is in the midst of a spiritual awakening and a moral renewal. And with your Biblical keynote, I say today, "Yes, let justice roll on like a river, righteousness like a never-failing stream.

"Now, obviously, much of this new political and social consensus I've talked about is based on a positive view of American history, one that takes pride in our country's accomplishments and record. But we must never forget that no government schemes are going to perfect man. We know that living in this world means dealing with what philosophers would call the phenomenology of evil or, as theologians would put it, the doctrine of sin.

There is sin and evil in the world, and we're enjoined by Scripture and the Lord Jesus to oppose it with all our might. Our nation, too, has a legacy of evil with which it must deal. The glory of this land has been its capacity for transcending the moral evils of our past. For example, the long struggle of minority citizens for equal rights, once a source of disunity and civil war, is now a point of pride for all Americans. We must never go back. There is no room for racism, anti-Semitism, or other forms of ethnic and racial hatred in this country.

I know that you've been horrified, as have I, by the resurgence of some hate groups preaching bigotry and prejudice. Use the mighty voice of your pulpits and the powerful standing of your churches to denounce and isolate these hate groups in our midst. The commandment given us is clear and simple: "Thou shalt love thy neighbor as thyself." But whatever sad episodes exist in our past, any objective observer must hold a positive view of American history, a history that has been the story of hopes fulfilled, and dreams made into reality. Especially in this century, America has kept alight the torch of freedom, but not just for ourselves but for millions of others around the world.

And this brings me to my final point today. During my first press conference as President, in answer to a direct question, I pointed out that, as good Marxist-Leninists, the Soviet leaders have openly and publicly declared that the only morality they recognize is that which will further their cause, which is world revolution. I think I should point out I was only quoting Lenin, their guiding spirit, who said in 1920 that they repudiate all morality that proceeds from supernatural ideas—that's their name for religion—or ideas that are outside class conceptions. Morality is entirely subordinate to the interests of class war. And everything is moral that is necessary for the annihilation of the old, exploiting social order and for uniting the proletariat.

Well, I think the refusal of many influential people to accept this elementary fact of Soviet doctrine illustrates an historical reluctance to see totalitarian powers for what they are. We saw this phenomenon in the 1930's. We see it too often today. This doesn't mean we should isolate ourselves and refuse to seek an understanding with them. I intend to do everything I can to persuade them of our peaceful intent, to remind them that it was the West that refused to use its nuclear monopoly in the forties and fifties for territorial gain and which now proposes 50-percent cut in strategic ballistic missiles and the elimination of an entire class of land-based, intermediate-range nuclear missiles.

At the same time, however, they must be made to understand we will never compromise our principles and standards. We will never give away our freedom. We will never abandon our belief in God. And we will never stop searching for a genuine peace. But we can assure none of these things America stands for through the so-called nuclear freeze solutions proposed by some.

The truth is that a freeze now would be a very dangerous fraud, for that is merely the illusion of peace. The reality is that we must find peace through strength.

I would agree to a freeze if only we could freeze the Soviets' global desires. A freeze at current levels of weapons would remove any incentive for the Soviets to negotiate seriously in Geneva and virtually end our chances to achieve the major arms reductions which we have proposed. Instead, they would achieve their objectives through the freeze.

A freeze would reward the Soviet Union for its enormous and unparalleled military buildup. It would prevent the essential and long overdue modernization of United States and allied defenses and would leave our aging forces increasingly vulnerable. And an honest freeze would require extensive prior negotiations on the systems and numbers to be limited and on the measures to ensure effective verification and compliance. And the kind of a freeze that has been suggested would be virtually impossible to verify. Such a major effort would divert us completely from our current negotiations on achieving substantial reductions.

A number of years ago, I heard a young father, a very prominent young man in the entertainment world, addressing a tremendous gathering in California. It was during the time of the Cold War, and communism and our own way of life were very much on people's minds. And he was speaking to that subject. And suddenly, though, I heard him saying, "I love my little girls more than anything—--- "And I said to myself, "Oh, no, don't. You can't—don't say that."

But I had underestimated him. He went on: "I would rather see my little girls die now, still believing in God, than have them grow up under communism and one day die no longer believing in God."

There were thousands of young people in that audience. They came to their feet with shouts of joy. They had instantly recognized the profound truth in what he had said, with regard to the physical and the soul and what was truly important.

Yes, let us pray for the salvation of all of those who live in that totalitarian darkness—pray they will discover the joy of knowing God. But until they do, let us be aware that while they preach the supremacy of the state, declare its omnipotence over individual man, and predict its eventual domination of all peoples on the Earth, they are the focus of evil in the modern world.

It was C.S. Lewis who, in his unforgettable "Screwtape Letters," wrote: "The greatest evil is not done now in those sordid 'dens of crime' that Dickens loved to paint. It is not even done in concentration camps and labor camps. In those we see its final result. But it is conceived and ordered (moved, seconded, carried and minuted) in clear, carpeted, warmed, and well-lighted offices, by quiet men with white collars and cut fingernails and smooth-shaven cheeks who do not need to raise their voice."

Well, because these "quiet men" do not "raise their voices"; because they sometimes speak in soothing tones of brotherhood and peace; because, like other dictators before them, they're always making "their final territorial demand," some would have us accept them at their word and accommodate ourselves to their aggressive impulses. But if history teaches anything, it teaches that simple-minded appeasement or wishful thinking about our adversaries is folly. It means the betrayal of our past, the squandering of our freedom.

So, I urge you to speak out against those who would place the United States in a position of military and moral inferiority. You know, I've always believed that old Screwtape reserved his best efforts for those of you in the church. So, in your discussions of the nuclear freeze proposals, I urge you to beware the temptation of pride—the temptation of blithely declaring yourselves above it all and label both sides equally at fault, to ignore the facts of history and the aggressive impulses of an evil empire, to simply call the arms race a giant misunderstanding and thereby remove yourself from the struggle between right and wrong and good and evil.

I ask you to resist the attempts of those who would have you withhold your support for our efforts, this administration's efforts, to keep America strong and free, while we negotiate real and verifiable reductions in the world's nuclear arsenals and one day, with God's help, their total elimination.

While America's military strength is important, let me add here that I've always maintained that the struggle now going on for the world will never be decided by bombs or rockets, by armies or military might. The real crisis we face today is a spiritual one; at root, it is a test of moral will and faith.

Whittaker Chambers, the man whose own religious conversion made him a witness to one of the terrible traumas of our time, the Hiss Chambers case, wrote that the crisis of the Western World exists to the degree in which the West is indifferent to God, the degree to which it collaborates in communism's attempt to make man stand-alone without God. And then he said, for Marxism-Leninism is actually the second oldest faith, first proclaimed in the Garden of Eden with the words of temptation, "Ye shall be as gods."

The Western world can answer this challenge, he wrote, "but only provided that its faith in God and the freedom He enjoins is as great as communism's faith in Man."

I believe we shall rise to the challenge. I believe that communism is another sad, bizarre chapter in human history whose last pages even now are being written. I believe this because the source of our strength in the quest for human freedom is not material, but spiritual. And because it knows no limitation, it must terrify and ultimately triumph over those who would enslave their fellow man. For in the words of Isaiah: "He giveth power to the faint; and to them that have no might He increased strength But they that wait upon the Lord shall renew their strength; they shall mount up with wings as eagles; they shall run, and not be weary."

Yes, change your world. One of our Founding Fathers, Thomas Paine, said, "We have it within our power to begin the world over again." We can do it, doing together what no one church could do by itself.

God bless you, and thank you very much.

---

*Sources:* https://en.wikisource.org/wiki/Evil_Empire_speech and https://www.reaganlibrary.gov/archives/topic-guide/evil-empire-speech-03081983

APPENDIX B

# President Ronald Reagan's Address to the Nation on Events in Lebanon and Grenada

## October 27, 1983

My fellow Americans:

Some two months ago we were shocked by the brutal massacre of 269 men, women, and children, more than 60 of them Americans, in the shooting down of a Korean airliner. Now, in these past several days, violence has erupted again, in Lebanon and Grenada.

In Lebanon, we have some 1,600 marines, part of a multinational force that's trying to help the people of Lebanon restore order and stability to that troubled land. Our marines are assigned to the south of the city of Beirut, near the only airport operating in Lebanon. Just a mile or so to the north is the Italian contingent and not far from them, the French and a company of British soldiers.

This past Sunday, at 22 minutes after 6 Beirut time, with dawn just breaking, a truck, looking like a lot of other vehicles in the city, approached the airport on a busy, main road. There was nothing in its appearance to suggest it was any different than the trucks or cars that were normally seen on and around the airport. But this one was different. At the wheel was a young man on a suicide mission.

The truck carried some 2,000 pounds of explosives, but there was no way our marine guards could know this. Their first warning that something was wrong came when the truck crashed through a series of barriers, including a chain-link fence and barbed wire entanglements. The guards opened fire, but it was too late. The truck smashed through the doors of the headquarters building in which our marines were sleeping and instantly exploded. The four-story concrete building collapsed in a pile of rubble.

More than 200 of the sleeping men were killed in that one hideous, insane attack. Many others suffered injury and are hospitalized here or in Europe.

This was not the end of the horror. At almost the same instant, another vehicle on a suicide and murder mission crashed into the headquarters of the French peacekeeping force, an eight-story building, destroying it and killing more than 50 French soldiers.

Prior to this day of horror, there had been several tragedies for our men in the multinational force. Attacks by snipers and mortar fire had taken their toll.

I called bereaved parents and/or widows of the victims to express on behalf of all of us our sorrow and sympathy. Sometimes there were questions. And now many of you are asking: Why should our young men be dying in Lebanon? Why is Lebanon important to us?

Well, it's true, Lebanon is a small country, more than five-and-a-half thousand miles from our shores on the edge of what we call the Middle East. But every President who has occupied this office in recent years has recognized that peace in the Middle East is of vital concern to our nation and, indeed, to our allies in Western Europe and Japan. We've been concerned because the Middle East is a powder keg; four times in the last 30 years, the Arabs and Israelis have gone to war. And each time, the world has teetered near the edge of catastrophe.

The area is key to the economic and political life of the West. Its strategic importance, its energy resources, the Suez Canal, and the well-being of the nearly 200 million people living there—all are vital to us and to world peace. If that key should fall into the hands of a power or powers hostile to the free world, there would be a direct threat to the United States and to our allies.

We have another reason to be involved. Since 1948 our Nation has recognized and accepted a moral obligation to assure the continued existence of Israel as a nation. Israel shares our democratic values and is a formidable force an invader of the Middle East would have to reckon with.

For several years, Lebanon has been torn by internal strife. Once a prosperous, peaceful nation, its government had become ineffective in controlling the militias that warred on each other. Sixteen months ago, we were watching on our TV screens the shelling and bombing of Beirut which was being used as a fortress by PLO bands. Hundreds and hundreds of civilians were being killed and wounded in the daily battles.

Syria, which makes no secret of its claim that Lebanon should be a part of a Greater Syria, was occupying a large part of Lebanon. Today, Syria has become a home for 7,000 Soviet advisers and technicians who man a massive amount of Soviet weaponry, including SS-21 ground-to-ground missiles capable of reaching vital areas of Israel.

A little over a year ago, hoping to build on the Camp David accords, which had led to peace between Israel and Egypt, I proposed a peace plan for the Middle East to end the wars between the Arab States and Israel. It was based on U.N. resolutions 242 and 338 and called for a fair and just solution to the Palestinian problem, as well as a fair and just settlement of issues between the Arab States and Israel.

Before the necessary negotiations could begin, it was essential to get all foreign forces out of Lebanon and to end the fighting there. So, why are we there? Well, the answer is straightforward: to help bring peace to Lebanon and stability to the vital Middle East. To that end, the multinational force was created to help stabilize the situation in Lebanon until a government could be established and a Lebanese army mobilized to restore Lebanese sovereignty over its own soil as the foreign forces withdrew. Israel agreed to withdraw as did Syria, but Syria then reneged on its promise. Over 10,000 Palestinians who had been bringing ruin down on Beirut, however, did leave the country.

Lebanon has formed a government under the leadership of President Gemayal, and that government, with our assistance and training, has set up its own army. In only a year's time, that army has been rebuilt. It's a good army, composed of Lebanese of all factions.

A few weeks ago, the Israeli army pulled back to the Awali River in southern Lebanon. Despite fierce resistance by Syrian-backed forces, the Lebanese army was able to hold the line and maintain the defensive perimeter around Beirut.

In the year that our marines have been there, Lebanon has made important steps toward stability and order. The physical presence of the marines lends support to both the Lebanese Government and its army. It allows the hard work of diplomacy to go forward. Indeed, without the peacekeepers from the U.S., France, Italy, and Britain, the efforts to find a peaceful solution in Lebanon would collapse.

As to that narrower question—what exactly is the operational mission of the marines—the answer is, to secure a piece of Beirut, to keep order in their sector, and to prevent the area from becoming a battlefield. Our marines are not just sitting in an airport. Part of their task is to guard that airport. Because of their presence, the airport has remained operational. In addition, they patrol the surrounding area. This is their part—a limited, but essential part—in the larger effort that I've described.

If our marines must be there, I'm asked, why can't we make them safer? Who committed this latest atrocity against them and why?

Well, we'll do everything we can to ensure that our men are as safe as possible. We ordered the battleship New Jersey to join our naval forces offshore. Without even firing them, the threat of its 16-inch guns silenced those who once fired down on our marines from the hills, and they're a good part of the reason we suddenly had a cease-fire. We're doing our best to make our forces less vulnerable to those who want to snipe at them or send in future suicide missions.

Secretary Shultz called me today from Europe, where he was meeting with the Foreign Ministers of our allies in the multinational force. They remain committed to our task. And plans were made to share information as to how we can improve security for all our men.

We have strong circumstantial evidence that the attack on the marines was directed by terrorists who used the same method to destroy our Embassy in Beirut. Those who directed this atrocity must be dealt justice, and they will be. The obvious purpose behind the sniping and, now, this attack was to weaken American will and force the withdrawal of U.S. and French forces from Lebanon. The clear intent of the terrorists was to eliminate our support of the Lebanese Government and to destroy the ability of the Lebanese people to determine their own destiny.

To answer those who ask if we're serving any purpose in being there, let me answer a question with a question. Would the terrorists have launched their suicide attacks against the multinational force if it were not doing its job? The multinational force was attacked precisely because it is doing the job it was sent to do in Beirut. It is accomplishing its mission.

Now then, where do we go from here? What can we do now to help Lebanon gain greater stability so that our marines can come home? Well, I believe we can take three steps now that will make a difference.

First, we will accelerate the search for peace and stability in that region. Little attention has been paid to the fact that we've had special envoys there working, literally, around the clock to bring the warring factions together. This coming Monday in Geneva, President Gemayel of Lebanon will sit down with other factions from his country to see if national reconciliation can be achieved. He has our firm support. I will soon be announcing a replacement for Bud McFarlane, who was preceded by Phil Habib. Both worked tirelessly and must be credited for much if not most of the progress we've made.

Second, we'll work even more closely with our allies in providing support for the Government of Lebanon and for the rebuilding of a national consensus.

Third, we will ensure that the multinational peace-keeping forces, our marines, are given the greatest possible protection. Our Commandant of the Marine Corps, General Kelley, returned from Lebanon today and will be advising us on steps we can take to improve security. Vice President Bush returned just last night from Beirut and gave me a full report of his brief visit.

Beyond our progress in Lebanon, let us remember that our main goal and purpose is to achieve a broader peace in all of the Middle East. The factions and bitterness that we see in Lebanon are just a microcosm of the difficulties that are spread across much of that region. A peace initiative for the entire Middle East, consistent with the Camp David accords and U.N. resolutions 242 and 338, still offers the best hope for bringing peace to the region.

Let me ask those who say we should get out of Lebanon: If we were to leave Lebanon now, what message would that send to those who foment instability and terrorism? If America were to walk away from Lebanon, what chance would there be for a negotiated settlement, producing a unified democratic Lebanon?

If we turned our backs on Lebanon now, what would be the future of Israel? At stake is the fate of only the second Arab country to negotiate a major agreement with Israel. That's another accomplishment of this past year, the May 17th accord signed by Lebanon and Israel.

If terrorism and intimidation succeed, it'll be a devastating blow to the peace process and to Israel's search for genuine security. It won't just be Lebanon sentenced to a future of chaos. Can the United States, or the free world, for that matter, stand by and see the Middle East incorporated into the Soviet bloc? What of Western Europe and Japan's dependence on Middle East oil for the energy to fuel their industries? The Middle East is, as I've said, vital to our national security and economic well-being.

Brave young men have been taken from us. Many others have been grievously wounded. Are we to tell them their sacrifice was wasted? They gave their lives in defense of our national security every bit as much as any man who ever died fighting in a war. We must not strip every ounce of meaning and purpose from their courageous sacrifice.

We're a nation with global responsibilities. We're not somewhere else in the world protecting someone else's interests; we're there protecting our own.

I received a message from the father of a marine in Lebanon. He told me, "In a world where we speak of human rights, there is a sad lack of acceptance of responsibility. My son has chosen the acceptance of responsibility for the privilege of living in this country. Certainly, in this country one does not inherently have rights unless the responsibility for these rights is accepted." Dr. Kenneth Morrison said that while he was waiting to learn if his son was one of the dead. I was thrilled for him to learn today that his son Ross is alive and well and carrying on his duties in Lebanon.

Let us meet our responsibilities. For longer than any of us can remember, the people of the Middle East have lived from war to war with no prospect for any other future. That dreadful cycle must be broken. Why are we there? Well, a Lebanese mother told one of our Ambassadors that her little girl had only attended school 2 of the last 8 years. Now, because of our presence there, she said her daughter could live a normal life.

With patience and firmness, we can help bring peace to that strife torn region—and make our own lives more secure. Our role is to help the Lebanese put their country together, not to do it for them.

Now, I know another part of the world is very much on our minds, a place much closer to our shores: Grenada. The island is only twice the size of the District of Columbia, with a total population of about 110,000 people.

Grenada and a half dozen other Caribbean islands here were, until recently, British colonies. They're now independent states and members of the British Commonwealth. While they respect each other's independence, they also feel a kinship with each other and think of themselves as one people.

In 1979 trouble came to Grenada. Maurice Bishop, a protege of Fidel Castro, staged a military coup and overthrew the government which had been elected under the constitution left to the people by the British. He sought the help of Cuba in building an airport, which he claimed was for tourist trade, but which looked suspiciously suitable for military aircraft, including Soviet-built long-range bombers.

The six sovereign countries and one remaining colony are joined together in what they call the Organization of Eastern Caribbean States. The six became increasingly alarmed as Bishop built an army greater than all of theirs combined. Obviously, it was not purely for defense.

In this last year or so, Prime Minister Bishop gave indications that he might like better relations with the United States. He even made a trip to our country and met with senior officials of the White House and the State Department. Whether he was serious or not, we'll never know. On October 12th, a small group in his militia seized him and put him under arrest. They were, if anything, more radical and more devoted to Castro's Cuba than he had been.

Several days later, a crowd of citizens appeared before Bishop's home, freed him, and escorted him toward the headquarters of the military council. They were fired upon. A number, including some children, were killed, and Bishop was seized. He and several members of his cabinet were subsequently executed, and a 24-hour shoot-to-kill curfew was put in effect. Grenada was without a government, its only authority exercised by a self-proclaimed band of military men.

There were then about 1,000 of our citizens on Grenada, 800 of them students in St. George's University Medical School. Concerned that they'd be harmed or held as hostages, I ordered a flotilla of ships, then on its way to Lebanon with marines, part of our regular rotation program, to circle south on a course that would put them somewhere in the vicinity of Grenada in case there should be a need to evacuate our people.

Last weekend, I was awakened in the early morning hours and told that six members of the Organization of Eastern Caribbean States, joined by Jamaica and Barbados, had sent an urgent request that we join them in a military operation to restore order and democracy to Grenada. They were proposing this action under the terms of a treaty, a mutual assistance pact that existed among them.

These small, peaceful nations needed our help. Three of them don't have armies at all, and the others have very limited forces. The legitimacy of their request, plus my own concern for our citizens, dictated my decision. I believe our government has a responsibility to go to the aid of its citizens, if their right to life and liberty is threatened. The nightmare of our hostages in Iran must never be repeated.

We knew we had little time and that complete secrecy was vital to ensure both the safety of the young men who would undertake this mission and the Americans they were about to rescue. The Joint Chiefs worked around the clock to come up with a plan. They had little intelligence information about conditions on the island.

We had to assume that several hundred Cubans working on the airport could be military reserves. Well, as it turned out, the number was much larger, and they were a military force. Six hundred of them have been taken prisoner, and we have discovered a complete base with weapons and communications equipment, which makes it clear a Cuban occupation of the island had been planned.

Two hours ago, we released the first photos from Grenada. They included pictures of a warehouse of military equipment—one of three we've uncovered so far. This warehouse contained weapons and ammunition stacked almost to the ceiling, enough to supply thousands of terrorists. Grenada, we were told, was a friendly island paradise for tourism. Well, it wasn't. It was a Soviet-Cuban colony, being readied as a major military bastion to export terror and undermine democracy. We got there just in time.

I can't say enough in praise of our military—Army rangers and paratroopers, Navy, Marine, and Air Force personnel—those who planned a brilliant campaign and those who carried it out. Almost instantly, our military seized the two airports, secured the campus where most of our students were, and are now in the mopping-up phase.

It should be noted that in all the planning, a top priority was to minimize risk, to avoid casualties to our own men and also the Grenadian forces as much as humanly possible. But there were casualties, and we all owe a debt to those who lost their lives or were wounded. They were few in number, but even one is a tragic price to pay.

It's our intention to get our men out as soon as possible. Prime Minister Eugenia Charles of Dominica—I called that wrong; she pronounces it Dominica—she is Chairman of OECS. She's calling for help from Commonwealth nations in giving the people their right to establish a constitutional government on Grenada. We anticipate that the Governor General, a Grenadian, will participate in setting up a provisional government in the interim.

The events in Lebanon and Grenada, though oceans apart, are closely related. Not only has Moscow assisted and encouraged the violence in both countries, but it provides direct support through a network of surrogates and terrorists. It is no coincidence that when the thugs tried to wrest control over Grenada, there were 30 Soviet advisers and hundreds of Cuban military and paramilitary forces on the island. At the moment of our landing, we communicated with the Governments of Cuba and the Soviet Union and told them we would offer shelter and security to their people on Grenada. Regrettably, Castro ordered his men to fight to the death, and some did. The others will be sent to their homelands.

You know, there was a time when our national security was based on a standing army here within our own borders and shore batteries of artillery along our coasts, and, of course, a navy to keep the sea-lanes open for the shipping of things necessary to our well-being. The world has changed. Today, our national security can be threatened in faraway places. It's up to all of us to be aware of the strategic importance of such places and to be able to identify them.

Sam Rayburn once said that freedom is not something a nation can work for once and win forever. He said it's like an insurance policy; its premiums must be kept up to date. In order to keep it, we have to keep working for it and sacrificing for it just as long as we live. If we do not, our children may not know the pleasure of working to keep it, for it may not be theirs to keep.

In these last few days, I've been more sure than I've ever been that we Americans of today will keep freedom and maintain peace. I've been made to feel that by the magnificent spirit of our young men and women in uniform and by something here in our Nation's Capital. In this city, where political strife is so much a part of our lives, I've seen Democratic leaders in the Congress join their Republican colleagues, send a message to the world that we're all Americans before we're anything else, and when our country is threatened, we stand shoulder to shoulder in support of our men and women in the Armed Forces.

May I share something with you I think you'd like to know? It's something that happened to the Commandant of our Marine Corps, General Paul Kelley, while he was visiting our critically injured marines in an Air Force hospital. It says more than any of us could ever hope to say about the gallantry and heroism of these young men, young men who serve so willingly so that others might have a chance at peace and freedom in their own lives and in the life of their country.

I'll let General Kelley's words describe the incident. He spoke of a "young marine with more tubes going in and out of his body than I have ever seen in one body."

"He couldn't see very well. He reached up and grabbed my four stars, just to make sure I was who I said I was. He held my hand with a firm grip. He was making signals, and we realized he wanted to tell me something. We put a pad of paper in his hand—and he wrote 'Semper Fi.'"

Well, if you've been a marine or if, like myself, you're an admirer of the marines, you know those words are a battle cry, a greeting, and a legend in the Marine Corps. They're marine shorthand for the motto of the Corps—"Semper Fidelis"—"always faithful."

General Kelley has a reputation for being a very sophisticated general and a very tough marine. But he cried when he saw those words, and who can blame him?

That marine and all those others like him, living and dead, have been faithful to their ideals. They've given willingly of themselves so that a nearly defenseless people in a region of great strategic importance to the free world will have a chance someday to live lives free of murder and mayhem and terrorism. I think that young marine and all of his comrades have given every one of us something to live up to.

They were not afraid to stand up for their country or, no matter how difficult and slow the journey might be, to give to others that last, best hope of a better future. We cannot and will not dishonor them now and the sacrifices they've made by failing to remain as faithful to the cause of freedom and the pursuit of peace as they have been.

I will not ask you to pray for the dead, because they're safe in God's loving arms and beyond need of our prayers. I would like to ask you all—wherever you may be in this blessed land—to pray for these wounded young men and to pray for the bereaved families of those who gave their lives for our freedom.

God bless you, and God bless America.

---

*Source:* https://www.reaganlibrary.gov/archives/speech/address-nation-events-lebanon-and-grenada.

APPENDIX C

# President Ronald Reagan's Remarks at a White House Ceremony Marking the First Anniversary of the Grenada Rescue Mission

## October 24, 1984

Together we celebrate today, with joy, an anniversary of honor for America—your rescue and the liberation of our neighbor, Grenada, from the grip of oppression and tyranny. Just one year ago, Grenada's Governor General Paul Scoon and members of the Organization of Eastern Caribbean States called for our help.

Using military force is, I'm sure you realize, the most serious decision any President must make. It's an awesome responsibility. But the evidence to me was clear. At stake was the freedom of 110,000 Grenadians, the security of the democracies of the Eastern Caribbean and, most important, the safety and well-being of you American medical students trapped by events that were totally beyond your control. So, we approved a military operation to rescue you, to help the people of Grenada, and to prevent the spread of chaos and totalitarianism throughout the Caribbean.

Side by side, with forces from neighboring Caribbean democracies, the brave young soldiers, sailors, marines, and airmen accomplished their mission. They went to Grenada not to conquer, but to liberate, and they did. They saved the people, they captured tons of Soviet military equipment, and they averted a hostage crisis before it happened. And then those combat troops left the island so the Grenadian people could start a new life and give peace, freedom, and democracy, and self-determination a chance.

But today over 100,000 Soviet troops are still ravaging Afghanistan. There is a fundamental moral distinction between the Grenada rescue mission and the Soviet invasion of Afghanistan—a brutal and bloody conquest that aims to destroy freedom, democracy, and self-determination. It's the difference between totalitarianism and democracy, between tyranny and freedom. And it gives all of us hope for the future to know that you see the difference that others should have seen from the very beginning.

During the latter part of the 1970s, America passed through a period of self-doubt and national confusion. We talked and acted like a nation in decline, and the world believed us. Many questioned our will to continue as a leader of the Western alliance and to remain a force for good in the world. But I believe this period of self-doubt is over. History will record that one of the turning points came on a small island in the Caribbean where America went to take care of her own and to rescue a neighboring nation from a growing tyranny.

Our brave military personnel displayed the same love of liberty and personal courage which has made our nation great and kept her free. And this courage and love of country is also what we saw in Beirut at virtually the same time. And we will always honor those brave Americans. Let no one doubt that those brave men were heroes every bit as much in their peacekeeping mission as were our men in the rescue mission in Grenada.

And we continue to see this devotion and commitment every day. On the demilitarized zone in Korea, on the NATO lines in Europe, at bases from Diego Garcia to Guam, and on our ships at sea, young Americans are proudly wearing the uniform of our country and serving with the same distinction as those who came before.

Cicero once said, "Courage is that virtue which champions the cause of the right." Well, with us today is a small contingent of military personnel, a few of the heroes who took part in the rescue mission—two each, from the Army, Navy, Air Force, and Marines. And four of these brave young Americans are here with me on the podium, and the other four are sitting among the students that they rescued. So, I thank them for joining us today, and thank all of you. We're very grateful to all of you.

Nineteen brave men died during the Grenada rescue, serving their country and the cause of freedom. One of them was Sean Luketina. He was a paratrooper seriously wounded by a rocket. He was evacuated to Puerto Rico, and there in the hospital slipped in and out of a coma. His father, Colonel Robin Luketina, a retired military officer who's here with us today, rushed to his bedside. And Colonel Luketina, I'm told that on one of those moments when your son regained consciousness, you asked him, "Sean, was it worth it?" And "Yes, Dad," he answered. And you asked again, "Would you do it again?" And he looked up at you and said, "Hell, yes, Dad." A few months ago, Sean died of his wounds. But he, Sean Luketina, gave his life in the cause of freedom. He did not die in vain. The young Americans he helped to rescue know that. The liberated people of Grenada know that. Grenada's neighbors know that. And Sean himself knows. So, let us honor him as he would have wished, by keeping faith with the policy of peace and deterrence that assures the survival of our freedom, keeps alive the hope of freedom for all the peoples of the world.

This is the meaning of peace through strength. And let us always remember that America is the land of the free, because we're the home of the brave.

To Sean and all the men and women who served the cause of freedom, and to all of you, all of you students who are dedicating yourselves to saving human life: you are the hope of America. You are all America's future. Thank you for what you do, and God bless you.

I know I've told this many times but, you know, when you get past 40, you have a tendency to tell the same story over and over again.

I just have to tell you a little story about Grenada here, and then I will get back to the office and go to work. This young lieutenant marine, flying a Cobra helicopter, was at Grenada and then went on to Beirut. And from Beirut he wrote back to the Pentagon to the *Armed Forces Journal*, and he said that there was one thing in all the news stories about Grenada that was so consistent and so repeated that he decided it was a code, and he was going to break the code.

That line was that Grenada produces more nutmeg than any other spot on Earth. So, he said, in breaking the code, number one, that is true—they produce more nutmeg than any other spot on Earth. He said, number two, the Soviets and the Cubans are trying to take Grenada. And number three, you can't have good eggnog without nutmeg. And number four, you can't have Christmas without eggnog. And number five, the Soviets and the Cubans were trying to steal Christmas. And number six, we stopped them.

---

*Source:* https://www.reaganlibrary.gov/archives/speech/remarks-white-house-ceremony-marking-first-anniversary-grenada-rescue-mission.

# Acknowledgments

A special thank you to all the people who made themselves available for interviews for this book including: Edwin Meese, Michael Reagan, Sal Russo, Christopher Lehman, K.T. McFarland, Lt. Col. Tony Shaffer, Mike Parnel, and Lt. Col Oliver North.

Also thanks to all those who provided guidance on this project including Greg Kelly, James Rosen, Craig Shirley, Andrew Brown, and Christopher Ruddy.

To the veterans of Operation Urgent Fury—every American owes you a debt of gratitude. Thank you.

# Notes

## PREFACE
1. https://www.margaretthatcher.org/document%2F108325
2. https://www.nytimes.com/1983/10/22/world/us-marines-diverted-to-grenada-in-event-americans-face-danger.html
3. https://www.marines.mil/Portals/1/Publications/U.S.%20Marines%20in%20Grenada%201983%20%20PCN%2019000309700.pdf
4. https://sofmag.com/operation-urgent-fury-the-1983-invasion-of-grenada/#:~:text=Strategic%20Setting,population%20of%20about%207%2C500%20inhabitants
5. https://www.washingtonpost.com/archive/politics/1984/10/25/memories-of-a-soldier-son/38bdc9de-90fa-45e3-98fa-7eac57ca176f/
6. https://airspacehistorian.wordpress.com/2018/07/30/operation-urgent-fury/

## CHAPTER 1
1. https://millercenter.org/the-presidency/presidential-speeches/december-17-1895-message-regarding-venezuelan-british-dispute
2. https://smallwarsjournal.com/jrnl/art/monroe-doctrine-21st-century-great-power-competition#_edn29
3. https://www.publishersweekly.com/978-0-671-64996-8
4. https://www.newspapers.com/newspage/633353739/
5. https://www.washingtonpost.com/archive/1980/09/19/argentines-sought-as-killers-of-somoza/4234833e-dfa6-404a-b2bf-1dbb6a37a440/
6. https://files.libcom.org/files/Cienfuegos-6.pdf; https://www.cia.gov/readingroom/docs/CIA-RDP90-00552R000100260008-6.pdf
7. https://www.nytimes.com/1982/07/29/world/around-the-world-grenadan-signs-pacts-with-soviet-officials.html
8. https://www.nytimes.com/1982/07/29/world/around-the-world-grenadan-signs-pacts-with-soviet-officials.html

9. https://www.cia.gov/readingroom/docs/CIA-RDP85-00024R000400310048-1.pdf
10. https://www.washingtonpost.com/archive/politics/1979/05/18/castro-returns-to-mexico-as-a-vindicated-hero/0e302625-6b75-46d2-a270-facec9bef6b0/
11. https://www.cia.gov/readingroom/document/cia-rdp11m01338r000400470013-5
12. https://www.cia.gov/readingroom/docs/CIA-RDP11M01338R000400470013-5.pdf
13. https://www.cia.gov/readingroom/docs/CIA-RDP11M01338R000400470013-5.pdf
14. https://www.washingtonpost.com/archive/local/1984/08/25/jewish-group-finds-no-anti-semitism-by-sandinista-regime/2042de6b-afb1-493e-9b8f-d09eda8d7242/

## CHAPTER 2

1. https://www.usnews.com/news/articles/2008/01/17/the-actor-and-the-detail-man
2. https://media.cleveland.com/politics_impact/other/1980-debate-day-after.pdf
3. https://www.upi.com/Archives/1980/10/30/Amy-Carters-concern-about-nuclear-warfare-and-the-strategic/1556341730000/
4. https://www.youtube.com/watch?v=mCaAiIb_ns
5. https://www.politico.com/magazine/story/2016/04/1976-convention-oral-history-213793/
6. https://www.politico.com/magazine/story/2016/04/1976-convention-oral-history-213793/
7. https://www.nashuatelegraph.com/news/local-news/2018/12/03/a-recollection-the-historic-1980-nashua-debate/
8. https://www.americustimesrecorder.com/2020/01/10/i-am-a-candidate-for-reelection-president-carter-enters-1980-race/
9. https://www.nytimes.com/1979/03/28/archives/brzezinskis-deputy-a-source-of-growing-influence-confrontation-with.html
10. https://www.washingtonpost.com/archive/politics/1978/09/08/defense-bill-veto-upheld-in-major-victory-for-carter/6a2ccf17-2bba-4f40-a5aa-659295612e0a/
11. https://www.washingtonpost.com/archive/politics/1980/12/31/up-to-reagan-or-iran/96315c84-dade-46e0-afb5-e6583a9e1706/

## CHAPTER 3

1. https://www.inquirer.com/philly/blogs/americandebate/Al_Haig_the_long_goodbye.html
2. https://tnsr.org/roundtable/policy-roundtable-reconsidering-alexander-haig/
3. https://www.nytimes.com/1981/05/31/magazine/how-haig-is-recasting-his-image.html
4. https://www.reaganlibrary.gov/public/digitallibrary/smof/president/presidentialbriefingpapers/box-001/40-439-5730647-001-023-2016.pdf.

5. https://books.google.com/books?id=qFy0CAAAQBAJ&pg=PA225&lpg =PA225&dq=%E2%80%9CYou+just+give+me+the+word,%E2%80%9D +Secretary+of+State+Alexander+M.+Haig+told+President+Ronald +Reagan,+%E2%80%9Cand+I%E2%80%99ll+turn+that+fucking+island +into+a+parking+lot.%E2%80%9D%C2%B9&source=bl&ots=9UJc6 HO1GX&sig=ACfU3U2HaCgiO8d5nwJwynkEV53H2Lg31Q&hl=en&sa =X&ved=2ahUKEwiAseiys6-DAxWvmmoFHcXxBPIQ6AF6BAgIEAM#v =onepage&q=%E2%80%9CYou%20just%20give%20me%20the%20word %2C%E2%80%9D%20Secretary%20of%20State%20Alexander%20M.%20 Haig%20told%20President%20Ronald%20Reagan%2C%20%E2%80%9C and%20I%E2%80%99ll%20turn%20that%20fucking%20island%20into%20 a%20parking%20lot.%E2%80%9D%C2%B9&f=false
6. https://www.washingtonpost.com/archive/politics/1981/03/22/haig-remarks -may-hinder-nuns-death-probe/0e5e732e-872a-4dd0-a929-8eaa806c3113/
7. https://www.upi.com/Archives/1981/03/18/Secretary-of-State-Alexander -Haig-said-Wednesday-that-four/7903353739600/
8. https://content.time.com/time/subscriber/article/0,33009,922441-2,00.html
9. https://adst.org/2014/03/al-haig-and-the-reagan-assassination-attempt-im -in-charge-here/https://web.archive.org/web/20080406153923/
10. http://www.time.com/time/magazine/article/0,9171,954230-22,00.html
11. https://web.archive.org/web/20080406153923/http://www.time.com/time/ magazine/article/0,9171,954230-22,00.html
12. https://adst.org/2014/03/al-haig-and-the-reagan-assassination-attempt-im -in-charge-here/
13. https://www.washingtonpost.com/opinions/when-reagan-was-shot-who-was -in-control-at-the-white-house/2011/03/23/AFJlrfYB_story.html
14. https://www.nytimes.com/1981/05/24/weekinreview/some-signals-for-reagan -that-honeymoon-is-over.html
15. https://www.thereaganfiles.com/19811221-nsc-33.pdf
16. https://tile.loc.gov/storage-services/service/mss/mfdip/2004/2004mcm01/ 2004mcm01.pdf
17. https://www.nytimes.com/1981/06/14/weekinreview/the-shadow-of-taiwan -follows-haig-to.html
18. https://www.reaganlibrary.gov/archives/speech/address-commencement -exercises-university-notre-dame
19. https://www.reaganlibrary.gov/archives/speech/interview-new-york-city -members-editorial-board-new-york-post
20. https://history.state.gov/historicaldocuments/frus1981-88v13/d195
21. https://www.reaganlibrary.gov/public/2023-05/40-096-6120362-003-010 -2023.pdf

## CHAPTER 4

1. https://www.nytimes.com/1976/03/07/archives/soviet-gerontocracy.html
2. https://www.washingtonpost.com/archive/politics/1981/03/04/soviet -union-retaining-old-team/462b85b3-576d-4c3a-88d9-e89a344b4c67/
3. https://www.nytimes.com/1976/03/07/archives/soviet-gerontocracy.html

4. https://www.washingtonpost.com/archive/politics/1988/05/29/reagan-gorbachev-two-paths-to-detente/8bec251e-7160-4599-a6e4-f527c4ff885a/
5. https://web.archive.org/web/20150328151950/http:/nsarchive.gwu.edu/NSAEBB/NSAEBB426/docs/3.The%201983%20War%20Scare%20in%20U.S.%20Soviet%20Relations-circa%201996.pdf
6. https://www.washingtonpost.com/archive/politics/1988/05/29/reagan-gorbachev-two-paths-to-detente/8bec251e-7160-4599-a6e4-f527c4ff885a/
7. https://www.washingtonpost.com/archive/politics/1980/06/16/a-buildup-in-us-forces/a7b162d0-f745-4a0b-993a-05e23f94f105/
8. https://www.washingtonpost.com/archive/politics/1988/05/29/reagan-gorbachev-two-paths-to-detente/8bec251e-7160-4599-a6e4-f527c4ff885a/
9. https://www.stateoftheunionhistory.com/2020/01/1977-gerald-ford-from-peace-with-honor.html
10. https://www.reaganlibrary.gov/reagans/ronald-reagan/time-choosing-speech-october-27-1964
11. https://www.brookings.edu/wp-content/uploads/1986/06/1986b_bpea_gately_adelman_griffin.pdf
12. https://policyoptions.irpp.org/magazines/the-best-pms-in-the-past-50-years/the-mulroney-years-transformation-and-tumult/
13. https://www.presidency.ucsb.edu/documents/address-commencement-exercises-the-university-notre-dame-0
14. https://web.archive.org/web/20150328151950/http:/nsarchive.gwu.edu/NSAEBB/NSAEBB426/docs/3.The%201983%20War%20Scare%20in%20U.S.%20Soviet%20Relations-circa%201996.pdf
15. https://cdn.theatlantic.com/media/archives/1986/09/258-3/132674176.pdf
16. https://history.state.gov/historicaldocuments/frus1981-88v03/d160
17. https://www.reaganlibrary.gov/archives/speech/address-members-british-parliament
18. https://apnews.com/article/ronald-reagan-republican-debate-election-2024-ce3d776fdd26bd23b3b9b7fe49e376af
19. https://web.archive.org/web/20150328151950/http:/nsarchive.gwu.edu/NSAEBB/NSAEBB426/docs/3.The%201983%20War%20Scare%20in%20U.S.%20Soviet%20Relations-circa%201996.pdf; https://books.google.com/books?id=6ahujvo6ukwC&printsec=frontcover#v=onepage&q=1941&f=false
20. https://en.wikipedia.org/wiki/Operation_RYAN
21. https://books.google.com/books?id=6ahujvo6ukwC&printseczaaa=frontcover#v=snippet&q=Marshal%20Dmitri%20Fyodorovich%20Ustinov&f=false
22. https://books.google.com/books?id=6ahujvo6ukwC&printsec=frontcover#v=snippet&q=Maclean&f=false
23. https://www.fordlibrarymuseum.gov/digital-research-room/library-collections/topic-guides/vladivostok-summit-meeting-arms-control
24. https://archive.org/details/yearsofrenewal00kiss_0/page/286/mode/2up
25. https://www.nytimes.com/1992/08/20/opinion/foreign-affairs-who-won-the-cold-war.html

26. https://theaviationgeekclub.com/viktor-belenko-who-defected-to-the-west-in-a-mig-25-foxbat-jet-fighter-has-passed-away/
27. https://www.upi.com/Archives/1983/10/07/The-CIA-Friday-branded-as-absolutely-ridiculous-and-utterly/1046434347200/
28. https://www.nytimes.com/1983/09/02/world/transcript-of-shultz-news-conference-on-the-korean-airliner.html
29. https://books.google.com/books?id=ck2A4Int8n0C&pg=PA50&lpg=PA50&dq=intelligence+agencies+%22have+no+compunction+about+fooling+you.%22&source=bl&ots=vdXBsF8VrJ&sig=ACfU3U3WZ15UYDtFUJJ1-LRbpfKAMB-gwA&hl=en&sa=X&ved=2ahUKEwi_yrbu1OKDAxU_lmoFHfieAGUQ6AF6BAgJEAM#v=onepage&q=intelligence%20agencies%20%22have%20no%20compunction%20about%20fooling%20you.%22&f=false
30. https://nsarchive.gwu.edu/briefing-book/russia-programs-russian-pages/2023-05-25/anatoly-s-chernyaev-diary-1983
31. https://www.pbs.org/wgbh/nova/missileers/falsealarms.html
32. https://flb.ru/info/27637.html

## CHAPTER 5

1. https://www.independent.co.uk/news/people/obituary-sir-eric-gairy-1247273.html
2. https://digitalcommons.fiu.edu/cgi/viewcontent.cgi?referer=&httpsredir=1&article=1035&context=laccopsd; https://www.nytimes.com/1974/01/06/archives/an-uneasy-grenada-to-get-independence-mounting-resistance-permits.html
3. https://global.uwi.edu/sites/default/files/bnccde/grenada/conference/papers/Baptiste.html
4. https://nsarchive.gwu.edu/document/19938-national-security-archive-doc-1-white-house
5. https://nsarchive.gwu.edu/document/19940-national-security-archive-doc-03-memorandum
6. https://www.jfklibrary.org/asset-viewer/archives/jfkwhp-1961-10-25-a
7. https://www.jfklibrary.org/asset-viewer/archives/jfkwhp-1961-10-25-a
8. https://nsarchive.gwu.edu/document/19938-national-security-archive-doc-1-white-house
9. https://nsarchive.gwu.edu/briefing-book/intelligence/2020-04-06/cia-covert-operations-overthrow-cheddi-jagan-british-guiana-1964#_ednref7
10. https://nsarchive.gwu.edu/briefing-book/intelligence/2020-04-06/cia-covert-operations-overthrow-cheddi-jagan-british-guiana-1964#_ednref8
11. https://nsarchive.gwu.edu/briefing-book/intelligence/2020-04-06/cia-covert-operations-overthrow-cheddi-jagan-british-guiana-1964#_ednref9
12. https://nsarchive.gwu.edu/document/19945-national-security-archive-doc-08-secretary
13. https://nsarchive.gwu.edu/briefing-book/intelligence/2020-04-06/cia-covert-operations-overthrow-cheddi-jagan-british-guiana-1964
14. https://nsarchive.gwu.edu/document/19946-national-security-archive-doc-09-national

## NOTES

15. https://docs.google.com/document/d/18fkzNVWLsbYF8IqYJQqlTHWL z9tKuxvg_ED6E4zLDiU/edit?tab=t.0
16. https://www.mylondon.news/news/nostalgia/ship-full-buses-sank-thames-24011934
17. https://www.cia.gov/readingroom/docs/CIA-RDP82R00025R000400220014-3.pdf
18. https://www.washingtonpost.com/archive/politics/1977/06/25/pleasant-poor-grenada-takes-lead-from-happy-barman/b6e390c7-e81f-4aa7-9ad2-19d404a7cf8b/
19. https://history.state.gov/historicaldocuments/frus1977-80v23/d304
20. https://www.latimes.com/archives/la-xpm-1997-aug-25-mn-25805-story.html
21. https://en.wikipedia.org/wiki/Tonton_Macoute
22. https://www.youtube.com/watch?v=98OOYZ6M7k0
23. https://nowgrenada.com/2023/01/this-day-in-history-21-january-1974-2-2/
24. https://www.vice.com/en/article/how-britain-might-have-deliberately-concealed-evidence-of-imperial-crimes/
25. https://www.google.com/books/edition/Faith_in_the_Face_of_Militarization/o9EoEAAAQBAJ?hl=en&gbpv=1&dq=%E2%80%9CIt+might+be+better+that+Mr.+Gairy+should+have+a+free+hand+to+keep+such+developments+under+control+in+an+independent+Grenada+than+that+we+ourselves+should+run+the+risk+of+becoming+involved+in+the+task.%E2%80%9D&pg=PT237&printsec=frontcover
26. https://www.vice.com/en/article/revealed-britains-top-secret-plan-to-invade-a-tiny-caribbean-island/
27. https://www.google.com/books/edition/Faith_in_the_Face_of_Militarization/o9EoEAAAQBAJ?hl=en&gbpv=1&dq=%E2%80%9CIt+might+be+better+that+Mr.+Gairy+should+have+a+free+hand+to+keep+such+developments+under+control+in+an+independent+Grenada+than+that+we+ourselves+should+run+the+risk+of+becoming+involved+in+the+task.%E2%80%9D&pg=PT237&printsec=frontcover
28. https://digitalcommons.fiu.edu/cgi/viewcontent.cgi?referer=&httpsredir=1&article=1035&context=laccopsd; https://link.springer.com/chapter/10.1057/9780230609952_3
29. https://www.youtube.com/watch?v=dPY5d9ptvvA
30. https://www.cia.gov/readingroom/docs/DOC_0000177663.pdf
31. https://history.state.gov/historicaldocuments/frus1977-80v23/d313
32. https://www.washingtonpost.com/archive/politics/1979/04/27/us-vs-cuba-on-caribbean-isle-of-grenada/ff9069cc-973f-4d94-9f38-76eacdca7c3c/
33. https://www.washingtonpost.com/archive/politics/1979/04/27/us-vs-cuba-on-caribbean-isle-of-grenada/ff9069cc-973f-4d94-9f38-76eacdca7c3c/
34. https://en.wikipedia.org/wiki/6th_Summit_of_the_Non-Aligned_Movement#:~:text=6th%20Summit%20of%20the%20Non%2DAligned%20Movement%20took%20place%20on,among%20the%20non%2D aligned%20countries.
35. https://aad.archives.gov/aad/createpdf?rid=5540&dt=2776&dl=2169
36. https://www.marxists.org/history/grenada/1973/manifesto.htm

37. https://www.reaganlibrary.gov/public/2023-10/40-219-6927378-007-004-2023.pdf
38. https://www.google.com/books/edition/Maurice_Bishop_s_Line_of_March_Speech_Se/mihIAQAAMAAJ?hl=en&gbpv=1
39. https://www.cia.gov/readingroom/docs/CIA-RDP86M00886R001500020008-9.pdf
40. https://www.nytimes.com/1981/08/01/world/us-and-allied-navies-starting-major-test-today-military-analysis.html
41. https://www.ausa.org/articles/we-were-there-reforger-exercises-designed-counter-soviet-threat
42. https://www.cia.gov/readingroom/docs/CIA-RDP90-00552R000505400106-2.pdf
43. https://www.cia.gov/readingroom/docs/CIA-RDP88B00745R000100140026-6.pdf
44. https://www.cia.gov/readingroom/docs/CIA-RDP90-00552R000202230073-4.pdf
45. https://digitalcommons.nyls.edu/cgi/viewcontent.cgi?article=1248&context=journal_of_international_and_comparative_law
46. https://www.usni.org/magazines/proceedings/1983/december/grenada-soviet-stepping-stone
47. https://www.cia.gov/readingroom/docs/CIA-RDP85M00364R000601010026-9.pdf
48. https://www.theatlantic.com/magazine/archive/1984/02/grenada-before-and-after/666836/
49. https://web.archive.org/web/20230327161950/https:/www.theatlantic.com/magazine/archive/1984/02/grenada-before-and-after/666836/
50. https://www.nytimes.com/1983/04/22/world/brazil-and-libyans-are-said-to-discuss-unloading-of-planes.html
51. https://web.archive.org/web/20170828064444/https://www.washingtonpost.com/web/20170828064444/https://www.washingtonpost.com/archive/politics/1983/04/06/grenadan-leader-says-airport-is-for-tourism/ff3715a9-15ad-4647-bc08-ff3e37a281a3/?utm_term=.99be04145cd2
52. https://archive.margaretthatcher.org/PREM19/PREM19-1048.pdf
53. https://grenadarevo.com/grenada-revo-02/
54. https://digitalcommons.fiu.edu/cgi/viewcontent.cgi?referer=&httpsredir=1&article=1035&context=laccopsd
55. https://www.cia.gov/readingroom/docs/DOC_0000652875.pdf
56. https://www.thenewtodaygrenada.com/local-news/layne-and-cornwall-identified-as-the-persons-who-put-maurice-bishop-under-house-arrest/
57. https://www.amazon.com/Ghostriders-1976-1995-Invictus-Salvador-Bosnia-Herzegovina/dp/1637581572
58. https://www.nytimes.com/1983/10/28/world/from-rescued-students-gratitute-and-praise.html
59. https://www.nytimes.com/1983/10/28/world/from-rescued-students-gratitute-and-praise.html
60. https://maint.loc.gov/law/mlr/Military_Law_Review/277865~1.pdf

## CHAPTER 6

1. https://www.jcs.mil/Portals/36/Documents/History/Monographs/Urgent_Fury.pdf
2. https://catalog.archives.gov/id/74614443
3. https://archive.is/vBpCM
4. https://www.google.com/books/edition/The_American_President/UxOnCgAAQBAJ?hl=en&gbpv=1&dq=%E2%80%9CYou+never+had+a+day+when+the+secretary+of+state+and+the+secretary+of+defense+weren%27t+at+each+other%E2%80%99s+throats,%E2%80%9D&pg=PT616&printsec=frontcover
5. https://www.golfdigest.com/story/he-wanted-to-talk-to-the-president-so-he-stormed-augusta-national
6. https://www.cfr.org/blog/when-america-attacked-syria
7. https://www.nytimes.com/1982/09/30/world/text-of-reagan-s-letter-to-congress-on-marines-in-lebanon.html
8. https://foreignpolicy.com/2014/02/07/when-reagan-cut-and-run/
9. https://foreignpolicy.com/2014/02/07/when-reagan-cut-and-run
10. https://www.washingtonpost.com/archive/entertainment/books/1997/03/09/the-contras-counter-intelligence-and-the-kgb/7388cfb0-a555-40ae-96e5-1b7d8ae89e33
11. https://history.state.gov/historicaldocuments/frus1981-88v12/d105
12. https://www.amazon.com/Never-Fight-Fair-Stories-Adventure/dp/089141519X
13. https://www.sandiegoreader.com/news/1990/oct/04/you-know-ken
14. https://www.jcs.mil/portals/36/documents/history/monographs/urgent_fury.pdf

## CHAPTER 7

1. https://archive.margaretthatcher.org/doc02/EC4228DFDB2243A4A96E53FE4132202D.pdf
2. https://newcriterion.com/article/the-special-relationship-past-present-future
3. https://www.reuters.com/article/idUS1717327354
4. https://www.margaretthatcher.org/document/110357
5. https://www.theguardian.com/theguardian/from-the-archive-blog/2011/jun/02/guardian190-thatcher-is-pm-1979
6. https://nsarchive2.gwu.edu/NSAEBB/NSAEBB374
7. https://nsarchive2.gwu.edu/NSAEBB/NSAEBB374
8. https://history.state.gov/historicaldocuments/frus1981-88v13/d190; https://history.state.gov/historicaldocuments/frus1981-88v13/d188#fn:1.7.4.4.12.463.14.4
9. https://www.margaretthatcher.org/document/110526
10. https://www.dailymail.co.uk/news/article-10781239/Margaret-Thatcher-threatened-NUKE-Argentina-unless-France-handed-Exocet-information.html

11. Don Oberdorfer. "US Envoy to Mideast Is Replaced," *Washington Post*, July 23, 1983.
12. https://www.margaretthatcher.org/document/109319
13. https://www.reaganlibrary.gov/archives/speech/statement-assassination-president-elect-bashir-gemayel-lebanon
14. https://www.youtube.com/watch?v=VMnQwhP0f68
15. https://en.wikipedia.org/wiki/Barry_Goldwater
16. https://archive.margaretthatcher.org/doc03/831023%201202%20MT%20to%20Reagan%20BEIRUT%20MARINE%20ATTACK%20THCR%203-1-33%20PART2%20f60.pdf
17. https://www.margaretthatcher.org/document/109278
18. https://www.nytimes.com/1983/09/30/world/us-deficit-worries-mrs-thatcher.html
19. https://www.margaretthatcher.org/document/109390
20. https://www.reaganfoundation.org/ronald-reagan/white-house-diaries/diary-entry-10211983
21. https://docs.google.com/document/d/1sgxImj204iPykbQ2G9Y31VR1s8w9rM3QS6vmtIplGV8/edit

## CHAPTER 8

1. https://www.miamiherald.com/news/nation-world/world/americas/article1956688.html
2. https://www.miamiherald.com/news/nation-world/world/americas/article1956688.html
3. https://docs.google.com/document/d/1pSwqemxubY-AiKCmmpRSKmSj_7QSZ0RQ-sBurDUqnK0/edit
4. https://www.govinfo.gov/content/pkg/GOVPUB-D114-PURL-gpo3814/pdf/GOVPUB-D114-PURL-gpo3814.pdf
5. Constantine C. Menges. *Inside the National Security Council: The True Story of the Making and Unmaking of Reagan's Foreign Policy*. Simon & Schuster 1998.
6. https://books.google.com/books/about/Ghostriders_1976_1995.html?id=0ZdkEAAAQBAJ&printsec=frontcover&source=kp_read_button&hl=en&newbks=1&newbks_redir=0#v=onepage&q&f=false
7. https://www.nytimes.com/1983/11/09/world/us-officers-give-invasion-details.html
8. www.erenow.org
9. https://www.amazon.com/Navy-SEALs-Their-Untold-Story/dp/0062336614
10. https://www.bendbulletin.com/localstate/30-years-ago-us-cuban-troops-fought-on-grenada-battlefield/article_31cb78f9-803f-5e66-830d-ded4e2a88885.html
11. https://www.upi.com/Archives/1983/10/27/Students-evacuated-from-Grenada-Marines-protected-us/3212983477191/

## CHAPTER 9

1. https://www.washingtonpost.com/archive/politics/1983/11/03/us-allies-join-in-lopsided-un-vote-condemning-invasion-of-grenada/5d979c34-41c2-4ddb-826b-eb6e5425749d
2. https://www.nytimes.com/1983/11/06/world/in-wake-of-invasion-much-official-misinformation-by-us-comes-to-light.html
3. https://www.youtube.com/watch?v=b5wfPlgKFh8
4. https://www.youtube.com/watch?v=kCOsnFw5wlc
5. https://www.cpr.org/2020/08/26/1986s-top-gun-drove-a-military-recruiting-boom-will-the-sequel-do-the-same
6. https://www.irishtimes.com/news/ireland/irish-news/thatcher-tried-to-deter-reagan-from-retaliation-on-lebanon-1.1481724
7. https://www.politico.com/story/2019/01/11/reagan-delivers-farewell-address-jan-11-1989-1088708
8. https://www.wsj.com/articles/the-day-the-evil-empire-retreated-1540422480

# PHOTOGRAPHY CREDITS

Page iv       Getty Images/Bettmann/Contributor

Page 2        Photo by Michael Evans/The White House/Getty Images

Page 4        Getty Images/Bettmann/Contributor

Page 24       Getty Images/Bettmann/Contributor

Page 50       Getty Images/Bernie Boston/Contributor

Page 84       Getty Images/Express/Stringer

Page 114      Getty Images/Keystone/Stringer

Page 116      Getty Images/Bettmann/Contributor

Page 170      Getty Images/Peter Jordan/Popperfoto/Contributor

Page 224      Getty Images/PA Images/Contributor

Page 260      Alamy/ZUMA Press

Page 262      Associated Press/stf

Page 330      Alamy/DOD Photo

Page 364      Top Alamy/DOD Photo; bottom Alamy/NB/ROD

Page 368      Photo by Boris Spremo/Toronto Star via Getty Images

# Index

Aaron, David L., 36, 37
ABC (ABC News), 45, 187
Abizaid, John, 306, 307
Acapulco, Mexico, 127
Adams, Tom, 166, 257
"Address to the Nation on Events in Lebanon and Grenada" (Reagan speech), 383–396
Afghanistan, 7, 35, 44, 45, 99, 138, 206, 339
AFL-CIO, 57, 180
Albert, William, 28
Albert Thomas Convention Center (Houston), 34
Albright, Madeleine, 358
Algeria, 152
Allen, Richard, 60–64
Allende, Salvador, 155
Allied Atlantic Command (NATO), 194
*Al-Watan* (newspaper), 19
American exceptionalism, 46, 92
American Institute for Free Labor, 180
American Revolution, 155
Anderson, John, 28
Andropov, Yuri, 86, 88, 89, 95, 99, 100, 102–106
Anglican Church, 143
Angola, 7, 44, 87, 186, 206, 348
Anti-Defamation League, 21
Antigua, 132
Antilles Islands, 118
Anti-Semitism, 21
Apartheid, 155
*Apocalypse Now* (film), 319
Argentina, 11, 14, 75–78, 232–237, 239–244, 252, 254
(*See also* Falklands War)
Argentine People's Revolutionary Army (Ejército Revolucionario del Pueblo, ERP), 10–13
Arlington National Cemetery, xxvii
Armentrout, Ernest, 282
Arms control, 27, 89, 93, 148, 149, 246, 252–254, 355, 358
Arms Control and Disarmament Agency, 36
Aruba, 117
Ascension Island, 233, 239, 240

415

Assad, Hafez al-, 245
Associated Press, 98
Association of Diplomatic Studies and Training, 68
Asunción, Paraguay, 7–8, 13, 14
Atkins, C. Scott, 266–267, 282–284, 292–294
Atlanta, Ga., 225
*The Atlantic*, 94
Augusta National Country Club, 188–190, 192, 196–199, 250
Austin, Hudson, 140, 162–165, 175, 183–184, 200, 341, 351
Australia, 339

Bahamas, 7, 118
Baker, Howard, 220
Baker, James, III, 61, 64, 79, 177, 184, 190, 208, 344–345
Balkans, 358
Banks, John, 14
Barbados, 123, 139, 162, 166, 180, 185, 191, 218, 257, 265–267, 298, 308, 316, 338, 343, 351
Barnes, Ben, 42
Battle of San Carlos, 241
Bay of Pigs, 6
Beatles, 226
Beausejour, Grenada, 266, 279, 283, 287
Begin, Menachem, 69
Beirut, Lebanon, xxii, xxiv, 79, 203, 210, 244, 247–248, 349
Beirut embassy bombing (Apr. 1983), xxii, 248–249
Beirut International Airport, 201
Beirut Marine Barracks bombing (Oct. 1983), 201–222, 250, 251, 350
Belenko, Viktor, 105
Belize, 141
Bell, Paul, 307
Bentsen, Lloyd, 146

Beqaa Valley (Lebanon), 247
Berlin blockade (1948), 112
Berlin Wall, fall of the, 356, 359
Bermuda Triangle, 127
Biden, Joe, 29
Bish, Milan, 180
Bishop, Angela, 138
Bishop, Maurice, 15–16, 87, 129, 133, 136–143, 145, 146, 150, 151, 153–166, 175, 176, 181, 182, 186, 189, 193, 195, 273–274, 282, 298, 314, 336, 339, 341, 342, 351, 365
Bishop, Rupert, 129, 134
Black Buck Raids, 240
Black Power Movement, 132
Bloody Monday (Grenada), 129–130, 134
Bloody Sunday (Grenada), 129–130, 134
Bloody Sunday (Northern Ireland), 131

*Bonnie and Clyde* (film), 226
Borge, Tomas "The Comandante," 12, 13, 19
Bornham, Forbes, 121
Boston, Mass., 225
Bourne, Martha, 55–56
Bouterse, Desi, 181
Boykin, Terry, 291, 292
Brady, James, 57, 61
Brady, Nicholas, 188
Bramel, Dave, 290
Brandeis University, 156
Brands, H. W., 346–347
Bremer, Jerry, 69–70
Brezhnev, Leonid, 86, 88, 99, 101–103, 148, 253
Brezhnev Doctrine, 329, 358
Bridgetown, Barbados, 257
British Commonwealth, xxii, 130, 153–154, 192, 336–338, 353

British Guiana (see Guyana)
Brussels, Belgium, 151
Brzezinski, Zbigniew, 36, 37, 44, 127
Bubiyan Island, 359
Bulgaria, 150, 175
Burnham, Forbes, 123–125
Burt, Peter, 354
Bush, George H. W., 33–35, 57, 62, 63, 66, 79, 184, 190–192, 245, 357, 359, 360
Butcher, Kenneth J., 211, 367
Butler, Rab, 125
Byrd, Robert, 220, 344
Byron, Denis, 351

California, 189, 226–228
Calliste, Grenada, xxv–xxviii, 306
Cambodia, 44
Camel cigarettes, 71
Camp David Peace Accords, 21, 38
Canada, xxi, 6, 92–93, 125, 137, 144, 151, 339
Cannon, Lou, 90
"Captain Santiago," 8–10
Cardenas, Oscar Osvaldo, 181, 342
Caribbean Broadcasting Corporation (CBC), 162
Caribbean Peacekeeping Force, 217
CARICOM, 337
Carlucci, Frank, 65
Carriacou (Grenadian dependency), 149
Carson, Johnny, 45
Carter, Amy, 26–28
Carter, Jimmy, and administration, 5, 7, 12, 14, 18, 20, 21, 25–28, 32, 33, 36–39, 45, 47, 59, 70–71, 91, 103, 127–128, 136, 137, 148, 154, 186, 265, 346, 358
Carter-Mondale Book, 59

Cascio, Richard, 322
Casey, William, 39, 64–66, 80, 150, 172, 177, 182
Castro, Fidel, 7, 11, 15–16, 18, 34, 53, 93, 120, 125, 141, 142, 146, 150–151, 155, 161, 165, 176, 181, 183, 186, 276–277, 282, 304, 340–342
Caterpillar Tractor, 66
CBS (CBS News), 36, 208, 344, 345
Central Intelligence Agency (CIA), 8, 10, 11, 13, 14, 37, 39, 54, 63, 76, 88, 93, 98, 99, 104, 107, 108, 120–126, 136, 146, 147, 150, 158, 171, 172, 175, 177, 181, 190, 200, 207, 208, 216, 234, 235, 258, 278, 280, 284
Chain, Jack, 93–94
Chamorro, Pedro, 6
Chaplin, Charlie, 67
Charles, Eugenia, 167, 272–274, 297–301
Charles, Sydney, 143
Charleston Air Force Base, 321
Chernenko, Konstantin, 88, 89, 355
Chernyaev, Anatoly, 110
Chicago, Ill., 225
Chile, 135, 155
China, 44, 63, 70–72, 228
Churchill, Winston, 91, 355, 361
Clark, William "Judge," 64, 65, 70, 80, 98, 171, 172, 174, 177, 188–189, 239, 245, 246
Cleveland, Ohio, 25, 28
Cline, Randy, 366
Cline, Randy E., 308
Clinton, Bill, and administration, 358
Coard, Bernard, 87, 154, 156–165, 175, 189, 341, 351, 352
Coard, Phyllis, 156, 159, 162–163, 351

418 INDEX

Coca-Cola, 71
Cold War, xxi
Coles, John, 153–154
Colombia, 7, 18
Communist Party of Great Britain, 156
Communist Party of the Soviet Union, 85, 86, 103
Communist Party USA, 156
Communists and communism, xxviii, 3, 11, 15, 17, 20, 43, 48, 70, 73, 90, 93, 95–99, 120–123, 146, 156, 178, 180–181, 183, 186, 205–206, 274, 348, 359, 362, 366
Compton, John, 137
*Confessions of a Nazi Spy* (film), 67
Congress, 18–21, 29, 37–38, 43, 55, 56, 63, 70, 76, 90, 91, 147, 171, 173, 174, 192, 202, 220–221, 249, 255–258, 273, 344, 348
 (*See also* House of Representatives; Senate)
Connally, John, 32, 42
Conservative Party (U.K.), 131, 225, 230, 231, 244, 338, 353
Contras, 155, 173, 235
Cornwall, Leon, 159
Costa Rica, 11, 18
Couch, Dick, 282
Couvillon, Michael, 270
Crisis Pre-Planning Group (CPPG), 182–183, 185–187, 212
Cruise, Tom, 347
Cruise missiles, 252, 254, 333
Cuba and Cubans, xxii, xxiv, xxv, xxvii, 6, 11, 18, 20, 30, 34–35, 37, 52–54, 87, 93, 118, 120, 121, 125, 137, 139, 141–155, 160, 161, 165–166, 174–178, 181, 183–187, 190, 192, 217, 268, 270, 272, 276–279, 289, 290, 299, 302–310, 317, 319, 321, 324, 325, 340–342, 348, 365, 366
Cuban Missile Crisis, 53, 85, 112, 149, 157, 354
Cuyahoga, Ohio, 27
Czechoslovakia, 97, 150, 160, 340

D'Aguilar, Peter, 124, 125
Damascus, Syria, 245
Darman, Dick, 345
Davis, Tony, 307
Deaver, Michael, 31
Defense Condition (DEFCON), 62
Defense Intelligence Agency (DIA), 63, 207, 278, 311
Delahanty, Thomas, 57
Delta Force (*see* U.S. Army Delta Force)
Democracy, 7, 46, 98, 173, 176, 180–182, 184, 205, 242, 244, 257, 274, 299
Democratic Party, 36–38, 42, 91, 220, 344, 356
Denmark, 145
*The Denver Post*, xxvi
Department of Defense, 54, 76, 144, 145, 171, 178–179, 193–194, 196, 204, 209, 238, 321, 324, 343, 357
Détente, 29, 47, 48, 57, 66, 90, 101–103
Diaz, Carlos, 277, 305, 342
DiLiberta, Joseph, 322–323
Directorate of National Intelligence (DNI), 80
Dobrynin, Anatoly, 102–103
Doherty, Bill, 180–181
Dolan, Anthony, 98
Dole, Bob, 31
Dominica, 118, 132, 185, 272
Dominican Republic, 121

Donaldson, Blair, 306–308
Donaldson, Sam, 47–48, 256
Douglas-Home, Lord, 121–123
*The Downing Street Years* (Thatcher), 253
Doyle, John, 322
Doyle, William, 282
Druze militias, 249
Duarte, José Napoleón, 43
Duke University, 52

Eagleburger, Lawrence, 177, 205, 206
East Germany, 97, 125, 150, 175, 187, 356
Egypt, 246, 339
Eisenhower, Dwight D., 356
Eisenhower Cottage (Augusta, Ga.), 188, 190
El Salvador, 17, 19, 20, 42–45, 52, 54–56, 88, 254, 339
Elizabeth II, Queen, 118, 138, 166, 240, 335
Epcot Center, 95
Epps, Gary, xxvii, 366
Erskine, Donald "Kim," 282–288
*Escape* (film), 67
Eskridge, Will, 327
ESPN, 198
Ethiopia, 44, 186
"Evil Empire" (Reagan speech), v–vi, 369–381
Exercise Ocean Venture '81, 144–146, 150

Falklands War, 75–78, 223, 232–244, 252, 254, 333, 335
Farfan, "El Gordo," 9–11
Faulkner, William, 73
Federal Bureau of Investigation (FBI), 55, 56, 63
Federal Elections Commission (FEC), 33

Federal Reserve Board, 17, 252
Fielding, Harvey, 295, 296–297
*The Fighting Seabees* (film), 307
First Chief Directorate (FCD), 100–101
First Gulf War, 360
Flanders, Ronald, 347
Flannery (pilot), 291
Florida, 18, 147
Ford, Gerald, and administration, 29–33, 63, 90–91, 103, 186, 190, 231
Fort Campbell, 264
Fort Frederick, 164, 286, 289, 302, 313, 314, 317
Fort McPherson, 208–209
Fort Rupert, 163, 164, 182, 341, 351
Fort Stewart, 209, 352
Foster, Jody, 61
France, 118, 145, 148, 202, 242–243, 247, 250, 253, 339
Fraser Institute, xxi
Freedom, 95–99, 180, 298, 356, 359, 361, 362
Frequente, Grenada, 276–278, 290–291
Fujian Province, 71

Gaddafi, Muammar, 14
Gairy, Eric Matthew, 15, 115, 117–120, 126–140, 142, 156, 273, 282, 353
Galbraith, John Kenneth, 92
Galtieri, Leopoldo, 233–235, 239
Gammon, Samuel, 58–59
Garfield, Bradley, xxii–xxv, xxviii
Gaza, 349
Gelb, Leslie, 104
Gemayel, Amin, 245, 348
Gemayel, Bashir, 203, 248
General Assembly (U.N.), 128, 138, 339

Geneva arms talks, 252
George Mason University, 26
Georgetown, Guyana, 120, 122, 124
Georgia, 30
*Ghostriders* (Walter), 275–276
Giguere, Pat, 313
Gipp, George, 72, 73
Global War on Terror, 358
Golan Heights, 349
Goldwater, Barry, 90, 91, 146, 249
*Golf Digest*, 198, 199
Gorbachev, Mikhail, 88, 89, 355–356, 362
Gordievsky, Oleg, 90, 99, 100
Gormly, Robert A., 211, 280, 281, 312
Grand Anse Bay (Grand Anse Beach), 165, 204, 276, 285, 311, 317, 320 321, 313
Grantley Adams Airport, 265
Graves, Dick, 208–209, 214–215
Great Britain, 149
(*See also* United Kingdom [U.K.])
Great Depression, 45, 46
*The Great Dictator* (film), 67
Greenland, 6
Grenada:
  construction of Point Salines airport in, 151–154
  and Cuba, xxiv, xxvii, 34, 37, 87, 137, 139, 141–155, 161, 165–166, 175, 183, 186, 192, 217, 268, 270, 276–279, 302–310, 317, 319, 321, 340–342, 365
  foreign policy of, under Maurice Bishop, 154–156
  Eric Gairy as prime minister of, 15, 115, 117–120, 126–140, 142, 156, 273, 282, 353
  independence movement in, 126–128
  independence of, after U.S. invasion, xxviii, 350–353, 358, 366
  Marxist revolution in, 15–16, 136–141
  Mongoose Gang in, 128–132
  New Jewel Movement in, 15, 87, 128–143, 152, 156–159, 161–164, 175, 176, 350
  overthrow and assassination of Maurice Bishop in, 156–167
  Soviet influence in, 34, 141–151
  *See also* (Operation Urgent Fury [OUF])
Grenada Assembly of Youth After Truth, 156
Grenada Manual and Mental Workers Union, 118
Grenada National Party (GNP), 126, 134, 139–140
Grenada United Labour Party (GULP), 118, 119, 126, 353
Grenier, Philip, 366
Grenier, Philip Sebastian, 326
Grenville, Grenada, xxv, 129, 264, 269, 311, 318
Gromyko, Andrei, 153
GRU, 99, 100
*Guardian*, 231
Guiana, 122, 123
Gulf of Tonkin incident, 194
Guyana (formerly British Guiana), 120, 121, 124–126

Habib, Philip, 69, 245, 247
Hagler, Ralph, 302–303, 325
Haig, Alexander, 44, 51–73, 75–81, 96, 181, 190, 232–241, 243–246
"Haig Incident," 58
Haiti, 128
Harris, Charlie "Smiley," 196–199
Harris, Harriet, 197

Hartman, Phil, 345–346
Harvard University, 92
Havana, Cuba, 16, 125, 138, 161, 340
Hayek, Friedrich, 230
Heath, Edward, 131, 229–230
Helms, Jesse, 29, 30, 184
Helsinki Accords, 66
Henderson, Nicholas, 243
Hersh, Seymour, 94
Heseltine, Michael, 334
Hilton Hotel (Washington, D.C.), 57
Hinckley, John, Jr., 57, 61, 361, 362
Hitler, Adolf, 88, 89, 102
HMS *Sheffield*, 240
Hollywood, 66–67, 227, 347
Holocaust, 66–67
Holt, Eric, 327
Hope, Bob, 45
House Foreign Relations Committee, 18, 221
House of Commons, 230, 231, 334, 338
House of Representatives, 18–21, 59, 91, 104, 173, 220–221, 249
Houston, Tex., 34–35
Howard, Timothy, 313
Howe, Geoffrey, 334–338
Hughes, Bob, 27
Hughes, G. Philip, 58, 60
Hull, Cordell, 191
Hungary, 160
Hunter Army Airfield, 269
Hunter College, 155
Hurlburt Field, 269
Hussein, Saddam, 359–361

ICBMs, 107
Ikle, Fred, 93, 183, 205
Indiana, 30
Inman, Bobby, 76, 78, 239–240

*Inner Circles: How American Changed the World* (Haig), 54
*Inside the National Security Council* (Menges), 17–18, 39, 169, 171, 357
Institutional Revolutionary Party (Partido Revolucionario Institucional, PRI), 17
Inter-American Treaty of Reciprocal Assistance (Rio Treaty), 192
International Harvester, 66
Iowa, 33
Iran, 7, 39–42, 349, 359
 (*See also* Islamic Revolution in Iran)
Iran hostage crisis, 25, 38–42, 45, 47, 190, 194, 265, 347
Iran-Iraq War, 41, 359
Iraq, 41, 152, 359–361
Islamic Revolution in Iran, 14, 25, 38, 39
Israel, 21, 69, 78, 79, 202, 228–229, 244–249, 252, 269–270, 339, 348, 349
Israeli Defense Forces (IDF), 244, 247, 248
*It Doesn't Take a Hero* (Schwarzkopf), 209
Italy, 202, 247
Ivers, Brian C., 306

Jagan, Cheddi, 120–126
Jamaica, 118, 132, 134, 155, 156, 167, 180, 185, 191, 298, 316
James, Liam, 158–160
Japan, 52, 104, 228, 339
*Jewish Press*, 21
Jews, 20–21
John Paul II, Pope, 65, 68, 73–74
Johnson, Lyndon B., and administration, 42, 49, 124, 125

Joint Chiefs of Staff, 179, 181, 184, 191, 193–196, 202–204, 207, 214, 220, 221, 246, 299, 323, 324
Joint Endeavor for Welfare, Education, and Liberation (JEWEL), 133, 157
Joint Special Operations Command (JSOC), 193, 195, 196, 204, 216, 218, 269, 304, 311
Jordan, 20, 339
Jordan, Robert, 165, 320
Joyce, Edward, 344

Kaiser Foundation Hospital (San Francisco), 226
Kamchatka Peninsula, 94, 104–105
Kansas City, Mo., 30
Kefauver, Estes, 32
Kelley, John, 264
Kelley, Paul X., 201, 202, 204
Kelly, John, 58–60
Kelly, Orr, 211
Kennedy, Charles Stuart, 68
Kennedy, John F., and administration, 42, 49, 53, 59, 120–124, 178, 184
Kennedy, Ted, 42
KGB, 86, 89, 99–101
Khalid, King, 79
Khmer Rouge, 44
Khomeini, Ayatollah, 38, 40–41
Khrushchev, Nikita, 7, 53, 85–86, 88, 178, 184
King, Martin Luther, Jr., 188, 226
Kirby, Jack, 27
Kirkpatrick, Jeanne, 65, 76, 109, 177, 234, 239, 240, 243, 273, 339
Kissinger, Henry, 29–30, 36, 37, 57, 64, 77, 103, 205, 228–229, 238, 243–244, 246

*Knute Rockne, All American* (film), 93
Kodak, 71
Kohl, Helmut, 254
Korean Air Lines Flight 007, 104–110, 253
Korean War, xxvi, 53, 54, 214
Kornienko, Georgi, 105
Kosygin, Alexei, 86
KQED-TV, 226
Kukielski, Philip, 282
Kuwait, 19, 359–360

Labour Party (U.K.), 124–125, 339
Land reform, 15, 135
Lannon, Kevin, 326, 327, 366
*The Larry King Show*, 27
Layne Dredging, 152
Lebanese Armed Forces, 203
Lebanon, xxii, 69, 79, 185, 187, 201–203, 205, 208, 244–251, 253, 255, 300, 347–350
(*See also* Beirut Marine Barracks bombing)
Leeward Islands, 118
Lehman, Christopher, 207, 255, 256
Lehman, John, 145
Lehrer, Jim, 28
Leyland, 125
Libya, 14, 150, 152, 175, 186, 187, 192
Lincoln, Abraham, 155
"Line of March" speech (M. Bishop), 141
"Little Havana," 276, 306, 309–310
London, England, 14
Londonderry, Northern Ireland, 131
Long, Admiral, 216
López Portillo, José, 18
Los Angeles, Calif., 225
*Los Angeles Times*, 227, 344
Lucas, Keith, 266–267, 290, 293, 367

Luketina, Sean P., 366
Lundberg, Kevin E., 211, 367

MacArthur, Douglas, 52
Maclean, Donald, 100
Macmillan, Harold, 120, 123, 124
Mahon, George, 38
Maine, 33
*Man Hunt* (film), 67
*The Man I Married* (film), 67
Mandi, Jorge, 19–20
Manley, Michael, 155
Mariel Cubans, 54
Marine barracks bombing, 203, 250
Marine One, 202
Marley, Bob, 268
Maronite Christian Phalange Party (Lebanon), 203, 248
Marryshow, Theophilus, 118
Marshall Plan, 226
Maryknoll sisters, 55–56
Maryland, 30
Maynard, Marlin, 308, 366
McCarthy, Timothy, 57
McCone, John A., 122
McDonald, Larry, 104
McDonald, Wesley, 193–196, 200, 203–204, 213–218, 311, 324
McFarland, K. T., 76–77, 238, 347, 357
McFarlane, Robert "Bud," 70, 80, 171, 177–179, 182, 185, 187, 189, 190, 194, 200, 202, 205, 213, 220, 234, 238, 245–247, 256–258, 272, 301
McGehee, Ralph, 107
McManaway, Clayton E., 68–70
McNeil, Francis, 257
Medicare, 25–26
Meese, Edwin, 54, 56, 64, 65, 67, 80, 234, 239, 255, 256

Menges, Constantine, 17–18, 39, 44–45, 64, 169, 171–187, 190–192, 200, 205–206, 208, 212–213, 220, 256, 258, 272–275, 297, 298, 301, 331–332, 357
Merlo, Gorriarán, 9–13
Merman, Ethel, 45
Metcalf, Joseph, III, 213–219, 230, 280, 295, 301, 311–316, 319, 323–325, 342–344, 351–352
Mexico, 7, 17–18, 20, 173, 174, 205
MGM, 67
MI5, 130
Miami, Fla., 7, 152, 225
*Miami Herald*, 10, 13, 268
Michael, Jim, 172, 173
Michel, Robert, 220
Michigan, 33
Middendorf, William J., Jr., 179, 180, 183
Miles, Simon, 52
Military Airlift Command, 195
Minnesota National Guard, 195
Mitterand, François, 112, 242–243
Mondale, Walter, 28, 36, 37, 59
"Mondale Mafia," 36–37
Moneron Island, 104, 105
Mongoose Gang, 128–132, 134–135
Monroe Doctrine, 5, 37, 53, 155
Montserrat, 185
Morris, Stephen L., 211, 367
*The Mortal Storm* (film), 67
Motley, Langhorne "Tony," 179, 206
Motley, Tony, 185
Movement for the Assemblies of the People (MAP), 133, 157
Mozambique, 44, 186
Muccia, Joe, 308
Mulroney, Brian, 92
Multinational force (MNF), 202, 203, 247–251

*My American Journey* (Powell), 358

NASA, 226
*Nashua Telegraph*, 33
National Archives (England), 130
National Association of Evangelicals, 95
National Intelligence Daily, 171
National Security Agency (NSA), 63, 108, 311
National Security Council (NSC), 29–30, 44, 51–54, 58, 60, 64, 65, 75–78, 80, 121, 147, 171–172, 174, 176–179, 181, 184, 185, 190, 191, 200, 205, 208, 212, 213, 238, 246, 257–258, 273, 297, 331
National Security Decision Directive 32 (NSDD 32), 95
Navy SEALs (*see* U.S. Navy SEALs)
*Navy SEALs: Their Untold Story* (Couch and Doyle), 282
Nazi Germany, 66–67, 88–89, 104
Nebraska, 30
Netherlands, 144, 145
*Never Fight Fair: Navy SEALs' Stories of Combat and Adventure* (Kelly), 211
New Criterion, 228
New Deal, 226
New Hampshire, 32, 33
New Jewel Movement (NJM), 15, 87, 128–143, 152, 156–159, 161–164, 175, 176, 350
New York City, 225
*New York Post*, 74–75
New York State, 55
*New York Times*, 15, 36–37, 42, 64, 83, 86, 88, 104, 144, 154, 165, 252

Nicaragua, 3, 5–7, 10–14, 17–21, 43, 87, 135, 142, 143, 148, 149, 152, 153, 155, 173, 178, 186, 206, 235, 272, 339
(*See also* Sandinistas)
Nimitz, Chester, 214
Nixon, Richard M., and administration, 36, 42, 51, 58, 63, 71, 103, 228
NJM Manifesto, 139
"Nobody's Backyard" speech (M. Bishop), 139
North, Oliver, 174, 184, 190–191, 200, 220, 258
North Atlantic Treaty Organization (NATO), 36, 52, 100, 144, 145, 194, 253, 339, 340, 353, 354, 358
North Carolina, 30
North Korea, 147, 150, 107, 340
North Vietnam, 194
Northern Ireland, 131, 350
Notre Dame University, 72–74, 93, 99
Nuclear Information Service (NIS), 354
Nuclear weapons, 27, 28, 32, 53–54, 61–62, 65, 74, 87, 89, 99–104, 106, 111–112, 148–149, 153, 178, 243, 253–254, 334–335, 353–356

*Oceans Ventured: Winning the Cold War at Sea* (Lehman), 145
Ogarkov, Nikolai, 104, 106
Oil markets, 17, 92
Oko (Soviet nuclear early warning system), 111–112
Omaha, Neb., 225
Oman, 246
O'Neill, Tip, 220
Operation Able Archer, 353–356

Operation Amber in the
  Amberdines, 145, 150,
  178–179
Operation Barbarossa, 88
Operation Desert Storm, 360
Operation Eagle Claw, 265
Operation Overlord, 265
Operation Peace for Galilee, 244
Operation RYaN, 99–101
Operation Urgent Fury (OUF),
  xxii–xxviii, 263–328
  assault on Richmond Hill
    Prison, 288–297
  casualties, 365–367
  fight for Little Havana, 302–312
  initial assault, 263–272
  and the media, 342–347
  and Organization of Eastern
    Caribbean States, 297–301
  Point Salines attack, 275–279
  preliminary consideration and
    planning, 176–193, 200,
    203–214
  and Radio Free Grenada,
    282–288
  reactions to, 255–258, 272–275,
    332–342
  Reagan's green-lighting of, 196,
    205
  rescue of medical students,
    317–328
  Schwarzkopf and, 209–210, 215,
    219, 301, 302, 311–312, 314,
    315, 318, 323–324, 327–328,
    352
  Paul Scoon rescued during,
    279–282
  and United Kingdom, 332–339,
    350
  USS *Guam* during, 301–302
  and Vietnam syndrome, 358
Operations Center (State
  Department), 60

Organization of American States
  (OAS), 18, 173, 179, 180,
  257
Organization of Eastern
  Caribbean States (OECS),
  167, 176, 185, 187, 189–191,
  257, 272, 274, 280, 297, 298,
  316, 332, 337, 342
Organization of Revolutionary
  Education and Liberation
  (OREL), 157
Orlando, Fla., 29, 95
Ortega, Daniel, 12, 13, 142
Ortiz, Frank, 128, 139
Osipovich (Soviet pilot), 109, 110
Ossining, N.Y., 55
Ottawa, Ont., 361
Ottinger, Richard, 55

Pakistan, 246, 339
Palestine Liberation Organization
  (PLO), 19–20, 79, 155, 203,
  244, 245, 247, 248, 252
Panama, 18
Paraguay, 7–8, 10, 11, 13, 14
Paramaribo, Suriname, 181
Parliament (U.K.), 96–98, 131,
  225, 231, 334–338, 361
Parnell, Mike, 263
Parr, Jerry, 57
Pastora, Eden, 11–12
Patterson, Robert, 195
PBS, 28, 346
Pearl Harbor, 191
Pearls Airport, xxiv–xxv, 151, 160,
  161, 204, 264, 268, 279, 311,
  314
Pentagon (*see* Department of
  Defense)
"People's Laws" (Grenada), 142
People's Progressive Party (PPP)
  (Grenada), 121–122, 124,
  125

People's Revolutionary Army (PRA), 140, 142, 157, 162–165, 175, 204, 267–268, 277, 279, 280–282, 285, 286, 289, 302, 305, 317, 321, 350, 365
People's Revolutionary Government (PRG), 136–139, 143, 151, 153–154, 156, 158, 159, 161, 164, 189
Pershing II missiles, 148, 149, 252, 254
Personnel Office (White House), 80–81
Peterson, Dale, 107
Petrov, Stanislav, 111–112
Philadelphia, Pa., 28
Pinochet, Augusto, 135
*Plain Dealer* (Cleveland), 26, 27
Plante, Bill, 208
Platt Amendment, 6
Plessy (defense contractor), 152
Podgorny, Nikolai, 86
Poindexter, John, 80, 171, 178, 182, 184, 200, 220, 258, 297, 301
Point Salines International Airport, xxv, xxvi, 16, 147–149, 151–153, 161, 175, 189, 194, 204, 210, 216–218, 264, 269, 272, 275–279, 281, 282, 290, 292, 294, 301, 303, 305–309, 312, 316–320, 323, 325, 341
Poland, 64–66, 97, 146
Politburo, 85, 86, 99, 340
*Politico Magazine*, 31
Pope Air Force Base, 265, 266
Port Stanley, Falkland Islands, 234, 241
Portugal, 144
Powell, Colin, 202, 357, 358
Powell Doctrine, 357–358
*Pravda*, 103
*La Prensa* (newspaper), 6

Press Room (White House), 61
Price, Paul, 290, 293
Puerto Rico, 145
Pym, Francis, 236, 237, 243

Quainton, Anthony, 21

Rademacher, Mark, 309, 366
Radio Free Grenada, 139, 162, 164, 282–285, 288, 315
Rajbhandary, Dinesh, 367
Rasch, Stewart, 321
Reagan, Colleen, 31–32
Reagan, Maureen, 31–32
Reagan, Michael, 31
Reagan, Nancy, 31, 32, 188, 228, 363
Reagan, Ronald, and administration:
assassination attempt, 56–64
and Augusta country club hostage crisis, 187–188, 196–199
and Beirut embassy bombing, 248–249
and Beirut Marine Barracks bombing, 202–203, 250–251
Maurice Bishop and, 154–155
China/Taiwan policy, 70–75
and Cold War politics, 64–68, 86–104, 112
and Falklands conflict, 75–78, 233–244
first televised press conference of, 47–48
and Grenada, 145–151 (*See also* Operation Urgent Fury [OUF])
and Al Haig, 51–52, 54, 78–81
inauguration of, 45–47
and Iran hostage crisis, 39–42
and Israeli invasion of Lebanon, 244–248

and KAL Flight 007 disaster,
 108–110
and legacy of Carter's foreign
 policy, 42–45
in the media, 345–347
and Monroe Doctrine, 53
and National Security Council,
 172–175, 178–180
and Nicaragua, 21
in 1980 campaign, 25–35
1982 trip to Europe, 68–70
and Ocean Venture '81 exercise,
 144–146
and Operation Able Archer,
 353–356
and Operation RYaN, 99–101
and Reagan Doctrine, 95,
 357–358
and Solidarity, 64–66
speeches by, v–vi, 369–400
Strategic Defense Initiative of,
 102–104, 153, 358
and Margaret Thatcher, xxii,
 226–232, 251–255, 257,
 332–334, 360–363
on victory, 23
*Reagan: The Life* (Brands), 346
Reagan Doctrine, 95, 357–358
*Reagan's War* (Schweizer), 98
Red Army, 89
Regan, Donald, 61, 188
Reich, Otto, 329, 358–359
"Remarks at a White House
 Ceremony Marking the First
 Anniversary of the Grenada
 Rescue Mission" (Reagan
 speech), 397–400
Republican National Convention
 (1976), 23
Republican Party, 30, 33, 35, 51,
 90, 91, 147, 174, 178, 179, 220,
 228
Restricted Interagency Group, 185

Reuters, 166, 230
Revolutionary Military Council
 (RMC), 163–165, 175,
 180–183, 200, 207, 216, 217,
 268, 302
Reykjavik Summit, 355
Richmond Hill Prison (Grenada),
 143, 207, 266, 279, 288–297,
 351
Riffley, Bill, 321–322
Ritz, Michael, xxv–xxvii, 367
Ritz, Michael F., Sr., xxvi
Ritz, William, xxvi
Roberts, Michael, 142–143
Robinson, Russell, 308, 366
Rockefeller, Nelson, 31
Rockne, Knute, 72
Rodgers, Silva Mercedes, 11
Roman Catholic Church, 54, 65,
 117, 133, 143, 315
Romick, Timothy, 309
Roosevelt, Franklin, and
 administration, 191
Roosevelt Corollary, 5
Roper, James, 261, 275–276
Rosen, James, 78, 79
Royal Air Force (RAF), 240, 354
Royal Navy, 241
Rusk, Dean, 49, 121–123
Ruth Howard, Grenada, 308

St. Christopher-Nevis, 185
St. George's, Grenada, xxii, 118,
 129, 156, 163, 183, 204, 207,
 279, 280, 288, 311–315, 323
St. George's University School of
 Medicine, 165, 176, 189, 264,
 276, 277, 282, 310–311, 317,
 331–332, 365
St. Lucia, 118, 132, 137, 151, 185
St. Vincent, 132, 185
Sakhalin Island, 105
San Francisco, Calif., 225, 226

*San Francisco Chronicle*, 227
Sanchez, Nestor, 147
Sandinistas, 7, 10–13, 17–21, 43, 152, 155, 173–174
*Sands of Iwo Jima* (film), xxiv
Sarbanes, Paul, 344
*Saturday Night Live*, 345–346
Saudi Arabia, 78, 246
Savannah, Ga., 269
Sazhenev, Gennadi, 157–158
Schamberger, Robert R., 211, 367
Scharver, Jeffery, 367
Scharver, Jeffrey, 313
Schieffer, Bob, 208
Schlesinger, Arthur, 92, 122
Schneider, William, 94
Scholtes, Richard A., 193, 203–204, 216–217, 304, 311
Schwarzkopf, Brenda, 210
Schwarzkopf, Norman, 208–210, 213–219, 301, 302, 311–312, 314, 315, 318, 323–324, 327–328, 343, 352
Schweizer, Peter, 98
Scoon, Esmai, 315, 316
Scoon, Paul, 138, 166–167, 266, 272, 279–282, 284–285, 312, 314–316, 352–353
Scott, James, 325
Sea of Japan, 105
Sea of Okhotsk, 105
Seaga, Edward, 180
Seagle, Jeb, 313, 367
Sears (rescued soldier), 327
Second Gulf War, 361
Secret Service, 57, 198–199, 273
Security Council (U.N.), 109, 192, 360
Seigle, Robert N., 325
Semcken, John, 347
Senate, 37–38, 59, 149, 173, 220–221, 249

Senate Armed Services Committee, 37–38
Senate Foreign Relations Committee, 54, 56, 221, 252
Senate Intelligence Committee, 146
Seoul, South Korea, 104
Shah of Iran, 17, 39
Shenkman, Rick, 26
Shiite militias, 249
Shirley, Craig, 30
Shultz, George P., 79–80, 108–110, 154, 177, 184, 187–191, 194, 202, 204, 213, 245, 246, 251, 272, 337, 346, 356
Simmons, Chris, 268
Singapore, 228
Situation Room (White House), 60–62, 171, 184, 191, 206–208, 220, 255, 258, 301, 334
Slater, Stephen, 366
Slater, Stephen Eric, 326, 327
Slavery and slave trade, 118, 155
Sloan, Larry, 290
Smith, Howard K., 34
Smith, Ray "E-tool," xxiii
Smith, William French, 213
Snyder, Alvin, 109
Sokol Air Base, 105
Solidarity, 64–65, 67, 97
Solzhenitsyn, Aleksandr, 29
Somoza Debayle, Anastasio "Tachito," 3, 5–13, 21, 135
Somoza Debayle, Luis, 6
Somoza García, Anastasio "Tacho," 6, 21
South Africa, 155
South Georgia, 232
South Korea, 187, 228
South Sandwich, 232
Soviet Bloc, 87, 150, 176, 192, 317, 339, 348, 352

Soviet Union, xxi, xxii, xxv, xxviii, 8, 15–16, 19, 20, 26–27, 29, 30, 34, 35, 37, 43–45, 47–48, 52–54, 61, 64–68, 74–75, 83, 85–112, 120, 138, 140–141, 144–155, 157, 158, 166, 174–176, 178, 186, 187, 192, 234, 244, 246, 252–255, 264, 272, 278, 285, 299, 300, 304, 308, 309, 313, 317, 325, 329, 339–340, 342, 348, 353–359, 362, 366
Space race, 226
Spain, 145, 232
Spanish-American War, 6
Speakes, Larry, 58, 207, 208, 274, 300–301, 344–345
Special Operations Forces, xxi–xxii, xxv, 218
Special Situations Group, 191, 192
SS-20 missiles, 148–149
Stahl, Lesley, 345
Stalin, Joseph, 29, 85, 88–90, 100, 102, 355
Standard Oil, 117
"Star Wars" (*see* Strategic Defense Initiative [SDI])
State Department, 7, 18, 44, 49, 51, 54, 58–60, 62–63, 68–69, 80–81, 94, 110, 121–122, 137, 143, 154, 169, 171–174, 177, 179–187, 189, 191, 192, 200, 205–208, 210, 216, 217, 225, 226, 233, 234, 245, 246, 272, 274, 280, 338
  (*See also individual secretaries of state*, e.g.: Haig, Alexander)
Stennis, John C., 38
Stewart, Jimmy, 45
Strategic Air Command, 93–94, 145
Strategic Arms Limitation Treaty (SALT), 27

Strategic Defense Initiative (SDI), 102–104, 153, 358
Stroessner, Alfredo, 14
Sugar production, 118
Summit of Non-Aligned Countries (Havana, 1979), 138
Suriname, 141, 148, 180–181, 342
Suslov, Mikhail, 86
Syria, 79, 152, 187, 244, 245, 247, 249, 252, 348

Tactical Operations Center (TOC), 271, 276
Taiwan, 70–72, 228
Taiwan Relations Act (1979), 70–71
TASS, 103, 166, 340
*Taxi Driver* (film), 61
Taylor, Wesley, 271, 276–278, 302, 303, 307
Tehran, Iran, 39, 47
Texas, 30, 38, 42
Thailand, 228
Thames River, 125
Thanksgiving Day (Grenada), 359, 366
Thatcher, Denis, 225
Thatcher, Margaret, xxi, xxii, xxviii, 77, 78, 92, 153–154, 223, 225–227, 229–239, 241–244, 247, 250–257, 332–338, 347–350, 353–356, 359–363
Thatcher Archives, 229
"A Time for Choosing" (Reagan speech), 91
*Time* magazine, 56
Tonton Macoute, 128
*Top Gun* (film), 347
*Top Secret Files on KGB Foreign Operations* (Gordievsky), 99
Torres Rizo, Julian, 341–342

430    INDEX

Tortolo, Pedro, 277, 304–305, 341–342
Tosh, Peter, 268
Totalitarianism, 74, 96, 356
Treasury Department, 61, 188, 256
Treaty of Paris (1763), 118
Trinidad, 117, 132
Trobaugh, Edward, 216, 318, 324–325
Troyanovsky, Oleg, 109, 110
Trudeau, Pierre, 92–93
Trujillo, Stephen, 326–327
Truman, Harry, and administration, 6, 32
Tunis, Tunisia, 238
Turner, Stansfield, 37, 39
20th Century Fox, 67
Twenty-Fifth Amendment, 60
Tyrell Bay, 149–150

UFOs, 127, 135
United Arab Emirates (UAE), 359
United Kingdom (U.K.), 69, 75–78, 90, 92, 96–98, 118–126, 130–133, 137, 144, 145, 148, 151–154, 156, 166–167, 192, 202, 229–244, 252–255, 332–339, 354–355, 361
    (*See also* British Commonwealth; Falklands War; Thatcher, Margaret)
United Nations (U.N.), 63, 69, 76, 97, 109, 128, 135–136, 238–240, 253, 339, 360
United Nations Charter, 192
United People's Party (Grenada), 134
Universal Declaration of Human Rights, 97
University of California at Berkeley, 226, 227
University of Leeds, 353
University of Sussex, 156
University of Toronto, 353
UPI, 27, 56
U.S. Air Force (USAF), 127, 145, 194, 195, 210, 217, 265, 270–272, 281, 307, 319, 321
U.S. Army, xxi, xxv, xxvi, 51–52, 145, 193–195, 214–216, 234, 263–269, 291, 292, 294, 301, 312, 318, 323–325, 366–367
U.S. Army Delta Force, xxii, 193, 195, 264–266, 279, 281, 282, 289–295, 303
U.S. Army Night Stalkers, 265–266
U.S. Army Rangers, xxi, xxv–xxvii, 145, 193, 195, 204, 215, 217, 218, 264, 269–272, 275–279, 290, 293–294, 302–311, 317, 319, 320, 323–328
U.S. Atlantic Command, 193, 194, 214, 311, 315, 317, 323–324
U.S. Atlantic Fleet, 194
U.S. Information Agency, 109
U.S. Marine Corps, xxi–xxv, xxviii, 5, 6, 145, 190, 193–196, 201–204, 208, 209, 214, 219, 232, 239, 245, 247, 248, 250, 251, 264, 268–269, 278, 279, 292, 294, 312, 313, 315–319, 321–323, 347–350, 367
    (*See also* Beirut Marine Barracks bombing)
U.S. Naval Academy, 6, 194, 214
U.S. Navy, 94, 106, 145, 148, 185, 193, 194, 211, 213–216, 218, 230, 288, 291, 294, 301, 312, 313, 319, 320, 326, 343, 347
U.S. Navy SEALs, xxi, 193, 195, 210–212, 216, 218, 264, 266, 270, 279–289, 304, 312, 315, 316, 367
*U.S. News and World Report*, 26
U.S. Steel, 197

*The U.S. Invasion of Grenada: Legacy of a Flawed Victory* (Kukielski), 282
USS *Caron*, 315, 320
USS *Eisenhower*, 238
USS *Enterprise*, 94, 347
USS *Fort Snelling*, 314
USS *Guam*, xxii–xxiv, 218–219, 264, 268, 280, 281, 291, 301–302, 311–316, 318, 319, 323, 327, 343, 351
USS *Independence*, 193, 208, 294, 295, 313
USS *Manitowoc*, 314
USS *Midway*, 94
USS *Moosbrugger*, 292
USS *New Jersey*, 202, 349
USS *Sprague*, 211, 212
USS *Theodore Roosevelt*, 38
USSR (*see* Soviet Union)
Ustinov, Dmitri, 100, 105

Vance, Cyrus, 37, 44, 127
Vargas Llosa, Mario, 17
Vatican, 65
Venezuela, 7, 18, 152, 190, 329
Ventura, Jose, 302–303, 305
Versailles, France, 69
Vessey, John, 193, 195–196, 200, 203, 204, 207–208, 213, 221, 300, 324
*Vice News*, 131
Vieques, Puerto Rico, 145
Vietnam, xxiii, xxvi, 44
*Vietnam Heroico* (Cuban vessel), 161, 175, 183
Vietnam Syndrome, 358
Vietnam War, 45, 53, 54, 89, 194, 196, 207, 214, 219, 225–226, 230, 264, 307, 347, 356
Virginia, 28
Vladivostok Summit, 103
Volcker, Paul, 252

Walesa, Lech, 5
Walker, Johnny, 210–211
*Wall Street Journal*, 329
Walt Disney World, 95
Walter, William, 275–276
Walter Reed Hospital, 126
War Powers Resolution, 192
Warbah Island, 359, 360
Warner Brothers, 66, 67
*Warriors of Disinformation: American Propaganda, Soviet Lies, and the Winning of the Cold War* (Snyder), 109
Warsaw Pact, 354
(*See also* Soviet Bloc)
*Washington Post*, xxvi, 10, 13, 18, 21, 38, 40, 55, 86, 89, 90, 127, 146, 152, 334
Watergate, 45, 347
Watt, James, 189
Wayne, John, xxiv, 307
Weinberger, Caspar, 54, 61–62, 65, 66, 76–80, 177, 184, 190, 193–194, 202–204, 213, 234, 238–239, 245, 247, 248, 255–256
Weisner, Admiral, 216
West Bank, 349
West Berlin, 187, 356
West Germany, 144, 145, 148, 254, 339, 356
West Point, xxvi
West Virginia, 30
*Where's the Rest of Me?* (Reagan), 90
Wiles, Lanny, 198, 199
Wilkinson, Howard, 26
Wilmington, Del., 225
Wilson, Harold, 124–125
Woodcock, Leonard, 71–72
World War II, 6, 46, 67, 88–89, 196, 264–265
Wright, James, 220

Xinhua, 71

Yamane, Mark, 306–307, 366
Yom Kippur War, 228–229
Young, Bill, 18–21

Yrurzum, Hugo Alfredo, 10, 11

Zeleny Island, 94
Zimbabwe, 339

# About the Author

**JOHN BACHMAN** is the host of NEWSMAX John Bachman Now and an award-winning journalist who has worked for more than two decades as a TV news producer, reporter, and anchor. He started as an intern at Fox 5 in Atlanta, then moved to WRDW in Augusta, GA, and then on to WPEC in West Palm Beach, Florida, and covered special assignments for CBS News, CNN, and Fox. Since joining NEWSMAX in 2011, Bachman has traveled throughout the United States and the world and won an award for the NEWSMAX HEROES documentary he wrote and produced, to commemorate the heroic acts of twenty-five ordinary Americans. He lives with his wife, Ariel, and three children in Tequesta, Florida.

For more information, visit https://www.newsmaxtv.com/n2.

## About the Editor

**CRAIG SHIRLEY** is a presidential historian and Reagan biographer. All told, he has written eleven books including six on Ronald Reagan and the *New York Times* bestselling *December 1941*. His wife, Zorine, also worked for Reagan and is now president of the Essex County Museum in Virginia. Together they enjoy sailing.